AF600545

THE CATHOLIC UNIVERSITY OF AMERICA
CANON LAW STUDIES
No. 122

SUPPLIED JURISDICTION ACCORDING TO CANON 209

AN HISTORICAL SYNOPSIS AND COMMENTARY

A DISSERTATION

Submitted to the Faculty of Canon Law of the Catholic University of America in Partial Fulfillment of the Requirements for the Degree of

DOCTOR OF CANON LAW

BY

FRANCIS SIGISMUND MIASKIEWICZ, J.C.L.
Priest of the Archdiocese of Boston

THE CATHOLIC UNIVERSITY OF AMERICA PRESS
WASHINGTON, D. C.
1940

NIHIL OBSTAT:
CLEMENT V. BASTNAGEL, J.U.D.
Censor Deputatus.

IMPRIMATUR:
✠ WILLIAM CARDINAL O'CONNELL
Archiepiscopus Bostoniensis.
Boston, May 9, 1940

COPYRIGHT 1940, BY
THE CATHOLIC UNIVERSITY OF AMERICA PRESS

PRINTED IN THE UNITED STATES OF AMERICA
BY THE WATKINS PRINTING CO., BALTIMORE

TO

HIS EMINENCE

WILLIAM CARDINAL O'CONNELL

IN

REVERENCE AND GRATITUDE

TABLE OF CONTENTS

Foreword 1

PRELIMINARY NOTIONS

Article I. Jurisdiction 3
A. *Definition* 3
B. *Division of Jurisdiction* 13
C. *Subjects of Jurisdiction* 18
Article II. The Supplying of Jurisdiction.. 21

HISTORICAL DEVELOPMENT

Article III. The Roman Law Influence 32
Article IV. The Pre-Gratian Development 41
Article V. The Influence of Gratian 47
Article VI. The Influence of the Glossators 50
Article VII. The Subsequent Development Up to the Code 55
A. *Application to Both "Fora"* 55
B. *Breadth of the Application of the Principle of Jurisdiction* 57
C. *Application to Cases of Delegated Power* 62
D. *Common Error* 67
I. Quality of the error 69
II. Place of the error 70
III. Subjects of error 72
IV. Extent of common error 74
V. The measure of common error.. 78
E. *Necessity of a Title* 81
F. *Probability of Fact and of Law* 87
I. Probability as a source of jurisdiction.. 90
II. Supplying in probability of fact or of law.. 98

Conclusions 104

Summary 106

CANONICAL COMMENTARY

Introduction

Article I. Conditions Requisite for the Supplying of Jurisdiction 115
A. *Common Error* 115
I. Introductory notions 115
1. Error and ignorance 115
2. Common 116
II. Traditional interpretation of common error 116
III. Interpretative error 121
1. Arguments against the strict interpretation of common error 124
2. Arguments for the interpretative theory 127
3. Highlights of the interpretative theory 128
IV. Appraisal of the interpretative theory 130
1. Textual arguments 133
2. Contextual arguments 135
a. Difficulties alleged against the traditional theory 135
b. Context of the Code 143
c. Sequels of the interpretative theory 148
V. Theory identifying error and ignorance 151
1. Gist of the ignorance theory 151
2. Evaluation and criticism of the ignorance theory 152
VI. Conclusion 156
1. General notions 157
a. The common good 157
b. Canon 209, a repetition of the old law 160
c. Canon 209, and *epikeia* 161
2. Qualifications of common error 163
a. Extent of common error 163
b. Quality of the error 168
(a.) Real 168
(b.) Probable 169
(c.) Explicit or implicit 169

(d.) Actual or virtual 169
(e) Practical or speculative 171
c. Measure of common error 172
d. Place of error 175
e. Subjects of error 176

B. *Doubt* 176
I. Doubt 178
II. Positive and probable 182
1. Pre-Code interpretation 184
2. Text of the Code 185
3. Consideration of the context of the Code..... 188
4. Involvement of the common good............ 191
5. The practice of the Rota 192
6. Conclusion 193
III. Doubt of law and of fact 194
1. Preliminary notions 194
a. Scope limited to ecclesiastical laws alone.. 194
b. Relation between canon 209 and canon 15.. 194
2. Doubt of law 196
a. Kinds of doubts of law 197
(a.) Intrinsic probability 197
(b.) Extrinsic probability 198
a° Private probability of law...... 199
b° Public probability of law....... 200
b. Examples 202
3. Doubt of fact 210
a. Decisions of the Roman Rota 212
b. Examples 217
4. Conclusion 219

Article II. Application of Canon 209 221

A. *In Reference to the Twofold Forum* 221
B. *In Reference to Ordinary and Delegated Power*...... 223
I. Jurisdictional power 224
1. In positive and probable doubt either of fact or of law 225
2. In common error 225

a. Ordinary power 225
b. Delegated power 230
(a.) Universal delegation 232
(b.) Delegation for one case 235
II. Assistance at marriage 239
1. Historical survey 239
2. Post-Code interpretation 248
a. Non-jurisdictional character of the act of assistance at a marriage ceremony 248
b. Applicability of canon 209 to marriage 250
c. Extent of application to marriage 256
(a.) Ordinary assistance 256
(b.) Delegated assistance 258
a° Pre-Code attitude 258
b° Attitude of the Code 260
a′ In doubt 260
b′ In common error 261
α Application to universal delegation to assist at marriage 263
β Application to assist at one marriage 271
III. Non-jurisdictional power 279
1. Non-jurisdictional power wielded by one who has an office 280
2. Purely dominative power 282
a. Pre-Code background 283
b. Post-Code doctrine 286
c. Conclusion 288

ARTICLE III. LICIT USE OF CANON 209 290
A. *Common Error* 290
I. Minister 291
II. The faithful 296
B. *Doubt* 298
C. *Penal Sanctions* 300
I. Imputability of the censure 302
II. The sanctions 303

III. Applicability of canon 209 303
IV. The necessary jurisdiction 305
V. Presumption 310

CONCLUSIONS 311

BIBLIOGRAPHY 313

ABBREVIATIONS 325

BIOGRAPHICAL NOTE 327

ALPHABETICAL INDEX 329

CANON LAW STUDIES 335

FOREWORD

Canon 209 in the Code of Canon Law constitutes ecclesiastical legislation which contains not only many but also highly important and far-reaching implications. Perhaps there is no other canon which has been—or which will continue to be—the source of so much concern for priests in the greater or lesser interests they may have as canonists. Certainly there are few, if any canons which have provoked so much argument and contention or have been the subject of so vastly diversified doctrinal interpretation. The ultimate reason for this state of affairs is the fact that in canon 209 there is not question of solving one isolated problem. On the contrary, an adequate solution of the problem of the applicability along with the extent of the application of canon 209 presumes necessarily, and depends upon, a previous solution of other problems which are inseparably interwoven in the texture and pattern of this suppletory principle. Since there are so many angles and, above all, so many possibilities of fact to which these angles can apply, it is easily seen that a complete explanation and a definitive solution of the problems offered by canon 209 may rightfully seem to transcend the capacity of any concentrated study upon a subject so thoroughly involved.

Despite the numerous intricacies which are latent within canon 209, the writer cherishes a hope that by his analysis of the main lines of historical evidence and by his application of legally acceptable principles in their proper mutual interrelationship, he may, as he presents the variously conceived difficulties, offer a fully workable basis for the correct juridical interpretation of this canon.

With such a purpose in view, therefore, this study of canon 209 will be made under the two general headings of its historical analysis and of its doctrinal commentary. The historical treatment, premised with the consideration of certain preliminary legal notions, which of necessity enter into the historical discussion, will attempt to trace the essential outline of fact and of law in the past in order to clarify the canonical concepts which gave rise to the law as it is now incorporated in the wording of canon 209.

The commentary will be devoted to a close study of this suppletory principle as it is found in the Code today. Consideration will first be given to the conditions under which the legislator will supply deficient jurisdiction. In this section considerable attention will be given to the much discussed problem of *common error* and to the less discussed, but equally important, problem of *positive and probable doubt*. Secondarily, an attempt will be made to define the limits of the applicability of the suppletory principle of canon 209, whether it is intended by the legislator to apply to merely jurisdictional power or whether it is intended to extend to other power and authorization which, though not public in character like that of jurisdiction, is required by the Church for the juridical validity of certain acts. And, finally, some consideration will be given to the ever present correlate of validity: i.e., liceity.

In the process of preparing this work the author has contracted obligations which it is his great pleasure now to acknowledge. First of all he wishes to express his profound and sincere gratitude to His Eminence, William Cardinal O'Connell, Archbishop of Boston, whose interest and generosity have made possible for him the pursuit of graduate studies at the Catholic University of America. He wishes also to acknowledge his indebtedness to the members of the Faculty of the School of Canon Law for their helpful direction and generous assistance at all times. The author wishes likewise to express his appreciation to the Reverend Alexander Ogonowski, pastor of Holy Trinity Parish of Lowell, Mass., for his innumerable acts of kindness and solicitude. To the Rt. Rev. Edward G. Murray, S.T.D.; to the Rt. Rev. Joseph C. Walsh, J.C.D., LL.D.; to the Rev. Dr. Eric F. MacKenzie, J.C.D.; to the Rev. Dr. Valentine F. Schaaf, O.F.M., J.C.D.; to the Rev. Dr. Thomas J. Reilly, Ph.D.; to the Rev. Dr. Eugene Dooley, O.M.I., J.C.D.; to the Rev. Dr. William J. Doheny, C.S.C., J.U.D.; and to the Rev. Dr. José Pando, C.M., Ph.D., grateful acknowledgment is made for advice, suggestions and kind assistance in the preparation of this work.

To these and to other friends, unnamed, sincere thanks are expressed. The kindness of them all has given much pleasure to the task of preparing this thesis.

PRELIMINARY NOTIONS

ARTICLE I. JURISDICTION

A. Definition

Although not all authors admit certainty on the point of its etymological derivation,[1] the Roman jurists generally held that *iurisdictio* is derived from two words: *ius* and *dicere,* which means *to say what is just* or *to make pronouncement on the law.* The words then imply an official act of declaring subjective rights and duties relative to the law. It is interesting to note one author's observation,[2] that even etymologically jurisdiction implies a certain power, a certain relationship between superior and inferior.

As for the civil definition, it may be of some benefit in the analysis of this thesis to arrive at the definition only after a study of its gradual growth and crystallization in the Roman law system.

The Romans recognized and distinguished a four-fold power in the state: *maiestas, imperium, iurisdictio,* and *notio.*[3] *Maiestas* denoted the supreme power which reposed in the people and was later in Roman history transferred into the hands of the Emperor. This *maiestas* was considered by the Roman jurists as the source and fount of all other power. *Imperium* was the power to coerce criminals, in a word, the *ius gladii,* or the power of the sword. *Iurisdictio* was the power of appointing a judge, of hearing a case, of judging its merits, or of carrying out a judgment. Finally, *notio* was the faculty of hearing and judging a case but not of carrying out a judgment.[4]

[1] Cf., e.g., Sebastianus Berardi, *Commenturia in ius ecclesiasticum universum* (Augustae Taurinorum, 1766), Tom. I, Disp. I, cap. 1: "Nolo esse sollicitus de grammaticali nominis derivatione, libenter relinquendo iis, qui liberiore otio abundant, investigationem, an jurisdictio abs *iure dicundo* an potius abs *iure et ditione* dicatur."

[2] Cf. M. Van de Kerckhove, O. M. Cap., "De notione jurisdictionis in jure romano,"—*Jus Pontificium,* XVI (1936), 49-65, esp. 49. Hereafter reference to the *Jus Pontificium* will be made by using the abbreviation *Jus Pont.*

[3] Berardi, *Commentarium in ius ecclesiasticum universum,* Tom. I, Disp. I, cap. 1.

[4] J. Raus, *De sacrae obedientiae virtute et voto* (Lugduni: Apud Emmanuelem Vitte, 1923), p. 77.

In the period of the Kings, all power was vested in the person of the king.[5] After the constitution of the Roman Republic, this fullness of power resided in the person of the consul.[6] Gradually, however, it came about that the consuls did not exercise all the duties and offices which their powers allowed. With the institution of the praetorship, while the consuls retained the power of voluntary jurisdiction, the contentious jurisdiction was assigned to the praetor.[7]

Power, then, was among the Romans a divisible term, a divisible factor in the task of proper government. Jurisdictional power was only one of the phases of power generically taken. This is a very important point to bear in mind throughout this entire study. For, it matters not whether it be civil or canonical jurisdiction under study, it will always be vitally necessary to appraise correctly the ambit of the term under analysis. And, secondly, the placing of all the power by the jurists in the people or in the Emperor gives a good inkling of the recognized sovereignty of the people and of the Roman Emperor over jurisdictional power. And this sovereignty ultimately explains how the term *jurisdiction* could and did widen according to the exigencies of the times and the good of the Roman people whose safety was ever considered the supreme law. There was, then, in brief, a consciousness on the part of the Roman jurists that the rules and conditions for the exercise of jurisdictional acts were not iron-clad or inflexible, but rather subject to revision and to change. To be sure, Rome was jealously careful of her laws. But Rome also knew how and to what extent to relax them when the common good of the people was imperiled.[8]

The widening of the ambit of jurisdictional power is perhaps best to be appreciated in a brief treatise such as this in parallel

[5] D. (1. 2) 2. 1, 14.

[6] D. (1. 2) 2. 16.

[7] D. (1. 2) 2, 17-19, 27. Cf. also M. Van de Kerckhove, "De notione jurisdictionis in jure romano,"—*Jus Pont.*, XVI (1936), 49-65.

[8] D. (14. 6); D. (47. 2) 52; D. (1. 14) 3. Cf. also Andrea Guarneri Citati, "Supplere, nei testi giuridici,"—*Studia et Documenta Historiae et Iuris*, I (1935), 153-187.

analysis with the successive reigns of the three great judiciary systems of Rome: the *legis actiones;* the formulary system, and the *cognitio extraordinaria.* In the first system the jurisdictional activity of the magistrate, or of the praetor, was limited to and coextensive with the pronouncement of a formula of sacred words *in iure* which rendered the activity of the litigants legitimate and juridical.[9] It gradually dawned upon the Romans that the extreme technicality and insufferable formalism of the *legis actiones* [10] made that system incapable of expansion and application to the new problems which were steadily growing in number and in importance with regard to foreigners and the Romans themselves. Eminently practical lawmakers, the Romans slowly turned towards a new system, which in all probability was first introduced by the *praetor peregrinus:* the formulary system.[11] As a result of this system, even though the activity of the magistrate was still limited to the trial *in iure,* the magistrate in time attained almost absolute control of the formulae, which he set forth in his praetorian edict and which had to be complied with by litigants. In virtue of this new power vested in him, the praetor could refuse an action where one lay at civil law, and in this manner he was able to dispose of what was obsolete in the *ius civile.* In the same way, he could grant an action but defeat it by inserting some defense, like fraud, etc. By granting actions where none lay at civil law, he could meet the needs of social development.[12]

What was doomed to bring an end to the formula system also paved the way for an even greater extension of the magistrate's jurisdictional power. That particular act was the Decree of Hadrian which deprived the praetorian edict of its pristine force. It must be remembered that the whole procedure by way of the formula depended upon the praetor, and when the time arrived that it was no longer possible for Rome to keep pace with the needs of the time by means of the praetorian edict, the formula, which

[9] G. (4. 16).

[10] G. (4. 11, 30).

[11] Cf. Leage-Ziegler, *Roman private law* (2. ed., New York: MacMillan and Co., Ltd., (1937), p. 399.

[12] Cf., e.g., G. (3. 180) ; (4. 46).

had no real existence apart from the praetor's edict, could hardly escape becoming as technical and stereotyped as the *legis actiones* which had preceded it. The subsequent procedure annihilated the time-honored division of a trail *in iure* and *in iudicio.* Now the trial was conducted throughout by a state official. And now, for thc first time, the judgment was no longer the *sententia* of a private person, but a *decretum* of a state official.[13]

Yet, despite all this progress and development, jurisdiction was still restricted to the judicial authority in the modern sense, or the power to take cognizance of causes and to decide them according to the law of equity.[14]

One cannot read the Novels of Justinian and note the numerous constitutions providing for the administration of the Church and containing the legislation of the early Councils and still deny that the Church wielded a real power and influence on Roman law. Among other things, these constitutions[15] reveal to us that the word *jurisdiction* was used in the sense of not mere judiciary competence, but of general administration—a sense that was altogether foreign to Roman law before this. It was rather in this sense that the Church adopted the term, and since the time of Gregory the Great (590-604), although in canonical terminology the word itself is not of frequent occurrence, it has been employed by canonists consistently to denote the whole power of government inherent in the juridically perfect society as such, both civil and ecclesiastical.[16]

Here it is eminently proper to place a little emphasis on the objective fact that, in the point just analyzed, one perfect society was aided by another perfect society. By her divine institution the Church is an external society, perfect, *sui iuris,* organically constituted, truly juridical and public. Her own proper law was borrowed from no one. But, as a matter of historical fact, it is evi-

[13] Cf. Leage-Ziegler, *Roman private law,* pp. 415-417.

[14] "La giurisdizione nel diritto romano era esclusivamente limitata alla decisione delle controversie giuridiche civili."—I. Glück, *Commentario alle pandette* (Milano, 1888), II, 5.

[15] N. (131. 3) ; N. 11; N. (120. 6).

[16] Reiffenstuel, *Ius canonicum universum* (Romae, 1843-1844), lib. I, tit. I, n. 29.

dent that on numerous occasions the Church appropriated the terminology and institutions of civil law insofar as they were convenient for her purposes.[17] Yet she always safeguarded the principle of her own social activity. If she did follow the civil law in many points, it must also be remembered that she played a powerful role in correcting, changing, elaborating many civil institutions. It is clear that the crystallization of the term *jurisdiction* was due in great part to the Church. In the pages that are to follow an attempt will be made to ascertain on what side, the civil or canonical, and in what measure credit is to be given for the development of the present day teaching on the supplying of jurisdiction according to canon 209.

First of all, it must be stressed that it would be a mistake to assume that with Gregory the Great or with his contemporaries the canonical concept of *iurisdictio* reached its full development. Such was not the case. From the seventh to the twelfth century, due to the changes wrought upon Roman law by germanic and consuetudinary law, the term *iurisdictio* passed almost entirely out of use. It was supplanted by other terms, such as *ditio, ius pontificis, administrationem habere*. However, all these and similar terms retained the signification of *administrative power in general.*[18] The twelfth and the thirteenth centuries, so well known for their numerous and valuable contributions towards the systematizing of so many sciences, clarified for posterity the concept of ecclesiastical jurisdiction. Thus Huguccio (†1210) [19] was the first to exclude from the comprehension of the term "jurisdiction" the notion of power to administer *temporal* goods. In this manner "jurisdiction" received the limited signification of a power within a spiritual orbit, of a power which extended to acts that were dependent upon the

[17] C. 1, X, *de novi operis denuntiatione,* V. 32; c. 28, X, *de privilegiis et excessibus privilegiatorum,* V. 33.

[18] Cf., e.g., c. 34, C. XXIV, q. 1; c. 10, D. XCVI; c. 52, C. XVI, q. 1; c. 1, C. XVI, q. II. Cf. also M. Van de Kerckhove, "De notione jurisdictionis in jure romano,"—*Jus Pont.,* XVI (1936), 63-65.

[19] *Summa,* glossa ad c. X, q. 1., introd., Cod. Vat. Lat. 2280, fol. 163 r' . . . as cited by Van de Kerckhove, "Notio jurisdictionis apud decretistas et priores decretalistas,"—*Jus Pont.,* XVIII (1938), 12.

power of Orders for their exercise. Again, after 1215, following Ambrose, canonists clearly distinguished the power of Orders from the power of jurisdiction. Having excluded from jurisdiction the notion of the administration of temporal goods, these canonists attributed to this term the meaning of a *public power of ruling a perfect society.*[20] Finally, it is to be noted that the first to identify the *potestas clavium* with the power of jurisdiction was Joannes Teutonicus (†circa 1240), who hesitantly ventured that he thought the *key* was *jurisdiction.*[21] As Van de Kerckhove points out, even at the late stage of the middle of the thirteenth century the distinction of the *forum internum sive sacramentale sive extra-sacramentale* did not yet appear.

In view of this analysis, it would appear, jurisdiction may be canonically defined as a public power, granted either directly by Christ Himself, or indirectly through the Church by lawful commission, of governing and leading the faithful towards the goal of eternal life.[22] Analyzing with Kearney[23] this definition, the reader notes that jurisdiction is a *public* power to distinguish it from a mere economic or dominative power such as is exercised by a husband over a wife, by a father over his children, or by a teacher over his pupils. Jurisdictional power was conferred by Christ upon the Church. From this source the Roman Pontiff has ever drawn the plenitude of this power. And having drawn from Christ, the Church, through the Pope, has traditionally conferred upon her subjects a share in that power by means of legitimate commission. This power, it must furthermore be noted, is exercised directly over the baptized only, since by baptism alone does man become a

[20] M. Van de Kerckhove, "De notione jurisdictionis apud decretistas et priores decretalistas,"—*Jus Pont.*, XVIII (1938), 11.

[21] *Summa ad decretum,* glossa ad dist. XX, c. 1., *Claves,* Cod. Vat. 658, fol. 5 r' " . . . Sed credo clavem jurisdictionem esse." as cited by M. Van de Kerckhove, "Notio jurisdictionis apud decretistas et priores decretalistas,"—*Jus Pont.,* XVIII (1938), 14.

[22] P. Maroto, *Institutiones iuris canonici* (Matriti: Editorial del Corazon de Maria, 1919), I, 66.

[23] *Principles of delegation* (Catholic University of America, Canon Law Studies, N. 57, Washington, D. C., 1929), p. 45.

subject of the spiritual kingdom, according to the words of the Apostle: "For what have I to do to judge them that are without?"[24] And the ultimate purpose of this power of jurisdiction is the salvation of the subjects who are members of Christ's Church on earth. In a word, as canon 196 states, the power of jurisdiction denotes the whole power of ruling, i.e., the *potestas regiminis,* which is present in the Church as a juridically perfect society.[25]

Very clearly, even this somewhat general concept of jurisdictional power, excludes any direct notion of the power of Orders *(ministerium)*. Her Sacramental ministry, which is concerned primarily with the individual good, is not essentially a part of the Church's *social* power. It can be social only in the sense that it is a social possession and that its use, which by Christ's disposition is a social duty, must like any social means be regulated by social authority.[26] Ottaviani[27] expounds more at length the points of difference between the power of Orders and that of Jurisdiction. In brief summary, these divergencies may best be aligned under three headings: *origin; properties;* and *proximate purpose.* In reference to *origin,* whereas the power of Orders is conferred by an external, sense-perceptible rite, the power of jurisdiction is granted by legitimate commission or institution. In view of its *properties,* one observes that the power of Orders is perpetual, validly exercisable notwithstanding and despite any authoritative prohibition, not delegable nor prescribable. Also notable is the fact that the power of Orders is always possessed in the same quantity and degree by all those who have been raised to an Order. On the other hand, the power of jurisdiction is a power possessed subject to the will of the proper superiors. It is a power that can be lost.

[24] I Cor., V, 12; cf. canons 12 and 87.

[25] Reiffenstuel, *Ius canonicum universum,* lib. I, tit. I, n. 29; Lega, *Praelectiones de judiciis civilibus* (2. ed., Romae: Ex Typographia Polyglotta, 1905), I, n. 41.

[26] G. Ryan, *The principles of episcopal jurisdiction* (Catholic University of America, Canon Law Studies, N. 120, Washington, D. C., 1940), p. 10.

[27] *Institutiones iuris publici ecclesiastici,* vol. I, *Ius publicum internum* (Ed. altera, Romae: Typis Polyglottis Vaticanis, 1935), pp. 219-222.

It is a power which can be curtailed in part of even wholly restrained. It can be acquired by delegation. And it can be, indeed it actually is, found in varying degrees among men who enjoy the same rank in the ecclesiastical hierarchy of Orders. As regards the *proximate purpose,* as Ryan points out, the power of Orders aims immediately at the sanctification of the individual, through means which give grace *ex opere operato.* Jurisdictional power has a more social purpose in view, i.e., to rule the actions of the members of a community.

The powers of Orders and of Jurisdiction are separable, although they can and do actually exist cumulatively in one and the same individual. Indeed, as canon 118 prescribes, clerics are the sole possessors of jurisdictional power under the ordinary law.

This effort to distinguish clearly between the power of Orders and that of jurisdiction had to be made for a clear delineation of the specific character of jurisdictional power. But there remains another power in the Church, i.e., dominative power, which it is also necessary to differentiate from purely jurisdictional power.

Suarez,[28] while admitting other points of distinction, considered the following three as the main differences. Dominative power is, first of all, essentially concerned with private persons, or members of an *imperfect* society. Jurisdictional power, on the other hand, is an essentially necessary attribute of a perfect society. It logically follows, therefore, that jurisdictional power possesses a stronger, more highly sanctioned power of coercion. The third difference is that, as a rule, dominative power is more for the convenience of the party endowed with it than for the party over whom it is exercised. Jurisdictional power, in further contrast, is essentially more social in character. The person in whom lies vested even the slightest participation of that power is obligated always to act for the good of the perfect society of which he is only a member.

Schmalzgrueber [29] has noted several excellent illustrations of dominative power. Among these he included the power of regular superiors to command their subjects to perform actions in accord

[28] *Opera omnia* (Venetiis, 1740-1757), *De legibus,* lib. I, c. 8.

[29] *Ius ecclesiasticum universum* (Romae, 1843-1845), lib. I, tit. 31.

with their constitutions, to declare vows invalid, to administer the properties and goods of the monastery or of the congregation, to arrange all things connected with the promotion of divine worship or for the welfare of their subjects. To these acts Saucedo[30] would add the power to accept new candidates or to expel unworthy members, as well as the power to punish deliquents by penal remedies and mild penalties.

Theoretically it is not difficult to distinguish dominative acts from the jurisdictional acts of legislation, punishment and judgment. But this differentiation is not always the same easy matter in practice. Thus, for example, Saucedo remarks, the superiors of non-exempt congregations do many things which, to him, seem to pertain to jurisdictional power. And yet these superiors have only dominative power.[31] Larraona strove to obviate this difficulty by defining dominative power as that power, which pertains to religious bodies, not inasmuch as they are, and are considered to be, segments of ecclesiastical society, but, on the contrary, as they are particular societies with in the Church, societies pursuing a particular purpose, subsisting under the authority of the Church and drawing thence their public status.[32] Thus Larraona notes that these societies are public only in the broad sense.

Finally, in this attempt to posit as clearly as possible the distinctive nature of jurisdictional power, a word or two must be added concerning expressions, like *competence* and *approbation,* which sometimes are confused with jurisdiction.

Competence in general implies jurisdiction; for, a judge is called competent who has the power of applying the law to certain persons in certain cases. Thus, properly considered, competence is jurisdiction over persons and their causes. Or, as Noval put it,[33]

[30] "Exercitium jurisdictonis et superiores laici ex ordine hospitalario S. Joannis de Deo,"—*Commentarium pro Religiosis,* XIII (1932), 59. Hereafter, reference to this periodical shall be made by use of the abbreviation *CpR.*

[31] *Op. cit.,—CpR,* XIII (1932), 60.

[32] Cf. *CpR,* VII (1926), 31.

[33] *Commentarium codicis iuris canonici,* Lib. IV, *De processibus,* Pars I, *De iudiciis* (Augustae Tauronirum: Marietti, 1920), n. 58.

competence in general is the limitation or the measure of jurisdiction. Thus judicial competence, for example, is the jurisdiction whereby the judge or a tribunal is able to settle some controversy. Using the term in this specific sense, Bouix noted that competence is identically the same as jurisdiction.[34]

As regards approbation, it is to be noted that from the Council of Trent up to the time of the Code, besides the power of Orders and jurisdiction, approbation was required for the validity of sacramental absolution. This consisted in the judgment of the Ordinary of the place concerning the fitness of the priest. This approbation had to be given by the Ordinary of the place where the confession was to be heard, while the jurisdiction was given as a rule by the bishop to whom the penitent was subject. In the new law this approbation is not required in the confessor as a distinct essential requisite for valid absolution. It is required in the bishop as a condition for the licit granting of jurisdiction.[35]

At this juncture there arises a problem which has caused very much concern and agitation among canonists, and a solution of which will determine to a great extent the applicatory force of canon 209. There is no question, as Smith points out,[36] that jurisdictional power includes the power to make laws, to inflict penalties, to execute sentences, to confer benefices. Certainly jurisdictional power, as has been seen, is distinctly separate from the powers of Orders and therefore the power of jurisdiction does not include the faculty to bless, to consecrate, to say Mass, to anoint, or to perform some other sacred function. The dispute is centered on whether or not jurisdiction includes the power to teach, to preach, to guard the faith, to protect morals, to buy, to sell, to possess, and

[34] Bouix, *Tractatus de iudiciis ecclesiasticis* (Parisiis, 1855), I, 245. Hereafter this work shall be referred to simply as *De iudiciis*.

[35] Noldin-Schmitt, *Summa theologiae moralis iuxta codicem iuris canonici* (21. ed., Oeniponte, 1932), III, n. 337 note. Hereafter this work shall be referred to simply as *Theologia moralis*. This edition shall be used in this work unless otherwise noted.

[36] *The penal law for religious* (Catholic University of America, Canon Law Studies, n. 98, Washington, D. C., 1935), p. 57.

to enter contracts. Chelodi[37] maintains vigorously that all these acts are within the scope of jurisdictional power. The exclusion of all these acts from the ambit of jurisdiction seems to him to narrow down too much the concept of jurisdiction and to be out of conformity with the dichotomy of power in the Church, which dichotomy, he notes, must be maintained in canon law. On the other side stand Cerato[38] and Cipollini,[39] who are loath to include these acts within the scope of jurisdictional power. Cappello[40] and Ciprotti[41] agree with Cerato and Cipollini and maintain the existence of administrative jurisdictional power in the Church. The great objection to the first opinion, as Smith clearly points out, is that it ignores entirely the dominative power.[42]

B. Division of Jurisdiction

The power of jurisdition is divided into many species:

1. In reference to the *forum* in which it is exercised, jurisdiction may be of the *external* or of the *internal* forum; for, while in other perfect societies the jurisdictional power extends to the individual members of the society only in relation to the society itself, the peculiar nature of the Church's purpose necessitates its extension to the individual's moral relation to God. Thus it is that external jurisdiction denotes the power which primarily and directly regulates the social actions of the faithful in respect to the public good and which merits recognition *coram Ecclesia* in its juridical and social effects. Internal jurisdiction signifies the power which primarily and directly regulates the moral actions and relations of the faithful in regard to the private good, and which obtains its sanc-

[37] *Ius poenale* (4. ed., Tridenti: Libr. Edit. Tridentum, 1935), p. 93, note 3.

[38] *Censurae vigentes* (2. ed., Patavii, 1921), n. 74.

[39] *De censuris latae sententiae* (Turini, 1925), lib, II, n. 27.

[40] *De censuris* (Augustae Taurinorum: Ex Officina Marietti, 1919), n. 91.

[41] *De consummatione delictorum attento eorum elemento obiectivo in iure canonico* (Romae: Apud Custodiam Libr. Pont. Instituti Utriusque Iuris, 1936), n. 61.

[42] *The penal law for religious,* p. 57.

tions *coram Deo* in its moral effects.[43] Jurisdiction in the internal forum is subdivided into *sacramental* and *non-sacramental* jurisdiction. The former is that which is exercised within the administration of the Sacrament of Penance or upon the occasion of such administration; the latter is that which is exercised outside or apart from the occasion of the administration of this sacrament.

2. In reference to the *manner* in which it is exercised, iurisdiction is either of a *contentious* or of a *voluntary* character, inasmuch as it is exercised either with or without a formal judicial process.

3. In reference to the extent of its application, jurisdiction is either *universal* or *particular.* It is universal when it is unrestricted and all-inclusive with regard to person, place and content. It is enjoyed solely by the Roman Pontiff. Even the Roman Congregations, Offices and Tribunals must function within restricted limits, at least in reference to the content of jurisdiction enjoyed by them. Jurisdiction is of a particular character when it is limited either to a certain group of persons, or to a special locality, or to a definite matter or content. Such is the jurisdiction possessed by any and every ecclesiastic inferior to the Roman Pontiff.

4. Jurisdiction is also divisible in reference to *title.* Since the term, "title," will occupy a particularly prominent place throughout this thesis, it is appropriate that at least a brief exposition of it be given for the proper understanding of the controversies which will be met in this study. It is readily understood that no one can posit a juridical act unless and until he has the necessary authorization or power to do so. This requisite, as the Romans put it, the *cause* wherefore one can act, is the title.[44] Or, as Van Hove phrases it,[45] a title is the instrument of proof of a juridical act or of the

[43] A. Van Hove, *Commentarium Lovaniense,* Vol. I, Tom. I, *Prolegomena ad codicem iuris canonici* (Mechliniae: H. Dessain, 1928), n. 32, note 1: "Potestas jurisdictionis stricte intelligitur potestas publica ad bonum commune directa. Quia potestas fori interni spectat bonum singulorum, ideo tantum vocatur potestas jurisdictionis, quia ordinatur potestate fori externi et acquiritur missione canonica quae est actus fori externi." Hereafter this work will be referred to as the *Prolegomena.*

[44] D. (5. 3); D. (24. 1) 54.

[45] *Prolegomena,* n. 10. Cf. also Lessius, *De iustitia et iure* (3. ed., Antuerpiae: Ex Officina Plantiniana, 1612), lib. II, cap. 29, n. 65.

quality in virtue of which one can take part in the performance of such an act. Let the reader be warned that the title is not to be confused with the document which contains the record of its bestowal.

As D'Annibale [46] observed, a title may be one of three kinds: true; colored; and putative. A title is, first of all, *true* when validly received from a fully competent superior. Thus, a pastor has a true title to his parish if the proper bishop legitimately installs him in parochial office. A title which is not true is either colored or putative. A *colored* title is one which has the appearance of a true title inasmuch as it is conferred by a competent superior. However, even though no defect appears in the concession of the title, it labors under an occult defect which vitiates it and renders it invalid. The defect may be on the part of the one granting, or of the one receiving it, or even in the manner of its conferring. The defect may be *on the part of the one conferring it,* as for example, if the one granting it should have been deprived of jurisdiction for some of the many causes like deposition, revocation, etc., which is still unknown to the public at large. The defect may be *on the part of the one receiving it,* as, for example, if the one receiving it were rendered by the law incapable of such reception because of an occult censure. Finally, the defect may arise *from the manner of its conferring,* as for example, if in the process there were substantial error or simony involved.[47] A *putative* title is present whenever a person pretends to be endowed with power—whether he does so in good faith or in bad does not make any difference—as long as this pretense is not objectively based upon the act of a legitimate superior.[48]

To illustrate this latter point, Sanchez proposes the case in which a municipal Council appointed a pastor, who then exercised the duties of his office for two whole years. Although this pastor was commonly received as true pastor by the faithful of his parish, still

[46] *Summula theologiae moralis* (2. ed., Mediolani, 1881), I, n. 79, footnote 73. Hereafter this work shall be referred to simply as *Summula.*

[47] Cf. Maroto, *Institutiones,* I, 730, 1.

[48] Cf. Benedict XIV, *Casus conscientiae* (Monasterii, 1856), IV, 515; Kearney, *The principles of delegation,* p. 122.

he had only a putative title and not a colored one precisely because this Council was not and had never been legally competent to make such an appointment.[49] Similarly Lehmkuhl indicated that the credentials falsified by a priest are not evidence of a colored title inasmuch as they have not emanated from the legitimate ecclesiastical authority.[50]

5. A further distinction arises from the manner in which the superior grants jurisdiction. Jurisdiction is *ordinary* if and when it is attached to an ecclesiastical office by law, so that the one who acquires the office automatically also acquires the jurisdiction connected with it. According to canon 197, § 1, two elements are conspicuous in ordinary jurisdiction: the power must be attached to an ecclesiastical office; and the connection with the office must be effected by the disposition of the law itself. In general it must be stated that the older authors insisted more upon the first element than upon the second.[51] Ordinary jurisdiction may in turn be *proper* or *vicarious*. The two enjoy a common element: they are attached to an office by the law itself. They differ in the fact that he who enjoys proper power, acts in his own name, e.g., a residential bishop, while he who enjoys vicarious power, acts in the name of him whose vicar he is, e.g. a vicar apostolic or general. In this, as Kearney well puts it, the vicar general resembles the delegate who likewise acts in the name of another; the delegate, however, does not act by virtue of a power attached by law to his office and in this differs from the vicar.[52]

Jurisdiction, as has already just been intimated, is *delegated* whenever it is derived by way of a commission from a person com-

[49] *Disputationum de sancto matrimonii sacramento libri tres* (Genuae: Apud Josephum Favonem, 1602), Tom. I, lib. III, disp. 22, n 63. Hereafter this work will be referred to as *De matrimonio*.

[50] *Theologia moralis* (11. ed., Friburgi Brisgoviae: Herder, 1910), II, n. 433; cf. also De Lugo, *Disputationes scholasticae et morales* (ed. nova, Parisiis, 1868), *De iustitia et iure*, Diss. XXXVII, n. 21.

[51] Cf. Hilling, "Begriff und Umfang der potestas jurisdictionis ordinaria und delegata nach geltendem Kirchenrecht,"—*Archiv für katholisches Kirchenrecht*, CIV (1924), 181-205. Hereafter this periodical will be referred to by the abbreviation *AKKR*.

[52] *The principles of delegation*, p. 55.

petent to bestow it. Thus the power of the delegate is not properly his own but that of the delegator. Delegation may proceed from the *Apostolic See* or from an inferior prelate. Delegation may be granted by reason of a *dignity* or *office,* or it may be granted by reason of *person.* In the first case it would be called *real* delegation; in the second, *personal.* It must be remembered that all delegation is personal since it is committed to a person. Hence in a real delegation the power is entrusted to a person, but by reason of his office. Such a delegation is regarded as passing from one incumbent of the office to another, yet always attributed to the person and not to the office. Delegation, however, that is conceded *electa industria personae* might aptly be called *strictly personal.* Furthermore, delegation may be *special* or *universal,* according as it is conceded for a particular case or for several determined cases, or according as it is granted for every species of power within the competence of the delegator, or at least for one determined class of affairs. Finally, delegation may be *ab homine* or *a iure.* This distinction was most frequent before the Code. The Code, however, does not employ this terminology, i.e., *a iure,* except in regard to censures.[53] Whether or not delegations, arising from the common law without the intervention of the delegator, still exist after the promulgation of the Code, is an object of great dispute among canonists.

6. In reference to *origin,* jurisdiction is either true or false. It is *true* whenever it really exists, whether it be directly true because it is founded upon a genuine title, or whether it be indirectly true when, lest in its absence grave harm redound to the faithful, it is supplied by the Church because of the common good. Jurisdiction is *false,* if in reality it does not exist at all, neither because of the presence of a true, genuine title nor because of a title indirectly conferred by the Church for purposes of supplying the deficient jurisdiction.[54]

[53] Canons 2245, § 2; 2252; 2253.

[54] J. Kelly, *The jurisdiction of the confessor* (Catholic University of America, Canon Law Studies, n. 43, Washington, D. C., 1927), pp. 5-6. Maroto, *Institutiones,* I, 574.

C. Subjects of Jurisdiction

Under the common law of the Church [55] clerics alone can obtain and exercise ecclesiastical jurisdiction. By definition a cleric is one who has been assigned to the Divine ministry by the conferring of tonsure.[56] It is this enrollment into the clerical state which renders him *capable of the reception* of ecclesiastical jurisdiction. Thus laics are excluded from participation in the jurisdictional power of the Church by the express, though implicit, provision of canon 118. This provision of the Code is not new but had its source in pre-Code custom and practice.[57]

However, this incapacity is not absolute, at least not so on the part of all laics. This general law may be and *de facto* is patently derogated by the special laws of the Code. Canon 239, § 2, for example, admits that a layman can be elected Pope, as in the history of the Church it has happened, and, should this occur, he receives supreme jurisdiction from the moment of his acceptation, before the consecration, ordination, or even tonsure. Moreover, there have been cases of delegation of jurisdiction to laymen in history, and there is no reason why the Church cannot do the same today. Indeed, the Bulls and Briefs, cited by Saucedo, establish beyond prudent question the fact that by privilege such a concession was made in regard to the Hospitalers of St. John. Not content with this, Saucedo proceeds to point out and to prove that, in fact, the superiors of any exempt, non-clerical religious order possess and wield truly jurisdictional power.[58] Thus, while laics are generally excluded from jurisdiction by canon 118, it is true that their incompetence can be remedied by special provision of the supreme legislator. But, as has been intimated above, there is some

[55] Canon 118: "Soli clerici possunt potestatem sive ordinis sive iurisdictionis ecclesiasticae et beneficia et pensiones ecclesiasticas obtinere."

[56] Canon 108, § 1.

[57] C, 12, X, *de rebus ecclesiae alienandis vel non,* III, 13: "Quum laicis, quamvis religiosis, disponendi de rebus ecclesiae nulla sit attributa potestas, quos obsequendi manet necessitas, non auctoritas imperandi."

[58] "Exercitium jurisdictionis et superiores laici ex Ordine Hospitalario S. Joannis de Deo,"—*CpR,* XIII (1932), 51-61; 106-114; 224-231; and 291-302.

question about the universal applicability of the last statement. The difficulty is concerned with the character of the incompetency of women. Clearly some, like D'Annibale,[59] openly taught that women and non-baptized persons were equally rendered incapable of jurisdiction by divine law. But others, like Bouix,[60] were not so certain of this. Thus Bouix, after an extensive study, made the following conclusions. While under the common law women are incapable of jurisdiction, this incompetency was never proven by anyone to rest upon the divine or the natural law. Nowhere in Sacred Scripture or in tradition, or in the very physical nature of woman, has an adequate argument been found in support of such a contention. At the most, women are banned from the exercise of jurisdictional acts by ecclesiastical law. Women could, and did, as the examples of the ancient abbesses prove, exercise jurisdictional power. However, Bouix warns, this is not to be construed as any other kind but a delegated power exercised in virtue of papal privilege.

These observations are important in the application of canon 209, inasmuch as there may be jurisdictional acts which do not require the power of Orders for effective performance, in which case the Church probably would supply even though the agent were not, strictly speaking, a cleric.

However, returning to the cleric, who after all is the ordinary recipient of jurisdictional power, the reader should keep a few other points clearly in mind. The censured, heretics and schismatics are not fit subjects of jurisdiction, inasmuch as their transgression has placed them outside the pale of active membership in the Church. Such persons are always forbidden to exercise jurisdictional power under the sanction that such an exercise will be an unlawful act. However, not always are their acts invalid. As canons 2265, § 1, n.2, 2275, and 2283 explictly state, it is only when such a person is a *vitandus,* or when a declaratory or condemnatory sentence has been executed against him that his jurisdictional acts will be invalid.

In closing this preliminary analysis, one more observation needs

[59] *Summula* (5. ed., Romae, 1908), I, p. 59.

[60] *Tractatus de jure regularium* (Parisiis, 1857), II, 452-464.

to be made. It may be remembered that, though any cleric whatsoever is immediately capable of all grades of jurisdictional power, this capacity may be limited by the prescription of law, human or divine, where there is a demand for the presence and possession of some sacred Order. Thus, for example, penitential jurisdiction assumes that the person who is to wield it already is invested with the priestly dignity and power of Orders.

ARTICLE II. THE SUPPLYING OF JURISDICTION

In virtue of Christ's commission [1] the plenitude of ecclesiastical jurisdictional power lies in the hands of the Church. This power, as has been clearly pointed out above, implies action and direction, be it legislative, judicial or coercive. It comprises the *public* power in virtue of which the Church is assigned the task of leading men back to God. With all this power at her command, the Church is left to her resources to marshal that power in whatever way may best serve her in attaining her one purpose on earth: the common salvation of mankind. Thus, speaking in the realm of possibility, one can readily admit that the Church could have granted vaster powers of jurisdiction to each and every priest, or she might have limited the number of acts demanding special power and authorization for their valid performance.

But such a lenient manner of action, though it might seem very desirable in a particular emergency, never enjoyed the approval of the Church. Her divine wisdom and her age-old experience has made her an ever more jealous stewardess of her Christ-bequeathed power. Dealing with men, with all their foibles and weaknesses, with their need of strict sanctions to help them along the path of probity and justice, the Church has found it necessary to be very careful in allowing others to share in her power. To protect the faithful against deception and to assure them of competent and worthy ministers, the Church has ever insisted, and still does insist, that those who are to minister unto the faithful in the name of Christ and of the Church, must first receive the approval and authorization necessary for the valid and licit performance of jurisdictional acts. She requires that they prove themselves worthy of the signal honor and capable of performing all the obligations and duties incumbent upon the minister of the Church. In a similar way, to warn the faithful against the insidious poison of some unholy practices, the Church finds it necessary to withdraw certain sins from the power of the ordinary priest to absolve. Thus, it

[1] Matt. XVI, 18; John XX, 22-23.

is readily seen how all these formalities, conditions and rules [2] are prompted not by any other reason but by the deep concern that the Church has for the good of her faithful. This last observation must be kept in mind always. And in this thesis such an understanding of the philosophy behind the Church's jurisdictional laws will serve as a helpful guide in any attempt to delineate the extent of the applicability of the suppletory principle.

The matter of jurisdiction, then, is very important. First, the necessity for it supplies the Church with strict sanctions against usurpers and incompetents. The possession of it is important also for the priest who, in acting without it, would not only posit invalid acts, but would run afoul of the rigid sanctions of the Church and of God. Finally, it is especially clear how important the use of it is to the faithful and what a great loss it would be for them to approach a priest adjudged to have faculties to absolve, confess and then upon their confession depart not knowing that they were still unabsolved.

This entire thesis will treat of such instances as the last one, i.e., instances in which, upon the presence or absence of jurisdiction, the very validity or the invalidity of the acts will depend. Thus it will be entirely out of the field of this discussion to treat of any acts the validity of which, as D'Annibale pointed out,[3] is never questioned, even though they were performed by a priest who was not juridically designated for these acts. For example, the conferring of solemn baptism and the administration of the sacrament of extreme unction are functions which belong to the office of the proper pastor of the person. In a wide sense, one might say that these acts fall within the range of that pastor's jurisdiction. Should acts like the two aforementioned be performed by another priest without the permission of the proper pastor, no doubt remains that under the normal circumstances they would be illicit. Nevertheless, *positis ponendis,* they would be valid. Such instances, then, it is repeated, will not fall within the scope of this treatment.

The general rule regarding the possession of jurisdiction for

[2] Cf., e.g., canon 877.
[3] *Summula,* I, n. 69.

validity was well summarized by Wernz-Vidal: there is no jurisdiction without a title.[4] And where, by mandate of the Church or her rightful representatives, jurisdiction is required for the validity of a certain act, there, if the minister acts without the proper jurisdiction, he acts fruitlessly because invalidly. In such individual instances it is useless to bring up as an argument for validity the presence of good faith on the part of the priest or of the individual.[5] For, as Toso [6] notes in adducing Celsus' principle,[7] the law is to be considered as continuing to have its effect even though in individual instance some inconvenience be suffered. The general good of the community, for which purpose the law is presumed to have been enacted, must prevail.

However, granted that the intricate jurisdictional system in the Church today has been prompted by the Church's desire to safeguard the Church and the faithful against the inroads of duplicity and incompetency, in a word, to promote the good order of the Church, then on the other hand certain extraordinary conditions cause the invalidity of the acts performed by one jurisdictionally incompetent demand that the Church let down the bars, relax the strictness of her jurisdictional sanctions and make special provisions for the validity of the acts performed under such extraordinary circumstances. For, as Kearney observed,[8] it will escape no one that a series of invalid acts, posited by an unauthorized agent, whether maliciously or in good faith, especially when distributed over a long period of time, will raise havoc in society. And to forestall such dangers and calamities,[9] provided that the necessary

[4] *Ius canonicum* (2. ed., Romae, 1928), II, n. 380.

[5] Cf., e.g., Jombart, "Consultations,"—*Nouvelle Revue Théologique,* XLVII (1920), 546. Hereafter reference will be made to this periodical by the use of the abbreviation *NRT*.

[6] "Jurisdictio quando ab ecclesia suppleatur,"—*Jus Pont.,* XVII (1937), 103.

[7] D. (1. 3) 4: "Ex his, quae forte uno aliquo casu accidere possunt, iura non constituuntur."

[8] *The principles of delegation,* p. 120.

[9] T. Sanchez, *De matrimonio,* Tom. I, lib. III, disp. 22, n. 5; Pirhing, *Jus canonicum novo methodo explicatum* (Dilingae, 1674-1678), lib. II, tit. 1, n. 83 ss.; Lega, *De iudiciis,* I, n. 355: ". . . Ratio illius provisionis repetitur a bono communi quod . . . pene irreparabilem pateretur iacturam."

conditions are verified, namely, common error or positive and probable doubt of fact or of law,[10] the necessary jurisdiction is *supplied* by the Church.

Etymologically, "to supply" *(supplere),* means to furnish that which is lacking in a given case. When one speaks of any power being supplied, one means that there is a furnishing by the Church of a power that would otherwise be lacking. The obvious question arises: How far and for whom can the Church supply, and how and under what circumstances does she supply?

It has been noted that the Church has the plenitude of jurisdictional power. Quite logically, then, her ability to supply is coextensive with the breadth of her power. Quite logically, also, in regard to the dispositions of the divine and natural law, which were not placed by Christ under absolute control and disposition of the Church, the Church must be considered incompetent to supply. Thus, for example, the Church can never supply the power of Orders. Hence, if a non-ordained person should pretend to absolve others, his act or acts could under no condition be validated by the Church in virtue of her suppletory principle. Nor can the Church supply the jurisdiction necessary to validate the jurisdictional acts performed by an agent destitute of reason, nor by a competent agent, simulating absolution.

In a similar manner the Church cannot ratify by means of the suppletory principle acts performed by non-baptized persons. For, the Church can touch no infidel either by law or dispensation. Only God can do that, as is evidenced by the fact that He gave every man the power to baptize a non-baptized person. Wherefore, not even the supreme power of the Church can avail anything towards the supplying in common error of the power of a non-baptized person. This incapacity exists *iure divino*. It is thus more radical than the incapacity of a woman to receive jurisdiction strictly so called. For the latter could be conferred by the Pope, provided that there would not be required simultaneously the power of sacred Orders, of which women are incapable by divine law.[11]

[10] Canon 209.

[11] Cf. Vermeersch, "Quam late locus sit can. 209 de Ecclesia supplente

Canon 209 is an instance in the Code which reveals that the Church does supply in conditions of common error or of a positive and probable doubt of fact or of law. In virtue of this supplying, the Church may grant jurisdiction to one who until now has not possessed any,[12] or to one who has some jurisdictional power but receives an extension of the same.[13] In either case, there are several points that must be kept in mind if one is to have a correct understanding of the suppletory principle.

First of all, the suppletory principle does not render an incompetent agent *habitually* competent. Thus, for instance, an invalidly elected bishop will never be the true bishop unless and until he is elected in the proper manner or has the matter sanated by the Holy See. In the same way, a person who has simoniacally obtained a pastorate or some other ecclesiastical office never becomes the true occupant of his chair by reason of mere tenure of that office. This is stressed by Ciprotti in his interpretation of canon 209 in reference to canon 2331, § 1.[14] What does happen is precisely this: every single time that this reputed bishop or pastor under the requisite conditions of canon 209 attempts the performance of a jurisdictional act, he receives the necessary jurisdiction *in actu*. Thus, he does not possess the jurisdiction one moment before nor a single moment after the performance of the action.[15] It does not matter how many acts he performs. The jurisdiction is always supplied in the self-same manner: *in actu*.

Secondly, it is to be noted that the Church supplies only those things which are pertinent to the *state and conditions of persons*.[16]

iurisdictionem in errore communi,"—*Periodica,* XXIII (1934), 59*-61*. However, as Vermeersch observes, certain canonists seem to hold that the Church could supply jurisdiction even in the case of a non-baptized person. Concerning this point cf., e.g., Trombetta, *Supplet ecclesia,* pp. 25-27. This certainly seems directly contrary to the general prescription of c. 201, § 1, and of c. 87.

[12] E.g., canon 882.

[13] E.g., canons 2252-2254.

[14] "De consummatione delictorum attento eorum elemento obiectivo,"—*Apoll.,* VIII (1935), 392, note 4.

[15] Cf. Lessius, *De iustitia et iure,* lib. II, cap. 29, nn. 65 and 68.

[16] D'Annibale, *Summula,* I, n. 79, not. 75.

In regard to this point certain authors, like Kearney,[17] add that the omission of formalities, required by the law for the validity of acts is not supplied for by the Church. Thus, supplied jurisdiction may make valid the absolutions of a putative confessor; but if a competent confessor should hear the confession of religious women outside the legitimate place for confession, his acts will be invalid and the Church will not supply. This opinion is open to some criticism, for in its phrasing it is a source of difficulty and confusion. First, it must be remembered that at any time when the Church supplies jurisdiction she does so because in the person conferring or accepting the jurisdiction, or in the manner of its bestowal or acceptance, some formality required by the law for validity was not observed. Hence it is erroneous to say that the omission of formalities required by law for validity is not supplied. As a matter of fact, there are no formalities of Church law which could not be supplied. Thus, for example, if a Pope were invalidly elected, once he were regarded by the world as Pope all of his jurisdictional acts would be valid.

What seems to be insinuated in Kearney's words and correspondingly deserves to be brought out is the following. A competent confessor comes into a convent and hears the confession of religious women in the proper place. The sisters all regard him as a properly authorized confessor. His acts are valid because he has faculties. And, in fact, in view of the consideration of him as confessor by the sisters, his acts would be valid even if he had no faculties. But, the moment he hears the confessions outside the proper place, he is arrogating to himself greater power than that of a *mere confessor*. For the Code requires the confessor of religious women to hear the confessions in a certain, legitimate place as a condition for validity.[18] He is arrogating to himself a power that is over and above the powers of the office which he is correctly or erroneously supposed by the sisters to possess.

[17] *The principles of delegation,* p. 121.

[18] Cf. *Pontificia Commissio ad Codicis Canones Authentice Interpretandos,* 28 Dec., 1927—*AAS,* XX (1928), 61. Hereafter this Commission shall be referred to by the abbreviation *PCI.*

Now, since an error of fact on the part of the sisters in regard to the priest's faculty to hear their confessions might easily arise, it is not hard to see that in the event of such error, the Church supplies. However, if the sisters were to conclude that the priest, as simple confessor, was capable of hearing validly their confessions outside the properly designated place, it seems the Church would not supply. For, in such a case is verified an error of law. And unless there be a positive, probable doubt about the priest's power to hear the confessions outside the legitimately designated place, confessions so heard will be invalid.[18a] Therefore, it must be concluded that any incompetency of a priest, caused by the omission of no matter what formalities of the law, will be supplied if there be probable common error concerning the priest in that specific capacity.

When the Church supplies jurisdiction in this manner, it is entirely wrong to refer to the act as at any time invalid. On the contrary, the act is valid from the very first instant of its performance, just as valid as if performed by one who legitimately and habitually possessed the power of jurisdiction. And it is on this particular point that the reader finds the specific difference between the supplying of jurisdiction according to canon 209 and convalidation,[19] and between canon 209 and radical sanation.[20] Both convalidation and radical sanation indicate actions of remedy applied only *after* the performance of acts which were invalid from the beginning up to the very moment of the convalidation or radical sanation.

Supplied jurisdiction, then, is a jurisdiction, be it ordinary or delegated, which is bestowed in an extraordinary manner,[21] without any formality, even perchance to people who are unfit and unworthy.[22] Thus the ordinary manner of bestowing jurisdiction is

[18a] More will be seen in detail about this point in the commentary about the supplying of jurisdiction in error of law.

[19] Canon 1133.

[20] Canon 1138.

[21] M. Coronata, *Institutiones iuris canonici* (2. ed., Taurini: Ex Officina Libr. Marietti, 1939), I, n. 291.

[22] D'Annibale, *Summula,* I, n. 78.

momentarily suspended. Without the usual test of the candidate and the subsequent approval by a responsible superior, the Code simply states that under the circumstances of common error or of positive and probable doubt of fact and of law the Church, or more properly the Supreme Pontiff, from whom all jurisdiction emanates and from whom all common law has its origin, supplies the necessary jurisdiction.

And yet one must not lose sight of the fact that there are other instances in the Code of extraordinary grants or extensions of jurisdiction. Such an instance, for example, occurs in canon 882 where the power of jurisdiction is granted to any and every priest, regardless of his personal status, to absolve any penitent from all censures and sins no matter how they may be reserved,[23] provided that there be a probable danger of death. Similarly, in canon 883 there is a prorogation of jurisdictional power on the sea to those who in their territory are already approved confessors. Likewise, similar extensions in regard to dispensation from matrimonial impediments and to assistance at marriage are evident in canons 1098, § 2, and 1043-1045. Other canons also make liberal allowances on the part of the legislator when the spiritual welfare of the penitent is permitted to outweigh the advantage of strict consistency in the law.[24] Thus canon 207, § 2, states that jurisdiction granted for the internal forum is still validly exercised if through inadvertence the priest has not noticed that the time for his faculties has expired or that he has taken care of the number of cases for which he had faculties. Canon 2247, § 3, maintains the efficacy of absolutions from certain reserved censures if and when given by priests ignorant of the reservation. Like these canons, canon 209 reveals the aim of the legislator to provide for the good of the faithful. But whereas each of the other canons is restricted

[23] It must be remembered, however, as the *PCI* decided, that the absolution granted in virtue of the power conferred by canon 882 is limited to the internal forum and cannot be extended to the external forum. Cf. *PCI*, 28 Dec. 1927—*AAS*, XX (1928), 61.

[24] O'Donnell, "When does the Church supply jurisdiction?"—*Irish Ecclesiastical Record,* XVI (1920), 500. Hereafter this periodical shall be referred to by the use of the abbreviation *IER*.

to cover particular cases, canon 209, while also demanding the presence of certain conditions for its functioning, exerts its force in regard to all sorts of jurisdictional acts. In addition, it serves, or rather it can serve, as a reflex principle whereby the other canons can be used in the event of a positive and probable doubt as to the existence of the conditions that the Code requires for their functioning.

HISTORICAL DEVELOPMENT

THE HISTORICAL DEVELOPMENT

Writers are universally agreed that until the Code came into effect in 1918 there was never any express legislation in any code of law, civil or canonical, concerning the doctrine of the supplying of jurisdiction as it is known to canonists today. At the same time it is equally agreed that the present law, as it is found in canon 209, is not an innovation, but rather the fruit and natural result of a growth and development in jurisprudential doctrine which is centuries old. Thus far, except for the work of Thomas Sanchez in the seventeenth century,[1] there have been few attempts to trace in detail a full picture of the historical development of this doctrine.

Present day commentators [2] have stressed to varying degrees the influence of Roman Law on canon law on this point of jurisprudential doctrine. At the International Juridical Congress, held in Rome in 1934, Charles Boucaud, noting how much of the Code of canon law, and especially of its fourth book, was borrowed terminology from Roman Law, wrote that he considered canon 209 a direct inheritance from the law of Roman.[3] In a similar vein

[1] *De matrimonio,* Tom. I, lib. III, disp. 22, nn. 1-65.

[2] J. Chelodi, *Ius de personis* (2. ed., Tridenti: Libr. Edit. Tridentum, 1927), n. 130; Maroto, *Institutiones,* I, 731; Wernz-Vidal, *Ius Canonicum,* II, n. 381, note 5; M. Lega, *Praelectiones de iudiciis civilibus,* I, n. 355; F. Cappello, *Tractatus canonico-moralis de sacramentis* (2. ed., Taurinorum Augustae: Marietti, 1929), II, n. 502; Coronata, *Institutiones iuris canonici,* I, p. 339, footnote 6; Kearney, *Principles of delegation,* p. 119; Kelly, *The jurisdiction of the confessor,* p. 120; A. Trombetta, *Supplet ecclesia seu commentarium in canonem* 209 *codicis iuris canonici* (Neapoli: Ex typis pontificiis M. D'Auria, 1931), p. 15, (hereafter this work will be referred to simply as *Supplet ecclesia*). Cf. also Bibliophilus, "Seculo XIV decurrente post indictam a Justiniano Aug. 'Digestorum' compilationem,"—*Jus Pont.,* X (1930), 267.

[3] "Relationes inter ius Romanum et codicem Benedicti XV,"—*Acta congressus iuridici internationalis* (Romae: Apud Custodiam Librariam Pont. Instituti Utriusque Iuris, 1937), IV, 48.

[4] L'erreur commune,"—*NRT,* L (1923), 169: "Si Barbarius ou même si le droit romain n'avait pas existé, L'Église aurait-elle admis peut-être un peu plus tard et dans circonstances un peu différentes, cette juridiction

Jombart[4] noted the dependence of the Church's doctrine upon the Roman precedent as it is recorded in the Digest of Justinian.[5]

It is of primary importance in tracing the history of this topic to determine the extent of this dependence. Was it a case of complete absorption? Or did the Church contribute something of her own also? It is impossible to arrive at a satisfactory answer unless and until a close study has been made of the Roman precedent and of its transition into canonical jurisprudence.[6]

The development, as it has actually occurred, is not easy to follow. In its process numerous and varying opinions have sprung up which are the source of much difficulty and concern to the student who attempts to understand or explain them. The fact of the jurists' disagreement is the direct and natural result of juristic theorizing which was allowed to go on free and untrammelled by any definitive pronouncement of positive law. The following inspection of the *Lex Barbarius* is intended as a means of accounting for much of the disagreement of the jurists and as a proof that the real, full development of the doctrine of the supplying of jurisdiction is in the last analysis the result of the Church's teaching on equity.

suppléé en vu du bien général? C'est infiniment vraisembable, mais, pour affirmer avec certitude, il ne faudrait rien moins que le science moyenne de Dieu."

[5] D. (1. 14) 3.

[6] T. Sanchez, *De matrimonio,* Tom. I, lib. III, disp. 22, n. 1; "Tota huius disputationis difficultas pendet ex intellectu L. Barbarius . . . 1 2 C. de sentent. & interloquut . . . c. ad probandum, de sentent., & re judic . . . Tota igitur difficultas versatur in horum textuum intelligentia . . ."

ARTICLE I. THE ROMAN LAW INFLUENCE

Justinian defined slavery as an institution of the *Ius Gentium,*[1] in which a person was, contrary to his nature, subject to the *dominium* of another person. But, as Leage-Ziegler note, in his definition[2] Justinian missed to some extent the Roman point of view, which did not require every slave to be owned. There were the *servi poenae* and the slaves of the *Fiscus* who were not owned. There were other such cases. So much was true, however, that the slave was the one human being who could be owned. Slavery, some contended, was a condition of rightlessness. But, as Leage-Ziegler further indicate,[3] this statement must be understood with reservations, for there seem to have been instances under the later classical influence, after the time of Antonius Pius (138-161), when the slave could get the protection of the law. Generally considered, however, it is true that a slave was both rightless and dutiless in law, although he was personally liable for crimes and civil wrongs. Certainly, then, if a slave could not hope for the ordinary ministrations of justice from the tribunals of Rome, how much less could he aspire in his condition to administer justice to others! The slave was neither free nor was he a citizen. Hence under the law he was completely beyond the pale of a potential candidacy for any public office. And Rome, proud and imperial Rome, it must be remembered, had strict ordinances against any unrightful usurpations of power.[4]

In the period of the *Ius Gentium,* about 50 B.C.,[5] the story of Barbarius was cast. While there are other instances in Roman law

[1] Inst. (1. 3) 2.

[2] *Roman private law,* p. 54. Cf. also W. W. Buckland, *A text-book of Roman Law* (2. ed., Cambridge: At the University Press, 1932), pp. 62-63.

[3] *Roman private law,* p. 53.

[4] Cf., e.g., C. (9. 26). Cf. also in regard to the incapacity of slaves: C. (10. 33) 2; (3. 1) 6; (7. 16) 11.

[5] Cf. G. Lopez, *Ottonis thesaurus iuris romani* (Basileae, 1744), Tom. III, 442. Cf. also E. Klebs, "Barbarius,"—Pauly-Wissowa's *Real-Encyclopädie der klassischen Altertumswissenschaft* (Stüttgart, 1897).

which helped to give rise to the principle *"error communis facit ius"*,[6] in none of these instances except in one[7] was there suestion of a *public office* or of acts which presumed the possession or exercise of the power of jurisdiction in any way. That case concerned an arbiter who, having been appointed as such by the magistrate, proceeded to give sentence despite the fact that he was truly a slave. Because he was considered free at the time when he passed the sentence, the sentence was to retain the force of a *res iudicata.* But more celebrated than any of these texts, and propounding the same doctrine, i.e., *"error communis facit ius"*, is the *Lex Barbarius.* This *Lex* was concerned with a case of *public* law. To it the greater part of jurisconsults point when they wish to demonstrate the efficacy of common error towards bringing about the validity of acts which, under the ordinary law, would be invalid.

Thus one can not help but agree that this *Lex Barbarius* is interesting for many reasons. Its rather unusual character in itself is intriguing enough to command attention. But more important in this study are the views and solutions proffered by the jurists of four periods: of Barbarius' day, of Ulpian's time, of the days of the rebirth of the Roman Law, and finally of this our own day as regards their respective understanding of this principle of Roman law and the motivating cause of its coming into existence and use. For each of these groups sheds some light of understanding, if not on the jurisprudence of Barbarius' day, then at least on the jurisprudence current in the days of its respective contemporaries.

The story of Barbarius was recorded in the Digest of Justinian:

> *"Ulpianus libro trigesimo octavo ad Sabinum.* Barbarius (Barbatius) Philippus, cum servus fugitivus esset, Romae praeturam petiit, et praetor designatus est, sed nihil ei servitutem obstetisse, ait Pomponius, quasi praetor non fuerit. At quin verum est, praetura eum functum et tamen videa-

[6] Cf., e.g., C. (6. 23) 1; Inst. (2. 10); C. (7. 45) 2; D. (14. 6) 3; N. (44. 1) 1-4.

[7] I.e., in C. (7. 45) 2.

mus: si servus, quamdiu latuit dignitate praetoris functus sit: quid dicemus? quae edixit, nullius fore momenti? an fore propter utilitatem eorum, qui apud eum egerunt, vel Lege, vel 'quo alio iure'. Et verum puto, nihil eorum reprobari: 'Hoc enim humanius est' cum etiam potuit populus Romanus servo decernere hanc potestatem: sed et si scisset servum esse, liberum effecisset. Quod ius multo magis in imperatore observandum est." [8]

Two points are to be kept in mind. First of all, as it is very clear, the passage concerning Barbarius does not refer to any previously drawn up general or specific statute law. Rather, it is only an exemplification of Roman jurisprudence, the application of a *ius non scriptum.* And secondly, critical editions [9] reveal the presence of two interpolated lines *"quo alio iure"* and *"hoc enim humanius est."* These interpolations were in all probability the result of the Christian influence which had reached its peak at the period of Justinian.[10]

They will have a definite place and value in this study; but for the time being they shall be omitted in the immediate consideration,

[8] D. (1. 14) 3.

[9] Cf. P. Krueger's edition of the *Corpus iuris civilis* ad D. (1. 14) 3 . . . which is cited above. Cf. also Lévy-Rabel, *Index interpolationum quae in Justiniani Digesti inesse dicuntur* (Weimar: Herman Boehlaus Nachfolger, 1929), ad D. (1. 14) 3.

[10] Cf. C. Hohenlohe, *Einfluss des Christentums auf das corpus iuris civilis* (Wien: Hölder, Pichler, Tempsky, 1937), pp. 130-131. Such also is the view of D'Angelo ("De aequitate in codice iuris canonici,"—*Periodica,* XVI [1927], 220-221) who followed Riccobono ("Cristianesimo e diritto privato," *Riv. di dir. civ.,* III [1911], 37ss.): "Sub influxu religionis aequitatem iustinianam aliam toto et coelo diverso fuisse ab aequitate classica. Methodo autem non autem comparativa, sed etiam, et maxime, exegetica (per examen interpolationum) ad hanc apodicticam conclusionem pervenitur . . . *humanius, tutius, commodius, aequius* . . . quae inveniuntur in plurimis fragmentis classicis a codificatoribus studio inveniuntur additae ad designandam *'humanitatem', 'pietatem', 'benignitatem',"* Riccobono refers to several specific instances as D. (;5. 3) 2. 5; (7. 8) 1; (50. 17) 173; (34. 1) 1. 22. According to him, this *humanitas* tempered the *ratio scripta* and corrected it. Cf. also U. Berlière "L'exércice du ministère paroissial par les moines dans le haut moyen-âge,"—*Revue Bénedictine,* XXXIX (1927), 227-250.

the object of which is to ascertain as closely as possible what Ulpian wanted to record.

According to Ulpian, Barbarius, a slave, fled from his master to Rome. Masquerading as a freeman and as a citizen, he succeeded in getting deeply enough involved in politics to seek the office of praetor. Ulpian tells us that he succeeded in his quest and was *designated* to this office. In this capacity Barbarius served for a number of years, when ultimately his true caste became known. Then arose the perplexing question concerning the many litigations which he had settled and the decrees that he had issued during the period of his tenure of this public office. Were they to be considered valid? Or were they to be considered invalid and was there a consequent need to reprobate them? There evidently was a problem. As has been briefly pointed out above, under the law a slave could not function as a magistrate and consequently all of his acts would be invalid.

As a matter of recorded fact the acts of Barbarius were not reprobated. Ulpian expressed a clearcut decision that he thought the acts were to be regarded as valid. He did not demand, nor did he indicate the necessity of, adjudication by a special court, which perhaps would validate or sanate his acts. Nor did Ulpian imply that his own words or authority lent these acts any power of validity. Rather, he might be said to have indicated that the customary manner of acting in such emergencies would be to consider these acts valid.

Granted that the acts of Barbarius were to be considered valid, the question now occurs: On what basis were the acts of a slave praetor to be considered valid? From the manner in which Ulpian proposed this case of Barbarius, as a problem that merited the close attention of a jurist, it seems that Pomponius over-simplified the entire difficulty when he stated that the slavery of Barbarius was no obstacle to Barbarius' acting as praetor. Certainly, Ulpian did not manifest any agreement with Pomponius' solution. But, while it is true that Ulpian did not give assent to the apparently over-simplified solution of Pomponius, it is also true that this text of Ulpian reveals no authentic word or words which would indicate the specific reason why the acts of Barbarius were to be regarded as valid.

Because of this incompleteness of the text of Ulpian, to this day there has been much and varied theorizing on the question proposed in the *Lex Barbarius*. In all such theorizing one must remember that to the Romans Law was not a philosophical but an eminently practical issue.[11] Thus it might very well have been that the sole reason for considering the acts of Barbarius as valid was mere utility and the wish to avoid all the difficulties which would inevitably arise in the event that these acts were to be declared invalid. On the other hand, it might also have been the equity which the Greeks had as a juridico-philosophical postulate,[12] which was to give an internal consistency to a body of precepts and related them to some unchangeable verity. This Grecian idea of equity the Romans had made the servant of their practices to such an extent that the entire *Ius Honorarium* stands as a monumental proof of Roman equity, i.e., of Rome's recognition that behind the strict letter of the law was another law, the law of the safety of the Roman people, which must always occupy the first place in rank and importance.[13] Or, as Modestinus, a contemporary of Ulpian, put it,[14] the proper concept of law and of equity cannot allow an interpretation of law to be so harsh and severe as to forget the paramount purpose of law, namely, the utility of men. According to Modestinus it would be a grave mistake to sacrifice the convenience and utility of men by a rigid adherence to the literal wording of the law.[15]

[11] Sosius d'Angelo, "De aequitate in codice iuris canonici,"—*Periodica,* XVI (1927), 220*-221*: "Quid sit aequitas in iure Romano classico, omnes sciunt: 'est vis quaedam realistica,' ope praetoris aliquid 'retribuentis' in concreto per suum imperium in conflictu inter ius et aequum."

[12] Cf. *Aristotelis opera* (Berlin, Academia Regia Borussica, 1831-1870), *Nicomachea Ethica,* V, cc. 9-10.

[13] Cf. Roscoe Pound, "The idea of law," *Jubilee law lectures,* 1889-1939 (The Catholic University of America, School of Law, Washington, D C., 1939), pp. 72-97, esp. p. 73.

[14] D. (1. 3) 25: "Nulla iuris ratio aut aequitatis benignitas patitur, ut quae salubriter pro utilitate hominum introducuntur, ea nos duriore interpretatione contra ipsorum commodum producamus ad severitatem."

[15] Cf. also E. Wohlhaupter, *Aequitas canonica* (Paderborn: Verlag Ferdinand Schoeningh, 1931), p. 27.

But surely, if Ulpian's own lines lack direct assertion of what prompted the considering of the acts of Barbarius as valid, the interpolations make a bold attempt to reveal the missing reason. According to these the reason was equity, which stood over and above the direct demands of positive law. And this was an evidence of the growing spirit of benignity in law. It revealed juristic technique which had attained a status of maturity. It revealed juristic minds which had become more and more conscious of the law behind laws. It revealed their confidence that the supreme lawgiver, whether it be the people or the Emperor, to whom in the final analysis belonged the sovereignty of power in these questions, was ready and willing in such emergencies to overlook the strict demands of law and to favor the good of the people.

The progress of the study and of the practice of the Roman law was definitely halted by the Germanic invasions and by the fall of the Western Roman Empire. Roman law was a forgotten field until it was once more brought into cultivation by the efforts of Irnerius in the eleventh century. At that period the jurisconsults brought up again from the ashes the story of Barbarius. It is important to note their observations, because they indicated a manner of jurisprudence prevalent at their time and because their studies and findings may well account for the transition of the doctrine of the supplying of jurisdiction into canonical practice.

As Bartolus a Saxoferrato († 1357) remarked,[16] the text of *Barbarius* was interpreted in a twofold manner: either according to the *glossa* or according to the ultramontane theory to which on this point Bartolus himself subscribed.[17]

Following the *glossa* of Vivianus,[18] and thus adopting the rea-

[16] Cf. *Omnia, quae extant, opera* (Venetiis: Sexta Editio Juntarum, 1590), Tom. I, fol. 32, ad D. (1. 14) 3, *prima lectura,* ad litteram *a.*

[17] *Omnia, quae extant, opera,* ad D. (1. 14) 3, *secunda lectura,* nn. 6-7.

[18] *Glossa* ad D. (1. 14) 3, ad v. *Barbarius,* "Tria dicit haec lex. Pone. quidam Barbari nomine, servus erat: fugit a domino suo, et Roman ivit, et praeturam petiit, et praetor est factus. His tria quaeruntur, an fuit praetor? et respondit quod sic ibi *sed nihil etc.* Item quaeritur an fuerit liber? et ad hoc non respondit sed dicit quod Romanus populus potuit servum liberum facere: et ex hoc colligitur, populum tacite voluisse eum liberum esse, et sic liber fuit, et multo magis potuisset Imperator."

soning of Pomponius as evidenced in the text of Ulpian, *"nihil ei servitutem obstetisse,"* one school of interpreters held that Barbarius was a true praetor, and free, and that consequently his acts were valid as a natural consequence of his official position.[19] As a matter of fact, their position has never been wholly disproved. Even in the seventeenth century T. Sanchez granted the possibility that the glossator's interpretation might have been correct.[20] But the more common view was that of the ultramontane jurists, who claimed that Barbarius was not a praetor *de iure* but merely *de facto.*[21] They pursued this statement arguing that Barbarius, if he had been praetor, could have been so only in one of two ways: either by the force of common law or in virtue of a dispensation. They reject the first possibility on the ground of his utter incapacity as a slave. Nor do they feel there is a sufficient reason to presume that dispensation had been granted to Barbarius. And Bartolus notes [22] that he could not understand why all the difficulty should, or would, have risen about the validity of Barbarius' acts, if he were truly the praetor. And so, arguing on that basis, Bartolus concludes [23] that, although Barbarius was not a true praetor and not free, still his acts were valid.

But even among this second group of commentators there was no agreement as to what was the ultimate basis for validity. Some held that public utility, the public authority of the superior, and the error on the part of the people were all three required for the validity of these acts. Others felt that the law itself implied a dispensation because of the public peril, and so the ultimate reason was public utility. Still others held that common error would suffice, especially in a judge with ordinary power.[24] For the present,

[19] Bartolus, *Omnia quae extant, opera,* ad D. (1. 14) 3, *secunda lectura,* nn. 1-3.

[20] *De matrimonio,* Tom. I, lib. III, disp. 22, n. 5.

[21] Bartolus, *Omnia, quae extant, opera,* ad D. (1. 14) 3, *secunda lectura,* n. 3. Among the foremost proponents of this ultramontane theory were: Petrus de Bellapertica († 1335), Iacobus de Ravagnis († 1296), Cynus Pistoriensis († 1337), and Gulielmus de Cuneo († 1335).

[22] *Omnia, quae extant, opera,* ad D. (1. 14) 3, *secunda lectura,* n. 4.

[23] *Omnia, quae extant, opera,* ad D. (1. 14) 3, *secunda lectura,* n. 6.

[24] Bartolus, *Omnia, quae extant, opera,* ad D. (1. 14) 3, *secunda lectura,* n. 7.

the important point to note is that all agreed that the public good was a factor to be reckoned with in preventing the enforcement of the strict letter of the law.

It has been evident in the short study just completed that, with the passing of the centuries, the jurists were becoming more and more articulate in their consciousness that the law behind laws is concerned with the protection of the good of the people for whom laws were and are enacted. They were becoming more and more convinced that the legislator did not intend any man-made laws to bind any longer if, when, and as the observance of that law or its enforcement would defeat the very purpose of its institution: namely, the public good.

Roman law chronologically was the first to give jurists a recorded example which could have been, and actually was, interpreted by the jurists of all ages as an instance when the strict jurisdictional law was set aside, because otherwise the public good would have been endangered. In the pages following it will become more apparent just how closely canonists have followed the *Lex Barbarius.* It is true that what Rome was and is interpreted by jurists to have done seems at this age to be what any truly developed law system should do. It also remains true, as Jombart points out,[26] that, considering the internal and external constitution of the Church, in all probability, even without the precedent of the *Lex Barbarius,* the Church would have evolved her principle of the supplying of jurisdiction. Still, with all these possibilities, credit is due Roman law for affording canonists a legal background for a practice of equity in similar cases. But, despite this, remembering the objective fact that jurists were not, and even now are not, agreed on what actually took place in the case of Barbarius, whether he became a true praetor or not, whether his acts were valid *ex rigore* or *ex aequitate,* one must draw the conclusion along the lines of Van Hove's statement: "It is not of such prime importance to know exactly what the Roman law decreed. It is far more important to appreciate the understanding of that decree by interpreters and their application of it to various circumstances

[26] "L'erreur commne,"—*NRT,* L (1923), 169.

. . . In addition (it must not be forgotten) that canon law contributed not a little towards the rounding out of juridical teachings which have been first uttered by Roman jurists."[20] Truly, fortified by her own innate principles of equity, with which she was endowed by her Divine Founder, and which consequently were far above the pagan concept of equity, the Church, as shall be seen, through the medium of her canonists, took this Roman precedent, and, according to her interpretation, applied it to similar cases in the sphere of ecclesiastical affairs.

[20] *Prolegomena,* n. 301.

ARTICLE II. PRE-GRATIAN DEVELOPMENT

In the preceding article considerable care was taken to show that in all probability the basis of the *Lex Barbarius* was the equity of the Roman law system. Forthwith, however, even greater stress was laid, in a manner that was intended to allay any and all suspicion to the contrary, on the point that the Church did not in any way directly borrow from the Roman concept of equity. The Church was endowed with her own proper principles of equity by her Divine Founder, principles of a supernatural character, which of their very essence and because of their supernatural source were more noble than those evolved by a purely pagan mind. But if this be so, then a very natural question presents itself. If the purely human concept of equity could and did evolve a kind of pagan jurisprudence that is manifest in the *Lex Barbarius,* how is it that the doctrine of the supplying of ecclesiastical jurisdiction made no appearance at all until the twelfth century? How is the similarity between the Roman remedy and the canonical teaching to be explained? These questions will be answered, not because it is an imperative task to explain the absence of any canonical doctrine concerning the supplying of jurisdiction until so late a date, but because the answers may help to explain Gratian's reference to the suppletory principle of the *Lex Barbarius* and account for the varying opinions that arose concerning this doctrine as to its scope and comprehension.

First of all, one must understand that, though the Church is by institution a divine organization, it is nevertheless headed and directed on earth by human beings to meet human needs. In its aspect as a human organization, therefore, the Church has been subject to progress and development. This has been eminently true in the matter of jurisdiction. Contrary to the statement of Lea,[27] the Church enjoyed from the very beginning a power of jurisdiction which was separate from the power of Orders.[28] For

[27] *A history of auricular confession and indulgences,* (Philadelphia: Lea Brothers and Co., 1896), I, 274.

[28] Matt. XVIII, 18; VI, 19; Council of Carthage (350), cc. 4-9; 11-12—

example, it may be pointed out that jurisdiction does not primarily entail the power to give disciplinary decrees; but, first of all, doctrinal decrees. Even Lea could not claim that no doctrinal decrees were given prior to the thirteenth century. And, while it is true that jurisdiction was not the product of scholasticism, it is likewise true that the notion and the expanse of the concept of jurisdiction was not always so well defined as it is today.

Abuses of usurpation of ecclesiastical authority existed in the Church from the earliest centuries of her existence.[29] The Councils strove to eradicate these evils by establishing severe sanctions against usurpers.[30] But as regards the acts performed by these usurpers for people who were unaware of their incompetency there was never raised any question about their jurisdictional validity. There was a material toleration of such acts. Wilches carefully adds that before Gratian there was no word of formal supplying of jurisdiction by the Church. In fact, he points out, there could not be any inasmuch the doctrine about jurisdiction was not yet fully developed.[31]

From the Council of Chalcedon (451)[32] to the Third Lateran Council (1179)[33] the distinction and separability of the powers of Orders and of jurisdiction were not too apparent, since by the

Harduin, I, 952-954; Council of Hippo (393), cc. 7. and 9—Harduin I, 953-954; Cyprian, *Ep. IX—MPL,* IV, 257. Cf. also Hallier, "De sacris electionibus et ordinationibus," — Migne, *Theologiae cursus completus* (Paris, 1864), XXIV, 162; Kober, *Die Deposition und Degradation nach den Grundsätzen des kirchlichen Rechts* (Tübingen, 1867), p. 6 ss; Petavius, *De ecclesiastica hierarchia libri tres* (Paris, 1643), lib. III, cap. 9, n. 10 and cap. 10, nn. 6-8.

[29] Bruns, *Das Recht des Besitzes im Mittelalter und in der Gegenwart* (Tübingen, 1848), p. 128 ss.

[30] Cf., e.g., Council of Nice (325), c. 15—*Coll. Regia,* I, 431; Council of Antioch (341), c. 21—*Coll. Regia,* I, 601; Council of Sardica (342), cc. 1-2—*Coll. Regia,* I, 637; III Council of Carthage (397), c. 20—*Coll. Regia,* I, 963. Cf. also Wilches, *De errore communi in iure romano et canonico* (Romae: Apud Pontificium Athenaeum Antonianum, 1940), pp. 67-68.

[31] *De errore communi,* p. 68.

[32] C. 5—Mansi, VII, 365; Harduin, II, 603.

[33] C. 5—Harduin, VII, 1676.

very act and at the very moment when jurisdiction was granted by canonical mission, the ordination was likewise performed.[34] In the parish where the cleric received his training, there also was he to exercise his future ministry. The Council of Chalcedon had established this norm for the Church at large, and the custom continued that only such candidates should be raised to sacred Orders whose pledge to abide permanently at the church for which they were to be ordained had been confirmed by the term of their willing service previously rendered there. According to the then current ecclesiastical discipline, ordination and assignment formed reciprocal elements of one indivisible canonical concept. The conferring of an Order upon a cleric necessarily involved his simultaneous appointment.[35]

It was the Third Council of the Lateran (1179) that brought into bold relief the distinction and separability of the two powers of the keys. In addition it should be remembered that it was also in the twelfth century that ecclesiastical jurisdiction was properly limited to the spiritual sphere.[36]

In the face of all these obscurities in the demarcation of Orders and of jurisdiction it is little wonder that there is no trace of the doctrine of the supplying of jurisdiction until the twelfth century. But there were always in the Church two elements present which led inevitably towards the steady, although gradual, evolution of a jurisprudence to which the Code eventually gave its official sanction.

These two elements were the innate equity of the Church and the principle of ecclesiastical jurists of following the canons of the law of Rome wherever Church legislation was lacking. The

[34] C. Badii, *Institutiones iuris canonici* (3. ed., Florentiae: Libreria Editrice Fiorentina, 1921), n. 143, note 2; Wernz-Vidal, *Ius canonicum,* II, n. 48, note 14; Claeys-Bouuaert, *De canonica cleri saecularis obedientia* (Lovanii, 1904), I, 7, note 4.

[35] Bastnagel, *The appointment of parochial adjutants and assistants* (Catholic University of America, Canon Law Studies, No. 58: Washington, D. C., 1930), p. 24. Cf. also footnote 10 on p. 24 and footnote 33 on p. 30 of this same work.

[36] M. Van de Kerckhove, "De notione jurisdictionis apud decretistas et priores decretalistas,"—*Jus Pont.,* XVIII (1938), 12.

understood proviso in all such imitation was, of course, that there be nothing in the civil law contrary or derogatory to the Church's teaching.[37] Therefore, with the clear division between the power of Orders and that of jurisdiction, with the development and growth of the system of *latae sententiae* penalties from the eighth century on,[38] and with the beginning in the eleventh century of the practice of superiors to reserve to themselves certain sins and censures,[39] one agrees with Creusen's observation that the principle of the *Lex Barbarius* was especially practical in the middle ages and at the beginning of the modern era, when the conferring of offices could be so easily nullified by reason of the presence of some unknown censure.[40] Such a practice even received express Pontifical approval.[41] And quite naturally the decretalists followed this same rule in their interpretation of law.[42] In reference to the dependence of canonical jurisprudence upon Roman law in the subject of the supplying of jurisdiction, St. Alphonsus Liguori (1787) made perhaps the most direct statement: *"Lex Barbarius*

[37] *Glossa anonyma* ad D. XX: "Argumentum iudicandum esse in causis ecclesiasticis tam secundum leges quam secundum canones et tunc observandas esse leges sicut canones. Quod verum est nisi leges obvenient canonibus: tunc enim eis abrenuntiandum est."

[38] Cf. Michiels, *De delictis et poenis* (Lublin: Universitas Catholica, 1934), I, p. 35.

[39] Cf. Van Espen, *Tractatus de censuris,* p. 62a; Schmalzgrueber, *Ius ecclesiasticum universum,* lib. V, tit. 39, n. 216.

[40] "Pouvoir dominatif et erreur commune," *Acta congressus iuridici internationalis,* IV, 187.

[41] Lucius III (1181-1185) decided: "Quia vero, sicut leges non dedignantur sacros canones imitari, ita et sacrorum canonum principium constitutionibus adiuvantur . . . mandamus, quatenus diligenter considerans, quod post denunciationem novi operis, sive iure sive iniuria aliquid construatur, legalibus debet constitutionibus demoliri. Et quia nulla ecclesia in praeiudicium est alterius construenda, negotium ipse secundum legem et canonum statuta non differas terminare." in c. 1, X, *de novi operis denuntiatione,* V. 32. The *glossa ordinaria* to this canon is in entire agreement. ". . . In causa ecclesiastica Leges possumus allegare ut, etiamsi canones deficiant, possit iudicari secundum Leges."

[42] Cf. A. Van Hove, *Prolegomena,* n. 94.

. . . qui textus, etsi civilis, tamen, cum non sit reprobatus a iure canonico, vim habet etiam in illo, ut habetur in c. 1, De novi operis nuntiatione. . ." [48]

[48] *Opera moralia Sancti Mariae De Liguori* (Ed. nova, Romae: Ex Typographica Vaticana a P. Leonardo Gaudé, 1905-1912), Tom. III, lib. VI, n. 572. Hereafter reference will be made to this work simply as *Theologia moralis.*

ARTICLE III. THE INFLUENCE OF GRATIAN

Gratian's *Decretum* was not a mere compilation of canons like the later books of the Corpus of Canon Law. It was not a collection of rules such as contemporary legal scholarship took the Digest to be and such as was the Code of Justinian. Gratian thought of his function, not as one of Justinian's compilers, but as that of one of the classical Roman jurisconsults who had worked out principles of law which were designed to meet cases that were not included within the four corners of any rule. Gratian played a great part in the revival of the Roman law in his capacity as a *magister* in the School of Bologna. His greatness as a jurist becomes apparent by means of the *dicta* which he repeatedly appended to the laws included in his collection. His character as a Roman jurist is manifest in cases where he shows a direct dependence upon Roman civil law. Both these traits become apparent in a famous *dictum* which was inserted by him after a statement which he attributed to the Synod of Rome in the fourth century.[1] The law which Gratian recorded said in effect that an infamous person should be neither a procurator nor a judge. In a word, infamy excluded a person from certain acts which partook of a public or jurisdictional nature. Gratian however added: *"Tria sunt quibus aliqui impediuntur ne iudices fiant. Natura, ut surdus, mutus, et perpetuo furiosus, et impubes, quia iudicio carent. Lege, qui senatu motus est. Moribus, foeminae, servi, non quia non habent iudicium, sed quia receptum est ut civilibus non fungantur officiis.*[2] *Verum si servus, dum*

[1] C. 1, C. III, q. 7. Cf. Ojetti, *Commentarium in codicem iuris canonici* (Romae: Apud Aedes Universitatis Gregorianae, 1931), lib. II, 216, note 2: "Canon iste in textu dicitur desumptus ex sancta Romana synodo sine ulla maiori determinatione; sed secundum Car. de Turrecremata, *Gratiani decretum* (Romae, 1726), II, p. 399, desumptus est potius ex capitulis Hadriani papae I, c. V, A. D. 785. At confer Berardi, *Gratiani canones,* part. I, c. 45.

[2] Note the almost verbal similarity of this part of the *dictum* with D. (5.1) 12: *"Paulus libro septimo decimo ad edictum.* Cum praetor unum ex pluribus iudicare vetat, ceteris id committere videtur. Iudicem

putaretur liber, ex delegatione sententiam dixit, quamvis postea in servitute depulsus sit, sententia ab eo dicta rei vindicatae firmitatem tenet." [3] Thus in the first part of the *dictum* Gratian noted the three ways in which a person was excluded from the position of judge: by nature; by law; by custom. He noted, however, that women and slaves were barred, not because of any inherent inability, but merely because law and custom had so decreed. Therefore, when Gratian said that a slave's acts could under certain conditions be held valid, he merely implied that human laws could be understood in certain circumstances as not binding. By his silence in regard to impediments of natural law, Gratian evidently intimated the immutability of the natural law and the consequent necessity of always fulfilling the requirements of natural law.

This *dictum* is important for many reasons. Chief of all is the fact that it served as the first juridicial expression of a principle which was destined to evolve into the complex teaching on the supplying of jurisdiction. Secondly, the almost literal dependence of Gratian on Roman civil law shows the extent of the study of that Roman law by Gratian and his contemporaries.[4] Thus, when Lucius III expressly approved the practice of following the prescripts of Roman law where canon law had as yet made no direct provisions, he gave official sanction to a

dare possunt, quibus hoc lege vel constitutione vel senatus consulto conceditur, lege sicut proconsuli. is quoque cui mandata est iuridictio iudicem dare potest: ut sunt legati proconsulum. Item hi quibus more concessum est propter vim imperii, sicut praefectus urbi ceteriqui Romae magistratus. Non autem omnes iudices dari possunt ab his qui iudicis dandi ius habet: quidam enim *lege* impediuntur, ne iudices sint, quidam *natura*, ut surdus, mutus: et perpetuo furiosus et impubes, quia iudicio carent. *lege* impeditur, qui senatu motus est. *moribus* feminae et servi, non quia non habent iudicium, sed quia receptum est, ut civilibus officiis non fungantur. Qui possunt esse iudices, nihil interest in potestate an sui iuris sint."

[3] Note the similarity of context and solution with those in D. (1. 14) 3, as quoted on pages 33-34.

[4] It is important to note that chronologically the Decree of Gratian antedated the text of Lucius III given in c. 1, X, *de novi operis denuntiatione*, V, 32.

practice which was already common in the days of Gratian. From this it becomes evident that at least Gratian accepted the equitable solution of the problem of Barbarius the slave as applicable to similar cases in canon law.

However, care must be taken that not too much be deduced from this *dictum.* Close examination shows that Gratian here gave a particular manifestation in operation of the principle of equity. How far Gratian intended this principle of equity to function cannot be ascertained definitely. On the other hand, it would also be uwarrantable to set the limits of its functioning according to the case mentioned in the second part of the *dictum.* Furthermore, it needs to be stressed that here we have the strictly private opinion of Gratian. And, while it may be said with great probability that there was a general trend among jurists to apply this doctrine, so characteristically Roman in its origin, to the sphere of canonical law, it would be a sad mistake to aver that the doctrine of Gratian was immediately the generally accepted teaching. The glossator clearly indicates that there was a real doubt entertained on this question. While the writers who favored Gratian's doctrine could strengthen their claims by certain provisions of law,[5] a certain group of writers still retained its doubts concerning the applicability of Gratian's doctrine on the ground of other laws.[6] It must be noted that, while there was a division in opinion regarding the general applicability of the doctrine, there seems to have been a positive stand taken against its applicability in the case of one who had been excommunicated and then performed jurisdictional acts while his spiritual plight was unknown. The basis for this contention lay in the fact that a slave had at least some rights to appear before the court, while the excommunicated person had no right whatsoever to make such appearance. It is of added interest to note that certain canonists would not apply this doctrine of Gratian even to the case of the slave. Thus the

[5] Cf. c. 19. X. *de iure patronatus,* III, 38; c. 2, X, *qui filii sint legitimati,* IV, 17; c. 108, C. I, q. 1.

[6] Cf. c. 4, C. XXIX, q. 2; c. 4, D. VIII.

glossator Joannes Faventinus († 1190) stated: *"Vel dic (quod verius credo) quod nec sententia servi teneret, nisi confirmata esset a principe."* [7]

In brief resumé one may say that there was yet in the period of Gratian no uniformity of opinion. Gratian opened the way. But even his opinion, powerful though it was despite its merely private character, did not gain immediate acceptance by all. The idea was too new and Gratian's exemplification of it too sketchy and indefinite.

[7] *Glossa,* ad c. 1, C. III, q. 7, *v. Dum putaretur.*

ARTICLE IV. THE INFLUENCE OF THE GLOSSATORS

The principle of the supplying of jurisdiction was not any more formally expressed in the Decretals than in the Decree of Gratian. However, the glossators on the Decretals give unmistakably clear evidence not only of the continued reception of this principle but also of gradual evolution of it. They reveal how bit by bit the principle was being extended in its application. The glossators reveal also, from the differences of opinion among themselves and from the subsequent reception of them on the part of later canonists, that there were still no authoritative pronouncements to guide or to restrain them in their interpretations. They reveal, above all, the new lanes of thought which were being opened up for the decretalists and their successors in turn to probe and explore more thoroughly.

As has been noted above, there was no formal expression of this principle of the supplying of jurisdiction in the Decretals. However, the doctrine seems to have been at least adverted to in a case upon which Pope Innocent III passed judgment towards the close of the thirteenth century.[1] In this case Innocent declared invalid the sentences pronounced by a judge who had been *publicly* excommunicated. At this juncture it is imperative to recall that in that era, in fact right up to the issuance of the Constitution *"Ad evitanda"* by Martin V in 1418,[2] all excommunication deprived the delinquent of jurisdiction.[3] Every excommunicate was juridicially an *excommunicatus vitandus.* Now the decision of Innocent implied, as Bernardus Parmensis de Bottone († 1263) interpreted it in his *glossa,* that the sentence

[1] C. 24, X, *de sententia et re iudicata,* II, 27.

[2] *Fontes, n.* 45.

[3] Hyland, *Excommunication, its nature, historical development and effects* (Catholic University of America, Canon Law Studies, No. 49: Washington, D. C., 1928), pp. 31-34; 36-47; T. Sanchez, *De matrimonio,* Tom. I, lib. III, disp. 22, n. 33, Cf. also E. F. MacKenzie, *The delict of heresy in its commission, penalization, absolution* (Catholic University of America, Canon Law Studies, No. 77: Washington, D. C., 1932), p. 12.

would have been valid if and when the excommunication had been occult. Then, if there had been common error, the Church would have supplied the necessary jurisdiction.[4] The *glossa* of Bernardus de Bottone is undoubtedly a sign of a distinct veering away from the flat, uncompromising contention of some jurists, as expressed by Joannes Faventinus († 1190),[5] namely, that in the case of one excommunicated there could be absolutely no invocation of the principle of the supplying of jurisdiction. It may not be premature to note at this juncture that the interpretation, as expressed by Bernardus de Bottone, did not enjoy a universal acceptance over the narrower interpretation expressed by Joannes Faventinus. As will be seen, authors still were to come forward who would tenaciously hold to the stricter limits of interpretation.

Aside from indicating progress in interpretation, this *glossa* in addition allows two other important deductions. First of all, it seemed to aver that only those who were ignorant of the impediment would profit from the doctrine of supplied jurisdiction.[6] Secondly, the *glossa* reveals the still existent rigor of discipline in regard to those who were *publicly* excommunicated.[7] Clearly there was no question of supplying in cases where the excommunication had been public.

While other *glossae* similarly revealed that the doctrine of the supplying of jurisdiction occupied the attention of canonists, they likewise indicated the uncrystallized character of opinion concerning it. For example, in reference to a case at Rouen,[8]

[4] *Glossa,* ad c. 24, X, *de sententia et re iudicata,* II, 27, ad *v. Innodatus* " . . . aliud si occulte: quia tunc nec ipse nec alii ipsum tenebantur vitare: quia divinare non poterant . . . unde cum communi opinione liber et absolutus habebatur et credebatur, quicquid interim facit, valet."

[5] *Glossa,* ad c. 1, C. III, q. 7, ad *v. Reprobari.*

[6] *Glossa,* ad c. 24, X, *de sententia et re iudicata,* II, 27, ad *v. Innodatus:* " . . . aliud si occulte: quia tunc nec ipse nec alii tenebantur vitare: *quia divinare non poterant."*

[7] This was in entire agreement with c. 7, X, *de immunitate ecclesiarum, coemeterii et rerum ad eas pertinentium,* III, 49, and a *glossa* on this text ad *v. Vigorem.*

[8] C. 54, X, *de electione et electi potestate,* I, 6.

which was decided against a certain priest, who, contrary to express conciliar provisions, had presumed to retain simultaneously two benefices, the text of the decision included the lines: *"In suae quoque salutis et multarum animarum dispendium praedictas parochiales ecclesias retinebat, quum earum cura, qua iam privatus fuerat ipso iure, ad eum nullatenus pertineret, et sic per ipsum eaedem animae damnabiliter sunt deceptae."* Interpreting these lines, a certain glossator correctly noted that, if a prelate ceased to hold a benefice, he no longer had any power of binding or loosing over his parishoners. But then, bringing up a very pointed and direct query as to the validity of absolutions given by such a prelate or of the penances imposed by him, the glossator wrote that in his opinion such acts were not valid. He indicated an awareness that the faithful still considered this prelate their lawful pastor. Yet, although he did not think the salvation of these people was endangered unto damnation, he attributed their being saved not to the power of the *keys,* as exercised by this prelate, but to power of the *faith* that they had at the time of the reception of his ministrations.[9] On the strength of these lines in the text and of the jurisprudential outlook expressed by the glossator, various interpretations and applications were made on such points as, e. g., whether the doctrine of the supplying jurisdiction was to apply to the internal forum or not, and whether it would apply when a title, once had, was lost. Thus a new series of problems was provoked by this *glossa.*

In regard to the need of a title the glossators said nothing to indicate that it was universally required or dispensed with by jurists. The cases in which mention of the principle of the supplying of jurisdiction was made all dealt with specific inci-

[9] *Glossa,* ad c. 54, X, *de electione et electi potestate,* I, 6, ad v. *Deceptae:* "Sed numquid valebit absolutio illius talis praelati sive poenitentia per illum imposita? Non videtur, quia nullam potestatem habet ligandi vel solvendi, sicut non valent sententiae a non iudice latae . . . In isto casu non credo quod perirent, non quia ille posset, sed *propter fidem* quam habebant de sacramento, cum crederent esse praelatum, et ita *in sola fide salvantur."*

dents where some sort of title had been present at one time or another. Of such incidents, and particularly of one, in regard to which the glossator points out that the quasi-possession of a prelature *by the permission of the pope* was sufficient reason for the application of the principle of the supplying of jurisdiction,[10] many commentators were to make much in demanding that a title be present before the principle of the supplying of jurisdiction could be invoked. The fact remains that the glossators did not directly indicate that the problem of the *titulus* had engaged their attention. Consequently no definite solution was offered by them for this problem.

Likewise, on the point of *error* no definite disquisition is to be found in the annotations of the glossators, although it is evident, from every citation wherein the glossators make reference to the principle under discussion, that they regarded error as an indispensably accompanying factor in the case. But on one point, it seems, there was some amplification over and above the doctrine of Gratian and the legislative text of the Decretals. It appears that the glossators recognized the possibility of an impediment being public in one place and not in another. Consequently they held that, if error were common in the place where the jurisdictional act was exercised, such a circumstance was reason enough to bring about the supply of needed jurisdiction.[11]

This brief study was primarily intended to show how the teaching on the supplying of jurisdiction, as received from Gratian, gradually evolved in its scope and comprehension. No doubt other *glossae* could be noted which canonists have cited in support of their particular contentions. But to treat all such *glossae* with all their possible insinuations would be a long, tedious task which would merely accentuate the fact that the teaching on the various points was still not uniform. An addi-

[10] *Glossa finalis* ad c. 43 X, *de electione et electi potestate,* I, 6: "Ponderant enim ut acta falsi praelati valeant, fuisse in quasi-possessione praelaturae de licentia Pontificis."

[11] *Glossa,* ad c. 21, X, *de iureiurando,* II, 24, ad *v. Observandus.*

tional reason for omitting any further inspection of the *glossae,* for the present at least, is the fact that in the following article the development of the doctrine will be traced and its tracing will necessitate occasional references to the glossarial teaching.

ARTICLE V. THE SUBSEQUENT DEVELOPMENT UP TO THE CODE

While the glossators did open up new avenues of thought in regard to the teaching of the supplying of jurisdiction, and while it is true that their contribution to the development of the doctrine is noteworthy, nevertheless it remains likewise true that they bequeathed to their successors a myriad of difficulties. This is noted not in any disparaging manner. One could hardly expect complete agreement on the part of the canonists on a point so new in jurisprudential practice as was that of the supplying of jurisdiction. If one were to add to this newness the further difficulty of an utter lack of directive official statements, one could not help but conclude that the progress made by the glossators is worthy of praise. They set the stage for further development, which shall now be noted along the different lines of the teaching on the topic under discussion.

A. Application to Both "Fora"

The principle of *Lex Barbarius,* as interpreted by canonists and as reiterated by the *dictum* of Gratian, treated of acts in the external forum. Naturally, since both texts had been so clear on this point, there was no doubt recorded regarding the application of the principle to the external forum in canon law. T. Sanchez (1550-1610) was able to call this opinion *most certain.*[1]

But it may also have been because of the very clarity of these two texts that commentators, who were inclined to follow slavishly their literal prescripts, doubted the applicability of this teaching to the internal forum. Bartolus († 1357) noted the doubt entertained by some of his contemporaries on this point [2] and T. Sanchez also noted that Paludanus († 1342) had cited certain writers who balked at the application of these principles of the supplying of jurisdiction *ad forum conscientiae.*[3] No

[1] *De matrimonio,* Tom. I, lib. III, disp. 22, n. 5.

[2] *Omnia, quae extant, opera,* ad D. (1. 14) 3, *secunda lectura,* n. 14.

[3] *De matrimonio,* Tom. I, lib. III, disp. 22, n. 12.

doubt those who felt inclined towards the literal interpretation of the two texts under consideration thought they found a veritable justification for their stand in the text of the Rouen case, treated in the preceding article, and in the *glossa* which had accompanied the word *"deceptae"*. Apparently there was a specific case, passed upon by the Pope, where despite the presence of a title and common error, the parishioners' salvation was seemingly not considered very seriously jeopardized.

However, this restrictive view did not have a general appeal. The greatest among the decretalists, such as Pope Innocent IV (1243-1254),[4] Hostiensis († 1271)[5] and Joannes Andreae († 1348)[6] did not see eye to eye with the glossator on the word *"deceptae."* On the contrary, they applied the principle of the supplying of jurisdiction also to the tribunal of penance, provided that there were concomitantly present with common error a title from the legitimate superior.[7] Panormitanus (Nicolaus de Tudeschis), also known as Abbas Siculus († 1453), likewise lent the force of his authority to this opinion. In addition he attempted to explain and to harmonize the words of the text and of the *glossa* with the position held by Innocent IV, Hostiensis, and Joannes Andreae.[8]

[4] Ad c. 54, X, *de electione et electi potestate,* I, 6, n. 3.

[5] ad c. 54, X, *de electione et electi potestate,* I, 6, ad *v. Damnabiliter.*

[6] ad c. 54, X, *de electione et electi potestate,* I, 6, n. 42.

[7] These authors belong to the school of canonists who demanded a title. As shall be seen in a subsequent article, the necessity of a colored title for the supplying of jurisdiction was questioned by many authors of weight and authority right up to the Code.

[8] C. 54, X, *de electione, et electi potestate,* I, 6, n. 20: "In glossa, in verbo *Deceptae,* ibi, *credo quod perirent,* etc. Signa istam particulam usque ad finem et numquam tradas oblivioni. . . . Unde dicit Innocentius quod non erant deceptae, quia ex quo habeatur pro praelato et tolerabatur a superiore, vere absolvebantur ab illo. Et ad textum potest dici, quod animae decipiebantur, quantum erat in isto praelato. Item potest dici, quod ex quo notorium erat illum non habere titulum canonicum in beneficio, quod vere decipiebantur animae, quia non datur tunc tolerantia. . . . Posset tunc circa dictum glossae dubitari, quid si aliquis esset intrusus, quod numquam habuisset superioris auctoritatem, dic quod non. . . . Sed in foro animae posset dici, quod sic, propter fidem sacramenti ex

From the decretalists this opinion passed down the centuries. Its universal reception is evident and authors continued to follow Panormitanus' manner of explaining the *glossa* to the word "*deceptae*" by offering the numerous possibilities that might have occurred in that case at Rouen,[9] and thus showing that the text and *glossa* did not necessarily mean to exclude from the application of the principle of the supplying of jurisdiction cases of the internal forum where common error and a title were present.

B. The Breadth of the Application of the Principle of Jurisdiction

The question of how far the Church could or would go in supplying jurisdiction was one of the most complex and perplexing to the canonists, at least until the issuance of the Constitution "*Ad evitanda*" by Martin V in 1418.[10] On the part of some canonists there was an apparently excessive liberality in extending the application of this principle, an astonishing heedlessness with regard to placing any limits on the Church's power to supply jurisdictional competency, or even on her capacity to make up for the deficiencies resulting from impediments inherent in the divine or natural law. On the part of others there was a very strict adherence to the literal wording of the texts of Ulpian[11] and of Gratian.[12] Between these two extreme tendencies was found a group that ever tried to be mindful of the potential extent and the limit of the Church's power and stressed more the spirit than the letter of the two texts just cited.

The extreme laxists held that, as long as common error and a title were present, even if there were present an impediment of

quo subditi credebant illum esse praelatum, praesertim cum non sit peccatum male intelligere ius positivum."

[9] Cf. Pignatelli, *Consultationes canonicae* (Coloniae Allobrogum: 1700), Tom. VI, Consultatio III, dubium I; M. Gonzales-Tellez, *Commentaria perpetua in singulos textus quinque librorum decretalium Gregorii IX* (Maceratae: 1756), Tom. I, lib. 1, tit. VI, cap. 54, n. 6.

[10] *Fontes*, n. 45.

[11] D. (1. 14) 3.

[12] C. 1, C. III, q. 7.

the divine law, the Church would still supply the necessary jurisdictional capacity to insure the validity of the jurisdictional acts performed. Thus Jason, at the end of the fifteenth century, asserted that, if a woman were by mistake elected to the Papacy, her jurisdictional acts would be valid if a title and common error were present.[13] Giovanni Francesco a Ripa († 1534) considered as safe the opinion that the absolutions of a non-priest would be valid if common error and the necessary title were present at the time of the acts. However, he did admit that the opposite opinion was safer.[14] Such, too, was the liberal conclusion of Mascardus († 1588),[15] although later in the same work he expressed a contradictory view.[16]

But while this group attributed such excessive power to the Church it must be recalled that Panormitanus had at an earlier time noted that there was a limit to the Church's power of supplying competence, that she had no power to supply it in any but the really jurisdictional sphere of affairs.[17] And, again, Panormitanus[18] and Felinus Sandeus († 1503)[19] further manifested the powerlessness of the Church over impediments of the natural law.[20] This general teaching, indicating limits to the Church's

[13] *Omnia opera,* ad D. (l. 14) 3, n. 64.

[14] *Responsa in quinque libros decretalium* (Venetiis: Apud Iuntas, 1569), "Tractatus de peste et de remediis ad conservandam ubertatem," fol. 57, nn. 45-46.

[15] *De probationibus* (Venetiis: Ex Officina Damiani Zenari, 1593), Tom. II, concl. 648, n. 14.

[16] *De probationibus,* Tom. II, concl. 648, n. 98.

[17] Ad c. 3, X, *de presbytero non baptizato,* III, 43: "In quibus iuribus nota quod communis error in dependentia a iurisdictione, non autem dependentia ab ordine, seu in istis sacramentalibus. In his enim attenditur veritas, et non opinio."

[18] Ad c. 13, X, *de rescriptis,* I, 3, n. 12.

[19] Ad c. 13, X, *de rescriptis,* I, 3, n. 4: "Non obstante aliqua iuris solemnitate, tamen non censetur remissa inhabilitas iuris naturalis, ut si est furiosus, surdus, etc. . . . Et ideo Baldus . . . dicit, quod contra defectus iuris non cadit dispensatio iudicis . . . Facit dictum Hostiensis . . . quod clausula supplens omnem defectum, non purgat tales defectus."

[20] Cf. Antonius Gabriellus, *Communes conclusiones* (Venetiis: Apud Minimam Societatem, 1593), Tom. I, lib. 1, concl. 8, n. 89.

power, found considerable confirmation in one of the canons of the Council of Trent wherein it was declared that the Church has no power over the matter and form of the Sacraments.[21] Obviously the erroneous concept, as expressed by Jason, Ripa and Mascardus, did not gain much headway. The excessive character of these assumptions led Sanchez uncompromisingly to label as *"prorsus a veritate aliena"* any opinion which claimed the validity of absolutions given by one who was not a priest.[22]

Of far graver complexity, and much more difficult for canonists to unravel, was the question of whether or not the Church would or could supply in the case of one who had been excommunicated. Here it will be of great aid to recall the contention of certain jurists, as expressed by Joannes Faventinus († 1190),[23] that the doctrine of supplied jurisdiction would not at all function in cases where the impediment of excommunication was present. Bernardus de Bottone in his *glossa,* however, indicated a trend of jurisprudence which held for the application of these principles in cases of occult excommunication.[24] This difference in the glossarial teachings quite naturally affected the juristic application of this principle in the cases of excommunication.

Some distinguished and held that, if one were excommunicated *before* assuming an office, his jurisdictional acts would be invalid simply because of his utter capacity to be the recipient of any favors from the Church.[25] The opposition to this opinion, as Sanchez noted, was vast and overwhelming; for the exception stipulated by them could not be justified by any law.[26]

Another group contended that, even if one were bound by an occult excommunication *after* gaining an office, the jurisdic-

[21] Sess. XXI, *de Sacramento Eucharistiae,* c. 2: "Praeterea declarat, hanc potestatem perpetuo in Ecclesia fuisse, ut in sacramentorum dispensatione, *salva illorum substantia,* ea statueret vel mutaret, quae susci pientium utilitati seu ipsorum sacramentorum venerationi, pro rerum, temporum et locorum varietati, magis expedire iudicaret."

[22] *De matrimonio,* Tom. I, lib. III, disp. 22, n. 27.

[23] *Glossa,* ad c. 1, C. III, q. 7, ad *v. Reprobari.*

[24] *Glossa,* ad c. 24, X, *de sententia et re iudicata,* II, 27, *v. Innodatus.*

[25] Cf. Sanchez, *De matrimonio,* Tom. I, lib. III, disp. 22, n. 30.

[26] *De matrimonio,* Tom. I, lib. III, disp. 22, n. 30.

tional acts would be invalid.[27] This contention clearly disregarded the *glossa* of Bernardus de Bottone. Against it stood a phalanx of jurisprudential authorities from the days of the decretalists onward. The tone of all this recorded objection was signalized by Pope Innocent IV. It was indicative of the effort to probe more deeply into the spirit and to test more profoundly the impelling motive of the juridical principles underlying the Church's power and readiness to supply whatever jurisdiction might have been wanting.[28] As Sanchez later remarked, this difficulty lost all of its legal cogency after the Council of Constance.[29] In virtue of the Constitution *"Ad evitanda"* of Martin V [30] the faithful were no longer bound to avoid excommunicated persons, unless and until their excommunication had been pub-

[27] Cf. Sanchez, *De matrimonio,* Tom. I, lib. III, disp. 22, n. 33.

[28] Ad. c. 35 X, *de sententia excommunicationis,* V, 39, n. 3: "Item dum tolerarentur in aliqua dignitate, et sunt occulti non nominatim excommunicati, satis videtur, quod possint excommunicare, beneficia conferre, litteras impetrare, quia hoc ipsa dignitas facere videtur et non persona excommunicati." Cf. also Bartolus, *Omnia, quae extant, opera,* ad D. (1. 14) 3, *prima lectura,* n. 7, and *secunda lectura,* n. 9; Hostiensis, ad c. 24. X, *de sententia et re iudicata,* II, 27, ad *v. Publice innodatus;* Joannes Andreae, ad c. 24, X, *de sententia et re iudicata,* II, 27, n. 8; Panormitanus, ad c. 24, X, *de sententia et re iudicata,* II, 27, n. 14.

[29] *De matrimonio,* Tom. I, lib. III, disp. 22, n. 32.

[30] *Fontes,* n. 45. The Constitution reads as follows: "Ad evitanda scandala et multa pericula, subveniendumque conscientiis timoratis, omnibus Christi fidelibus tenore praesentium misericorditer indulgemus, quod nemo deinceps a communione alicuius in sacramentorum administratione, vel receptione, aut aliis quibuscumque divinis, vel extra; praetextu cuiuscumque sententiae aut censurae ecclesiasticae (*aliter:* seu suspensionis aut prohibitionis) a iure vel ab homine generaliter promulgatae, teneatur abstinere, vel aliquem vitare, ac interdictum ecclesiasticum observare. Nisi sententia vel censura huiusmodi fuerit in vel contra personam, collegium, universitatem, ecclesiam, communitatem, aut locum certum, vel certa, a iudice publicata vel denunciata specialiter expresse: Constitutionibus Apostolicis et aliis in contrarium facientibus non obstantibus quibuscumque: salvo, si quem pro sacrilegio et manuum iniectione in clerum, sententiam latam a canone adeo notorie constiterit incidisse, quod factum non possit aliqua tergiversatione celari, nec aliquo iuris suffragio excusari. Nam a communione illius, licet denunciatus non fuerit, volumus abstineri, iuxta canonicas sanctiones."

licly promulgated or expressly declared by an ecclesiastical judge, or unless their excommunication as a notoriously known fact resulted from their notorious sacrilegious attack upon a cleric.[31]

According to another interpretation, similar to the one just treated, the principle of the supplying of jurisdiction had no place whatsoever in the case of an occult heretic. Consequently all of his acts were to be considered invalid.[32] As in the above case, the weight of authority was against this stand. And whatever doubt there might have been before the Council of Constance was wholly dispelled by the Constitution *"Ad evitanda"* of Martin V.[33]

While these opinions were restrictive of the Church's power, another group, insisting on a literal interpretation of a case settled by Innocent III in 1174,[34] went to the other extreme of interpretation defending the validity of acts performed by one publicly excommunicated. They noted that in this case there had been a condemnation of a *delegated* judge who had been publicly excommunicated. They argued against the extension of this decision to cases where *ordinary* judge would be bound by the same impediment. And in their defense they advanced an old decision of the Rota.[35] However, this teaching was diametrically opposed to the decretal *"Adversus consules,"*[36] and to the glos-

[31] Cf. also Felinus Sandeus, ad c. 24, X, *de sententia et re iudicata,* II, 27, n. 6; Navarrus, *Opera omnia* (Venetiis: Apud Ioannem Guerilium, 1618), Tom. I, *Manuale Confessariorum,* cap. IX, n. 10, where he states that since the Constitution *"Ad evitanda"* of Pope Martin V all earlier contrary speculation on this point was ended. For the time prior to this Constitution, Navarrus admits that the opinion of men like Calderinus (†1365), denying the validity of acts performed by occult excommunicates, might have been defended as tenable. After the Council of Constance (1414-1418) the opposite opinion demanded recognition.

[32] Cf. Sanchez, *De matrimonio,* Tom. I, lib. III, disp. 22, n. 25.

[33] *Fontes,* n. 45.

[34] C. 24, X, *de sententia et re iudicata,* II, 27.

[35] Cf. Sanchez, *De matrimonio,* Tom. I, lib. III, disp. 22, n. 24.

[36] C. 7, X, *de immunitate ecclesiarum, coemeterii, et rerum ad eas pertinentium,* III, 49: The Fourth General Council of the Lateran (1215) was here speaking of the excommunicated rectors of churches: "Adiicimus ut constitutiones et sententiae quae a talibus vel de ipsorum mandato

sarial teaching.[37] No wonder that almost universal teaching of the canonists was against the theory! [38]

Finally, a certain group of canonists contended that the acts performed by one who possessed a title to a parish, but who was under occult excommunication, would be valid if concomitant common error were present; not so, however, if these jurisdictional acts were performed by one who acted only out of a special commission or delegation. They looked upon the office of a delegate as a private one. And they felt, as Sanchez noted, that ". . . in regard to those things which are done by a private individual, there is no difference whether the individual be secretly or publicly excommunicated. Nor does common error avail anything in such a case.[39] This then brings up a question as to the applicability of the principles of the supplying of jurisdiction to cases of delegated power, which shall be treated in the immediately following number.

C. Application to Cases of Delegated Power

The fact that public welfare inspired the jurisprudential teaching evidenced by the *Lex Barbarius* and the *dictum* of Gratian was aparent to all canonists from the beginning. On this point all agreed. However, this same agreement did not exist among canonists with regard to the circumstances under which public utility was involved.

Despite the fact that Gratian clearly applied the suppletory principle to a slave who was regarded free and who, having been *delegated,* passed sentence,[40] and notwithstanding the fact that

fuerint promulgatae inanes et irritae habeantur, nullo umquam tempore valiturae." Cf. also c. 12, X, *de exceptionibus,* II, 25, and c. 14, *de sententia excommunicationis, suspensionis, et interdicti,* V, 11, in VI°.

[37] *Glossa,* ad 7, X, *de immunitate ecclesiarum, coemeterii, et rerum ad eas pertinentium,* III, 49, ad *v. Tempore:* "Sic patet, quod sententia a tempore excommunicationis lata nulla est, nec etiam convalescere potest, immo si detegatur post sententiam, quia si aliquis fuerit *publice* excommunicatus, retractatur sententia."

[38] Cf. Sanchez, *De matrimonio,* Tom. I, lib. III, disp. 22, n. 36.

[39] *De matrimonio,* Tom. I, lib. III, disp. 22, n. 26.

[40] C. 1, C. III, q. 7.

Innocent III in his decree implicitly applied this same teaching to a delegated judge,[41] certain canonists balked at the application of the principles of supplied jurisdiction to cases of delegated power. They felt with Celsus [42] that the laws were instituted because of public utility and consequently were not to be invoked in cases that did not concern the public good at all. And these canonists placed delegated power in just that category, as if it were the equivalent not of a public but of a private power. Thus, Innocent IV, writing of a certain process, which concerned judges who proceeded to pass judgment on the basis of falsified letters which was declared to be *"irritum . . . et inanem"*, forces the question: should these acts have been considered valid because of the ignorance of the nuns for whom the judges acted? Innocent answered in the negative. In his mind, when merely a single case had been delegated to someone, the public welfare was not at all at stake.[43] In agreement with Innocent was Joannes Andreae. Writing of the same case as Innocent, Joannes also concluded: *"Hic fuerit tantum una causa, non est multa subiectorum utilitas."* [44] And, as Panormitanus has recorded,[45] Guillermus de Cuno († 1335) held the same opinion in cases of delegation for individual instances, but not in delegations *ad universitatem causarum,* since the latter were considered equivalent to ordinary power.

Innocent's view was certainly a restrictive view of the scope of the application of the *Lex Barbarius* and of the *dictum* of Gratian. His view was diametrically opposed to that of Guillelmus Durantis († 1296) who expressly taught that the acts of a delegated arbiter or judge would be valid even though he were

[41] C. 24, *de sententia et re iudicata,* II, 27.

[72] D. (1. 3) 4: "Ex his, quae forte uno aliquo casu accidere possunt, iura non constituuntur."

[43] Ad c. 22, X, *de rescriptis,* I, 3, n. 1: "Sed dic illa tolerata propter utilitatem multorum, qui habuerunt necesse agere apud eum cum praefecturam teneret, et praesidiatum . . . his autem cum causa tantum una commissa sit, non est multa utilitas subditorum. Unde propter hoc non est tolerandus iste processus, item hic nullam habet iurisdictionem."

[44] Ad c. 22, X, *de rescriptis,* I, 3, n. 14.

[45] Ad c. 22, X, *de rescriptis,* I, 3, n. 10.

occultly incompetent.[46] Bartolus challenged this interpretation of Innocent IV: *"Et puto quod nisi unicum actum, ille actus valeret, et de aequitate."* [47] As Bartolus explicitly wrote, he considered two factors as necessary for the application of the principle of the supplying of jurisdiction: common error and the authority of the superior. Baldus de Ubaldis († 1400) declared himself as favoring the application of these principles to delegated power.[48] And Baldus, while he held, like Bartolus, that the two important factors for the supplying of jurisdiction were common error and the authority of the superior, added what Bartolus undoubtedly by oversight did not mention, namely, that it was sufficient in determining the public welfare to consider the quality of the office rather than the number of individual acts exercised in that office.[49] Furthermore, Joannes ab Imola († 1436) elaborated his opposition to Innocent's view thus: "Public utility is sufficiently at stake even though immediately the interests of only one person are involved: because it is of grave concern to the state that justice be measured out to each and every one." [50] Finally, as Panormitanus († 1453) observed: "It can be said that, by the very fact that a superior has entrusted a case to someone, public law and public utility are automatically involved, inasmuch as he has granted the commission in virtue of public law." [51] And Panormitanus in the same text related the general opposition in his day to the interpretation of Innocent: "Modern authorities commonly impugn this dictum of Innocent." Felinus Sandeus († 1503) likewise noted the same fact in his writings.[52] This teaching of the applicability of the suppletory principle in cases of common error even in regard to a delegate was subsequently continued, as is

[46] *Speculum iuris* (Venetiis, 1577), Pars I, lib. I, partic. I, *de arbitro et arbitratore,* § differt, n. 10.

[47] *Omnia, quae extant, opera,* ad D. (1.14) 3, *secunda lectura,* n. 7.

[48] *Opera omnia,* ad D. (1.14) 3, *prima lectura,* n. 35. "Unum non omitto."

[49] Cf. Felinus Sandeus, ad c. 22, X, *de rescriptis,* I, 3, n. 3.

[50] Cf. Felinus Sandeus, ad c. 22, X, *de rescriptis,* I, 3, n. 3.

[51] Ad c. 22, X, *de rescriptis,* I, 3, n. 10.

[52] Ad c. 22, X, *de rescriptis,* I, 3, n. 3.

evidenced by authors like Antonius Gabriellus,[53] Mascardus,[54] Reiffenstuel,[55] Schmalzgrueber,[56] Ballerini,[57] and Lehmkuhl.[58] A practical application of this doctrine by certain canonists will be seen in the treatment of the problem of the applicability of this suppletory principle to delegated assistance at marriage.

But while the common opinion of canonists turned against Innocent's teaching on the point of his general exclusion of any and all delegated power from the applicability of the principles of the supplying of jurisdiction, not all of the opposing doctors agreed on the extent of applying this principle to delegated power. Several, including Antonius de Butrio († 1408), Joannes ab Imola († 1436) and Dominicus de Sancto Geminiano († before 1436),[59] held that this doctrine would hold and apply only if the defect were in the *person,* and not at all if it were in the *form,* or in the commission. They argued that if an indifferent toleration of the acts of a delegated judge were intended by the law, why, given a defect in the delegated judge's jurisdiction, was he required by law to pronounce himself a competent judge?

Panormitanus[60] weighed carefully this objection. He noted, first of all, that this requirement of the judge to pronounce himself competent in a given case was not peculiar to merely delegated judges. Even the ordinary judges were required to do this. Panormitanus could not see why, if common error were able to effect the validity of the acts of Barbarius, the same should not apply in the case of anyone delegated for some jurisdictional act. He thereupon drew up two possibilities for the presence of error

[53] *Communes conclusiones,* lib. I, concl. 8, n. 33.

[54] *De probationibus,* concl. 648, n. 57 ss.

[55] *Ius canonicum universum,* lib. I, tit. 3, n. 234.

[56] *Ius ecclesiasticum universum,* lib. I, tit. 1, n. 20.

[57] *Opus theologicum morale,* V. 335.

[58] "Kirchliche Jurisdiktion und das Supplieren derselben," *Zeitschrift für katholische Theologie,* VI (1882), 677.

[59] Cf. Felinus Sandeus, ad c. 22, X, *de rescriptis,* I, 3, n. 3; Panormitanus, ad c. 22, X, *de rescriptis,* I, 3, n. 10; Sanchez, *De matrimonio,* Tom. I, lib. III, disp. 22, nn. 17-18.

[60] Ad c. 22, X, *de rescriptis,* I, 3, n. 10.

in a test case of the point at issue. First of all there could be common error in regard to the source of jurisdictional power. Thus, the faithful might falsely think that their bishop possesses a certain power or that he is a true bishop. In a case such as this Panormitanus felt that if the bishop delegated someone for a certain act, the delegate would act validly since the bishop's delegation was valid because of common error and of common utility. Indeed, Panormitanus pointed out, this would be a true parallel of the case in the *Lex Barbarius*. Secondly, there could be error in the mind of one person only, and clearly in such a case an error of this character could not contribute validity to the acts, precisely because the utility of many, or the public good would not be endangered.

But, granted that the error was common, Panormitanus evidently could not understand why the principle of public utility did not apply in a case wherein there was question of the power or competency of a delegated judge. For, as has already been noted above, he felt that the very fact that the delegation had been conferred in virtue of public law, public law itself and public utility were thereby at stake. Yet, he admitted that, *if* there were no probable ignorance (the context of the text indicates he meant *error*), the process ought not to obtain as valid. Nevertheless, having granted that the suppletory law should not apply where the requisite common error were not present with regard to the one delegated, Panormitanus immediately subjoined that there was always the possibility for such a common error to be present, and so he added ". . . *forte possit dici valere processus, nisi ius in poenam casset.*" In the last analysis, then, Panormitanus was not against the application of the principle of the supplying of jurisdiction to cases of delegated power. Rather he seemed to favor it. But he wondered if in such cases the conditions would be fulfilled which were required for the functioning of this principle.

Felinus Sandeus modified this concession of Panormitanus.[61] According to him, if the commission were "*simpliciter surreptitia*" and no exception had been made against the one dele-

[61] Ad c. 22, X, *de rescriptis,* I, 3, n. 3.

gated, as long as he were tolerated, the process would be valid. If the commission came from a false rescript, that is, not from a legitimate authority at all, then the *Lex Barbarius* could in no way apply.[62] And if the rescript were obtained from a legitimate superior but still remained null, then the trial would be invalid unless and until the delegate had pronounced upon his competence. Sanchez, a century and a half later, wisely noted this line of argumentation and stated in a more positive manner what Panormitanus ventured rather hesitantly, *"Sed verius est, quando vitium est circa commissionem factam a legitimo superiore, dum communiter id vitium ignoratur, valere gesta per delegatum, nisi ius in poenam casset."* [63] His ultimate reason for this view was that here were present all the requisites for the supplying of the jurisdiction: the authority of the superior and common error. He remarked very emphatically: *"Non est maior ratio, quando error est vitii personae, vel vitii commissionis: cum utrumque vitium possit probabiliter, vel crasse ignorari."*

Such was the evaluation of what was the constituent element of public utility. That difference of opinion was to prevail even up to the time of the present Code. The question of the *vitium commissionis* will come up for treatment again in the number dealing with *common error.*

D. Common Error

Ulpian's recording of the *Lex Barbarius* in the Digest of Justinian [64] revealed what a great rôle the factor of error played in the solution of the unusual case of Barbarius. The words *"quamdiu latuit"* and *"et si scisset servum esse, liberum efficisset"* clearly indicate that the Romans were deceived into considering Barbarius a true praetor and that their dealings with him as an official of Rome were occasioned by their error concerning his true status. The solution, that is, the decision on the part of the

[62] Here is an apparent insistence on the part of Felinus Sandeus that the delegate have some species of title from a legitimate superior. Though the two questions are very closely interrelated, the treatment of the necessity of the title will be deferred until a subsequent number.

[63] *De matrimonio,* Tom. I, lib. III, disp. 22, n. 19.

[64] D. (1.14) 3.

jurisconsults to consider his official acts as valid despite his servile condition, indicates that the error on the part of the people was, if not the entire, at least a partial, reason for the suspension of the normally strict Roman laws regarding status, public office and jurisdiction. However, the extent of this error of the people is not clearly manifest in the text itself. Still, the context seems to indicate that this error, although it may not have been universal, was at least rather general. It appears that the number of people affected by the actions of this Barbarius was comparatively large, large enough, in fact, to occasion an unmistakably general solicitude on the part of the jurists about the validity of Barbarius' acts, his judgments and decrees.[65] Indeed, there were instances in Roman law when error of a few was disregarded. Thus, for example, if anyone by error approached a praetor who was not qualified to hear his case, the consent to have him as judge could not effect the validity of that praetor's sentence.[66]

But, in the case of Barbarius reason itself demanded that the error be considered at least in some degree as common error; for the official position of Barbarius was, after all, a public charge. In the normal course of events his office was bound to bring him even into direct contact with many of his subjects, who in their needs and difficulties had to turn to him for official aid and ministration. Indications, therefore, are strong that in the case of Barbarius a goodly number of people had been affected in their dealings with this slave-praetor. And for this reason the jurists argued that the strict enforcement of the written law, which in the last analysis had been drawn up for the public utility and good, would not attain but rather defeat its primary purpose. The textual indications become clearer in the *glossa* of Accursius († 1260).[67] Drawing from the rescript of Hadrian[68] and a sentence of Paulus,[69] Accursius summed up

[65] D. (1.14) 3: " . . . quae edixit . . . quae decrevit."

[66] D. (2.1) 15. Cf. also D. (50.17) 116, 2.

[67] *Glossa*, ad D. (1.14) 3, ad *v. Functus sit.*

[68] C. (6.23) 1: "Testes servi . . . omnium consensu liberorum loco habiti sunt."

[69] D. (33.10) 3: " . . . et error facit ius."

the extent of the influence of error in an axiom which has retained its force up to this day: *"Communis error facit ius."* Apparently, while the concept of common error did not exist so clearly in the minds of the jurists in the days of Barbarius, there is no question of a definite crystallization of this notion in the period of the Roman glossators.

Unlike Ulpian, Gratian in his memorable *dictum*[70] merely indicated that here would hardly be sufficient reason for not heeding the requirements of the ordinary law regarding competency and jurisdiction, unless and until there had been a deception of the people whose welfare and interests would be placed in jeopardy, if the strictness of the written law were observed and enforced. And, as in the case of Ulpian's text, so in the reference to the *dictum* of Gratian the glossator defined more clearly the concept of the extent and import of this deception.[71] Thus from the glossators of the Roman law and of the Decree of Gratian the term *common error* came down the centuries.

Several notes concerning this common error must be observed in any serious effort to gauge its part in the progressive development of the doctrine on the supplying of jurisdiction.

I. Quality of Error

Almost from the beginning canonists were generally agreed that the error had to be one which had a probable basis in its occurrence and real existence, not an error which resulted from supineness of intellect or crassness of understanding. The latter kind of error was specifically excluded inasmuch as it potentially implied the equivalent of knowledge in all cases of normal human intelligence.[72] Perhaps the clearest summary of the teaching of the canonists has been phrased by Panormitanus: "*. . . tolerantur gesta propter errorem communem . . . aut erat ignorantia probabilis, et sustinetur propter ignorantiam . . . aut erat probabilis, sed crassa et supina, et tum actus est nullus si impedi-*

[70] C. 1, c. III, q. 7.

[71] *Glossa,* ad c. 1, c. III, q. 7, ad v. *Dum putaretur:* "Ecce quantum communis opinio operatur."

[72] C. 2, *de constitutionibus,* I, 2, in VI°.

mentum ex se inducit nullitatem." This distinguishing quality of error remained clearly stressed by almost all canonists of later times.[74]

II. Place of Error

Was it sufficient for error to be common in the place where the jurisdictional act was performed or would the fact that the error was not universal preclude the possibility of the application of the suppletory principles of the *Lex Barbarius* and of the *dictum* of Gratian?

Palacios (Joannes Lupus de palaciis rubeis, † after 1503),[75] for example, felt that, once a person had been a notorious or denounced excommunicate in any part of the world, he could never plead the existence of common error in any region of the world as a justification of the valid character of the jurisdictional acts he performed there. His reason was that such notoriety or denunciation placed one wholly outside the ambit of the Church's toleration. Thus he concluded that the Church would not supply the jurisdiction which was wanting. On this point, however, he and his school stood almost alone. Contemporary canonists adopted a kinder, broader view, namely, that it would suffice for error to be common in the place where the jurisdictional act was performed. The basis of their view was rooted in the objective facts underlying the story of Barbarius and the *dictum* of Gratian. Surely Barbarius' condition had been known to his intimates and acquaintances. The same could be

[73] Ad c. 13, X, *de rescriptis,* I, 3, n. 12. Cf. also c. 8, X, *de dolo et contumacia,* II, 14, nn. 42 and 45; Felinus Sandeus, ad c. 13, X, *de rescriptis,* I, 3, n. 5, where he indicates that he is substantially following the words of Panormitanus and that this opinion is in accord with Innocent IV and other canonists of that period.

[74] E. g., Felinus Sandeus, ad c. 13, X, *de rescriptis,* I, 3, n. 5; Lessius, *De iustitia et iure,* lib. II, cap. 29, dub. 8, n. 67; Sanchez *De matrimonio,* lib. III, disp. 22, n. 9; Pirhing, *Jus canonicum,* lib. II, tit. 1, sec. 3, q. 1, n. 84; Schmalzgrueber, *Jus ecclesiasticum universum,* lib. II, tit. 1, n. 20; Pichler, *Jus canonicum,* Tom. I, lib. II, tit. 1, n. 18; D'Annibale, *Summula,* I, n. 79, note 73; *Praelectiones iuris canonici habitae in seminario sancti Sulpitii,* Tom. I, n. 285.

[75] As cited by Sanchez, *De matrimonio,* Tom. I, lib. III, disp. 22, n. 33.

said of any slave whose condition would be a public fact at least in his section of the country.

The glossators, too, had been aware of this sort of reasoning, as they show very clearly. According to one *glossa* the fact of the notoriety of an act in any given place would not ban a special mode of procedure at law in another place if at the time and at the place of the positing of the jurisdictional act there was a common error about the true condition of the agent.[76] The decretalists generally held that the existing impediment or incompetency of an agent nevertheless admitted the application of the principle of the supplying of jurisdiction as long as the hindrance affecting the agent remained a secret in the place where the jurisdictional act was exercised.[77] They nevertheless recognized the existence of doubt on the part of some commentators concerning the correctness of this generally accepted interpretation. According to Panormitanus the commentator Antonius de Butrio († 1406) belonged to the ranks of those who were hesitant about accepting the commonly received explanation. But in justice to the latter it should be pointed out that on occasion he too revealed a strong leaning towards the broader and kindlier interpretation.[78] The broader interpretation prevailed to such an extent that Sanchez was able to write without any reservation that it would suffice for the error to be common in that place when the action was posited.[79] Common error,

[76] *Glossa,* ad c. 21, X, *de iureiurando,* II, 24, *v. Observandus.*

[77] Panormitanus, ad c. 13, X, *de rescriptis,* I, 3, n. 13: "Sed circa hoc vertitur notum dubium, quod si impedimentum erit notorium in uno loco et in alio ubi actus gestus occultus? Refert Paulus de Liazariis († 1356) se habuisse a Ioanne Andreae († 1348) quod actus detur sustineri propter probabilem ignorantiam, quod erat in loco, quod est semper menti tenendum. Et quamquam d. Antonius de Butrio († 1406) videtur dubitare, *ego puto illud dictum verissimum,* propter dictam legem Barbarius . . . nam verisimile est, quod in partibus suis erat notorium illos esse servos, et tunc actus sustinetur, si in loco iudicii putabantur liberti."

[78] Antonius, ad c. 13, X, *de rescriptis,* I, 3, n. 12; also ad c. 24, X, *de sententia et re iudicata,* II, 27, n. 11. Cf. also Panormitanus, ad c. 24, X, *de sententia et re iuricata,* II, 27, n. 11.

[79] *De matrimonio,* Tom. I, lib. III, disp. 22, n. 9. Cf. also n. 10, where Sanchez clearly marked the commonness of this opinion, noting as he

then, as existing at the place and at the time of the performance of the jurisdictional act was the requirement eventually agreed upon by canonists in relation to the Church's supplying of the needed jurisdiction.

III. Subjects of the Error

A point closely related to the one just treated caused difficulty in the application of the suppletory principle. Granted that common error had to be present, and granted that sufficient error was really present to demand the application of the doctrine of the supplying of jurisdiction, would it be necessary for those who were to profit from this law to be among those who were deceived?

Certain canonists, as Sanchez pointed out,[80] emphasized the fact that in both the *Lex Barbarius* and in the *dictum* of Gratian, the jurisprudence turned in favor only of those who were ignorant of the true status of the one acting in a jurisdictional capacity. They stressed the importance of the words *"quamdiu latuit"* [81] and *"si servus, dum putaretur liber."* [82] Their position apparently received confirmation from the *glossa*, *"Quia divinare non poterant vitium occultum."* [83] And on this score they felt that if a person had a putative title and there were a concomitant common error, the doctrine of the supplying of jurisdiction would indeed function but *only* with regard to those who were ignorant of the occult impediment. Among these were Baldus de Ubaldis († 1400),[84] Felinus Sandeus († 1503),[85] Antonius Gabriellus († 1555),[86] Covarrubias († 1577),[87] Navarrus († 1586),[88] and

did that he was following the teaching of Panormitanus, Antonius, Socinus († 1367), and other canonists. Cf. also *Communes conclusiones Antonii Gabrielli Romani*, Tom. I, conclusio 8, n. 12.

[80] *De matrimonio*, Tom. I, lib. III, disp. 22, n. 40.

[81] D. (1. 14) 3.

[82] C. 1, C. III, q. 7.

[83] *Glossa*, ad c. 24, *de sententia et re iudicata*, II, 27, *v. Innodatus*.

[84] *Opera omnia*, ad c. 24, X, *de sententia et re iudicata*, II, 27, *v. Innodatus*.

[85] Ad c. 35, X, *de rescriptis*, I, 2, n. 40.

[86] *Communes conclusiones*, Tom. I, lib. 1, concl. 8, n. 32.

[87] *Opera omnia*, ad c. 24, *de sententia excommunicationis, suspensionis, et interdicti*, V, 11, p. 1, § 6, n. 8.

[88] *Opera omnia*, Tom. I, *Manuale confessariorum*, cap. IX, n. 10.

others.[89] This opinion, however, gradually lost ground. Prosper Fagnanus († 1678) was perhaps its last notable defender.[90]

But what Sanchez termed the more probable opinion, which he also followed,[91] veered away from the literal reading of the texts of Ulpian and of Gratian. It argued that laws, by their nature, do not concern themselves with the error or ignorance of one or two people. Just as a particular error does not suffice to validate the acts of an incompetent judge, so too the knowledge of a particular person cannot hinder the validity of acts by the same judge, if the necessary conditions are fulfilled.[92] Such was the interpretation of by far the greater number of canonists, evidenced since the time of Sanchez by Basilus Pontius († 1629),[93] J. Sanchez [or Sanctius] († 1624),[94] Pichler († 1736),[95] Lessius († 1623),[96] Bouix († 1870),[97] and Craisson († 1881).[98] Among these canonists, however, as Sanchez pointed out,[99] the greater doubt concerned the validity or invalidity of a sacramental confession knowingly made to one who was a denounced excommunicate or a notorious aggressor of a cleric. Sanchez summed up the more commonly held opinion when he ventured that such confessions would be valid as far as the confessor's jurisdiction was concerned; but it would be invalid because of the *obex* on the part of the penitent. Basilius Pon-

89 Cf. Sanchez, *De matrimonio,* Tom. I, lib. III, disp. 22, nn. 42-44.

90 Ad c. 1, X, *de schismaticis et ordinatis ab eis,* V, 8, n. 134.

91 *De matrimonio,* Tom. I, lib. III, disp. 22, n. 41.

92 Cf. Sanchez, *De matrimonio,* Tom. I, lib. III, disp. 22, nn. 42-44.

93 *De sacramento matrimonio tractatus* (2. ed., Bruxellis: Ioannes Moercercius, 1627), lib. V, cap. 20, nn. 6-9.

94 *Selectae, illaeque practicae disputationes de rebus in administratione sacramentorum* (Venetiis: Apud Bertanos, 1639), Disp. 44, n. 3. Hereafter this work will be referred to simply as *Selectae disputationes.*

95 *Jus canonicum* (Ravennae, 1741), Tom. I, lib. II, tit. 1, n. 18.

96 *De iustitia et iure,* lib. II, cap. 29, dub. 8, n. 68.

97 *Tractatus de iudiciis ecclesiasticis,* p. 134.

98 *Manuale totius iuris canonici* (5. ed., Pictavii, 1877), Tom. I, n. 301. Here this author explicitly notes that this is a probable opinion, contrary to Fagnanus and others of that school of thought.

99 *De matrimonio,* Tom. I, lib. III, disp. 22, n. 46.

tius,[100] and Joannes Sanchez[101] went even a trifle farther and held that one could, even knowing of the impediment of the confessor, approach him and validly seek absolution. Pontius and J. Sanchez believed that the penitent would be placing an *obex* to the proper reception of the sacrament only if he knew that the confessor would commit a sin by administering the sacrament.

IV. Extent of Common Error

In this process of the crystallization of the doctrine regarding the supplying of jurisdiction there were two points concerning error which have caused much discussion. The first of these difficulties revolved about the question whether the doctrine would apply only in error of fact or whether it would apply also in error of law. The second was concerned about the question whether the error in form or commission would preclude the applicability of this principle.

First a few notes shall be made concerning the question of the application of the suppletory principle to common error of law and to common error of fact. Canonists have always readily admitted the supplying of jurisdiction in common error of fact inasmuch as the disposition of the *Lex Barbarius* specifically referred to an error of fact.[102] Indeed, an examination of the more ancient pre-Code authorities and a close study of the examples which they constantly adduced to illustrate their understanding of, and their teaching concerning, the suppletory principle[103] lead one to believe that as a body they did not extend the applicability of this principle beyond cases of common error of fact. As a matter of fact many of the older canonists very specifically declared that the Church would not supply

100 *De sacramento matrimonii tractatus,* lib. V, cap. 20, nn. 6-9.

101 *Disputationes selectae,* Disp. 44, n. 3.

102 Cf. Verricelli, *Quaestiones morales et legales,* Tr. II, q. XXV, n. 12.

103 Cf. Sanchez, *De matrimonio,* Tom. I, lib. III, disp. 22, nn. 33 and 37. On this point it is well to note that these older authors agreed despite their differences in opinion on other scores. Cf. A. Salvador, "Error communis et iurisdictionis suppletio ab ecclesia," *Boletin Eclesiastico,*—— XVII (1939), 176-177. Hereafter this periodical shall be referred to by the abbreviation *BE.*

in common error of law. In their opinion the Church would not supply because, in the ultimate analysis, error of law can be avoided whereas such is not the case with error of fact. Clearly voicing this sentiment were authors like Federicus de Senis, [104] St. Antoninus († 1459),[105] Cajetan († 1534), Mascardus († 1558) and Garcias († post 1613).[106] The others, it seems quite clear, were content to labor under the assumption that the Church would supply only in common error of fact. This contention is brought out in some measure by Sanchez when he wrote, "The acts of an occult heretic, provided there be verified common error of fact together with a true or a putativé title, are valid." [107]

Very manifestly Sanchez regarded as accepted by all the principle, *"Circa factum error facit ius."* [108] In a very precise manner († 1672) likewise [109] reflects the generality of this teaching. The significance of this doctrine was especially clearly exemplified by Fagnanus who, like Sperelli, lived in the seventeenth century.[110] Apply this doctrine to the Ruthenians, he carefully stated their position in the Church, their knowledge that they were cut off from the unity of the Church, and their possible conviction that theirs was the Catholic religion. He noted, then, that they were ignorant, not of the *fact,* but of the

104 As cited by A. Sperelli, *Decisiones fori ecclesiastici* (Coloniae, 1667), Dec. XXXI, n. 11.

105 "Confessionarium," c. 176 Prologi apud Cappelli, *Lexicon Abbreviaturarum* (Milano, 1899), pag. LXI.

106 *De beneficiis ecclesiasticis* (Venetiis, 1618), Par. V, c. IV, n. 304.

107 *De matrimonio,* Tom. I. lib. III, disp. 22, n. 6.

108 Compare with the *glossa* to the Roman text of the *Lex Barbarius:* "Circa factum error communis facit ius."—*Glossa* ad D. (1. 14) 3 ad *v. Reprobari.*

109 *Decisiones fori ecclesiastici* (Coloniae, 1667), Dec. XXXI, n. 11: "Dispositio leg. Barbarius Philippus procedit si erratur in facto, secus si in iure. Cum decisionis ea potest reddi ratio, quia conclusio dict. leg. Barbarius procedit dumtaxat, quando error est in facto, secus si erretur in iure, ut originaliter docuit Feder. de Senis in cons. 112, num. *nihil* 5, ver. *et si dicatur,* quem sequitur Francisc. igr. in rubr. ff. de oper. nov. nunc., concl. 648, n. 100."

110 Ad c. 1, X, *de schismaticis et ordinatis ab eis,* V, 8, n. 135.

jus. And as long as they were ignorant of the *jus* the doctrine of the supplying could not be applied to them. However, if any one of their ministers were mistakenly considered still to be a true Catholic, then, the error being about the fact, this doctrine would apply. As many authors have already pointed out, the opinion followed by Fagnanus was based upon the regula, "*Ignorantia facti, non juris excusat.*"[111]

Protagonists of this school continued right up to the time of the Code. Thus Maupied († circa 1878)[112] was able to write that, even in his day, the *majority* of authors insisted upon common and probable error of fact and taught that common error of law, no matter how probable it might be, would not suffice. They, too, after the fashion of Fagnanus, followed the rule that ignorance of the fact, and not of the law, excuses. They were convinced that, were the Church to supply in common error of law, she would be encouraging contempt for her laws. Maupied agreed that their reasoning was quite sound and valid in questions of clear and certain laws. But he also remarked that *many* canonists felt that, if common error were founded upon a truly probable opinion about an obscure law, the Church would supply the necessary jurisdiction.

As Salvador quite accurately observed,[113] members of this school for the most part came from amongst the comparatively more recent pre-Code authors. There is no doubt that this doctrine was developed simultaneously with the growth of the system of probabilism. Already in the time of Verricelli it was commonly taught that an error about a law which was obscure and doubtful was considered the same as an error of fact.[114]

Among the proponents of this newer school of canonists were Lessius († 1623),[115] Schmalzgrueber († 1735),[116] De Angelis († 1881),[117] Icard (†1893)[118] and D'Annibale († 1892).[119]

[111] Reg. 13, R. J., in VI°.

[112] *Juris canonici compendium*, Tom. I, col. 278.

[113] "Error communis et iurisdictionis suppletio ab ecclesia,"——*BE*, XVII (1939), 177.

[114] *Quaestiones morales et legales*, Tr. II, q. XXV, n. 12.

[115] *De iustitia et iure*, lib. II, cap. 29, n. 67. Speaking of jurisdictional

But it must be adequately emphasized that the authors of this school did not propound this doctrine without due distinctions and limitations. Even a cursory study shows that they did not admit that jurisdiction would be supplied if the common error should concern a law that was clear and certain.[120] They uniformily insisted that the error be truly probable.

Like these canonists, who have just been adduced, Bouix[121] also clearly held that the Church would supply in doubt of law as well as in doubt of fact. But Bouix stood apart from them in this respect, namely, that he did not demand that the error of law be probable. He took exception to Schmalzgrueber's statement that the Church would not supply the jurisdiction necessary for the validity of the acts of a putative judge if and when the common ignorance about the existence or validity of the title or about a *clear and certain law* were due to *crassness* or *supineness* on the part of those in error. Bouix insisted that any such qualification of common error was superfluous since, in his opinion, there simply could not be common error so crass or supine that the Church must be considered as not supplying.

In summary it might be said that all of these canonists but developed the doctrine that an error about a law which was obscure and doubtful was to be considered an error of fact. They enjoyed the support of all the probabilists who considered it licit to use probable jurisdiction. Aligned with them were also the anti-probabilists though on different grounds. The authority of both groups offered a grave reason for considering this doc-

acts performed by one without the necessary power of jurisdiction he wrote: "Si id occultum ratione communis ignorantiae fuisset, non fuissent irritae . . . Nec refert, quod id proveniat ex errore iuris: modo sit probabilis et causat errorem facti."

116 *Ius ecclesiasticum universum,* lib. II, tit. I, n. 20.

117 *Praelectiones,* II, tit. I, n. 24.

118 *Praelectiones iuris canonici* (7. ed., Parisiis, 1893), Pars I, p. 507.

119 *Summula,* I, n. 79, note 73.

120 Cf., e. g., Schmalzgrueber, *Ius ecclesiasticum universum,* lib. II, tit, I, n. 20; De Angelis, *Praelectiones,* II, tit. I, n. 24; Icard, *Praelectiones iuris canonici,* Pars I, p. 507; D'Annibale, *Summula,* I, n. 79, note 73.

121 *De iudiciis,* pp. 132-133.

trine as already tempered by common use even before the Code appeared.[122] But of this probable jurisdiction more will be said in detail in the section that will deal with the doubt of fact and of law.

The second difficulty alluded to above had to do with error in form or in commission. T. Sanchez had mentioned the difficulty in regard to a delegate, the validity of whose jurisdictional acts was questioned strongly despite the presence of the commission and of common error.[123] Craisson, obviously following Sanchez,[124] made the same exception, refusing the application of the principle of supplying because, as he put it, a title was then lacking. This interpretation of Craisson certainly did not reflect the common teaching of canonists. His *a priori* exception carried little, if any, weight with authors who did not demand a title for the Church's supplying of jurisdiction.[125]

V. The Measure of Common Error

Before the present Code there was no issuance of any definition to guide canonists in measuring the presence of common error. Nor was there ever a sufficient unanimity among them to result in a natural crystallization of the idea of *common error.*

It seems to have been well accepted by the time of T. Sanchez that for the verification of common error there was no need of the presence of universal error.[126] So also was it accepted that the error of one or two or a few did not suffice to form a common error.[127] Indeed, as Jombart well put it, between *moral*

[122] *Praelectiones juris canonici habitae in seminario sancti Sulpitii* (6. ed., Parisiis: Apud Victorem Lecoffre, 1886), Tom. I, n. 285.

[123] *De matrimonio,* Tom. I, lib. III, disp. 22, n. 53.

[124] *Manuale totius juris canonici,* Tom. I, n. 304.

[125] Cf. pp. 81-87 of this work.

[126] *De matrimonio,* Tom. I, lib. III, disp. 22, n. 5.

[127] Pirhing, *Jus canonicum in quinque libros distributum* (Dillingae, 1674), lib. II, tit. 1, sec. 3, q. 1, n. 84; De Angelis, *Praelectiones iuris canonici ad methodum decretalium Gregorii IX exactae* (Romae, 1877-1891), lib. II, tit. 1, n. 24; Schmalzgrueber, *Ius ecclesiasticum universum,* Tom. II, Pars I, lib. II, tit. 1, n. 20.

unanimity and the *small number* there lay vast open zones where most varied opinions were able to take their place.[128] Naturally, then, such an undefined and undetermined point gave rise to all kinds of theorizing.

Some authors made no effort whatsoever to enlarge upon the term *common error,* either because it seemed very clear or because in their day the various possibilities of complications in the application of this doctrine had not yet occurred.

Others declared themselves for *moral unanimity*. Among these were Reiffenstuel († 1703),[129] who admitted that error was common even if some of those present at the nuptial ceremony were aware that the ministering priest had no proper jurisdiction, and Schmalzgrueber († 1735),[130] who admitted the presence of common error even if the confessor were in bad faith.

Others demanded that a *greater part* of the faithful be in error. Among these were Leurenius († 1723),[113] and Gennari († 1914).[132]

Still another group was content that common error was present if *many* were in error.[133]

Lega († 1935) not long before the appearance of the Code summarized the teaching of canonists on common error very succinctly: "Since it is the public authority which supplies the defect of jurisdiction in a putative judge, certainly common error is required: for common law is intended to provide for the common good; for the incidental error of some does not merit a general provision: in this nearly all agree."[134]

In the midst of such a generally accepted manner of explaining the presence of common error, the really revolutionary char-

128 "L'erreur commune,"—*NRT,* L (1923), 171.

129 *Ius canonicum universum,* lib. IV, tit. III, n. 76.

130 *Ius ecclesiasticum universum,* lib. II, tit. I, n. 22.

131 *Ius canonicum universum* (Augustae Vindelicorum, 1737), Tom. II, lib. II, tit. 20, . 610.

132 *Consultazioni morali-canoniche-liturgiche* (Romae, 1902), Cons. LXIX.

133 Cf. Lehmkuhl, *Theologia moralis,* II, n. 504.

134 *De iudiciis ecclesiasticis civilibus,* n. 355.

acter of Bucceroni's concept stands out in bold relief.[135] Bucceroni († 1918) abandoned the hitherto traditionally accepted requirement that the *common error* be *actually* committed in the minds of the entire community, or of the greater part of the community, or even of many. He abandoned this theory because, he felt, it entailed too many inconsistencies and difficulties. Arguing his point Bucceroni took under consideration the case of a priest without faculties successively giving absolution to a certain number of people in a community. If it were true that the *common error* had to be actually common, when could one with certainty establish the presence of such actual common error? It would certainly be difficult to draw the line, on one side of which one could state positively that there was not *common error* and on the other side of which one could just as positively aver the presence of *common error.* There would always be a few cases about which one could not help but be uncertain. However, even if one could accurately determine that after such and such a time common error *actually* were present, would it not be true that the benignity of the Church would not benefit those persons who received absolution before the error had been actually committed by a sufficient number of people to become *common?* Furthermore, once the error had become actually *common,* undeniably the first person who thereafter received absolution would be validly absolved. But Bucceroni could not see how the required conditions of *common* good and *common* error could be considered to coexist in the case of such a single individual. In view of such difficulties Bucceroni discarded the theory which required *actual* error. Instead he taught that the requirements of the common error and of the public good were fulfilled from the very first absolution of the priest. It was sufficient, according to him, that there be present a *fundamentum erroris* which could and in the normal course of events would lead people into error.

[135] *Casus conscientiae* (4. ed., Romae: Ex Typographia Augustiniana, 1901), p. 568.

E. Necessity of a Title

The *Lex Barbarius*[136] and the *dictum* of Gratian[137] both cited examples wherein, besides common error, the authority of the superior was also in some way present. It is a matter of common agreement that from the beginning the authority of the superior has always been considered the normal source of public power, such as is the power of jurisdiction. The theory of supplied jurisdiction postulated situations that were not normal. The question presented itself to canonists: Was that title, apparent in the texts of Ulpian and of Gratian, always to be insisted upon before invoking the suppletory doctrine? Or was this authorization to be dispensed with?

From the treatment thus far it has become clear that the above cited texts did not propound any general statute laws but gave particular manifestations of a jurisprudential practice. As on all other disputed points, canonists had to decide for themselves whether or not the words of the texts were to be explained restrictively in the scope of their application, or whether they were to be regarded as encouraging a more expansive application and as indicating a liberal mentality in the lawgiver which allowed an advance beyond the limits of the text. It is undeniable, as Leurenius[138] and Schmalzgrueber pointed out,[139] that the texts themselves seemed to favor the school of canonists who held for the necessity of a title.

Bartolus († 1357) was perhaps the first who clearly drew a sharp outline of this dispute. His appraisal and solution of the problem was destined to wield a great influence on his pupils and on the canonists who were to follow. Bartolus himself felt that this law should be so understood that for its proper functioning the fulfilment of two conditions had to be verified: the conferring of the office by an *authorized* superior and the pres-

[136] D. (1. 14) 3: "Cum populus Romanus etiam servo potuisset decernere hanc potestatem."

[137] C. 1, C. III, q. 7: "Servus dum putaretur liber, *ex delegatione* sententiam dedit."

[138] *Ius canonicum universum,* Tom. II, lib. II, tit. 20, q. 610.

[139] *Ius ecclesiasticum universum,* lib. II, tit. 1, n. 21.

ence of common error.[140] His disciples, Baldus[141] and Jason,[142] two leading exponents of the Bartolist school, followed the opinion of their master on this point. And Bartolus' opinion was in full accord with that of Pope Innocent IV who likewise demanded the presence of a title.[143] Such, too was the opinion of Joannes Andreae who, like Innocent, clearly demanded the confirmation of the superior.[144] In fact, such was the general teaching of all the decretalists, as is further evidenced in Panormitanus[145] and Felinus Sandeus.[146] It appears that not even a single decretalist has yet been found who *clearly* stood against the requirement of a title in addition to common error for the application of these suppletory norms to acts that were properly jurisdictional.[147] The general position of the decretalists was manifestly followed by the greater part of the sixteenth and seventeenth century canonists, as evidenced by the clear texts of men like Navarrus († 1586),[148] Covarrubias († 1577),[149] T.

140 *Omnia, quae extant, opera,* ad D. (1. 14) 3, *prima lectura,* n. 7: "Modo quaerere restat, an communis utilitas, et publica auctoritas superioris, et error populi, et omnia ista tria essentialiter requirantur ad validitatem actorum. Et videtur quod sufficit superioris auctoritas cum quasipossessione libertatis . . . E contra videtur, quod periculum multorum dispenset haec lex, et sic sit finalis ratio, publica utilitas, vel quasi. E contra videtur, quod sufficit error communis, qui facit ius, et maxime in iudice ordinario."

141 Baldus de Ubaldis, *Opera omnia,* ad D. (1. 14) 3, *prima lectura,* n. 9.

142 Jason, *Opera omnia,* ad D. (1. 14) 3, n. 50.

143 Ad c. 43, X, *de electione et electi potestate,* I, 16, n. 11: "Nam ubi aliquis est intrusus in aliqua ecclesia sine auctoritate superioris, qualis est omnis non confirmatus, puta quia sua auctoritate occupavit, vel aliorum potentum, quicquid facit non tenet . . . nec potest bonam fidem allegare nisi confirmationem vel institutionem habuerit superioris." Cf. also n. 3. Also cf. ad c. 17, X, *de electione et electi potestate,* I, 6, n. 3.

144 C. 43, X, *de electione et electi potestate,* I, 16, n. 28.

145 Ad c. 43, X. *de electione et electi potestate,* I, 16, n. 11: "Nec communis error iuvat, ex quo deest auctoritas superioris. Nam *Lex Barbarius* praeallegata fundat se super communi errori, et super auctoritate superioris."

146 Ad c. 22, X, *de rescriptis,* I, 3, n. 3: " . . . habet locum si concurrat auctoritas superioris et error communis."

147 It is designedly noted that there are no texts which *clearly* and

Sanchez († 1610),[150] and Reiffenstuel († 1703).[151] Fagnanus (1598-1687) likewise insisted upon the presence of the title.[152] And while Benedict XIV (1740-1758) did not clearly reject the theory which asserted that the Church would supply in common error alone, he did cite the opinion of Fagnanus as worthy of commendation. He noted likewise that his opinion was followed by the Sacred Congregation of the Council.[153] Such was the interpretation, then, that was commonly held up to the time of the Code.

But even within this school of authors, who demanded the presence of a title in addition to common error, there was an attempt to further clarify their stand. It was not sufficient that the title come from any superior whatsoever. It had to be conferred by the *proper* superior.[154] And even when one had been legitimately elected, if the confirmation of the proper superior were required, there would be no title until and unless that confirmation were made.[155]

There were two other points regarding title which caused much controversy, but which were quite well determined by the time of the advent of the Code. One group claimed that if a title legitimately secured were lost by reason of a delict or were

convincingly establish this point. As the reader will soon see, several texts of Innocent, Hostiensis, Joannes Andreae and Felinus Sandeus have been adduced by authors as arguments for demanding only common error. These texts, however, are not so clear and definite as to establish with certainty that these authors did not require the presence of a title together with common error. Cf. on this point J. de Cardenas, *Crisis theologica* (Venetiis, 1700), Pars IV, Diss. II, art. V, n. 152; Cf. also T. Sanchez, *De matrimonio,* Tom. I, lib. II, disp. 22, n. 48; Didacus Antonius Frances, *Tractatus de intrusione* (Lugduni, 1660), q. XLVI, n. 5.

148 *Opera omnia,* Tom. I, Manuale, Cap. IX, n. 11.

149 *Opera omnia* (Antuerpiae: Apud Ioannem Meursium, 1628), *Practicae questiones,* Cap. XIX, n. 9.

150 *De matrimonio,* Tom. I, lib. III, disp. 22, n. 49.

151 *Ius canonicum universum,* lib. II, tit. I, Par. VIII, n. 199.

152 Ad c. 1, X, *de schismaticis et ordinatis ab eis,* V, 8, n. 130.

153 *Institutiones ecclesiasticae* (Ed. tertia latina veneta, Venetiis, 1788), Tom. II, Institutio LXXXIV, n. XX.

154 Sanchez, *De matrimonio,* Tom. I, lib. III, disp. 22, n. 50.

155 Sanchez, *De matrimonio,* Tom. I, lib. III, disp. 22, n. 52.

secretly revoked, then the doctrine of the supplying of jurisdiction would no longer apply. As has been seen in a previous section, the more common and more probable opinion was strongly in opposition to this view. Another group contended that if there were an error in the solemnity or in the form of the conferring of the title, the title could not be considered *coloratus* and therefore the suppletory doctrine would not apply. But Sanchez indicated the presence of another view: that this contention would not be acceptable once a confirmation of a proper superior had been given.[156]

Yet, while theories requiring the presence of a title from a legitimate superior retained a numerous following,[157] there slowly emerged another group of canonists who taught that common error alone was sufficient for the application of the suppletory principle. Already in the days of Bartolus[158] there was a tendency to hold that the *ratio finalis* of the *Lex Barbarius* was the public good and that the authority of the superior was not an indispensable condition. Numbered among these contenders were Petrus de Bellapertica († 1308) and Cynus Pistoriensis († 1337). Sanchez similarly made mention of a trend of thought in this direction.[159] As Sanchez notes in review, these jurists based their belief upon instances in Roman Law[160] and in Canon Law,[161] wherein the law provided for the validity of certain acts, although there were present only possession of an office and common error. These authors brought out as confirmatory

[156] Sanchez, *De matrimonio,* Tom. I, lib. III, disp. 22, nn. 55-53.

[157] Cf., e.g., Mascardus, *De probationibus,* Tom. II, concl. 648, n. 130; Lessius, *De iustitia et iure,* lib. II, cap. 29, n. 65; Tuschi, *Practicae conclusiones* (Lugduni, 1634), Tom. III, concl. 330, n. 8; De Coninck, *De sacramentis et censuris* (Antuerpiae, 1619), Tom. II, disp. VIII, dub. 3, n. 22; Santi, *Praelectiones juris canonici* (Ratisbonae, 1886), lib. II, tit. 1, n. 14; Maupied, *Juris canonici universi compendium,* Tom. I, Pars II, lib. 1, cap. VI, Par. 2, n. 2.

[158] *Omnia, quae extant, opera,* ad D. (1.14) 3, *prima lectura,* nn. 5 and 7.

[159] *De matrimonio,* Tom. I, lib. III, disp. 22, n. 48.

[160] N. (44.1).

[161] C. 24, X, *de electione et electi potestate,* I, 6; and c. 19, X, *de iure patronatus,* III, 38.

of their stand the teaching of Innocent IV, of Hostiensis, of Joannes Andreae, and of Felinus Sandeus, who, while treating of the case of the *tabellio* (i. e. a notary), in Roman law, commonly held that the acts of such a *tabellio,* who did not have a proper appointment, would nevertheless be valid. But as Sanchez noted in his criticism,[162] none of these authors referred to a strictly jurisdictional act. For this reason Sanchez did not even admit the probability of this doctrine, but called it outright a false doctrine.

However, a contemporary of Sanchez, Basilius Pontius, did not agree with him. Pontius noted frankly that the only argument in favor of Sanchez' stand was the textual reading of the *dictum* of Gratian and of the *Lex Barbarius.* His own approach was over and above this superficial appreciation of these two texts. He felt certain that the correct mode of interpretation was to note what the law could do, what the law has done, and finally to stress at all times that the impelling force of the supplying of jurisdiction was public utility. Pontius pointed out that the law had already admitted of ways other than the direct grant of title by which jurisdiction could be obtained. He pointed to the force of prescription and custom in this regard. He also retained the parallel case of the *tabellio* to lend force to his stand. But his clinching argument was that the public utility demanded the supplying of jurisdiction in cases of common error alone as much as in cases where the title was present in addition.[163] Basilius Pontius may be designated as the first author of weight who brought out in their fullness the arguments supporting the claim of the sufficiency of common error alone for the supplying of jurisdiction.

The two theories grew apace. It would be a mistake to say that the proponents of the theory which demanded the presence of a title grew any weaker in numbers or in influence. That would not be true. Even up to the time of the Code theirs was considered the more common and more probable theory, even by those who championed the opposite view.[164]

[162] *De matrimonio,* Tom. I, lib. III, disp. 22, n. 54.

[163] Pontius, *De sacramento matrimonii tractatus,* lib. V, cap. XX, nn. 1-9.

[164] Diana, *Omnium resolutionum moralium tomi decem* (Venetiis: Ex

But while this theory which required the presence of a title stood its ground, the theory requiring only common error also gained strength. There is undeniable evidence that canonists and moralists were becoming more and more convinced that the literal words of the *Lex Barbarius* and of the *dictum* of Gratian did not express the full law. Their conviction grew that the true interpretation of the extent of the suppletory power lay in the understanding of the *mind* of the law. Thus it was that Diana († 1663), having noted the long succession of imposing authorities who insisted upon the presence of a title, did not follow their view. He noted the comparative newness of the theory to which he inclined. "Let confessors observe this, because this opinion is *new* and *sufficiently probable.*" And he added: "Greater provision is made for the common good by this opinion than if, in addition to common error, a title were also necessary."[165] Gobat († 1679), too, admitted its probable character.[166] Cardenas († 1684) made the same admission, although he conceded that the opinion was not certain.[167] Frances († 1682) noted that both opinions were probable and defensible, and added: "Yet the more liberal opinion cannot be denied, since the opinion of Joannes Sanctius and of Basilius Pontius is founded upon strong argument, and therefore, I would not dare to reject it."[168] Leurenius († 1723), after adverting to the existence of the dispute, revealed the attitude of certain authors

Typographia Balleominiana, 1728), Tom. I, Tr. III, Res. 19, n. 1; Gobat, *Operum moralium tractatus octo priores* (Duaci: Apud Josephum Derbaix Bibliopolam, 1700), Tr. VII, Casus III, n. 106; Cardenas, *Crisis theologica sive disputationes,* Pars IV, diss. II, cap. VI, art. V, n. 149; Frances, *Tractatus de intrusione,* Q. XLVI, n. 12; Alphonsus, *Theologia moralis,* Tom. II, lib. VI, Tr. IV, cap. II, dub. 3, n. 572; D'Annibale, *Summula,* I, n. 79.

[165] *Omnium resolutionum moralium tomi decem,* Tom. I, Tr. III, Res. 19, n. 2.

[166] *Operum moralium tractatus octo priores,* Tr. VIII, Casus 3, n. 106.

[167] *Crisis theologica sive disputationes selectae,* Pars IV, Diss. II, cap. VI, art. V, n. 151.

[168] *Tractatus de intrusione,* XLIV, n. 12.

like Engel († 1674)[169] and Pirhing († 1679)[170] who, though they held that a title was necessary for the functioning of the doctrine of the supplying of jurisdiction, nevertheless strove to moderate their teaching by admitting the validity of acts performed without a title, if *good faith* were present at the time of the act.[171] Perhaps the strongest avowal of the strength of this theory since the days of Basilius Pontius († 1629) was that of Schmalzgrueber († 1735). He admitted that the wording of the texts of Ulpian and of Gratian favored the school that demanded a title. But he insisted that, if one were to follow the *mens* of the legislator, then the opposite theory would appear not only "not improbable, but more probable indeed."[172] St. Alphonsus († 1787) admitted that the opinion which claimed the sufficiency of common error alone without title was "deservedly probable."[173] The opinion of Schmalzgrueber and of St. Alphonsus had reasons and authority enough to leave Ferraris († ca. 1760)[174] and Bouix († 1870)[175] more or less at a loss to choose between the two interpretations. The uncertainty as to what explanation was to be followed drew from Lehmkuhl († 1917) a very revealing admission of inability to choose between them: ". . . and since we have no ecclesiastical law which commands this to be done, nor any agreement among the Doctors in accepting it, it is not certain."[176] Such was the situation until the Code was to make its appearance.

F. *Probability of Fact and of Law*

By the dawn of the sixteenth century the basic principle of the doctrine of the supplying of jurisdiction was a universally received and almost incontestable juridical principle. True, it

[169] *Collegium universi iuris canonici* (Beneventi, 1760), lib. III, tit. V.

[170] *Jus canonicum,* lib. II, tit. 1, sec. 3, q. 1, nn. 83-87.

[171] *Ius canonicum universum,* Tom. II, lib. II, tit. 20, q. 610.

[172] *Ius canonicum universum,* lib. II, tit. I, n. 21.

[173] *Theologia moralis,* Tom. II, lib. VI, cap. II, dub. 3, n. 572.

[174] *Prompta bibliotheca* (Venetiis: Apud Gasparem Stori, 1782), v. *"Confessarius"*, n. 39.

[175] *Tractatus de iudiciis ecclesiasticis,* Tom. I, p. 134.

[176] *Theologia moralis,* n. 504.

obviously was not fully developed. Canonists were not agreed on the extent and scope of its application. Thus, for example, some demanded the presence of a title together with common error for its functioning; others were content that common error alone was the indispensable condition. And so the disputes continued. Yet, in all this mêlée of canonical interpretation it must be remembered that these differences were really inspired by the varying appreciations on the part of the canonists of how the public good would best be served.

As has already been seen, jurisdiction was not an invention of Scholasticism but an historically recognized possession of the Church which she has enjoyed and made use of since the days of her Divine Founder.[177] However, with the growth and spread of the Church there was a corresponding development in canonical jurisprudence. There was an increase in rules and regulations concerning the acquisition, retention and extension of jurisdictional power. This general development was particularly remarkable between the twelfth century and the time of the Council of Trent. Quite naturally, then, as Suarez († 1617) observed, there was soon an ever-recurring stream of doubts and difficulties about the possession and sufficiency of jurisdictional power. Frequently as such problems, i. e., those involving doubtful jurisdiction, arose in the exercise of ordinary jurisdictional power, infinitely more often did they arise in the exercise of delegated power.[178]

However, it seems that little recognition was given to the problems of doubtful jurisdiction by authors who preceded Suarez. A few writers, like Panormitanus († 1453), did consider the question, but only in passing.[179] But for the most part the authors either did not at all consider the question of doubtful

[177] Cf. Conc. Trid., Sess. XIV, *de poenitentia,* cap. 7.

[178] F. Suarez, *Opera omnia* (Ed. nova, a Carolo Berton: Parisiis, Apud Ludovicum Vives, 1861), Tom. XXII, *De poenitentia,* Disp. XXVI, sec. vi, n. 1. Hereafter this work will be referred to simply as *De poenitentia.*

[179] Cf. Panormitanus, ad C. 43, X, *de electione et electi potestate,* I, 16, n. 12, where he considered the case of one who doubted whether or not he had been deprived of jurisdiction. Panormitanus held that acts performed in such a state of doubt would be valid.

jurisdiction or relegated it to a very insignificant place of consideration. In the meantime there had sprung up a universal custom on the part of confessors to absolve with only probable jurisdiction, that is, to act on the conviction that when they did so the validity of the sacrament was still sufficiently safeguarded.[180]

In view of so general an assumption that the probable possession was a sufficient basis for the valid exercise of jurisdiction, e. g., in the confessional, it becomes readily apparent that the question remained not merely one of speculative interest but became one of grave practical import. And so, when in the latter half of the sixteenth century this issue, which had been smouldering for some time, did break out, it occasioned disputes that were to be bitter and protracted.[181]

This section will be devoted to an analysis of this dispute. The treatment is intended to show how slowly probability emerged as a recognized source of jurisdictional power. Not without reason does Castillon observe: "This study in effect cannot be made without encountering difficulty, because the theories about the supplying of jurisdiction in general, and especially about the supplying of probable jurisdiction in particular, elaborated as they were bit by bit, are filled with confusion and misunderstandings." [182] An attempt, however, shall be made to clear the obscurities and unravel the difficulties sufficiently to mark the highlights in the development. First of all the general question of the supplying of jurisdiction in cases of probability shall be treated. Then particular attention shall be given to the extent of this supplying, namely whether the suppletory principle was acknowledged as functioning solely when accompanied

180 Cf. Suarez, *De poenitentia,* Disp. XXVI, sec. VI, n. 7: "Est autem universalis Ecclesiae usus ut sacerdotes secure utantur hujusmodi jurisdictione probabili in hujus sacramenti administratione." For confirmation, cf. also: De Lugo, *Disputationes scholasticae et morales,* Tom. V, Disp. XIX, sec. II, n. 35; Castropalao, *Opus morale* (Lugduni: Sumptibus Gulielmi Barbier, 1682), Tom. I, Tr. I, D. II, P. V, n. 9.

181 Cf. Trombetta, *Supplet ecclesia,* p. 19.

182 "La probabilité de fait en matière de juridiction pénitentielle,"—*NRT,* XLIV (1912), 545.

with a doubt of law, or only in connection with a doubt of fact, or also in the presence of either of them.

I. Probability as a Source of Jurisdiction

Conscious of the gravity of the problem, Suarez delved into it searchingly. In his analysis he found it necessary to distinguish purely negative doubt (*dubium proprie dictum*) and probable doubt (*dubium improprie dictum*).[183] As regards *purely negative* doubt, following what he called a general and certain rule, Suarez held that it was insufficient to effect the validity of the jurisdictional acts performed with it. He insisted that it would be entirely illicit to use such a jurisdiction, unless and until there were an obvious necessity for so doing, a necessity not only on the part of the minister but also on the part of the penitent. And even then Suarez insisted that the absolution be given *sub conditione,* with the obligation on the part of the penitent to confess anew at the earliest opportunity to a confessor who was in certain and unmistakable possession of jurisdiction.[184]

As regards *probable* doubt, Suarez defended the plausibility of the opinion which held that the exercise of a jurisdictional act was licit when accompanied by such a doubt.[185] He felt that it was "very likely" that the minister could exercise such a probable jurisdiction *ex tacita Ecclesiae concessione.* In addition he felt that in such a case of probability the minister might perhaps obtain jurisdiction in virtue of the well known suppletory principle of the *Lex Barbarius.* But Suarez insisted upon

[183] *De poenitentia,* Disp. XXVI, sec. VI, n. 1.

[184] *De poenitentia,* Disp. XXVI, sec. VI, nn. 2-3. Purely negative doubt was really excluded by all authors. Cf. e. g., De Lugo, *Disputationes scholasticae et morales,* Tom. V, Disp. XIX, sec. II, n. 28; Bonacina, *Opera omnia* (Venetiis, Sumptibus societatis, 1687), Tom. I, Disp. V, Q. V, sec. II, par. III. These and all other recognized authors agreed in their demand that the doubt have some probability. Disagreement set in among these selfsame authors because of their concepts of what qualities a truly probable opinion should have, namely, must it be an opinion publicly known and held in the world of canonists and moralists, or may it be a private judgment of some one or few persons, based upon solid grounds and capable of rendering the opinion publicly tenable?

[185] *De poenitentia,* Disp. XXVI, sec. VI, n. 5.

true probability. And to be truly probable an opinion had to be based upon more than merely private ignorance and error. To be truly probable, according to Suarez, an opinion had to be in conformity with the extrinsic, *common opinion of the doctors.* Suarez found a corroborative argument in the universal practice of confessors who absolved with merely probable jurisdiction; for, as Suarez noted, universal custom in canon law has always been a sufficient sign of jurisdiction. Thus in a word, a minister could use probable jurisdiction only under certain conditions. Two important points regarding this use must here be noted:

(1) Suarez recognized the difficulty of the problem of probable jurisdiction. However, in his solution of the difficulty he almost entirely disregarded this probability as a source of jurisdiction. His demands of what should constitute true probability tended to identify this probability with common error. And consequently, if the suppletory principle of the *Lex Barbarius* applied at all, it did so in virtue of common error and not of probability itself. A further consequence was that the useful probability, that is, in as far as the supplying of jurisdiction was concerned, was narrowed down to public probability of law. Thus there seemed to be a definite rejection and exclusion of the utility of merely private probability of law or of fact.[186]

(2) It must be remembered that Suarez never gave this solution his entire approval. He never considered it any more than merely probable. He expressly said: *"Est quidem hic dicendi modus probabilis, non tamen certus, et hoc ipso non omnino tollit dubium, nec dat rei certitudinem, quam quaerimus."* [187]

A contemporary of Suarez, T. Sanchez († 1610), treating of the authorization and jurisdiction necessary for the proper assis-

[186] *De poenitentia,* Disp. XXVI, sec. VI, n. 7.

[187] *De poenitentia,* Disp. XXVI, sec. VI, n. 8. This uncertainty of Suarez was shared by others as well, e.g., by Salas († 1612), one of his contemporaries. Taberna († 1686), who made note of this, concurred: "Licet certum sit quod [ecclesia] possit supplere, tamen tantum probabile est quod de facto suppleat."—*Synopsis theologiae practicae* (Ed. ultima, Coloniae Agrippinae, 1705), Pars III, Tr. IV, cap. VI, Q. 8.

tance at marriage and for the giving of absolution, stated that it was safe in practice to regard as valid acts performed with a probable jurisdiction, because this opinion could be held as morally certain. Sanchez thus reveals a more profound sense of security than does Suarez with regard to the certainty inherent in the proposed opinion. Like Suarez, however, Sanchez juridically defended his opinion through his concept of probability. According to him, it mattered not if there were conflicting opinions about the presence or the sufficiency of jurisdiction in a given case. He even admitted the possibility that the opinion denying the presence or the sufficiency of the jurisdictional power might be the true one objectively. His point was that, as long as the objective truth were not apparent, as long as the opinion asserting the presence or the sufficiency of jurisdiction were solid enough to win the assent of *prudent men,* the acts performed in virtue of it would be valid. The reason was that there would be thus present a common error and a presumed title. A few interesting points are also to be noted about the opinion of Sanchez:

(1) In the examples adduced by Sanchez it is clear he considered that the probability of jurisdiction required for validity could equally be verified in doubts of fact as well as in doubts of law.

(2) Even though, like Suarez, Sanchez confused probability with error, he differed from Suarez in this: the error was not necessarily the error of authorized doctors, but could be that of any prudent men.

(3) A natural consequence of this was that the probability which he recognized as adequate could rest upon questions of fact.[188]

Another writer of the same period, Bonacina († 1631), took a different point of view. His chief contribution lay in the fact that he placed probability and common error on an equal footing as agencies for the supplying of jurisdiction. Bonacina drew a parallel between the efficacy of common error and that of probability without allowing the former to absorb the latter. Prob-

[188] *De matrimonio,* Tom. I, lib. III, disp. 22, n. 65.

ability, according to him, was of itself the immediate and sufficient title of jurisdiction. The ultimate title was the good of the faithful, but without any recourse to common error.[189]

These opinions were markedly different. But despite, or perhaps because of, these differences the net result of the work of these three pioneers was the clear formulation of this problem of probable jurisdiction for the moralists and canonists of a subsequent age: if a priest, having only a probable jurisdiction, proceeds to exercise it, does this probability give him a certain and indubitable title of jurisdiction?

The lines of argumentation, as suggested in the analyzed texts above, all found their followers. Following them, canonists and moralists were divided into two main camps. Not a few, as T. Tamburini († 1675) pointed out,[190] held that probability *alone* would not be a sufficient guaranty of undisputed jurisdiction. These evidently followed the line of reasoning suggested by Suarez and Sanchez. Perhaps the most comprehensive appraisal of this group's teaching was later drawn by J. Cardenas († 1684). He flatly asserted that any opinion holding that probability of itself could prepare the way for the exercise of a certain and indubitable jurisdiction was false and subject to condemnation. Cardenas

[189] *Opera omnia, De sacramento poenitentiae,* Disp. V, Q. V, sec. II, Punct. III, n. 11: Having stated how the Church supplied jurisdiction in cases where there was common error plus an apparent title, Bonacina added: "Sicut etiam supplet, quando adsunt duae contrariae opiniones probabiles de iurisdictione, quarum una defendit sacerdotem habere potestatem absolvendi illique opinioni adhaeret sacerdos, tunc enim ecclesia supplet iurisdictionem, quam antea re ipsa confessarius non habebat. Ratio est, quia non est maior ratio, cur ecclesia suppleat iurisdictionem quando adest error communis, et titulus coloratus sine impedimento iuris divini, et naturalis, et non suppleat quando sacerdos sequitur opinionem probabilem asserentem confessarium habere iurisdictionem, alioquin in hoc casu eadem incommoda sequerentur Ecclesia non supplente iurisdictionem quando adest titulus coloratus et error communis."

[190] *Opera omnia* (Venetiis, 1702), Sec. II, *De sacramentis,* lib. IV, *De poenitentia,* Cap. V, Par. VIII, n. 11. Hereafter reference to this work will be made simply as *De poenitentia,* inasmuch as the present study is concerned solely with this section of the work.

was fully aware from the reports of the Roman theologians how through the agency of the Sacred Congregation of the Holy Office Pope Innocent XI had emphasized the powerlessness of the Church over the substantial elements of the sacraments. While Cardenas admitted the Church's stewardship of Christ's power on earth and granted that the Church possessed the plenitude of power in conceding, extending, or restricting jurisdictional competence, he nevertheless emphasized that the jurisdiction which was required by the Council of Trent for the valid administration of the sacrament of penance [191] was a requirement not merely of ecclesiastical but of divine origin. Thus he argued that if an opinion, regarded as probable, were to prove objectively false, then an essential element for the constitution of the sacrament of penance would be lacking. Thus the absolution would be frustrated in its desired effect.[192]

As has been intimated above, Cardenas observed that probability *alone* did not furnish a certain and indubitable title of jurisdiction. He and by far the greater number of his school were willing to admit the presence of such a certain and indubitable title of jurisdiction if some other factor were to re-enforce the probability and thus endow it with sufficient certainty for safe application in practice. Three such factors he enumerated:

(1) True probability, that is, probability in the sense expounded by Suarez. In such a case moral certainty would obtain in virtue of the common opinion of the doctors. Against the security of even this opinion some theologians and canonists continued to hold out. It has been noted how Suarez himself did not consider this solution certain and convincing. Salas also shared this doubt.

[191] Sess. XIV, *De poenitentia*, cap. 7.

[192] It is evident that Cardenas alluded to the following proposition condemned by Pope Innocent XI: "Non est illicitum, in sacramentis conferendis sequi opinionem probabilem de valore sacramenti, relicta tutiore, nisi vetet lex, conventio, aut periculum gravis damni incurrendi. Hinc sententia probabili tantum utendum non est in collatione baptismi, ordinis sacerdotalis, aut episcopalis." Cf. Denzinger-Bannwart-Umberg, *Enchiridion Symbolorum* (21-23 ed., Friburgi Brisgoviae: Herder, 1927), n. 1151.

And of course this argument had no appeal for those who with Paludanus († 1342) claimed that the suppletory principle of the *Lex Barbarius* was not to be extended to the internal forum.

(2) The supplying of the defect of jurisdiction by the Church *ex ratihabitione de praesenti.* To this the authors concluded from the fact that the Church was a witness of the universally accepted possibility of the exercise of probable jurisdiction and still tolerated it.

(3) The indirect absolution from grave sins. This the authors commonly asserted. They felt that any simple priest could absolve from venial sins without any authorization. If a penitent approached such a priest in good faith, the priest could absolve directly from the venial sins and indirectly from mortal sins.[193]

On the other hand, as Tamburini also pointed out,[194] many others held, after the manner of Bonacina, that probability was of itself, apart from common error, a sure guaranty of jurisdiction. Among these scholars perhaps the boldest champion was Verricelli († 1656). He was so convinced of the truth of his own opinion that he termed the opposite view utterly false and improbable.[195] Tamburini († 1675), who followed Verricelli, was an almost equally ardent adherent of this opinion.[196] Tamburini gave as his reason why he considered this opinion the more probable the fact that universal custom gave jurisdiction.[197] Thus this universal custom was the principal argument upon which these scholars rested their claim of certitude of jurisdiction in cases of probability.

[193] Cf. Cardenas, *Crisis theologica,* Pars IV, Diss. II, Cap. VI, Art. III, Q. III, nn. 137-146.

[194] *De poenitentia,* Cap. V, Par. VIII, n. 3.

[195] *Quaestiones morales legales in octo tractatus distributae* (Venetiis: 1653), Tract. II, Quaest. XXV, n. 5.

[196] *De poenitentia,* Cap. V, Par. VIII, n. 3.

[197] *Glossa,* ad c. 13, X, *de foro competenti,* II, 2, ad *v. Vel consuetudine:* "Nota quod consuetudo dat jurisdictionem." This was often repeated by canonists and even given formal recognition in the Council of Trent, Sess. XXII, *de reformatione,* cap. 3: "Si alicui ex praedictis dignitatibus in Ecclesiis Cathedralibus, vel Collegiatis, de jure, seu *consuetudine,* jurisdictio, administratio, vel officium non competat, etc."

Such were the two main lines of thought concerning the supplying of jurisdiction by the Church in cases of probability. There was a third group which answered in a firm negative to the question of whether one could administer the sacraments with merely probable jurisdiction. To this school belonged Concina († 1756). He saw in the condemnation of Innocent XI an absolute and universal condemnation of any and every use of merely probable jurisdiction whenever the validity of the sacraments was at stake. He argued that the Pope did not limit his condemnation to case of doubt in regard to the matter and form of the sacraments. For that reason Concina would not agree with the probabilist view as held by Filliuccius († 1622), Reginaldus (Renaud, † 1623), Lessius († 1623), Bonacina († 1631), Coninck († 1633), Diana († 1663), La Croix († 1714), and others even though he recognized the importance of these men. He would not agree with their view because he felt the distinction was unwarrantable whereby they interpreted the condemnation of Pope Innocent XI as not applying to cases of probable doubt concerning the possession or non-possession of jurisdiction necessary for the valid and licit administration of a sacrament.[198] Antoine († 1743) and Elizalde († 1678) held views similar to that of Concina.[199]

In the period of a little more than a century between Tamburini († 1675) and St. Alphonsus Liguori († 1787) it seems that there was no new theorizing on this question. As St. Alphonsus has shown in a comprehensive review,[200] the differences noted above were perpetuated by an unending succession of new adherents. St. Alphonsus analyzed the prevalent opinions. The unreservedly dissenting opinion of Concina he did not consider worthy of the trouble of refutation. He held also that the opinion which identified probability with common error was unconvincing. His

[198] *Theologia christiana* (Neapoli, 1775), Tom. IX, lib. II, *De sacramento poenitentiae,* Diss. II, cap. V, n. 2, and § III, n. 2: "Non modo adest fundamentum certum, sed neque probabile talis praesumptionis."

[199] Cf. St. Alphonsus Liguori, *Theologia moralis,* Tom. III, lib. VI, n. 573.

[200] *Theologia moralis,* Tom. III, lib. VI, n. 573.

reason was that at best the opinion which defended the supplying of jurisdiction in common error alone was not beyond dispute. He rejected, too, the solution which assumed the direct absolution from venial sins and the indirect absolution from grave sins. It seems that St. Alphonsus felt there was some real value in the argument for the supplying of jurisdiction *ex ratihabitione de praesenti,* namely, from the fact that the Church witnessed in practice the assumption of jurisdiction by confessors, in view of which they could absolve although possessing only probable jurisdiction, and gave her assent thereto. This solution seemed to probe the very core of the question studied. According to it the ultimate reason why the Church gave her assent was the salvation of souls; the immediate title was nothing beyond probability itself. But the solution which was most impressive to Liguori was the one based on the universal custom of accrediting probable jurisdiction for use in the confessional. However, like Salas and Suarez, St. Alphonsus would not allow the exercise of such jurisdiction except in grave necessity or for reasons of great utility.

Such, then, were the different theories on the rôle of probability in the performance of jurisdictional acts. Certainly, from the days of St. Alphonsus to the appearance of the Code the legal factor of probability was ever more and more received as a guaranty for suppletory jurisdiction. But as Bucceroni († 1918),[201] Lehmkuhl († 1917) [202] and D'Annibale († 1892) [203] have indicated, the most commonly used argument to support the claim that in probable jurisdiction there was inherent the guaranty of an assuredly real jurisdiction was the fact of its customarily and universally accredited usage.

In conclusion it may be admitted that there was as yet no general agreement. Nor was there any explicit demarcation or segregation of probability as of itself furnishing a sufficient guaranty for the presence of real jurisdiction. It remains true,

201 *Casus conscientiae,* p. 567.
202 *Theologia moralis,* n. 505.
203 *Summula,* I, n. 80.

of course, that other factors concerned with error and other items implied by custom were recognized as capable of association with probability so as to bolster its questionable claims. But it is not always evident in the pre-Code writers just how much of a rôle these items and factors played in their minds. It is also not always clear that the authors accepted these circumstances in a merely subsidiary capacity, as did Bonacina († 1631) [204] and Elbel († 1756), who plainly drew the validity of acts performed with probable jurisdiction from the moral guaranty of the *probability itself* and from the knowledge that along with its realization of the general attitude of mind the Church assented to the practice which resulted therefrom.[205]

II. Supplying in Probability of Fact or of Law

Pondering the problem of the efficacy of probable jurisdiction as a guaranty of real jurisdiction, the moralists and canonists were confronted with still another question that was closely allied with the first, in fact dependent upon the answer to the first: if any suppletory force was to be admitted in the case of merely probable jurisdiction, would this be verified only in doubts of law, or solely in cases of doubt of fact, or perhaps in the presence of either of these doubts? Evidently those whose rejection of probable jurisdiction as a possible guaranty for real jurisdiction was an outright one were not concerned with this problem at all.[206] Practically all the others, who held probability in some way or other to be endowed with suppletory power, agreed that this supplying force would be realized in cases where there was a *dubium iuris.* No such agreement existed in regard to cases where there was a *dubium facti.*

[204] *Opera omnia, De sacramento poenitentiae,* Disp. V, Q. V, sec. II, Punct. III, n. 11.

[205] *Theologiae moralis tripartita* (Venetiis: Sumptibus Societatis, 1733), Conf. XII, nn. 310-311.

[206] E.g., Concina, Antoine, Elizalde. In reference to these cf. St. Alphonsus Liguori, *Theologia moralis,* Tom. II, lib. VI, n. 573, and footnote *a.*

Sanchez[207] and Bonacina[208] made use of examples which illustrated not only doubts of law, but also doubts of fact. Both authors, and especially Bonacina, left the impression that the suppletory principle would function in any case of probability, whether derived from a doubt of law or from a doubt of fact. On the other hand, although Suarez[209] made use of similar examples, yet it also appears that he narrowed down the concept of probability which would make available any suppletory force to such cases as involved only public doubts of law. This is but a natural conclusion drawn from his insistence that a status of true probability can arise only from the common teaching of the doctors, and that its existence must consequently be evaluated through the norm of its conformity with their common opinion. This conclusion seems further to be confirmed by the fact that Suarez expressly rejected any and every personal error or ignorance as a basis for the probability here under discussion. The personal judgment of the minister, no matter how sound, apparently carried no weight with Suarez in this matter.[210] In the meantime many others[211] treated the question of probability only in general, without drawing any distinction between probability arising from doubt of fact or from doubt of law.

Perhaps one of the first and clearest declarations that the suppletory principle of probability would function in a *dubium facti* as well as in a *dubium iuris* was that of Verricelli. His statement came apparently in direct answer and opposition to the limitations placed by Aversa († 1657) and Salas († 1612). These writers had claimed that the supplying of jurisdiction would be verified only in doubt of law and not at all in doubt of fact. Verricelli, on the contrary, held that, regardless of the basis of

207 *De matrimonio,* Tom. I, lib. II, disp. 22, n. 65.

208 *Opera omnia, De sacramento poenitentiae,* Disp. V, Q. V, sec. II, Punct. III, n. 11.

209 *De poenitentia,* Disp. XXVI, sec. VI, nn. 1 and 5.

210 *De poenitentia,* Disp. XXVI, sec. VI, n. 7.

211 E.g., Castropalao, *Opus morale,* Tom. I, tr. I, p. II, Punct. V, n. 9; Lessius, *De iustitia et iure,* lib. II, cap. 29, n. 68; and Taberna, *Synopsis theologiae practicae,* Pars. II, Tr. IV, cap. VI, Q. 8.

the probability of an opinion, be it the extrinsic authority of the doctors, or the solid, intrinsic arguments considered by one learned man, a minister could use such a probable opinion licitly and, in fact, as he himself put it, *"validissime."* He expressly held for the application of the suppletory principle to probabilties *"circa ius"* and *"circa factum"* because, as he himself phrased it, "*. . . uterque error est inculpabilis et caveri a Populo nequit.*" [212]

This opinion of Verricelli appealed to Tamburini, who followed it. For two reasons Tamburini deplored the limitation placed by Aversa († 1657) and Salas († 1612). First of all, such a limitation served only to engender scruples. Secondly, it tended to disregard entirely the probable character of an opinion. Tamburini himself felt that the reasons which argued for the character of an opinion did so absolutely, without such restrictions and limitations.[213] Gobat († 1679) did not dare deny the probability of either opinion, but also refrained from any absolute approbation of either.[214] Cardenas seemed to lean towards the belief that, even in question of fact, probability would guarantee the validity of jurisdictional acts, provided the doubt was altogether invincible.[215] Elbel, like all other moralists and canonists, required the presence of a prudent probability. Yet he clearly wrote: "For when a priest according to a truly probable opinion thinks that he actually possesses jurisdiction over this or that penitent, or over this or that sin . . . then (even though perchance the opinion should be really erroneous and false) the Supreme Pontiff is considered and piously believed to concede the jurisdiction for the act, and this he does to avoid graver inconveniences and peril to souls." [216] Elbel evidently drew the guaranty of validity for jurisdictional acts from the probability itself and from the knowledge which the Church has of the accredited use made of probable jurisdiction. Thus Elbel accepted any probability, even

[212] *Quaestiones morales et legales,* Tract. II, Quaes. XXXV, nn. 11-12.

[213] *De poenitentia,* Cap. V, Par. VIII, nn. 7-10.

[214] *Operum moralium libri tres* (Venetiis, Sumptibus Iacobi Bertonis, 1698), Tom. I, T. VII, n. 117.

[215] *Crisis theologica,* Par. IV, Diss. II, Cap. VIII, art. II, n. 525.

[216] *Theologia moralis tripartita,* Conf. XII, nn. 310-311.

that derived from a factual doubt, since the passage cited above indicates his conviction that the personal judgment of a confessor in a particular fact carried as much weight as a juridical opinion held by the doctors.

A contextual study of Billuart († 1757) [217] and of Wigandt († 1708) [218] seems similarly to reveal that they held for the suppletory efficacy in a case of factual doubt as well as in a question of juridicial doubt.

But, on the other hand, following the apparent restriction of Suarez, La Croix († 1714) [219] expressly associated the suppletory force exclusively with a *dubium juris,* insinuating "... *ut opinio probabilis sit circa communem quaestionem juris et non pure facti privati.*" La Croix was followed by many, including Sporer († 1714)[220] and Sasserath († 1775).[221]

It is a remarkable fact that St. Alphonsus Liguori, in treating of the subject of probable jurisdiction,[222] did not make any note of the distinction of the *dubium iuris* and *dubium facti.* This is particularly arresting when one remembers with what meticulous care St. Alphonsus habitually sought to portray controverted points in proper contrast and relief. Castillon [223] regarded this omission on the part of St. Alphonsus as an indication that the controversy had to a great extent subsided. And, moreover, he took it as an indication that St. Alphonsus himself held that the probability which arose from a factual doubt and the probability which sprang from a juridical doubt equally warranted

[217] *Summa Sancti Thomae hodiernis academiarum moribus accomodata* (Ed. nova, Parisiis: Apud V. Palme, no date), Tom. VII, Disp. VI, art. IV, p. 2.

[218] *Tribunal confessariorum* (3. ed., Venetiis: Apud Niccola Pezzano, 1717), T. XIII, Examen V, q. 8, n. 91.

[219] *Theologia moralis,* Tom. II, lib. VI, Pars I, n. 118.

[220] *Theologia sacramentalis* (3. ed., Salisburgi, 1711), Pars III, Cap. VI, Sec. I, nn. 715-722.

[221] *Cursus theologiae moralis* (6. ed., Augustae Vindelicorum, 1787), Pars IV, Tr. I, Diss. V, q. 1, n. 120.

[222] *Theologia moralis,* Tom. III, lib. VI, nn. 571 and 573.

[223] "La probabilité de fait en matière pénitentielle,"—*NRT,* XLIV (1912), 675.

the effecting of validity in jurisdictional acts. Finally Castillon noted with a certain amount of satisfaction the fact that Bucceroni († 1918),[224] who himself did not incline to the application of suppletory force in a case of probability derived from a mere factual doubt, nevertheless admitted that St. Alphonsus[225] may well have singled out the probability derived from the *dubium facti* rather than that arising from the *dubium iuris,* for he wrote: "Thus, although generally the saintly Doctor speaks of probable jurisdiction, still it appears he had in mind probability *of fact* rather than *of law.*"

But, even apart from the acceptance of Castillon's viewpoint, certain it is that the canonists and moralists of the nineteenth century furnished a new impetus to the controversy. Certain writers, like Gury († 1867)[226] and Gousset († 1866),[227] while they did not distinguish between the *dubium juris* and the *dubium facti,* seem almost certainly to have held both kinds of doubt on an equal plane as far as the supplying of jurisdiction was concerned. But undoubtedly the plainest defense of both kinds of doubts as a basis for supplied jurisdiction was that of D'Annibale († 1892). Inasmuch as there has been some question of whether D'Annibale himself was responsible for this change of opinion which was introduced only in the third edition of his work, in order to forestall any difficulty of explanation it will be best to consult the work of Bucceroni († 1918), who surely cannot be adduced as a partisan proponent or ardent abettor of the opinion of D'Annibale.[228] Bucceroni plainly admitted that D'Annibale, in retracting his older opinion, expressed in the third edition of his work the statement: "Jurisdiction is supplied in a case of doubt, provided that the doubt is not merely negative, but positive and truly probable . . . whether *of law* . . . or *of fact.*" That D'Annibale did not always hold this view is indicated by the words following: ". . . *secus ac olim censui.*" However, Buc-

[224] *Casus conscientiae,* p. 567.

[225] *Theologia moralis,* Tom. III, lib. VI, nn. 571 and 573.

[226] *Compendium theologiae moralis* (7. ed., Romae, Ex Typographia Polyglotta, 1882), Tom. II, n. 549.

[227] *Théologie morale* (10. ed., Paris, 1855), Tom. II, n. 484.

[228] *Casus conscientiae,* pp. 567-568.

ceroni also noted that D'Annibale contradicted himself in another section of the same work. Treating of the sacrament of penance and specifically of the jurisdiction required on the part of the confessor, D'Annibale clearly stated that the Church supplies in cases of common error and in cases of probability of law *but not in cases of probability of fact.*[229] This lapse of D'Annibale was in all likelhood inadvertent; for Ojetti († 1932), when he asserted that jurisdiction is supplied in probability of fact as well as in a probability occasioned by a doubt of law, adduced D'Annibale as an unquestioned supporter of this view.[230]

At best one must admit that the authorities who held for the equality of the *dubium juris* and the *dubium facti* were not very numerous. They existed, one might say, only in sufficient numbers to compel Bucceroni's direct admission that there were not lacking those who affirmed such an equality,[231] to which he could nevertheless add that, as a matter of truth, this was not commonly admitted. According to him this was because the same universal practice and custom of the confessors could not be adduced in reference to the probability of fact that could be claimed in relation to the probability of law. Indeed even a summary inspection of the authors of the nineteenth and early twentieth centuries reveals the vastly preponderant number of authors who limited the supplying of jurisdiction to cases of probability arising from a doubt of law. Among these authors one might point to a few who enjoyed profound esteem and weighty influence during the period in which they lived, such as Kenrick († 1863),[232] Van der Velden († 1857),[233] Génicot († 1900),[234] Lehmkuhl († 1917),[235] and Noldin († 1922).[236]

[229] *Casus conscientiae,* p. 567; D'Annibale, *Summula* (3. ed., Romae, 1892), Tom. III, n. 321.

[230] *Synopsis rerum moralium et iuris pontificii* (Romae: Ex Typographia Polyglotta, 1899), ad v. *"Iurisdictio."*

[231] *Casus conscientiae,* Tom. II, p. 567.

[232] *Theologia moralis* (Mechlinae, 1861), Tr. XVIII, nn. 147-152.

[233] *Principia theologiae moralis* (Tornaci, 1882), Tom. II, Pars II, n. 287 . . . nn. 1 and 3.

[234] *Theologiae moralis institutiones* (6. ed., Bruxellis: A. Dewit, 1909), Tom. II, n. 330.

[235] *Theologia moralis,* Tom. II, nn. 503 and 505.

[236] *Theologia moralis* (5. ed., Oeniponte, 1904), III, nn. 356-358.

CONCLUSIONS

Before the appearance of the preparatory drafts of the Code there was no statute law in either Roman or Canon Law concerning the doctrine of the supplying of jurisdiction. When canon 209 was finally formulated, it represented many centuries of jurisprudential development.

From the earliest beginnings in both Roman and Canon Law there has ever been a consciousness on the part of jurisconsults and canonists that the supreme legislator had sovereign power over the concession, increase and restriction of jurisdictional competence. As the centuries passed there was a remarkable and steady growth and clarification of the jurist's conviction that the supreme legislator would not exact the strict fulfillment of the jurisdictional laws and requirements if, when and as such rigid enforcements were to redound to the general harm of the subjects. Such were the fundamental convictions of Roman jurisconsults and ecclesiastical canonists. Out of these convictions, which received the stamp of at least tacit approval from their legislator, gradually evolved the doctrine of the supplying of jurisdiction as it is known in Canon Law today.

The Canon Law jurisprudence on this subject dates back to the famous *dictum* of Gratian. This *dictum,* proposed under the influential, though private, name of Gratian, was readily received. Textually at least the *dictum* resembled the *Lex Barbarius* of Roman Law.

The exact influence of Roman jurisprudence on Canon Law in this respect it is not easy to ascertain, principally because the question of what actually happened in the *Lex Barbarius* has always been and still is a matter of controversy and speculation. Some jurists, after the fashion of Pomponius and of the glossators, virtually denied any need of this supplying of official competence in the person of Barbarius by the direct claim that he had been really a praetor and a free citizen. On the other hand, others, such as the ultramontane jurists, whom Bartolus and almost all of the canonists followed, maintained that Barbarius had never been any more than a slave. Consequently, if Barbarius' official acts were to be considered valid, this validity was due to the juridical presumption that the legislator, ever solicitous for the common good, would not enforce the jurisdictional laws in all their strictness, but would supply whatever competency was required for the valid performance of the acts.

The Church never officially reprobated the logic of the latter interpretation. On the contrary, by her silence the Church seemed to give her approval to such an understanding and exercise of the principle of the supplying of jurisdiction. Thus, amidst this silent approval on the part of the Church the doctrine of the supplying of jurisdiction gradually became crystallized. The process, however, was very slow and there emerged many differences of interpretation on the part of the canonists. One school of canonists followed strictly the literal wording of the *Lex Barbarius* and of the *dictum* of Gratian. Another insisted that these two texts were not yard-sticks with which to find an exact measure of the scope of the application of this teaching. The latter group preferred to look upon these texts as manifestations of the legislator's habitual attitude in reference to the degree of strictness with which he wished the jurisdictional laws to be observed. They insisted, therefore, that to interpret the scope of the suppletory doctrine, it was only necessary to bear in mind always what the intention of the lawmaker would be in each individual case.

On some points there was a general assent from the beginning:

A. The fact that public utility and the general good required the relaxation of the ordinary rules of jurisdiction.

B. The fact that this teaching would apply only to acts performed in virtue of a public office.

C. The application of this doctrine to the external forum.

D. The application of this doctrine to ordinary power.

E. The necessity of a common error. But the determination of what constituted *common error* was never a matter on which universal agreement could be found.

On other points there was controversy:

A. In some cases the differences slowly vanished, e.g.,

a. The application of this doctrine to the internal forum, to confession, etc.
b. The application of these principles to excommunicates, to those suspended and interdicted.

B. In other cases there was never sufficient agreement to term any opinion commonly received, e.g.,

a. Concerning the necessity of a title.
b. Regarding the application of this teaching to delegated power. This question revolved upon whether or not the exercise of such power would sufficiently endanger the public good to warrant the invocation of the suppletory principle.

The sixteenth century saw the extension of this principle to cases of probable jurisdiction. At first, if any suppletory power was admitted in cases of probability, it was only because probability was not considered a separate title of jurisdiction, but was confused with *common error* and *custom.* There was only a gradual severance of probability from common error and custom, i.e., probability considered as a separate title of jurisdiction. But even just before the Code the argument which invoked custom as a title was very commonly adduced and it was not always clear that probability alone or as something apart was regarded as a sufficient guaranty for the supplying of deficient jurisdiction.

In regard to the supplying of jurisdiction in cases of doubt, all who held the application of the general doctrine insisted that there be present a *positive* probability. But, then, some held that the supplying of jurisdiction would hold only in a doubt of law. Others insisted that it would apply also in a doubt of fact.

SUMMARY

The development of the canonical teaching began in the Universities. The theory thus developed was adopted from the schools as a doctrine. Students, when entering upon ecclesiastical offices, applied the suppletory doctrine in practice. Thus there was built up a customary mode of action which obtained the force and application of customary law.

CANONICAL COMMENTARY

INTRODUCTION

Canon 209: In errore communi aut in dubio positivo et probabili sive iuris sive facti, iurisdictionem supplet Ecclesia pro foro tum externo tum interno.

Canon 209 marks admittedly the first appearance of the suppletory principle as a statute law in ecclesiastical legislation. In virtue of this canon the doctrine which has long been held as probable on the authority of the doctors received the official sanction of the supreme ecclesiastical legislator. As authors indicate quite generally, it is evident that by the insertion of this canon into the Code of Canon Law the supreme legislator wished to put an end to many pre-Code uncertainties and disputes, as, e.g., in reference to the necessity of a colored title, the extent of the supplying in doubt, etc.

Of all the disputes that have arisen in the process of the development of the suppletory principle perhaps the most bitter and prolonged argument was centered about the necessity or non-necessity of a *colored title* in addition to common error. As has been seen in the preliminary notions and in the historical analysis, pre-Code authors quite commonly taught that the Church supplied only when with common error a colored title was also verified. On the opposite side, however, another powerful, though numerically smaller, contingent equally firmly contended that a colored title was not necessary and that common error of itself was a sufficient basis and reason for admitting the benefits of the suppletory principle.

Here it will be helpful to recall in brief review that the term *colored title* had a very definite, restricted meaning. Technically it denoted a title which was actually, though for some reason invalidly, conferred by a legitimate superior competent to confer it. Thus a colored title was always clearly distinguishable from a merely putative *(putativus)* or fictitious *(existimatus)* title, which would be present whenever a person pretended, in good or in bad faith, to be endowed with jurisdictional power while in reality the pretense was not based upon the required commission or institution by the legitimate superior.[1]

The Code is significantly silent concerning the necessity of a colored title. A few commentators, even after the appearance of the Code, still insist upon the necessity of the presence of a colored title.[2] However, this teaching has not a large following. On the contrary, it has been, and is, felt by almost all authors that the silence of the Code in regard to the necessity of a colored title is very significant and must be construed as *prima facie* evidence of the suppression of the need of such a colored title in every case in which the Church would supply the necessary jurisdiction.[3]

At the beginning of this discussion on the title, attention was deliberately riveted upon the fact that a *colored title* had a very technical meaning around which revolved all the pre-Code controversy. In the pre-Code understanding of the suppletory principle all authors required common error. Some required also the colored title. But even those who rejected the necessity of a colored title demanded some foundation for the common error,[4]

[1] Kearney, *The principles of delegation*, p. 122.

[2] Cf., e.g., Burke, *Competence in ecclesiastical tribunals* (The Catholic University of America, Canon Law Studies, n. 14: Washington, D. C., 1922), p. 13.

[3] S. R. R., *Nullitas matrimonii*, 22 Novembris, 1927, *coram R. P. D. Andrea Jullien*, dec. LI—*Decisiones*, XIX (1927), 456: " . . . nam, hodie, attento citato canone 209, ut Ecclesia suppleat in errore communi, non requiritur titulus coloratus." Cf. also e. g., Cappello, *De sacramentis*, III, n. 663, 5; Carberry, *The juridical form of marriage* (The Catholic University of America, Canon Law Studies, n. 84: Washington, D. C., 1934), p. 55; Wernz-Vidal, *Ius canonicum*, II, n. 381; Blat, *Commentarium textus iuris canonici* (Romae, 1921-1927), II, n. 158 (hereafter this work shall be referred to as *Commentarium*); Arregui, *Summarium theologiae moralis* (12. ed., Bilbao, 1934), n. 688 (hereafter this work will be referred to simply as *Summarium*). See also Badii, *Institutiones*, I, n. 49, 1; Kearney, *The principles of delegation*, p. 123; Simon, *Faculties of pastors and confessors* (New York, 1922), p. 18; Fink, "Eheassistenz und allgemeiner Irrtum,"—*Theologie und Glaube*, XXVI (1934), 587; Salvador, "Error communis et iurisdictionis suppletio ab ecclesia,"—*BE*, XVII (1939), 91.

[4] Cf., e. g., Billuart, *De poenitentia*, D. VI, art. 4, § 1.

since they realized that error in a multitude simply cannot arise without something tangible or sense-perceptible to produce it. "*Nihil in intellectu nisi prius in sensu.*"[5] Thus, it may be concluded that there was no dispute before the appearance of the Code on the point that common error in regard to someone's possession of jurisdictional power, before it could come into being, postulated the existence of some sort of a title. The disputed point was whether or not the title had to be *colored* in the technical sense explained above. The Code by its silence settled the controversy in the negative.

However, today, as in the days of Billuart, common error is scarcely conceivable without some apparent title. That consideration has prompted certain authors, like Ferreres[6] and Pruemmer,[7] who admit that the Code no longer requires a *colored* title, simultaneously to maintain that in practice common error cannot be verified unless and until there be present at least some *apparent* title. Certain other authors, like Cocchi,[8] go even further. They claim that, despite the theoretical non-necessity of a colored title, in practice error cannot be common unless a colored title be present. In regard to such claims Wernz-Vidal[9] admit that in the exercise of some jurisdictional power, such as the exercise of ordinary power in the external forum, it may be difficult for common error to be verified without the presence of a colored title. But he hastens to add that this difficulty would not be the

[5] St. Thomas, *De veritate,* 10, 6, 2m: "Dicitur cognitio mentis a sensu originem habere, non quod omne illud quod mens cognoscit, sensus apprehendat, sed quia ex his quae sensus apprehendit mens in aliqua ulteriora manducitur sicut etiam sensibilia intellecta manducant ad intelligibilia divinorum."

[6] *Compendium theologiae moralis ad normam codicis iuris canonici* (14. ed., Barcinone: Eugenius Subirana, 1928), II, n. 651, II. Hereafter this work will be referred to as *Compendium.*

[7] *Manuale iuris canonici* (3. ed., Friburgi Brisgoviae, 1922), p. 123, q. 90.

[8] *Commentarium in codicem iuris canonici* (Taurinorum Augustae: Marietti, 1922), *De personis,* Pars I, Sec. I, n. 133. Hereafter reference to this work will be made by the word *Commentarium.*

[9] *Ius canonicum,* II, n. 381, footnote 6.

same in regard to the exercise of jurisdictional power in the internal forum, to which is particularly applicable D'Annibale's statement: "... *quod titulus nec exhiberi vulgo, nec peti solet.*"[10]

In conclusion, therefore, it may be conceded that common error in regard to the existence or the validity of an office or jurisdiction is wont to arise among people because the priest or bishop in question has a colored title. Still, this does not furnish sufficient grounds to draw the conclusion and to support as irrefragable the general principle that a colored title is always required and that common error apart from it does not suffice. Common error, of and by itself is sufficient. The legislator, as Cappello points out,[11] is not concerned with the cause of the common error. He is satisfied that a common danger can exist even independently of the instances of the presence of a colored title. And, therefore, once common error is present and a common peril is verified, he declares that the Church will supply jurisdiction. Thus he seems to regard a colored title at most as a fruitful occasion of such error. It is precisely in this sense that one must understand canon 209, which expressly requires only common error.[12]

In a similar manner the legislator terminated the dispute concerning the supplying of jurisdiction in doubt by decreeing that the Church does supply in positive and probable doubt whether of law or of fact.

However, several difficulties still persist. In one way the persistence of these problems is perfectly understandable; for, it can hardly be conceived how the Church could, even if she wanted to, draw a sharply accurate, mathematical line of demarcation for all the problems that arise in relation to the application of the suppletory doctrine, which problems, because of the relativity of the circumstances under which they occur, cannot be handled in exactly the same manner at all times. By her apparent unwillingness to set down principles too inflexibly it seems that

[10] *Summula,* I, n. 79, note 73.

[11] *De sacramentis,* II, n. 496.

[12] Lega-Bartocetti, *Commentarium in iudicia ecclesiastica iuxta codicem iuris canonici* (Romae, 1938), I, p. 211.

the Church wishes the canonist to judge each and every case, as it arises, in accordance with the textual and contextual significance of canon 209. These difficulties, e.g., the true concept of common error and of positive and probable doubt of fact and of law, the extent of the application of this canon, and finally the conditions required for its licit use will, in turn, receive detailed treatment.

Two points may well serve as a prelude to the discussion that is to follow. First of all, canon 209 is an explicit confirmation and adaptation of a fundamentally ancient principle. In view of this fact it is necessary to bear in mind that, in accordance with the prescripts of canon 6, nn. 2-4, the old interpretation of this doctrine must be followed unless strong textual or contextual evidence can be adduced to show that the legislator intends to abandon or to alter the pre-Code understanding and application of the suppletory principle. Secondly, it is likewise evident that, as previously by the interpretation of canonists, so today in virtue of positive disposition of law, it is determined that the Church will supply jurisdiction in the two cases: 1) in common error; 2) in positive and probable doubt of fact as well as of law. Nevertheless, as authors point out, this does not deny a cumulative force to the simultaneous existence of these two conditions. Re-ënforced one by the other, the two may exist side by side and conspire towards the effective attainment of the one purpose: the supplying of the jurisdiction necessary for the validity of the act or acts posited. One might well ask whether or not the expression *sive iuris sive facti* modifies *in errore communi.* Because a satisfactory reply necessarily involves certain distinctions, it is best to defer the answer to this question until a later time when detailed attention will be given in the commentary in regard to the applicability of the suppletory principle to common error of law and of fact.

As a last word in this introductory section, some explanation is in order concerning the character of this suppletory law. Under one aspect it is an exception in relation to the ordinary law. Under another aspect it may be considered as a favor, contemplating the common good of the community in its first half and the welfare of the priest, specifically, in its latter half. In virtue of the fact that all jurisdictional power is divided into power that is ordinary or delegated,[13] the supplied power of canon 209 must be regarded as a delegation from the law (*delegatio a iure*). Such is the commonly accepted view of the authorities.[14]

[13] Canon 197, § 1; Kearney, *The principles of delegation*, p. 61.

[14] Cf. e. g., Kelly, *The jurisdiction of the confessor*, p. 117. Noldin-Schmitt, *Theologia moralis* (21. ed., Oeniponte, 1932), III, n. 345, 1 (hereafter this work will be referred to simply as *Summa*); Cappello, *De sacramentis*, II, n. 486; Wernz-Vidal, *Ius canonicum*, II, n. 379; J. Stocchiero, "De jurisdictione vicariorum paroecialium,"—*Jus Pont.*, XI (1931), 221.

ARTICLE I. CONDITIONS REQUISITE FOR THE SUPPLYING OF JURISDICTION

A. Common Error

Canon 209 basically reproduces an old law. This incontestable fact presents the following probem in the interpretation of canon 209. How far is this new law to follow the understanding and the interpretation of the old suppletory principle by pre-Code authorities? How far, if at all, does the legislator purpose to deviate from that interpretation in the New Code? This will be the core of the discussion now to occupy the attention of the reader. In turn, consideration will be given to the traditional interpretation before the Code, to the attempts of certain schools of canonists to establish that the present law is to be interpreted more benignly, and finally, an effort shall be made to evaluate these proposals in the light of the rest of the Code. However, as a preface to these considerations, for purposes of a better understanding of the issues involved, the following definitions and descriptions will be offered.

I. INTRODUCTORY NOTIONS ABOUT COMMON ERROR

1. *Error and Ignorance*

The opposite of truth, or true knowledge, is *error*, or erroneous belief. Error necessarily implies the possession of some ideas about the object thought of, and is the disagreement of the judgment which the mind has formed about the thing, and to which it adheres, with the thing or reality in question.

On the other hand, the absence of knowledge in a being capable of possessing it is called *ignorance*. Either the mind does not possess any ideas at all about the matter in question, in which case it is absolutely or totally ignorant, i.e., in a state of *nescience* regarding the thing; or, possessing some ideas about the thing, it does not know what is the proper relation to establish between these, and thus is partially ignorant, and in *doubt.*[1] But about doubt more will be given in detail when that phase of canon 209 will be given separate attention.

In regard to error, Kearney has given a few descriptive definitions which will be helpful to the reader.[2] They are based on the divisions of intention, used constantly by moralists:

> 1. *Interpretative* error is that which has never existed actually; it is merely a fiction. It would now be verified if conditions were otherwise. It is, therefore, nothing real; it is merely presumed. Thus, a fact of its nature public, but which has never come to the attention of a community, is merely interpretative knowledge until such a time as it actually becomes known.
>
> 2. *Virtual* error is that which was once actual and now continues to exist at least subconsciously, just as a virtual intention was once actual and now continues to exert its influence.
>
> 3. Error *de facto* is that error which is either actual or virtual since virtual error too implies the *fact* of error.
>
> 4. Error *de iure* is that which is a fiction of law. It is not factual. Thus, a fact that of its nature would lead many into error is not *common error;* yet, to this phase the law could attach such a meaning, if the legislator so willed. Such is only interpretative error.

2. *Common*

Etymologically, *common* means belonging or pertaining to a community at large, public. It signifies something prevalent or general, belonging to many or to a majority.

II. THE TRADITIONAL INTERPRETATION OF COMMON ERROR

In the historical analysis it has been observed how the authors clearly distinguished between *title* and *common error.* Without any doubt these two formed separate and distinct concepts in the minds of ancient canonists. While some of them required also the presence of a colored title, *all* insisted upon the presence of *common error.*

[1] St. Thomas, *In Sent.,* IV, 30, 1, 1; 49, 2, 5, 8m; *Summa theol.,* I-II, 76, 2; *De malo,* 3, 7c; 8, 1, 7m; *Post Anal.,* I, 27a. Cf. also P. Coffey, *The science of logic* (New York: Peter Smith, 1938), II, p. 211.

[2] *The principles of delegation,* p. 128.

Prescinding at this stage from the fact that among pre-Code authors the greatest discrepancy existed in reference to the *number* who must be in error in order that such an error be called *common*, prescinding also from the fact that many authors do not lengthily discuss common error, which, as Kearney with much justification argues,[3] should serve as evidence that they did not understand the term in any abnormal, fictional sense, one may adduce ample and irrefutable evidence in support of the fact that the old authors thought and wrote of common error in its true, literal sense.

Sanchez,[4] for example, qualified common error as the error whereby a person was *considered* a true judge. Clearly, then, Sanchez demanded something more than mere ignorance. He required *ignorance in action,* which is philosophically the true concept of error. Furthermore, Sanchez clearly noted that the *error of one person or another* could occur under two conditions, namely, such an error could arise when the fact of the impediment was or was not known to the general public. Sanchez felt that, if the error were made on the part of a few while the rest of the people remained in ignorance, the inconveniences and scandals would not follow which the suppletory principle was intended to forestall. As regards the first possibility Sanchez felt that, in view of the common knowledge about a defect, the error of one person or of another would be neither just nor probable, and hence had no right to the protective provision of the suppletory principle.

In a similar way Pirhing[5] noted that the mere fact of a person's possession of a judicial office or of some public power was insufficient to warrant the supplying of deficient jurisdiction. According to Pirhing two other conditons had to be fulfilled. The error had to be *public,* or *common.* In other words, the defect of the judge's competence had to be of such an occult nature that he was still *commonly* regarded as a true and legitimate official. Like Sanchez, Pirhing adverted to the fact that *the error of one or of another or of a few did not suffice.*

[3] *The principles of delegation,* p 124.
[4] *De matrimonio,* lib. III, disp. 22, n. 5.
[5] *Jus canonicum,* lib. II, tit. 1, n. 83 ss.

Thus, also, Schmalzgrueber[6] reiterated the same opinion as Sanchez and Pirhing in his contention that the error had to be *probable, public* or *common* on the part of the people. Like these two, Schmalzgrueber demanded something more than negative ignorance or possible common error. He specifically qualified as true common error the error whereby the people considered an incompetent judge a true judge.

Such was likewise the consistent teaching of Schmalzgrueber's contemporaries: Reiffensteul († 1703),[7] Wigandt († 1708),[8] and Mayr (Cherubin).[9]

Apparently, then, the ancient canonists, as exemplified by the several that have just been mentioned, regardless of their disagreement as to the necessity or non-necessity of a colored title, concurred in the concept that something more than negative ignorance was required, something more than the foundation of a public fact whereby under normal conditions others indiscriminately would also be led into error. Lega[10] recorded in his day how all agreed that the error of a few did not merit the general provision of the suppletory principle.[11]

Thus, as Toso[12] concluded, when the old jurists asserted that *the error of one or of another or of a few* did not suffice for the application of the suppletory principle, it is most clearly apparent that they spoke of *factual* error, of error really existing in the

[6] *Ius ecclesiasticum universum,* lib. II, tit. 1, n. 20 ss.

[7] *Ius canonicum universum,* lib. II, tit. 1, n. 198.

[8] *Tribunal confessariorum et ordinandorum* (Pisauri, 1760), tract. XIII, exam. V, q. VIII.

[9] *Trismegistus iuris pontificii* (Augustae Vindelicorum, 1742), Tom. III, lib. IV, tit. 26, n. 82.

[10] *De iudiciis,* I, n. 355.

[11] Cf., e. g., Pontius, *De matrimonio,* V, cap. 19, n. 14; Billuart, *De poenitentia,* Dist. VI, art. 4, § 1; Reiffenstuel, *Ius canonicum universum,* lib. IV, tit. III, n. 76; Ferraris, *Prompta bibliotheca,* ad v. "*Jurisdictio,*" n. 32; Scavini, *Theologia moralis,* III, n. 374—all of these were agreed that the error of a few is particular, and not common, and the Church will not supply.

[12] "De errore communi ad normam can. 209,"—*Jus Pont.,* XVIII (1938), 166.

nature of things, and not of error that was merely interpretative. For, this error, as they proposed it, is to be understood to be on the part of all or, contrariwise, as not having existed at all. Likewise *the error of one or of another* may be understood either as a truly factual error, or as a merely potential error. Now, if in the case of error by one or two that error was construed by the authors as a truly factual error, then, in a similar fashion, the common error of which they spoke was also a truly factual error. For there is the same *ratio* in either case. It would be illogical to oppose potential common error to factual particular error as they are not contrary ideas. That is why canonists were wont to require that a person be popularly or commonly considered as the true and legitimate judge. And, in the event that anyone ventured to interpose that the factual error of one person sufficed, provided the adjuncts of the case were such that others would themselves be necessarily led into error, then these same canonists, in answer to such a claim, would doubtless have called such an error merely private and particular, but certainly not a common error.

That such is a correct understanding of the concept of the older canonists in regard to common error is most commonly admitted by men who substantially sided with Toso [13] as well as those who disagreed with him.[14]

Indeed, this traditional concept of the older canonists received confirmation from the Sacred Congregation of the Council.[15] This

[13] E. g., Kearney, *The principles of delegation,* p. 123; Jombart, "L'erreur commune,"—*NRT,* L (1923), 538-539; Nevin, "Does doctrine concerning the supply of jurisdiction in *common error* apply in the case of matrimony?"—*Australasian Catholic Record,* XIV (1937), 144. Hereafter reference to this periodical will be made by using the abreviation *ACR.*

[14] E. g., Trombetta, *Supplet ecclesia,* p. 17; Wernz-Vidal, *Ius canonicum,* II, n. 381; Guns, "L'erreur commune,"—*NRT,* L (1923), 539; Fink, "Eheassistenz und allgemeiner Irrtum,"—*Theologie und Glaube,* XXVI (1934), 592; *L'Ami du Clergé,* XLII (1925), 105-106; XLVII (1930), 647; Vermeersch-Creusen, *Epitome,* I, n. 322, 4.

[15] "Caesaraugustana matrimonii," 10 Mar., 1770, in *Thesaurus resolutionum sac. congregationis concilii quae prodierunt anno 1770,* Rmo. P. D. Francesco Xaverio De Zelada Secretario (Romae: Ex Typographia

Congregation applied the principle of common error to a matrimonial case which involved a priest, who after the death of a certain pastor assumed the burdens of the parish. Among his acts was assistance at a certain marriage. The assistance of said priest was declared valid in view of the provisions of the suppletory principle. And it must be noted that, in establishing the existence of common error, the Sacred Congregation as not satisfied with the presence of pure ignorance on the part of the people. Apparently neither the public exercise of parochial functions, nor the colored title, were of themselves deemed sufficient grounds for the application of the suppletory principle. On the contrary, the Congregation methodically proceeded to examine whether or not *at the time of the marriage ceremony* the parishioners *considered* that the priest was their proper pastor. To establish the fact of the existence of common error at that time the Congregation carefully selected more than thirty parishioners from *different groups and ranks* to testify to the existence of such an error at the time of the marriage ceremony. And only when it was thus proved that the *error* was common in the parish *at the time when the ceremony took place and not afterwards,*[16] only then did the Congregation decree the suppletory principle applied in this case. Indeed one cannot overemphasize the fact that the Congregation was interested in the time of the verification of the common error. For the report of the case shows clearly that the six witnesses, who had been brought forth in the first instance to testify against the priest, were considered poor witnesses precisely because their testimony

Bernabò, et Lazzarini [1770], Tom. XXXIX, 51-56. Cf. Pallotini, *Collectio omnium conclusionum et resolutionum quae in causis propositis apud S. Congregationem Cardinalium S. Concilii Tridentini interpretum prodierunt* (Romae, 1887), XIII, v. "*Matrimonium,*" XV, n. 90, for digest.

[16] "Nec dubitare posse asserit [i. e. Defensor], quin *tempore contracti Matrimonii* Sacerdos Guillen habitus ab omnibus fuerit Regens Parochialis Ecclesiae S. Laurentii, cum id jurejurando deposuerint triginta, et ultra Testes Parochiani ex omni caetu, atque ordine decerpti, qui plenissimam constituunt communis opinionis probationem."—*Thesaurus,* XXXIX, 52.

did not refer to the time of, or before, the marriage ceremony.[17] As Kearney well points out,[18] since this is an authentic decision on the part of the Holy See, it may be regarded as a true norm. And, as has been seen, this norm was in accord with the teachings of the authors who lived in the period preceding its issuance and, undoubtedly must have served as a real guide for those canonists who belonged to a later period. It is no wonder then that Lega could speak in his day of such agreement on the part of the canonists in reference to the literal interpretation of common error.

III. INTERPRETATIVE THEORY

Unquestionably there has been, particularly in the last decade, a very strong trend among canonists to depart from what they almost unanimously concede has been the traditional, pre-Code interpretation of common error. When Bucceroni[19] first proposed his novel and, in view of the hitherto prevalent interpretation, liberal concept of common error, it appears that he received very little support from contemporary scholars. As Toso observes, and as later shall be seen in detail in this treatise on common error, not even his fellow Jesuits, like Wernz or Ojetti, not even Vermeersch, though he himself was preeminently a moralist like Bucceroni, espoused Bucceroni's point of view on this particular question.[20] Even Cappello, who in time became this theory's most ardent supporter, lacked at first the assurance of certainty which he later felt and expressed in regard to this thesis.[21] Kelly was able to refer to these canonists as of *recent* appearance.[22] At as late a date as 1925 *L'Ami du Clergé*[23] admitted freely that the thesis of the

[17] "Deinde de singulorum depositione aggrediens, observat [i. e. Defensor] ex iis nonnullos, qui Parochiani sunt eorum dictum non coarctare ad tempus Matrimonii, vel ante illius celebrationem, sed loqui *de tempore posteriori*."—*Thesaurus*, XXXIX, 53.

[18] *The principle of delegation*, p. 126.

[19] *Casus conscientiae*, p. 568.

[20] "De errore communi ad normam can. 209,"—*Jus Pont.*, XVIII (1938), 166.

[21] Compare *De sacramentis* (Romae, 1923), II, n. 665 and *De sacramentis* (Ed. altera, Romae, 1929), II, Pars I, n. 490.

[22] *The jurisdiction of the confessor*, p. 124.

[23] XLII (1925), 105-106.

interpretative error lacked authority, but also subjoined confidently and, as events proved, prophetically, that the support of the authors would come in due time. And this support did come. With much justification do Brys [24] and J. Creusen [25] remark that this interpretative theory is *commonly* admitted and may even be said to boast of a numerically larger following than the school of canonists insisting upon the stricter, traditional interpretation of common error. Cappello,[26] Vermeersch-Creusen,[27] at least since the second edition of their work, and Beste [28] and Gougnard,[29] for example, regard the interpretative error theory as *certain*. Sabbetti-Barrett [30] maintain that this theory *can with complete security be admitted*. To Coronata [31] this theory *appears* capable of successful defense. And Wouters,[32] Davis [33] and Aertnys-Damen [34] consider it *very probable*. In view of such an imposing arrary of canonists and moralists, Fink [35] considered the theory as *practically certain*, while Jone [36] felt himself constrained to admit that such a mass of authority was at least indicative of a *doubt of law*, in which case the Church would supply according to the second part of canon 209. In a similar manner Jombart, acknowledging the

[24] "Error communis,"—*Collationes Brugenses*, XXXV (1935), 61-62. Hereafter reference to this periodical will be made by using the abbreviation *Coll. Brug.*

[25] *Acta congressus iuridici internationalis*, IV, 183.

[26] *De sacramentis*, II, Pars I, n. 490.

[27] *Epitome* (6. ed., Mechliniae: Dessain, 1937), I, n. 322.

[28] *Introductio in codicem* (Collegeville, Minn.: St. John's Abbey Press, 1938), ad canonem 209.

[29] *Tractatus de matrimonio* (7. ed., Mechliniae, 1931), p. 191.

[30] *Compendium theologiae moralis* (34. ed., New York: Pustet Co., Inc., 1939), n. 770, q. 12.

[31] *Institutiones*, I, n. 492.

[32] *Manuale theologiae moralis*, I, n. 103, II, 1, a.

[33] *Moral and pastoral theology* (London: Sheed and Ward, 1935), III, 249-250.

[34] *Theologia moralis* (11. ed., Turin: Marietti, 1928), II, n. 359.

[35] "Eheassistenz und allgemeiner Irrtum,"—*Theologie und Glaube*, XXVI (1934), 586.

[36] "Error communis und Suppletion der Beichtjurisdiktion,"—*LQS*, LXXXI (1928), 141.

strength of the arguments for and against the interpretative theory, conceded that a doubt of law existed on that point and that the Church would supply.[37] Such men of repute, together with a vast host of others [38] have joined in maintaining the theory which Vermeersch-Creusen were the first to designate with the name *interpretative*. However, admitting that there are many who hold this theory, one should not be too credulous in accepting the lists of supporters that many of these protagonists claim. Thus, with ample reason, for example, does Claeys-Bouuaert [39] call De Smet [40] to task for listing Vermeersch and Jombart among the authors who favor the theory of error which is common only virtually, i.e., in the sense of being only in a potential stage as contraposed to actual existence. As shall be seen, Vermeersch certainly insisted upon the verification of real, common error, for the necessity of a *factum already perceived by many,* not merely apt to cause others to fall into error as they saw it.

This interpretative school of canonists and moralists contends that its stand is in conformity with both the text and the context of canon 209, with the words and the mind of the legislator. If they deviate, as they do, from the strict interpretation of common error, they claim to do so only because they are convinced that a strict interpretation could never be regarded as a satisfactory juridical basis or norm whereby to judge the applicability or non-

[37] "L'erreur commune,"—*NRT,* L (1923), 176.

[38] Cf., e. g., Grazioli, "De errore communi et de defectu iurisdictionis in confessario,"—*Palestra del Clero,* X (1931), 177-178; P. Necchi, "La giurisdizione nell'errore commune,"—*Palestra del Clero,* VII (1928), 279-280; Trombetta, *Supplet ecclesia,* p. 6; "Questioni proposte,"—*Perfice munus,* XIV (1939), 38-39; *Nederlandsche katholieke Stemmen,* XXVIII (1928), 44-48; Guns, "L'erreur commune,"—*NRT,* L (1923), 539; *L'Ami du Clergé,* XLVII (1930), 135-137; *Adloff,* "L'erreur commune et la juridicion suppléée,"—*Bulletin Ecclésiastique du Diocèse du Strasbourg,* XLVI (1927), 254 ss.; Couly, "La juridiction suppléée du canon 209," *Le canoniste,* XLVII (1925), 456; Wernz-Vidal, *Ius canonicum,* II, n. 381; Arquer, *El error común y la jurisdicción eclesiastica* (2. ed., Barcelona: Editorial Poliglota, 1927), nn. 14-16.

[39] "De conceptu erroris communis in canone 209,"—*Jus Pont.,* XVI (1936), 163.

[40] *De sponsalibus et matrimonio* (4. ed., Brugis: Beyaert, 1927), n. 109.

applicability of the suppletory principle. In their opinion the strict theory belies the benignity of the legislator and of his Code and runs counter to the very purpose of the suppletory principle: the good of all the faithful.

Perhaps this group's reasoning and the weight and import of their arguments will most effectively be brought out and best appreciated by taking into account first the negative considerations, i.e., the objections to the strict theory, and then by offering the positive arguments upon which the theory has been reared until it has assumed its present stature.

1. *Arguments Against the Strict Interpretation of Common Error*

The interpretative school of canonists briefly points out that the strict interpretation supports and defends the literal interpretation of common error, i. e., the error thus must be *actual* and must be entertained on the part of at least *many* of the faithful. But, they argue, if such were the true meaning intended by the legislator, then, since this would be a condition upon which the very validity of the jurisdictional acts would depend, an inquiry would of necessity have to be made in each indivdual instance to ascertain the sufficiency of the *number* of those who have really erred or are in error. To do that all the members of a parish or all the inhabitants of a community would need to be questioned; for, how else could the true state of affairs be known? But a task of this sort would be too exacting, too involved and difficult, in fact, altogether impossible in practice.[41]

In the first place, so they contend, who will authoritatively determine what figure will satisfactorily fulfill the requisite *number* of those in error. Certainly the authors are not in agreement on this score. Even those who have made a real attempt at greater clarity and practicability by admitting that the error of *many* will suffice, are not agreed about how and when *many* may be said to be in error. Consequently, because of such uncertainty and vagueness in regard to this essentially important condition, the interpretative school of canonists firmly contends it is not permissible to agree

[41] Cappello, *De sacramentis,* II, Pars I, n. 490, 2; Wernz-Vidal, *Ius canonicum,* II, n. 381; Coronata, *Institutiones,* I, n. 292, 1, a.

that the Church has intended to subordinate the validity of her absolutions, etc. to a norm so inadequately clear, so vague, so practically impossible to determine with any degree of assurance.[42]

In the second place, granting for the sake of argument only, that a definite figure or a percentage has been agreed upon, even then one will not always find it a simple task to ascertain the presence of the error of the necessary number of people. For, certainly it would be necessary to distinguish those in error from those who are in mere ignorance, and then those truly in error from those whose error is crass and supine.[43] It would be necessary to exclude the non-baptized of a certain locale, and it would not be clear as to whether the twenty, thirty or forty percent of the non-practicing Christians should be included or excluded.[44]

Such indeed are some of the difficulties arrayed against the wisdom of requiring the error to be real and common in the strict traditional sense. Wernz-Vidal go even further. Writing in reference to confession,[45] they venture to remark that many people do not approach the confessor, many do not even think of so doing, many are not even conscious of his presence or even of his existence, and therefore can hardly be expectd to err about his possession of the required jurisdiction. It was on this score that Coronata [46] stated that common error need not be present, and should not be required, precisely because it could almost never be verified. On the same grounds Guns [47] concluded emphatically that he could not subscribe to any such norm, not only because of its utter inutility but, even more, because of its utter lack of juridical foundation. *L'Ami du Clergé* [48] with much the same vehemence refused to accept such a norm because, in addition to all other reasons that can be adduced, in the last analysis, it would be practically impossible to arrive at an objective knowledge of the existence

[42] *L'Ami du Clergé,* XLII (1925), 102-103.
[43] Toso, "De errore communi,"—*Jus Pont.,* III (1923), 151.
[44] Guns, "L'erreur commune,"—*NRT,* L (1923), 538.
[45] *Ius canonicum,* II, n. 358, 9.
[46] *Institutiones,* I, n. 292.
[47] "L'erreur commune,"—*NRT,* L (1923), 537.
[48] XLII (1925), 104.

of such common error on the part of the people. For, certainly, the faithful would not be expected to make the necessary computation; it is none of their concern, nor is it within their province so to do. Nor will the confessor be capable of so doing; for, what does he know of the mentality of the faithful in things that concern him?

Pursuing this train of thought, Cappello[49] states that, granted that such a detailed interrogation could be made in a particular case, this would afford no argument in favor of the strict interpretation. For the law by its very nature is not concerned with cases that are so extraordinary and particular, but with cases which are wont to occur commonly and usually.

It is very clear among authors such as these that they regard the requisite of strict common error as untenable. And they note that, though these difficulties would be real and formidable in any case, they would be infinitely multiplied in large cities, in vast cathedrals.[50] And then, any attempt at such interrogation would be ludicrous, would engender scrupulosity and would not fit in with the age-old and proven wisdom of the Church.

Added to such arguments in proof of the impracticability of so vague a norm regarding common error, as expounded traditionally, and the moral, if not physical, impossibility of ascertaining the existence of any such common error, is the blunt charge that any such strict demand, i.e., for actual error on the part of at least many before the Church could be considered to commence the supplying of jurisdiction, is entirely subversive of the very purpose of law: to provide for the common good of the faithful. Such, as one may easily recall, was the ultimate reason for Bucceroni's defection from the traditionally accepted opinion on common error.[51] He could not reconcile himself to the belief that the Church would say that a number of successive individual absolutions would be invalid, and that at a certain time after these instances of invalidity the Church would begin to supply the defi-

[49] *De sacramentis,* II, Pars I, n. 490, 3.

[50] Cappello, *De sacramentis,* II, Pars I, n. 490, 4; Guns, "L'erreur commune,"—*NRT,* L (1923), 537.

[51] Cf. *Casus conscientiae,* p. 568.

cient jurisdiction. Why the borderline case should profit at the expense of so many invalid absolutions seemed to jar Bucceroni's concept of the benignity of the Church. It also seemed quite an anomaly to him that in that border-line case, that is, as soon as the error of many had been actually verified, the Church would consider the common good involved, but would not do so in any of the cases which preceded. This objection of Bucceroni can easily be seen perpetuated in the works of the innumerable authors who followed him in this view. Thus, for example, Wernz-Vidal [52] substantially reiterate Bucceroni's thesis, insisting that the Church could not be said to supply for the common good, if she did not supply until after many have already suffered from invalid confessions. They add that very often the sufficient number may be reached only at such a time when there is little if any use for the remedy.

2. *Arguments for the Interpretative Theory*

Many canonists are content to point out the above analyzed difficulties of the strict interpretation and to hold them as a sufficient reason for departing from its doctrine and a sufficient basis for embracing the more lenient view on the question. Others, however, add to these negative observations what they regard as direct and positive arguments, or at least indications, in support of their liberal contentions.

Thus, some [53] emphasize that, by the insertion of canon 209 into the Code, the legislator wished to cut short all controversy in regard to this supplying of jurisdiction. He wished to clarify the law so as to rid priests and the faithful of undue anguish and anxiety.

Others point out that, since the whole Code teems with patent manifestations of sympathy and benignity towards the safety of the faithful and the peace of mind of the clergy, particularly of confessors, as can be noted, for example, by the simplification of the sacramental discipline, there is valid reason for regarding the privilege of canon 209 in the light of this benignity and interpret-

[52] *Ius canonicum,* II, n. 381.

[53] E. g., Cappello, *De sacramentis,* Pars I, n. 490, 5; Gougnard, *Tractatus de matrimonio* (7. ed., Mechliniae: Dessain, 1931), p. 191.

ting it with leniency and consideration for all involved.[54] Others, furthermore, contend that the present era offers new problems whcih demand a more considerate application of canon 209. Thus *L'Ami du Clergé*[55] notes that of late the practice of confessing much more frequently than in the past has grown, that nowadays people are accustomed to confess to almost any priest they meet, and not to their own proper pastor as they were wont to do in the past almost exclusively, that today the people are not aware of the normal requirements as regards jurisdiction, whereas in the past, when they were more closely grouped about their priests, these normal requisites were known to them.

But with whatever arguments they fortify themselves, the members of this interpretative school feel, with varying degrees of assurance, that their more liberal concept is in full accord with the words and sense of canon 209 and the mind of the legislator.

3. *Highlights of the Interpretative Theory*

In general, the proponents of this theory do not demand for the verification of common error that many must err *de facto,* but that, in view of the circumstances, many could or would be drawn into error. In other words, the *fact* of error on the part of many is not necessary; a *foundation,* a *cause,* a *basis,* which, if allowed to run out its natural course, would necessarily lead others into error, suffices. Hence, as Kearney points out,[56] *common error* becomes a mere fiction of law; for, according to this theory, the error need not be *common,* nor in fact need there be *error* at all in actuality.[57] Yet, despite this patent disregard for the literal significance of these two words, the proponents of this theory are convinced that theirs is the interpretation intended by the legislator.

[54] *L'Ami du Clergé,* XLII (1925), 105.

[55] XLVII (1930), 136.

[56] *The principles of delegation,* p. 127.

[57] Cf., e.g., Cappello, *De sacramentis,* II, Pars I, n. 491, 4, where he speaks of *antecedent* common error arising because of certain adjuncts or circumstances. Likewise cf. A. Salvador's sharp criticism of Cappello about this point in: "Error communis et iurisdictionis suppletio ab Ecclesia,"—*BE,* XVII (1939), 246.

The full appreciation of this interpretative theory, of its merits, and its defects, will not be treated until later. But at this stage it may be helpful to interject this one observation. Under the interpretative theory error need not be actual; hence, in strictly abstract psychological terminology, it can not be virtual either since virtual error is a false judgment which, once elicited, perseveres in the mind even though momentarily the mind does not advert to its presence.

This substitute for actually common error is not presented by all authors in the same manner. Thus, for example, Bucceroni [58] declared it as his opinion that it is sufficient for error to be common *de jure* in *actu primo,* that is, the circumstances must be such that, following the natural course of events, a certain fact will lead many into error. Vermeersch-Creusen [59] state a little more clearly that the error is common once a basis of a *public* nature is posited for it. Vidal [60] is still clearer in his expression when he states that common error already exists when a *public fact* is posited which of its very essence is capable of leading into error, not one or a few, but all persons indiscriminately. Vidal accepted this conception without any hesitation and considered it so certain that he made use of it in the Gregorianum, the Papal University in Rome.[61] In a similar way Cappello declares that it is sufficient if under the circumstances many will of necessity be drawn into error.[62] As an example Cappello cites the case of a priest *in a public church,* in a *confessional,* with the *permission of the rector,* prepared to hear confessions. Such would be a sufficient basis, according to Cappello, for the Church to supply jurisdiction, even though only a few persons, or even one, or even none be present in the Church at the time. And Adloff [63] professes that *virtual* common error suffices, and that it exists even in a case in which merely

[58] *Casus conscientiae,* p. 568.

[59] *Epitome,* I, n. 232.

[60] *Ius canonicum,* II, n. 381.

[61] Cf. Jone, "Error communis und Suppletion der Beichtjurisdiktion,"—*LQS,* LXXXI (1928), 141.

[62] *De sacramentis,* II, Pars I, n. 490.

[63] "L'erreur commune et la juridiction suppléée," — *Bulletin Ecclésiastique du Diocèse de Strasbourg,* XLVI (1927), 254 ss.

the name of the priest is attached to the confessional, though none of the faithful advert to the fact. Similarly Couly[64] speaks of error as *virtually* affecting a community when a priest by entering a confessional offers his services for any approaching penitent. On the basis of such a *virtual* error *L'Ami du Clergé*[65] claims that every penitent who enters a confessional, every penitent who begs a priest to hear his confession, is validly absolved regardless of the existence of error on the part of the many.

IV. APPRAISAL OF THE INTERPRETATIVE THEORY

While a host of authorities has been shown to lean towards the interpretative theory, a vast numbers of others cling tenaciously to the stricter, traditional concept of common error. Among the latter are numerous canonists[66] and moralists[67] of great authority

[64] "La juridiction suppléée du canon 209,"—*Le canoniste*, XLVII (1925), 456.

[65] XLII (1925), 104.

[66] Cf., e. g., Badii, *Institutiones*, n. 149, note 1; Chelodi, *Ius de personis*, n. 130; Cocchi, *Commentarium*, lib. II, Pars I, sec. I, n. 132; Schrattenholzer, "Beichtjurisdiktionszweifel,"—*LQS*, LXXX (1927), 331-333; Ojetti, *Commentarium in codicem iuris canonici*, lib. II, ad can. 209, n. 2; Woywod, *A practical commentary on the Code of canon law* (New York, 1925), I, 80; Bączkowicz, *Prawo kanoniczne* (2. ed., Nakładem Ksiezy Misjonarzy, 1924), I, n. 468; Grabowski, *Prawo kanoniczne według nowego kodeksu* (2. ed., Lwów: Tow. Biblioteka Religijna, 1927), p. 168; Jone, "Error communis und Suppletion der Beichtjurisdiktion,"—*LQS*, LXXXI (1928), 140; Perathoner, *Das kirchliche Gesetzbuch sinngemäss wiedergegeben und mit Anmerkungen versehen* (4. ed., Brixen, 1926), p. 118; Triebs, *Praktisches Handbuch des geltenden kanonischen Eherechts* (Breslau, 1933), p. 575; Eichmann, *Lehrbuch des Kirchenrechts auf Grund des Codex* I. C. (4. ed., Paderborn, 1934), I, p. 170; A. Toso, "De errore communi ad normam can. 209,"—*Jus Pont.*, XVIII (1938), 166-169; F. Claeys-Bouuaert, "De conceptu erroris communis in canone 209,"—*Jus Pont.*, XVI (1936), 159; Knecht, *Handbuch des katholischen Eherechts* (Freiburg im Breisgau: Herder, 1928), p. 625; Sägmüller, *Lehrbuch des katholisches Kirchenrechts* (Freiburg i. Br., 1930), p. 437; J. Nevin, "Does doctrine concerning the supply of jurisdiction in *common error* apply in the case of matrimony?"—*ACR*, XIV (1937), 144; Wilches, *De errore communi*, p. 198; A. Salvador, "Error communis et iurisdictionis suppletio ab ecclesia,"—*BE*, XVII (1939),

and repute. With authorities thus ranged on both sides, it becomes immediately clear that if any definitive solution is to be reached concerning the character of the common error necessary for the applicability of the suppletory principle, the differences of opinions must be studied and their basic reason put to a rigid test and examination.

At the outset it must be observed that there are several points in common between the protagonists of both schools. Both agree that canon 209 is a favor, a clear evidence of the legislator's benignity and concern for the welfare of the faithful. Both, while they admit that the silence of the Code is to be interpreted as an express, though implicit, argument that a colored title is no longer required, believe that in the last analysis there must be some foundation for the existence of common error. And, finally, both agree on the literal meaning of the terms *common* and *error*. But beyond that the differences begin. One school attempts to adhere to the literal significance of these terms while the other strives equally earnestly to draw away from such an interpretation, to regard *common error* more as a technical term, a fiction of law, which connotes something more extensive than its literal denotation. And before proceeding any further, it must be admitted that both these schools sincerely attempt in different fashions to safeguard what they conceive as the common good of the faithful.

242; Dalpiaz, "Vicariis cooperatoribus ipso iure potestas non competit assistendi matrimoniis,"—*Apoll.*, VII (1934), 81.

[67] Cf., e. g., Ferreres, *Compendium theologiae moralis ad normam codicis iuris canonici* (14. ed., Barcinone: Eugenius Subirana, 1928), II, n. 651, II (hereafter this work will be referred to as *Compendium*); Marc-Gestermann-Raus, *Institutiones morales Alphonsianae* (18. ed., Lugduni: Typis Emmanuelis Vitte, 1927), n. 1761 (hereafter this work will be referred to as *Institutiones*); Pighi, *Cursus theologiae moralis* (4. ed., Veronae, 1926), lib. IV, n. 289; Merkelbach, *Summa theologiae moralis ad mentem D. Thomae et ad normam iuris novi* (2. ed., Parisiis: Typis Desclée, De Brouwer et Soc., 1935-1936), III, n. 586 (hereafter this work will be referred to as *Summa*); Vermeersch, *Theologia moralis, principia, responsa, consilia* (2. ed., Brugis: Charles Beyaert, 1926-1927), III, n. 459 (hereafter this work will be referred to as *Theologia moralis*); Noldin-Schmitt, *De sacramentis*, III, n. 247.

In this attempt to appraise the two theories, and to be able to select one or the other as the more probable, since the interpretative theory is the more recent of the two while the traditional one was already long established before the Code, consideration will first be given to the text of canon 209. Then the contextual reasons proffered by the authors of the interpretative school will be analyzed. Finally consideration will be given to the sequels of the interpretative doctrine.

The Interpretative Theory in the Light of the Text and Context of Canon 209

According to canon 18 ecclesiastical laws are to be understood according to the proper meaning of the words considered in their text and context. If their meaning should remain doubtful and obscure, recourse must be had to parallel places in the Code, if there be any, to the purpose of the law and the circumstances attending it, and to the mind of the legislator. But, over and above that, the Code makes an added provision in regard to old laws which have been incorporated in the new Code. Thus canon 6, n. 2, specifically states that such canons which restate the old law without change must be interpreted upon the authority of the ancient law, and, therefore, in the light of the teaching of the old approved authors. This canon further states in n. 4, that in the event of a doubt as to whether the canon in the Code differs from the ancient law the old law must be upheld.[68]

The most superficial study reveals that the interpretative theory contradicts the unanimous teaching of the pre-Code jurists. In addition, it must be pointed out that, as has been already illustrated, most, if not all, of this school *knowingly* and *willingly* deviated from the pre-Code teaching on common error. Thus, Guns,[69] for example, admitted that the pre-Code authors seem to have required the existence of real and factual common error, but he felt justified in veering away from that teaching because, as he noted, the majority of these pre-Code authors scarcely envisaged the case where the colored title was not present. Hence, since the Code

[68] Cf. pages 160-161.

[69] "L'erreur commune," *NRT*, L (1923), 539.

affirms that jurisdiction may be supplied even though in a specific case a colored title be not possessed by the one about whose jurisdictional competence there is a common error, a more free and advantageous interpretation of common error is entirely in order. Thus, also *L'Ami du Clergé*[70] seemed to be convinced that the *sympathy* of the new law, as exemplified by canons 207, § 2, and 209, was sufficient reason for the abandoment of the more severe, complicated, hardly practicable traditional theory. Thus, it is apparent that this defection from the traditionally accepted doctrine became a fact because the authors felt that the new law, if not in letter, at least in spirit departed from he old and confirmed such an interpretation. Was and is such the case?

1. *Textual Arguments*

The Code's phraseology, *in errore communi . . . supplet Ecclesia,* reproduces a time-honored phrase, which had its roots in a *glossa* of Accursius († 1260),[71] and which up to the time of the appearance of the Code always and—with the exception of Bucceroni—universally accepted in a definite sense, as has been seen above. The phrase, or more appositely the traditional intrepretation of that phrase, had official approbation on at least one occasion when the Sacred Congregation of the Council used that interpretation in settling a marriage case on Mar. 10, 1770.[72]

Therefore, when the Code made use of this traditionally accepted term and incorporated it without any change, there was immediately in that very fact a strong indication that the legislator intended to make no change. His reiteration without change might rather be looked upon as a confirmation of the old doctrine. Thus, if any argument is to be drawn from the text as it stands in the Code today, it is bound to turn against the theory that would assume that the legislator is in favor of an innovation. For, had the Code adopted any other meaning or meant to create a fiction of law, the legislator could and would have given some inkling of his purpose.[73]

[70] XLII (1925), 105-106.

[71] *Glossa* ad D. (1. 14) 3 ad v. *Functus sit.*

[72] Cf. Pallotini, XIII, v. *Matrimonium,* n. 90.

[73] Kearney, *The principles of delegation,* p. 129.

Many authors [74] of the interpretative school would draw an argument in their favor from the very presence of canon 209 in the Code, regardless of how this cannon might be worded. They contend that the existence of canon 209 in the Code is *prima facie* evidence of the legislator's wish to put an end to all controversies, and thus also to the controversy on common error, and consequently the interpretative theory may be regarded as upheld by the Code. There is a two-fold answer to this contention, according as one admits or denies that there existed such a controversy at the time of the Code's coming into being. Merkelbach [75] and Claeys-Bouuaert,[76] for example, admit that the legislator did want to solve the controversies already existing. However, apparently relying on the fact that Bucceroni's theory was for a long time lost for the lack of renowned champions to support it, they deny that any such controversy existed in regard to common error. They maintain that the legislator could not have looked back upon this controversy on common error since it had not yet arisen, that it can not be supposed that the legislator intended what had not yet been proposed by anyone and what he could not even suspect. Kearney's answer [77] is perhaps more satisfactory, because he assumes that the legislator was conscious of the dissident voice of Bucceroni on this question. Kearney notes that the legislator clearly settled three distinct controversies: the Church now supplies a.) without a colored title; b.) in doubt of fact as well as of law; and c.) in both *fora*. It is to be presumed that the legislator settled also the controversy stirred up by Bucceroni.[78]

He settled it by iterating the time honored phrase, "*Ecclesia supplet in errore communi,*" without any change. Thus it was that the settlement upon which Cappello and his confrères insist was made. But it was made to the discomfort of those who would hold the interpretative theory which was fathered by Bucceroni.

[74] E. g., Cappello, *De sacramentis,* II, Pars I, n. 490, 5.

[75] *Summa,* III, n. 586.

[76] "De conceptu erroris communis in canone 209,"—*Jus Pont.,* XVI (1936), 162.

[77] *The principles of delegation,* p. 131.

[78] Cf. *Casus conscientiae,* p. 568.

As further argument that the textual formation of canon 209 must be understood as evidence that *common error* must be taken in its strict sense, one might note how, despite, a lapse of more than one hundred and fifty years, the tribunal of the Rota in 1927 [79] clearly followed the Sacred Congregation of the Council in the manner it proceeded to establish the existence of common error, as required for the functioning of the suppletory principle, *at the time of the positing* of the jurisdictional or quasi-jurisdictional act.[80] In this case the Rota gives no evidence of being satisfied with the fact that the soldiers *could have* very easily fallen into the mistaken judgment that Father Chadim was still their military chaplain. On the contrary, the Rota was very careful to establish, on the testimony of two irreproachable witnesses, that the soldiers, as a matter of fact, *were all persuaded* that Father Chadim was *their pastor,* in fact, so much so that they used to come to him for whatever religious ministrations they needed.[81] And, to establish this point beyond any question of prudent doubt, the Rota went on in detail to examine all the adjuncts, all the circumstances of *persons,* of *place* and of *time.* Certainly this care on the part of the Rota is an authoritative indication that a mere *fundamentum erroris is not* constitutive in itself of error in the sense of c. 209.

2. *Contextual Arguments*

a. Difficulties Alleged Against the Traditional Theory

Perhaps the most commonly alleged reasons for the abandonment of the traditional concept of common error are centered in the difficulties which make that interpretation seem too severe and, therefore, impracticable. First of all, as has been seen above, the

[79] S. R. R., *Nullitas matrimonii,* 22 Nov., 1927, *coram R. P. D. Andrea Jullien,* dec. LI—*Decisiones,* XIX (1927), 453-465.

[80] S. C. Conc., 10 Martii, 1770, *Caesaraugustana matrimonii—Thesaurus resolutionum,* XXXIX (1770), 51.

[81] " . . . et legionarii, quemadmodum antea ita demum, Iosephum Chadim *habuerunt non modo uti sacerdotem sed uti sacerdotem 'suum',* quem nempe *adibant* pro negotiis suis religiosis explendis, et in specie pro matrimoniis ritu catholico celebrandis."—S. R. R., *Decisiones,* XIX (1927), 460.

champions of the interpretative theory emphasize how difficult it would be in every case to ascertain the presence of common error. Secondly, as has also been seen, they contend that to demand real and factual common error before the Church will begin to supply is tantamount to destroying the very purpose of the law's existence: the common good. For, they point to the case in which the people are not gathered as a body before confessions are begun to be heard by an unauthorized priest, but come into the Church one by one, and they seem extremely horrified when they are told by supporters of the stricter interpretation that, unfortunately, until and unless there be error that is common, these individual confessions are to be considered invalid.

To wave aside their objections as entirely groundless would be as foolhardy and as unreasonable as to admit them without further ado as a forceful, clinching argument against the continuance of the traditional concept of common error. The fact and the simultaneous justification of the regrettable invalidity of those confessions which were heard before common error was established will be treated more in detail in the following article. As for the necessity and extreme utility of having the concept of common error clarified, even the proponents of the traditional doctrine agree that such a thing is highly to be desired. For, while it is true that the old canonists most clearly show that they demanded the presence of real, common error, it is equally a fact that they did little to delineate and clarify the term *common error*.[82] And the difficulty persists to this very day, so that often there are found cases in which it is difficult to make a certain judgment concerning the *commonness* of the error. However, the mere citing of such a difficulty brings forth no serious or overwhelming argument against the maintenance of the traditional theory.[83]

But, while there is some difficulty in this regard in the traditional doctrine, it is highly questionable whether it is as grave as

[82] Jombart, "L'erreur commune,"—*NRT,* XLII (1920), 547.

[83] Cf. Cavigioli, "Teologia morale,"—*La Scuola Cattolica,* Series VI, XVI (1930), 218.

the interpretative school of canonists would seem to insinuate.[84] True, the error must be common. But this concept is not garbled or stretched beyond its ordinary meaning when the error of *many* is intepreted as being *common*. This term *many*, in its turn, may be taken either absolutely or in relation to a certain parish or community. Further, supporters of the traditional theory are not in favor of mathematical, physical computation and precision.[85] They view the case not mathematically but *morally*.

Indeed, in many cases, as Vermeersch noted,[86] the error may be already common before the jurisdictional acts are begun to be posited; for example, when the pastor publicly announces the advent of Father George to hear confessions in the parish. The judgment about Father George's competency to hear confessions in the parish on the day stipulated is common among the parishioners from the very moment of the announcement. If upon his arrival, Father George finds out that the necessary faculties had not been procured for him, but, despite this, proceeds to hear confessions, there is no question but that every confession that he hears in that parish at that time is heard validly in view of the common error which really, though perhaps only virtually, persists among the parishioners and which renders any and all of them liable to approach Father George to have him hear their confessions.

In other cases, as Claeys-Bouuaert contends,[87] a certain computation may be arrived at by a prudent priest without any laborious calculating. For, usually the answer will become apparent either from a morally sufficient number of people or from a morally deficient number of them. If a case should arise in which it is diffi-

[84] Cf. A. Salvador, "Error communis et iurisdictionis suppletio ab ecclesia,"—*BE*, XVII (1939), 246.

[85] Cf., e. g., Claeys-Bouuaert, "De conceptu erroris communis in canone 209,"—*Jus Pont.*, XVI (1936), 162; Oesterle, *Praelectiones*, pp. 112-113; Dalpiaz, "Vicariis cooperatoribus ipso iure potestas non competit assistendi matrimoniis,"—*Apoll.*, VII (1934), 80-81.

[86] *Theologia moralis*, II, n. 459.

[87] "De conceptu erroris communis in canone 209,"—*Jus Pont.*, XVI (1936), 162.

cult to eradicate all doubt on the matter, then certainly the second phase of canon 209 will come into play. Claeys-Bouuaert further suggests that those cases will be very rare in which, given the facts, a true probability of doubt will not be present. But, he continues, in the event that such should be the case, what juridical argument can be proffered as an inducement to veer away from the clear, decisive words of this canon and their genuine meaning? Obviously, personal predilections cannot supplant the enacted dictates of the law in this matter. A false sympathy would but merit recrimination if, in trying to insure the welfare of an individual in a specific case, one were ready to tolerate the upheaval of the entire jurisdictional system, and thus deprive the legislator of a strong sanction against interlopers and intruders.

In the same manner that the authors of the interpretative theory challenge the value of the traditional theory because of its practical difficulties, the proponents of the latter school can hurl back similar charges, and indeed of a graver nature, against their opponents. It is patent that most of the supporters of the interpretative school do nothing more than state their predilection for this theory. They offer no legal reasons to justify their regarding of common error as a pure fiction of law. And of those who do make such attempts there is not one whose reasoning is not strained to the breaking point.[88]

Cappello, for example,[89] asserts that "by the very fact that the *cause* of the error is *public*, the error can likewise, and with reason, be called *public* or *common*." First of all, this statement confuses the terms *common* and *public*. Consideration shall be given to this point presently. The second point to be noted is that Cappello

[88] Cappello has undeniably attempted to marshal up the arguments for the interpretative theory to the best advantage. It is interesting to note, therefore, A. Salvador's words in: "Error communis et iurisdictionis suppletio ab ecclesia,"—*BE*, XVII (1939), 247: "Sic igitur ex huc usque allatis argumentis in favorem sententiae P. Cappello relinquitur non agi in casu de doctrina certa et undequaque probata, sed *doctrina cui nullam probabilitatem tribuimus,* ipsam existimando ut *omnino falsam,* etsi de cetero sit proposita ab hocce clarissimo Auctore."

[89] *De sacramentis,* II, Pars I, n. 490, 3, 1.

offers no reason or justification for his obviously arbitrary conclusion.[90] In a similar way Vermeersch-Creusen[91] consider that, once a fact is *publicly* posited, which may lead others into error, the error is not to be considered merely private but public. Wernz-Vidal[92] share this opinon. They observe, first, that it is not required for common error that many actually go to confession. Granted! *Servatis servandis,* this does not conflict with any concept that supporters of the stricter interpretation might have in this regard. But, for Wernz-Vidal to leap from this statement to the conclusion that therefore, once there is posited a *public* fact which may lead others into error, common error is *already* present reflects an attempt on their part to close a gap in logic without the aid of a logical connecting link.

The crux of their difficulty lies in the meaning of the term *public,* Surely, if the fact is posited in the presence of many, the error is already common *de facto.* Such is the understanding of the term among all people, in all tongues, that the fact be perceived or known by many.[93] But as Cappello,[94] Vermeersch-Creusen,[95] and Wernz-Vidal[96] emphatically assert, they do not demand that the error be actually had on the part of many. They are content with the presence of a *fundamentum* which must be *public,* but public in a sense foreign to the genuine concept of this word. When do they consider a fact to be public? Is it public because it is posited in a public place, as in a church? Does it matter whether the church

[90] Concerning this argument, cf. A. Salvador, "Error communis et iurisdictionis suppletio ab ecclesia,"—*BE,* XVII (1939), 245: "Hinc circumstantia quae potest a multis cognosci, si de facto non cognoscitur, nullo modo dici potest publica, nam haec duo implicant: *'posse aliquid cognosci'* et *aliquid esse cognitum'.* Ergo hocce primum argumentum nullum habet sensum."

[91] *Epitome,* I, n. 322, 4.

[92] *Ius canonicum,* II, n. 381.

[93] Claeys-Bouuaert, "De conceptu erroris communis in canone 209,"—*Jus Pont.,* XVI (1936), 159-160; A. Salvador, "Error communis et iurisdictionis suppletio ab ecclesia,"—*BE,* XVII (1939), 245.

[94] *De sacramentis,* II, Pars I, n. 490.

[95] *Epitome,* I, n. 332, 4.

[96] *Ius canonicum,* II, n. 381.

be in the heart of a city, or will a deserted country mission suffice? Is it public simply because it can be proved by two witnesses? Cappello[97] indicates that the very fact that a priest sits in a confessional, in a public church, constitutes an antecedent common error *even before any of the faithful approach him.* The authors of the interpretative theory have as yet failed to agree among themselves in determining when the notion of *publicity* is really verified.[98]

One thing is certain. If a mistaken judgment is made by a few, there is particular error. The mere fact that a set of circumstances *might* cause others to fall into the same false judgment can not be used as a valid argument to consider the mere possibility of common error already actualized, i.e., even before many have fallen into the error. The potentiality of error simply cannot be identified with the actuality of error. True, common error would be present . . . *if* . . . the error were actually committed by many.[99] But that is as far as that statement can go. *A posse ad esse non valet illatio.* Interpretative error is unreal, non-existent, therefore utterly incapable of effecting the supplying by the Church of whatever jurisdiction might be necessary to insure the validity of a jurisdictional act.[100] The conclusion of the interpretative theory, therefore, is not factual but a mere deduction of the mind. There are innumerable elements which can avert the community from making any judgment whatsoever and thus from committing actual error, or even cause the community to learn the truth about a certain priest's incompetency. Thus, the interpretative error proves nothing, lends nothing of itself towards the formation of truly common error. Something else must be present before actual error becomes realized. Therefore, as Toso well put it, it will be appropriate to descend from the clouds and to investigate whether or not a community has

[97] *De sacramentis,* II, Pars I, n. 491.

[98] Kearney, *The principles of delegation,* pp. 129-130.

[99] Vermeersch, *Theologia moralis,* III, n. 459.

[100] *L'Ami du Clergé,* XLVII (1930), 648, footnote 2.

erred; otherwise a positive judgment in this regard can not be had.[101]

Amidst all this objecting to the conclusions of the authors of the interpretative schools as regards the efficacy of the *fundamentum* in establishing the existence of common error as demanded by canon 209, it must always be clearly understood that the traditional doctrine, and all of its supporters, grant readily that a public foundation *can* provoke and facilitate the error of many. But, *per se* this foundation can not produce this effect where, as a matter of objective fact, only a few know of this fact. According to the genuine meaning of the words *common error,* a real, not a merely possible or interpretative error is supposed and demanded.

A further discrepancy protrudes itself in the teaching of the supporters of the interpretative theory. Cappello,[102] Vermeersch-Creusen [103] and Wernz-Vidal [104] all substantially agree that private error will have no effect towards inducing the Church to supply. And yet, as has been seen, they all reduce the concept of common error to an error which *factually* is only private. Thus by mere cavilling they come to a point where they hold what they profess to deny, i.e., that the error of one or a few is sufficient, or that even no error is required provided that some evidence exist to indicate the possibility of common error.

A similar inconsistency on the part of the supporters of the interpretative theory is found concerning the usage of the term *virtual* error. As has been seen, *virtual* error is understood to be error which, once actual, continues to exist at least subconsciously, just as a virtual intention is an intention which was once actual and continues to exert its influence. Now, as has been just shown, in general the proponents of the interpretative theory require a mere public foundation for error. Hence, according to their concept, common error is entirely a fiction of

101 "De errore communi ad normam can. 209,"—*Jus Pont.,* XVIII (1938), 167.

102 *De sacramentis,* II, Pars I, n. 487, 5.

103 *Epitome,* I, n. 322, 4.

104 *Ius canonicum,* II, n. 381.

law; for, it is neither *error* nor *common.* Yet they maintain that this is what the law means by the term *common error.* Such error was never *actual;* therefore, it can not be conceived as *virtual,* since *virtual* is that which, once actual, still perseveres even though only subconsciously. And yet, authors like Adloff [105] profess that virtual error suffices. And Adloff accepts as an example the case in which the name of a priest is attached to a confessional, although none of the faithful advert to the fact. He holds that the Church will supply from the moment that this sign is put up. Strangely enough this author indicates very clearly the great difference existing between this case and the case where a public announcement is made to a congregation; yet, he calls both *virtual* error. If words are to retain their proper meaning, then the first example cited by Adloff cannot be said to have caused *virtual* common error; for, no error has been committed actually and, hence, no error exists virtually. Similarly, Couly [106] speaks of virtual error as affecting a community the while he points to the case of a priest entering a confessional for the sake of waiting upon any approaching penitents. But here again, it must be admitted, *actual* error need not have occurred. Now, if it did not occur, then also it never became existent, and if it never became existent, then likewise it could never eventuate in *virtual* error.[107]

In brief resumé, if it can be said—and it is a fact that can not be denied—that there is some difficulty entailed in the ascertainment of common error according to the traditional mode of interpretation, in all fairness it must also be admitted that the difficulty is a natural one, a difficulty one must expect to find in any norm that is intended for so many and such variable kinds of cases. It must be admitted that the difficulty is inherent in the problem itself. On the other hand, difficulties of the interpretative theory are difficulties resulting from an attempt to

[105] "L'erreur commune et la juridiction suppléée,"—*Bulletin Ecclésiastique du Diocèse de Strasbourg,"* XLVI (1927), 254 ss.

[106] "La juridiction suppléée du canon 209,"—*Le canoniste,* XLVII (1925), 456.

[107] Cf. Kearney, *The principles of delegation,* pp. 127-128.

break away from a traditionally accepted doctrine. They are difficulties which border closer and closer upon pure absurdity according as the individual authors venture to reduce *common error* to greater and greater insignificance. And it must be said that for such veering away from the traditional concept no limit can properly be set, precisely because it seems that the interpretative school has substituted its personal feeling of *how they would want the law* to be interpreted for the ordinary legal and objective norms which the law maintains must be followed.

b. Context of the Code

Another very familiar argument on the part of the interpretative school is that their apparently liberal view is in utter accord with the sympathy of the legislator as exhibited in the entire Code of Canon Law. But upon closer study of the various indications of the mind of the legislator in regard to the entire jurisdictional system, a strong suspicion, if not a full conviction, enters one's mind to the effect that there is little objective basis for such claims on the part of the authors who propose their interpretative doctrine.

Though the Church has received the plenitude of jurisdictional power from her Divine Founder, her present day system of granting a share in that power to different members of her clergy and of requiring the possession of such power for the valid performance of certain acts was developed and adopted only gradually as a means adequate enough to meet the different emergencies and needs in the Church. The system was adopted primarily as a means of helping the Church fulfill her mission and thus to realize her purpose on earth; the spiritual good of *all* the faithful.

Now, when the Church demands the presence of an authority, or jurisdiction, in any minister as a condition requisite for the valid performance of certain jurisdictional acts, such a jurisdictional regulation of the Church may well be regarded as an equivalently invalidating or inhabilitating law.[108] And one may

108 Cf. canon 11.

note by way of a comparison, which suggests itself, that such jurisdictional laws are, to all intents and purposes, as strict and as strongly to be enforced, as the laws which proclaim diriment matrimonial impediments of ecclesiastical origin.[109] No amount of good faith, no matter how inculpable, be it on the part of the contractants or on the part of the priest assisting at the marriage ceremony, would or could be considered as a barrier sufficiently strong to prevent a declaration of nullity in the case. The law is rigidly upheld simply because it was enacted in the first place for the *common* good. For that reason the law is rigorously enforced, even though in a given case it might very easily happen that much sorrow or grief may come upon an individual on that account. In the same way it can be said that, just as good faith or error is no substitute for a dispensation from a matrimonial impediment, so also good faith or error of themselves without the legislator's direct intervention, are not valid substitutes for the possession of jurisdiction. As without the proper dispensation a marriage would be declared invalid, so without jurisdiction a jurisdictional act could never be considered valid. Unless and until the Church furnishes that necessary jurisdiction, that act will always remain invalid.

However, it cannot be gainsaid that, as in the case of matrimonial impediments, so too in regard to her jurisdictional laws the legislator has given innumerable signs of benignity and of grave concern for the good of the faithful. Above all he has always been careful that his restrictions should never defeat, by their consistency and rigidity, their chief and ultimate purpose: the common good. Thus, as conclusive proof for this contention, one may point to such canons as 207, § 2; 882; 2247, § 3; and 209. In all of these instances an otherwise non-existent jurisdictional power is specifically provided, or supplied, to insure the validity of the jurisdictional acts performed. The legislator makes such provisions because it is entirely within the scope of his power to do so.

109 Cf. canon 1680.

Yet, as Cappello himself observes and admits,[110] it does not follow that the Church supplies in all those cases in which she can supply. The Church supplies exclusively in those cases in which she expressly, or at least tacitly, manifests her will to supply. And it is to be noted that in each and every case wherein the Church makes special provisions, as in the canons just mentioned above, she indicates that she wants it to be understood very clearly that she actually does not intend to supply in any and all cases. Thus, in virtue of canon 207, § 2, a priest absolves validly when he acts in inadvertence to the fact that the grant of his jurisdictional power has lapsed. But, this canon is careful to specify that the priest will act validly in only the two following cases: when he has inadvertently failed to notice: 1) that the period for which his jurisdiction was granted has expired; 2.) that the number of cases for which he was authorized has already been acquitted. Even a further restriction is placed by canon 207, § 2: its enabling concession applies exclusively to the *internal forum.*

In the same manner canon 882 grants most extraordinary powers to any priest. But, again, this grant applies only when he is to wait upon a penitent who is *in danger of death.* Likewise canon 2247, § 3, determines that, if a confessor in *ignorance of a reservation* should absolve a penitent from a censure and the sin, the absolution from the censure is to be regarded as valid *except in cases of censures reserved in the most special manner to the Holy See* as well as of *censures imposed and reserved "ab homine".* In other words, though undeniably the legislator is benign and extremely provident for the common good, the very care he exhibits in marking off the limits of these instances of his kindness is the very best indication that outside of those limits the ordinary rules must be applied.

The sum and substance of these observations is precisely this: any theory which regards *common error* as a pure fiction of law, in fact any attempt to minimize the quality or the quantity of the *common error* literally demanded by the text of canon 209

[110] *De sacramentis,* II, Pars I, n. 487.

cannot securely be followed unless it can be shown conclusively, *beyond all prudent doubt,* that the legislator countenances such a veering away from the pre-Code understanding of this phrase. The evidence of the legislator's intent—and this must be stressed time and again—must be *conclusive, beyond a prudent doubt;* for in doubt the clear prescript of canon 6, n. 4, must be followed.

As a result, an extension of the favor granted by the former law may not be arbitrarily assumed; it must be juridically proved. This the interpretative theory thus far has failed to do. The traditional theory of common error has proved its contention, and the Church has recognized that the true concept of any ecclesiastical law should never allow the faithful in general to suffer grave harm because of the jurisdictional incompetency of a minister of the Church, even though that incompetency was initially brought about by the Church herself for the selfsame common good of the faithful. These deductions were in full accord with the true concept of natural equity. And it is true that the Code does not, and can not, if it is to fulfill properly its legislative rôle, ignore the fact that natural equity is a factor always to be considered. But that is just the *crux* of the entire controversy. Can it be shown that the contention of the interpretative school is a postulate of natural equity, which the legislator must recognize? The main argument of the interpretative school is that the Church would and could not be assumed to allow a series of confessions to be invalid just because they were heard before the error became actually common. Why not? It is not a question of the Church's being able to supply in such a case just as soon as the *public fact* of the interpretative school is posited; for she could supply if only she wanted to do so. Nor is it true that the Church does not want to help an individual in his need. No! when the danger of death approaches, the Church willingly helps and supplies jurisdiction to any and every priest for any of the faithful.

But in cases other than those covered by canon 882 the Church rightly notes that there is not the same degree of emergency.

As Grosam explains,[111] the Church does not wish to endanger any soul by *limiting* jurisdiction. In fact she does not limit the priest's jurisdiction. He simply has none. And there are no grounds why the Church should feel obliged to supply him with jurisdiction that is lacking. First of all, it can be argued that in those cases outside the danger of death, which are often adduced in discussion as so critically important for the penitent etc., and which are argued to be important enough for the Church to relax her rules, those who urge that the Church make such extraordinary provisions could much more easily procure the necessary jurisdiction or prevail upon individuals to approach some other priest already empowered and capable of attending to their difficulty. For, if a case is important enough to warrant definite action by the Church, certainly *a fortiori* no attention that a mere individual can give should be considered by him as burdensome. There should not be any difficulty in the ordinary case for the priest to explain his incompetence. For people are used to hearing of incompetence and lack of necessary jurisdiction among civil officials. They should not find it strange that the Church has similar laws. Thus, in short summary, the Church will not in individual cases involving merely individual benefits supply an unauthorized confessor with the necessary jurisdiction to ensure the validity of his absolutions granted in confessions which he heard before the error concerning his unauthorized status was both actual and common, simply because it is not the mind of the legislator to relax jurisdictional discipline when the evil consequences for the general public would ultimately far outweigh the individual hardships of a few.[112] Any plea to the contrary on the part of the interpretative school is merely an arbitrary asser-

[111] "Der Beichtvater ohne Jurisdiktion,"—*LQS*, LXXXI (1929), 120-124.

[112] Dalpiaz, "De conceptu erroris communis iuxta canonem 209,"—*Apoll.*, VII (1934), 490-491; cf. also Suarez, *De poenitentia*, Disp. XXVI, sec. 6, n. 7; O'Neil, "The meaning of *common error*,"—*IER*, XXI (1923), 300; O'Donnell, "When does the Church supply jurisdiction?"—*IER*, XVI (1920), 499-502; Kearney, *The principles of delegation*, p. 132; Ferreres, *Compendium*, II, n. 651.

tion which has not been, and appears incapable of being substantiated by any truly sound and juridically valid argument.

c. Sequels of the Interpretative Theory

Added to the arguments already adduced against the juridical value of the interpretative theory is the contention of its ultimate inexpediency in view of the dangerous sequels that would follow in its train. The basic reason is precisely the fact that the authors championing the interpretative school differ so radically, if not in the statement, at least in their application and exemplification of their principle that the term *common error* is to be regarded in a technical sense, treated as a legal fiction rather than as a realized fact. The natural result of such disagreement is the eventual creation of the barest minimum required for the application of the first part of canon 209.

Guns,[113] for example, while he was personally opposed to this opinion, attests that a certain learned contemporary of his considered a sufficient basis for common error present once a priest accedes to a penitent's request to go to confession to him, even if the church or the chapel should otherwise be deserted. Such extreme views on the matter are not exceptional. For *L'Ami du Clergé*[114] also made the unqualified claim that every penitent who enters a confessional and confesses to the priest stationed therein and that every penitent whose confession is heard by a priest whom he has asked to hear him is validly absolved regardless of whether a factual error is or is not entertained on the part of many people. And in its article it goes on to say that this opinion alone exactly portrays the true meaning of common error. Cappello[115] himself, while he modifies his claims when he states that common error can scarcely be had in the case of a priest delegated for *one* marriage, maintained that common error would be verified if and when a priest, with consent of the pastor of the church, were in a confessional of a public church,

113 "L'erreur commune,"—*NRT,* L (1923), 540.
114 XLII (1925), 101-106.
115 *De sacramentis,* III, n. 671.

even if he should hear only a few penitents or even none. In Cappello's opinion the circumstances created an *antecedent* common error in virtue of which all the confessions would be valid.[116] As Toso observes, a theory that goes to such extremes obviously lends itself to arbitrary usage and is a wide-open door to most absurd conclusions.[117] "For, according to such a vague standard as a *quoddam fundamentum,* there is no reason why the mere wearing of the ecclesiastical garb, or the fact that a *cleric* performs some jurisdictional act, or that the act is performed in a parish church, or in a confessional, or in any public place no matter how deserted, or the fact that the proper form and ritual are observed, or that the cleric makes a peremptory declaration that he acts legitimately, should not be considered as sufficient basis to create the sufficient common error." In the light of such reasoning hardly any jurisdictional act could be posited invalidly. Dalpiaz [118] points out that only acts which are secretly posited—and these under the conditions mentioned would be rare indeed—would be invalid. Thus all those carefully phrased jurisdictional regulations and sanctions would wield their effect in only such exceptional instances. Kearney [119] observes that in virtue of the interpretative theory any priest could absolve anywhere. It would be sufficient for him to declare himself prepared to hear confessions.[120] But such a theory, as Kearney objects, would be a peril to the rigid laws, promulgated for the common good, on the need of jurisdiction, be it ordinary in virtue of its inherence in some ecclesiastical office or be it delegated by the proper authority after a proper examination and due approval. Similarly the force of invalidating laws would be weakened. The whole system of those clear, strict and grave regulations, with which the Church wishes the structure of ecclesiastical jur-

[116] *De sacramentis,* II, Pars I, n. 491, 4.

[117] "De errore communi ad normam can. 209,"—*Jus Pont.,* XVIII (1938), 166-167.

[118] "Vicariis cooperatoribus ipso iure potestas non competit assistendi matrimoniis,"—*Apoll.,* VII (1934), 81.

[119] *The principles of delegation,* p. 131.

[120] Vermeersch, *Theologia moralis,* III, n. 459.

isdiction to be protected and preserved, would be laid open to most arbitrary violation. The strict norms for jurisdictional acts in general [121] and for jurisdictional acts of the internal [122] and of the external [123] forum would thus be rendered meaningless,[124] nugatory and practically useless. For, if it be a public fact merely to enter a confessional, then it is likewise a public fact to stand at the altar to assist at a marriage or to sit in the usual tribunal prepared to pass sentence. Thus validity would be extended to invalid nuptials and void judicial sentences, since the suppletory principle is not restricted to the internal forum of the confessional, but extends to all other jurisdictional acts, and also to acts like assistance at marriage, which are considered by a goodly number of authors to be covered by canon 209 in virtue of canon 20.[125]

But surely canon 209 cannot be regarded as an ubiquitous law, scurrying through the Code to nullify the provisions of invalidating laws.[126] Canon 209 must rather be interpreted in the light of the whole Code and of the comprehensive outlook of the legislator, in favor of the common good, for the safeguarding and preservation of which the laws concerning jurisdictional competence and incompetence alike were enacted. Conversely the laws of jurisdiction are not to be interpreted in the light of ordinary needs on the part of a particular person; for, as has been seen above, if these needs are accompanied by the danger of death, then canon 882 makes liberal provisions. In any other case which is not such an acute emergency, there is always some other means to take care of the person's spiritual problems.

In summary, then, it may be stated that the general upheaval of the entire jurisdictional system which would undeniably follow

[121] Canons 196-210.

[122] Canons 872-890.

[123] Canons 1043-1045; 1049; 1052; 1094-1096; 2236 ss.

[124] Dalpiaz, "De conceptu erroris communis iuxta canonem 209,"—*Jus Pont.*, XVIII (1938), 491.

[125] Cf., e. g., Claeys-Bouuaert, "De conceptu erroris communis in canone 209,"—*Jus Pont.*, XVI (1936), 160.

[126] Kearney, *The principles of delegation*, p. 131.

upon the adoption of the interpretative theory, should serve not only as a sufficient deterrent, but also as a most effective sanction, against embracing and then reducing to practice any such perilous theory. The summary reason militating against the well-meaning but misappropriated solicitude of the interpretative theory is that no conclusive evidence has been adduced to show that the legislator wishes to extend the notion of common error to the extreme limits set for it by that theory. On the contrary, it seems clear that the legislator has set his own limits in accordance with the demand which natural equity makes in relation to the preservation not of the individual but of the public and common good of the faithful. In view of this consideration the legislator feels that the exceptional and possible harm of the few must give place to the ordinary and certified benefit of the many. Any other ruling must correspondingly appear to him as unwarranted. The evil consequences of a relaxation of the general ecclesiastical discipline in the realm of jurisdictional law far outweigh the personal hardships of a few individuals.[127]

V. THEORY IDENTIFYING ERROR AND IGNORANCE

The practical difficulty of determining the extent of the prevailing error for the functioning of the suppletory principle according to the traditional concept of *common error* has led many canonists to espouse the interpretative theory.[128] This trend of thought which caused so many to interpret common error as a mere fiction of law led a newer school of canonists to maintain further that the suppletory principle functions not only in common error but even *in common ignorance.*

1. *Gist of the Ignorance Theory*

The theory is composed of three elements which are contained in the following propositions:

I. That in common ignorance as well as in common error the Church will supply jurisdiction;

[127] Kearney, *The principles of delegation,* p. 132.

[128] Cf. Wernz-Vidal, *Ius canonicum,* II, n. 359, note 9.

II. That the presence of a public foundation for this ignorance is not necessary in order that the Church supply jurisdiction;

III. That not only when this common ignorance is *de facto* objectively present will the Church supply jurisdiction, but also when it is merely prudently and honestly thought to exist regardless of the objective truth of this judgment.[129]

2. *Evaluation and Criticism of the Ignorance Theory*

As one studies the three elements of this theory, one sees almost immediately that it rests or falls according as it succeeds or fails to establish that the Church does supply jurisdiction in common ignorance as well as in common error. Despite the probable character which this theory has in the eyes of certain canonists, it must be confessed that the theory labors under difficulties which make it untenable.[130]

First of all, the fact that *error* and *ignorance* differ philosopically is readily admitted by champions of the ignorance theory.[131] Error signifies a false judgment whereas ignorance expresses merely an absence of knowledge. The two, admittedly, are so closely correlated that error never exists without ignorance, for ignorance is the cause of error, the *matrix erroris,* or that from which error takes rise. It is because a man lacks a true knowledge of an object that he makes a false judgment concerning it. Therefore error properly so called is *ignorance in action.*[132] In a word, error is a *positive* act of the mind, by which something is misapprehended. Ignorance implies no act of cognition; it is an *absence* of knowledge. While error presupposes ignorance, ig-

[129] Kelly, *The jurisdiction of the confessor,* p. 128; Cf. also references to canonists of this school in: Oesterle, *Praelectiones iuris canonici* (Romae: In collegio S. Anselmi, 1931), pp. 112-113; Dalpiaz, "Vicariis cooperatoribus ipso iure potestas non competit assistendi matrimoniis,"—*Apoll.,* VII (1934), 82.

[130] Salvador, "Error communis et iurisdictionis suppletio ab Ecclesia,"—*BE,* XVII (1939), 180; Toso, "De errore communi,"—*Jus Pont.,* III (1923), 150.

[131] Cf., e. g., Kelly, *The jurisdiction of the confessor,"* pp. 128-129.

[132] Toso, "De errore communi."—*Jus Pont.*, III (1923), 150.

norance may well be conceived without error. In a word, ignorance is nothing; error is something.[133] The process of reasoning whereby one accepts ignorance in its philosophical, strictly negative sense and thereupon makes it convertible with error (i.e., having the same juridical effects) is as fallacious as it is unique.

It can scarcely be maintained that a glance at the history of the suppletory law will reveal that, while the Church used the time-honored phrase *in errore communi,* she meant *in ignorantia communi.*[134] First of all, as Kearney indicates,[135] and as has already been seen in the historical section of this thesis, it seems more tenable to hold that the Roman people were not only ignorant of the servile condition of Barbarius, but at the same time practically believed him to be their praetor. That note of ignorance carried into action is more evident in the *dictum* of Gratian.[136] Yet, even though it were granted for the sake of argument that the Romans were purely ignorant of the status of Barbarius and that the same idea could be deduced from the *dictum* of Gratian, it must be remembered that these two instances of the application of the suppletory principle can never be regarded as the full pre-Code law. In fact, they just happened to be seeds, as it were, which ripened into fruit after a slow but steady growth. The canonical teaching, as contained in the Code today, represents their latest, and perhaps even their final, development into legal maturity. And as has been seen in the section which proves in detail that among pre-Code canonists it was readily and universally admitted that *real error* of the faithful had to be present,—and this understanding received the official confirmation of the Sacred Congregation of the Council—[137] the traditional concept of common error has been tenaciously maintained since the promulgation of the Code by the present day champions of the

[133] Kearney, *The principles of delegation,* p. 133.

[134] Kelly, *The jurisdiction of the confessor,* p. 130.

[135] *The principles of delegation,* p. 134.

[136] C. I, C. III, q. 7: "Servus, dum *putaretur* liber . . . "

[137] "Caesaraugustana matrimonii," 10 Mar., 1770—*Thesaurus,* XXXIX, 52-53.

traditional idea, and its continued currency is at least frankly admitted by thoroughgoing opponents of this stricter view. The Code is not to be regarded so much as confirming the *Lex Barbarius* or the *dictum* of Gratian, but rather as confirming the principle underlying these two juridical facts in the measure and to the extent to which recognized authors and teachers had developed its understanding before accepting and approving it as a juridical norm. And thus, if the Code is at all considered to affirm pre-Code doctrine—and such is the case—then it must necessarily be concluded that something more than mere negative ignorance is required by the law for the functioning and application of the suppletory principle.

It is true that many authors after the Code have uttered statements to the effect that in law error and ignorance may be likened one to the other, that in law both have the same juridical effects.[138] But, as a matter of fact, a contextual study of these authors shows that when they make such a statement they are not speaking of negative ignorance, but of ignorance *as affecting human acts.*[139] Clearly, ignorance in its purely philosopical, negative conception cannot influence or cause an act. A negative cause is an absurdity. When, however, an agent posits an act which he would not posit were he cognizant of certain facts he *acts* in ignorance. He errs. Only such ignorance, i.e., ignorance to which a judgment can be added, can be understood to be convertible with error. The authors cited by Kelly can be understood in precisely this one sense, namely, as speaking of *ignorance that has occasioned a false judgment,* and not of inert, negative ignorance.[140] Certainly, then, it cannot be said that authors like Badii, Vermeersch-Creusen, Maroto or Wernz-Vidal

138 Cf. Kelly, *The jurisdiction of the confessor,* p. 129, footnote 29.

139 Kearney, *The principles of delegation,* p. 133.

140 Cf. canon 104. Note context especially in Cappello, *De sacramentis,* II, n. 529: " . . . Ignorantia . . . hic sumitur . . . prout nempe in actiones humanas *actualiter influit.*" Cf. also: Badii, *Institutiones,* I, n. 87; Vermeersch-Creusen. *Epitome,* I, n. 197; Maroto, *Institutiones,* I, 402; Wernz-Vidal, *Ius canonicum,* II, n. 39.

militate in the ranks of those who uphold the identity of error and of ignorance as regards their juridical effects.

In a similar way Kearney [141] disposes of the argument drawn from the fact that canon 2202, § 3, states that "What is said of ignorance holds also in reference to inadvertence and error." For, here there is also question of *ignorance in action,* since a violation of a law must be an act. If, however, the material violation is the result of an inadvertent omission, it cannot properly connote error but merely ignorance. Moreover, if any argument is to be deduced from the wording of canon 2202, § 3, Kelly, and all who follow him, must admit that inadvertence is likewise to be considered as convertible with error. If this be so, in the same sense that Kelly would identify error and ignorance, why does canon 207, § 2, provide for the supplying of jurisdiction in cases of inadvertence to the lapse of a formerly possessed jurisdiction? Why this explicit provision if it is already included in canon 209? And why such careful, accurate delimiting of canon 207 by the legislator, since canon 209, according to Kelly's understanding, would in its breadth and scope go far beyond the provisions of canon 207, § 2? Thus, it is at least difficult to see how this principle which identifies error and ignorance can be regarded as "officially recognized in the fifth book of the Code."

Again, it must be remembered that this canon is to apply to activities of both *fora.* If the ignorance of the people can be supposed to exist in regard to the competence of a priest to hear confessions, how much more so can a general ignorance be presumed as existent in regard to other, less known details of Church Law. If any and all jurisdictional activity is to be considered as valid because of the verification of *common ignorance,* what jurisdictional act could ever be called invalid? Even if the parties involved in a certain transaction knew that they were acting against the law, the general ignorance of the people would render their acts valid, according to the ignorance theory. In fact, a jurisdictional act would be invalid only when the group, in general, would know a certain priest was unlawfully arrogating

[141] *The principles of delegation,* p. 134.

to himself a jurisdictional power which was not his. And it must be admitted, the knowledge of the common people in regard to jurisdictional laws is not too broad. It does seem like stretching the rules of interpretation unduly when one goes so far as to assume that the legislator made laws for the rare case. It must be remembered that the purpose of law is to enact rules and regulations for the normal run of events.

Finally, even if one were to admit the presence of a certain degree of probability in the ignorance theory, one would still not have sufficient reason to espouse it. For the task which remains to be discharged, because it is so imposed by the direct precept of canon 6, nn. 2 and 4, is to prove *beyond all prudent doubt* that it is not only common error, but common ignorance as well, that suffices to bring the suppletory principle of canon 209 into effective operation. As long as this cannot be incontestably established and demonstrated, it simply must be assumed that the legislator wishes the traditional concept of common error to be retained.

VI. CONCLUSION

From the foregoing evaluations and criticisms of the interpretative and of the ignorance theory, it is quite apparent that the traditional concept of common error must be retained. Indeed, even though one were to grant that the innovators' theories enjoy some degree of probability and of consequent feasibility, canon 6, n. 4, must be remembered. Thus in reality there is no *dubium iuris* which could be solved in favor of the other theories by the use of the second phase of canon 209.

The attempt to analyze closely and to evaluate fairly the worth of the various contentions naturally invites the reader to expect that a synopsis, as it were, of the main features of common error will subsequently be offered here. That is indeed forthcoming. But, before launching upon that task, one should bear in mind several very important points, which will prove invaluable aids in the undertaking.

1. *General Notions*

a. The Common Good

The Church's ecclesiastical laws, with their invalidating sanctions, have been constituted for the common good of the faithful. Such is the necessary qualification of any law.[142]

Some identify the *common good* as something proper, not to the members of a society collectively taken, but to the society itself, inasmuch as it is a being subsistent in itself, a substance, a *suppositum* of an intellectual person or a real person having a proper *bonum.*[143] This *bonum* is not the sum of all the *bona* which pertain to the individual members of a society, but a certain ordering towards the attainment of the purpose of the society, i.e., not only of the members but also of their external *bona,* some of which are due to the society, others of which are distributed by the society among the members. In fact, it is an ordering of the *bona* which pertain to the members insofar as the *bona* are of benefit to all. And this ordering is ruled by the higher rule of morality by which man is directed towards his final destiny.[144]

Others understand the *common good* as the good of all the members not singly but collectively taken, inasmuch as society is something accidental inhering in a multitude of people, which, although it does not exist without the individuals, still adds something to them, namely, an order among them, a subordination of the individual good to the common good. This school views common good as the complexus of the *bona et iura* so ordered that the individuals might *universally* reach their proper destiny. And this ordering concerns those items which fall within the scope of the society's power.[145]

Irrespective of the comparative merits of these two views, one point evidently they have in common: both recognize the private

[142] Cf. Celsus in D. (1.3) 4.5.

[143] R. Kaibach, *Das Gemeinwohl und seine ethische Bedeutung* (Düsseldorf, 1929), pp. 44-56.

[144] Kaibach, *op. cit.,* pp. 99-115.

[145] Van Hove, *De legibus,* n. 82.

good as something subordinate and subservient to the common good.

Now, the Church as a perfect *necessary* society, has rights, i.e., the *iura socialia* which prevail over the sum of the rights of her members. Thus, the Church can put its membership under obligation even though the members be unwilling to yield thereto, and the Church can ordain the execution of disciplinary matters which of themselves are not necessitated by any individual's claims for his own full human happiness and welfare. True, the individual members of the Church have as their goal the gaining of a happy eternity. Simultaneously, however, it is not only the purpose but also the duty of the Church as a society to lead all these individuals to that destiny of salvation. So at all times it must be remembered that the means of sanctification were not entrusted by God to the individual but to the Church. The Church, then, has a right which extends farther than the rights properly belonging to the individual faithful.[146] Therefore, although it is readily admitted that, if she so willed, the Church could have carried on her mission without her system of invalidating jurisdictional laws and could even now abrogate their force, still it cannot be denied that the existence of such jurisdictional sanctions in the Code is open evidence of her will that such laws continue. No one can seriously and sanely challenge the wisdom of the Church in retaining these laws, for she has a venerable experience and the unceasing guidance of the Holy Ghost with her. It is precisely in the milieu of these factors—her experience, her prudence, and her sagacious solicitude as sublimated from on high by a divine guidance—that the Church has decided upon her present jurisdictional system as the best human manner of insuring an adequate order for her social discipline, especially in the matter of providing for the faithful a clergy duly equipped to minister to their spiritual needs in a fully accredited fashion.

If her legislation shoud at times cause some inconvenience or even spiritual loss to a private person, this must be regarded as a

[146] Ottaviani, *Ius publicum internum,* I, 76-77 and footnote 14 on p. 77.

simple, inevitable concomitant of human legislation. It must be noted withal, that in her kindness the Church has remembered to make many special provisions against such inconveniences.[147] But she can not be expected to make such provisions for every case. Even though she admittedly has the power to do so, she could not do so and still maintain the vigor and strength of the system which, after all, she has invoked to safeguard a common good. In making her choice between mutually exclusive benefits the Church can do naught else but tolerate the occurrence of individual inconveniences if she has set her hand to the definite task of maintaining and promoting the common welfare. And. to be promoted effectively, the common welfare must be allowed to exercise its rightful claims even at the expense of personal loss and individual detriment. Otherwise the jurisdictional laws of the Church and their attached sanctions would in reality become meaningless, since any disregard of them could be connived at whenever there was at stake in any way at all a person's spiritual welfare in as far as it called for the utmost and fullest assurance of effective help. Therefore it is a mistake for authors to stretch the applicability of canon 209 so far as to frustrate almost every jurisdictional law in the Code.

It might be profitably repeated that the Church provides generously for the spiritual good even of individuals when they are in danger of death.[148] As for the rest, she makes other specific provisions for definite instances, which she is careful to define with utmost accuracy. In most of the other cases, for which the Church makes no such special provision, examination often reveals that the difficulties can be handled in the normal manner, i.e., by seeking and obtaining the necessary authorization from the competent superiors.

But over and above this, where the rare cases exist which are not provided for by law, the loss of souls does not necessarily follow. The following reflections will bear this out:

[147] E. g., canons 882, 209, etc.

[148] Cf., e. g., canons 882, 1043-1045; 2252, etc.

1. The sacraments are the usual, not the exclusive channels of grace. God, Who knows the hearts of man, can provide in the unusual way for the unusual case.[149]

2. Penitents frequently make acts of perfect contrition, or are already in the state of grace.

3. The Sacrament of Extreme Unction remits sin.[150]

4. The sacraments of the living confer *gratiam primam* to those who approach them in good faith with attrition; penitents, moreover usually approach the Eucharistic Table at the first opportunity.

These facts, not forgotten by the legislator, go to show that although the Church does not supply jurisdiction so lavishly as some authors would desire, she is ever the *pia Mater Ecclesia.*[151]

b. Canon 209, a Repetition of the Old Law.

As has often been repeated, canon 209 is admittedly a new law only insofar as it represents the first statutory formulation of the suppletory principle. The doctrine, the jurisprudence of this principle, however, antedates canon 209. Since the Code *verbatim* received the *in errore communi . . . supplet ecclesia,* the presumption is that the legislator intended no substantial changes in the interpretation of the *error communis.*[152] And to all who would attempt to justify any deviation from the traditional concept it may be remarked that the burden of proof lies upon them. They will have to establish *beyond a prudent doubt* that the legislator wished to treat *error communis* in a new sense.

149 Reiffenstuel, *Ius canonicum universum,* lib. III, tit. XLIII, n. 3.

150 James, V, 15.

151 Kearney, *The principles of delegation,* pp. 136-137.

152 Salvador, "Error communis et iurisdictionis suppletio ab ecclesia,"—*BE,* XVII (1939), 85: "Revera huius canonis 6 dispositiones optime applicari possunt et debent ad nostrum institutum iuridicum, quia etiamsi non ageretur de iure scripto, canon ille non loquitur exclusive de tali iure, praesertim in nn. 2, 3 et 4, ubi ius debet sumi maiori extensione, videlicet non solum pro iure scripto, sed etiam non scripto. Hoc ipsum quoque apparet eo quod in supradictis numeris legislator non adhibet verbum 'lex', sed verbum 'ius', quod pro utroque iure merito intelligi atque interpretari potest." Cf. also Kearney, *The principles of delegation,* p. 136; Wilches, *De errore communi,* p. 203; Blat, *Commentarium,* I, n. 55, 2°.

Until they furnish such proof, their claim must be rejected in view of the explicit demand of canon 6, nn. 2 and 4.

c. Canon 209 and *Epikeia*

One may well agree with Toso[153] that the lax interpretation of canon 209 is traceable to the misconception concerning jurisdictional laws on the part of certain moralists.[154] However, though it is really superfluous to say so after having noted many ranking moralists among the post-Code supporters of the traditional concept of common error, it may be good policy to repeat that this liberal and extensive interpretation is not common to all moralists, nor is it restricted to moralists alone.

The important point to bear in mind is that jurisdiction, in the sense that was carefully designated in the preliminary notions, is a juridical factor and that jurisdictional laws are at least equivalently invalidating or incapacitating laws.[155] Thus, in the same manner that a dispensation is necessary for a person to marry validly in the presence of a diriment ecclesiastical impediment, so too the requisite faculty, the required power, or jurisdiction, is necessary to posit validly a jurisdictional act. Those, who have not that power, even should they possess all other qualifications, simply cannot validly act.

This jurisdiction the Church alone can grant. As has been seen, the Church normally is very careful in allowing persons to share in its use. Nevertheless, over and above her normal manner of distributing such power, there are instances in the Code, of which canon 209 is only one, where the Church grants the necessary jurisdiction in an extraordinary way by supplying it in order that thus certain jurisdictional acts may be valid. But in such cases the Church carefully delineates the limits of the grant and the conditions under which the grant is effective. Outside these limits there is simply no title of jurisdiction. And to argue in a given case that the legislator does not intend the

[153] "De errore communi ad normam can. 209,"—*Jus Pont.*, XVIII (1938), 166.

[154] Cf., e. g., Bucceroni, *Casus conscientiae*, p. 568.

[155] Canon 11.

jurisdictional law to bind because of the trying and difficult circumstances that the case might involve, even if the law clearly indicates otherwise, is pointless. For it must be remembered, as Suarez pointed out,[156] that there is no identity between laws that are merely prohibitive and laws that are invalidating. The prohibition by its very nature admits an excuse of ignorance or of moral inability, and thus frequently ceases in a moral case; for, if one correctly views it, in almost every interpretation of a law by *epikeia,* some moral inability intervenes. The invalidating law, on the contrary, is not based upon obligation, does not require the will or the power of the subject, but rather induces in a person a certain inability or even incapacity—even though he be unwilling to acknowledge it—which can not be taken away by mere excuse. Then, again, in laws that are merely preceptive or prohibitive, there is not necessary for the common good that same uniformity in the observance of the law. But in jurisdictional laws *it favors the common good more to preserve the law absolutely inviolable than to avoid some personal inconvenience in any one case.*

This of course is understood as not applying if an invalidating law is enacted in favor of a private person, or if, out of the observance of an invalidating law, a common harm should follow in a certain place, or if laws when violated entail a consequence of invalid action only upon subsequent authoritative declaration. Neither the first nor the third of these cases is contemplated by the norm of canon 209. This canon has an operative effect only amid the conditions verified in the second case. That is precisely the reason that the norm of canon 209, which envisages the existence of a *common* error out of which a *common* harm would result,[157] cannot be interpreted as becoming diminished in its motive force and application just as soon as it comes face to face with inconveniences of a merely private nature.

[156] *De legibus,* 1, V, c. XXIII, n. 4.

[157] Cf. Maroto, *Institutiones,* I, 242; Noldin-Schmitt, *Theologia moralis,* I, n. 160, 3; Sosio d'Angelo, "De aequitate in codice iuris canonici,"—*Periodica,* XVI (1927), 210*-224*, and especially p. 223*.

2. *Qualifications of Common Error*

a. Extent of Common Error

There can be no doubt whatsoever concerning the importance of solving properly the question whether this canon is applicable to *common error of law* or whether it is to be restricted in its application to *common error of fact.* As the historical analysis has indicated, canonists always agreed that this suppletory principle functions in circumstances of common error of fact. Likewise the historical study has shown that with the growth of the system of probabilism canonists developed more and more the doctrine that the Church supplies under certain conditions even in common error of law. The conditions upon which the great majority insisted were that the error be truly probable, and that the error be concerned with a law that was not certain and clear.

To comprehend adequately the question under discussion it is necessary to furnish at least a general description of *error of law* and of *error of fact.* If and when the faithful of a certain parish *know with certitude* that a certain title is present and that this title is productive of specific jurisdictional powers,—e.g., if they know with certainty that X is their proper pastor and that in virtue of his position he has ordinary power to hear the confessions of his parishioners—in such a case the faithful are said to have knowledge *of the fact and of the law* concerning the title of their pastor's jurisdiction. But, if these people should consider with equal certainty that their proper pastor has, in virtue of his parochial office, the power to excommunicate members of his parish, then they are in *error of law* concerning the nature of their pastor's jurisdictional title. Again, if these same faithful know the law and the nature of the pastor's jurisdictional title, but believe that X is their proper pastor while in reality he is not such, then they are *in error of fact* concerning the existence of the pastoral title. Finally, if the faithful believe both that he is their proper pastor, when in reality he is not such, and that as pastor he can excommunicate members of his parish, then the people *in error of fact and in error of law.*[158]

Obviously one could adduce examples of such errors almost interminably. One must therefore be satisfied to give a general rule concerning such errors, which rule, it is hoped, will cover every case in which they occur. If there be question about the existence or the valid possession of a certain office or jurisdiction, then there is *error of fact.* If there be error about the nature of a certain title or the competency of which it is productive, then there is *error of law.* In instances where both these errors are verified, one has *error of law and error of fact.*

As Salvador observes,[159] this question is not brought up by all canonists who treat of the topic of the supplying of jurisdiction in cases of common error.[160] While a few canonists, like Chelodi,[161] are content, after the fashion of Bouix,[162] to state simply and without adducing any reasons that the Church supplies in common error of fact and in common error of law, by far the greater number of post-Code authors insists that the error of law must be truly probable. Indeed, it is interesting to note how closely authors like Wernz-Vidal,[163] Coronata,[164] Blat,[165] Vermeersch[166] and Vermeersch-Creusen[167] follow D'Annibale,[168] not only in his teaching on this point, but even in the very wording of his opinion. All of them insist with the regularity of a trip-hammer that the error of law must be *probable.* Perhaps the clear-

[158] A. Salvador, "Error communis et iurisdictionis suppletio ab ecclesia,"—*BE*, XVII (1939), 179. Cf. also, Toso, "De errore communi,"—*Jus Pont.*, III (1923), 150.

[159] "Error communis et iurisdictionis suppletio ab ecclesia,"—*BE*, XVII (1939), 175.

[160] Cf., e. g., Wilches, *De errore communi*, pp. 192-198; Badii, *Institutiones*, n. 149.

[161] *Jus de personis*, n. 130.

[162] *De iudiciis*, pp. 132-133.

[163] *Ius canonicum*, II, n. 381.

[164] *Institutiones*, I, n. 292.

[165] *Commentarium*, II, n. 158.

[166] *Theologia moralis*, III, n. 459.

[167] *Epitome*, I, n. 284.

[168] *Summula*, I, n. 79, note 73.

est summary of the problem is the one offered by Vermeersch-Creusen.[169]

To begin with, Vermeersch-Creusen observe that an *error of law* can be of benefit to no one unless and until that error be *probable,* i. e., of such a character as to be capable of gaining the assent of a prudent man. It is of paramount importance carefully to note that, while Vermeersch-Creusen readily concede that a probability of law would be interpreted with much greater latitude in the case of a child, or of a woman or of a soldier, they are not so willing to admit the existence of a probability about a law which is not difficult *and* which is known *per se* to all the inhabitants of a certain place.

It is by no means a far-fetched conclusion to state that by their insistence upon true probability all of these authors rule out from the benefits of the suppletory principle that kind of common error which is not truly probable, a common error which is not based upon reasons strong enough to gain the assent of a prudent man. In a word, crass or supine ignorance of a law would never suffice to occasion an error which is truly probable.

In the light of such a teaching, in the event that a large group of parishioners disregarded all truths of religion, never troubled themselves about going to church and avoided any and all contacts with messengers of things spiritual, would the Church rally to their aid in the event that they should fall into error of law about someone's jurisdictional competence? In reference to this question Jombart,[170] closely following Schmalzgrueber,[171] De Angelis [172] and Bargilliat,[173] does not consider such culpable error as truly probable and, therefore, contends that the suppletory principle would not apply to such error so culpably occasioned by the negligence of these persons. Toso,[174] Guns [175] and Ojetti [176] give

[169] *Epitome,* I, n. 322, 3.
[170] "L'erreur commune,"—*NRT,* L (1923), 176.
[171] *Ius ecclesiasticum universum,* lib. II, tit. I, n. 20.
[172] *Praelectiones,* II, tit. I, n. 24.
[173] *Praelectiones,* I, n. 204, d.
[174] "De errore communi,"—*Jus Pont.,* III (1923), 150.
[175] "L'erreur commune,"—*NRT,* L (1923), 537.
[176] *Commentarium,* ad c. 209, n. 2.

clear evidence that theirs is substantially the same view. In the same manner does Santamaria view this case.[177]

In a comparatively recent and thought-provoking article,[178] wherein he considers the question of the applicability of the suppletory principle to common error of law and of fact, Salvador admits fully that the Church supplies in cases of *probable* error of law. However, he insists that the Church supplies not in virtue of common error of law, but in virtue of the doubt of law which exists in such a case. Thus according to him the Church does not supply in cases of common error of a clear and certain law. He substantiates his claims with the following arguments:

1.) The more ancient pre-Code canonists, even in their understanding of a colored title, demanded some sort of an intervention of an ecclesiastical superior. The conferring of an office or the commission of jurisdictional power on the part of such a legitimate superior was, in their understandng, a factor necessary to constitute a title, regardless of whether it proved to be true (*verum*) or apparent (*apparens*). It is manifest that these canonists wrote of error of fact, and not of error of law, when they considered the question of the extent of the applicability of the suppletory principle.

2.) The examples cited by the older authors to explain the functioning of the suppletory principle were concerned with instances of error of fact.

3.) Error of law, particularly common error of law, can in no way be justified, whereas error of fact commonly has full justification since it is almost impossible to detect.

4.) Those who hold that the Church does supply in common error of law provoke a confusion of the two parts of the supple-

177 "Titulum habere factum est particulare quod nemo tenetur cognoscere. Ius vero est aliquid quod omnes tenentur cognoscere; si vero non cognoscitur (quod evenit propter culpam propriam), nec debemus exigere ab ecclesia ut iurisdictionem suppleat: dantur enim alia media ad errorem depellendum."—*Commentarium ad codicem iuris canonici* (Typis non editum, Manilae, 1932), ad can. 209, 706—as cited in *BE,* XVII (1939), 181, footnote 17.

178 "Error communis et iurisdictionis suppletio ab ecclesia,"—*BE,* XVII (1939), 175-183.

tory principle of canon 209. They qualify common error of law with expressions; such as these: *error probabilis; error iustus et probabilis; error circa ius obscurum et dubium; error communis iuris ex probabilitate ortus; error iuris, dummodo non crassus et supinus.* If error of law arises from such causes, whence can doubt of law arise?

On the strength of these arguments Salvador insists that, when there is common error concerning a certain and clear law—and he admits that this can happen, though it will occur only very rarely—the Church will not supply for any deficiency in the jurisdiction required for the validity of an act. For, according to him, the legislator is concerned with the ordinary, and not with the extraordinary contingencies aising from events of a most rare occurrence.

On the strength of these considerations it seems highly reasonable to conclude that the Church does not supply in common error about a clear and certain law. By way of illustration one may note the fact that the law clearly demands that a priest be duly authorized to hear confessions. Since this law is so clear, one could not term any common error concerning its existence as probable. Therefore the Church in all probability does not supply in cases of such common error. The Church supplies only in common error of fact, that is, in common error about the existence or the valid possession of a certain office or jurisdiction. Thus the common error must, first of all, be particularized, i.e., about a priest or bishop who is considered to possess some definite title of jurisdiction or to be legitimately exercising whatever jurisdictional title he might possess.[179]

[179] Vermeersch, *Theologia moralis,* III, n. 459: " . . . Nuntio dato de proximo adventu missionarii ad praedicandam missionem, tam verus missionarius qui sine iurisdictione missionem incipiat, quam sacerdos qui, adveniens, falso putetur esse nuntiatus missionarius, propter errorem communem confessiones valide excipere possunt. Sed quod ignotus et non communiter exspectatus sacerdos a fideli rogetur audire confessionem et eam revera, etiam in ecclesiae confessionali audiat, non ideo iurisdictio ab Ecclesia supplebitur, cum nullus error formaliter vel fundamentaliter sit communis." Cf. also Noldin-Schmitt, *Theologia moralis,* III, n. 347; Claeys-Bouuaert, "De conceptu erroris communis in canone 209,"—*Jus Pont.,* XVI (1936), 160.

b. Quality of Common Error

(a.) Real

The common error about the existence or about the valid possession of ecclesiastical jurisdiction by any cleric, priest or bishop etc., must be *real* or factual, and not merely interpretative. There must be a false judgment on the part of the people of the community. And on this score great pains must be taken to distinguish carefully between the *existence* of a common error and the *proof* of its existence as a common error. The existence of the error may be proved juridically even by the testimony, of two capable and reliable witnesses.[180] The commonness of the error is proved by the absence of any cause of doubt and by the presence of circumstances which rendered the error inevitable.

For the existence of real common error two elements are required. First of all, there must be some *fundamentum,* some cause which is capable *per se* to lead the community into error. Then, in addition, the community must *de facto* err. To bring about this common error it is quite evident that the cause or the *fundamentum* of the error must be *public*. However, publicity *de iure*—as is the case with all ecclesiastical offices—does not suffice. The cause must be public *de facto.* It must be seen or perceived directly or learned about indirectly from others. Secondly, the error must be of such a character as to be a possible source of harm to any or to all of those who participate in it.[181] Wherefore, unless perhaps by way of exception there be question of an action which directly involves a community,[182] as, for example, in case of a general dispensation *per modum actus* from abstinence, or of a general granting of an important indulgence, the error must be concerning the *habitual* power of jurisdiction of some one. For, were a person limited to one act and in reference to one person, e.g., an individual dispensation, then *per se* the interest of many would not be involved.

[180] Cf., e. g., S. R. R., *Nullitas matrimonii,* 22 Nov. 1927, *coram R. P. D. Andrea Jullien,* dec. LI—*Decisiones,* XIX (1927), 453-465.

[181] Toso, "De errore communi ad normam can. 209,"—*Jus Pont.,* XVIII (1938), 167.

[182] Cf. Vermeersch, *Theologia moralis,* III, n. 459. Cf. likewise p. of this work.

But more concerning this point will be seen in the article dealing with the application of the principle of canon 209.

(b.) Probable

The common error must be *probable.* In other words, it must arise not because of crass and supine ignorance on the part of the people but because the reason, of the *fundamentum,* which occasions the error, is of such a character as to be capable of gaining the assent of prudent men.

(c.) Explicit or Implicit

For common error to be real it is not at all necessary that many of the faithful form an *explicit* judgment to the following effect: I believe that that priest, whom I now see, has the powers necessary to hear my confession, etc. On the contrary, it is enough if many, morally taken, fall into error at least in an *implicit* or confused fashion (*modo saltem confuso et implicito*).[183] Thus the author in *L'Ami du Clergé,*[184] while he is uncompromisingly opposed to the supporters of the interpretative school, considers that *common error* truly exists once the *cause* of the error is *publicly* posited. From the context of the article and from a footnote it is clear that *L'Ami du Clergé* understands this *public* positing in the genuine concept of the word i. e., in the sense of something posited in such a manner as to be actually seen by many. In the same way Jombart notes how many errors of the mind exist in a latent, confused state. Yet, when the occasion arises, a person invariably acts on the basis of the error no matter how implicit it might be.[185]

(d.) Actual or Virtual

Error postulates a false judgment. At the moment when the mind forms such a judgment and as long as it adverts to the judgment's presence the mind is said to be in *actual error.* Thus, if a body of people, assembled in a church, considers that a certain

[183] Claeys-Bouuaert, "De conceptu erroris communis in canone 209,"—*Jus Pont.*, XVI (1936), 160.

[184] XLVII (1930), 648.

[185] "L'erreur commune,"—*NRT,* L (1923), 173-174.

missionary, who has in reality for some reason or another failed to secure the necessary faculties, is at a certain moment legitimately exercising his power to grant them a special indulgence, this group is in actual error. And, clearly, in such a case, *positis ponendis,* there is no difficulty about the applicability of the suppletory principle.

But, while it is perfectly true that the Church demands real or *factual* common error and not merely interpretative error, lest others, after the fashion of *L'Ami du Clergé,*[186] fail to present this demand in its proper context, it must be emphasized that this error need not be *actual.* For, as Kearney observed,[187] the condition of common error *de facto,* and not simply *de iure,* can exist even though here and now many of the faithful do not elicit a false judgement or consciously advert to the presence of a judgment previously made. For the Code does not require actual error. All that it requires is that they be in error in such a way that their error might cause them to seek the ministrations of an incompetent minister. It is therefore enough for the faithful to have formed an erroneous judgment and to labor under this false impression or persuasion; they must be so mentally disposed that when asked, they would actually advert to the previously made judgment and respond that this particular agent is a confessor, a pastor, a judge, or the like. This suffices because the error, *which was once actual,* has not been corrected nor entirely dissipated by the lapse of time, but perseveres *virtually* and continues subconsciously to wield its influence.

As Jombart would put it,[188] the elements of an actual false judgment are present in the minds of the faithful, ready to leap out of the subconscious and to become clearly and formally expressed. As an example one might consider the case of a pastor who secured his parochial office invalidly and never had the defect remedied. The entire parish considers him the true pastor. But, in routine of their daily existence these parishioners do not constantly advert

186 XLII (1925), 102.
187 *The principles of delegation,* p. 125.
188 "L'erreur commune,"—*NRT,* L (1923), 174.

to their conviction that he is their pastor. But, should any one ever ask them who their pastor is, they would unhesitatingly inform the questioner. Thus the false judgment, once elicited, continues to wield its influence even in the subsconscious. And on that account every one readily agrees that every parochial function performed by such an intruder would be valid, provided that all of the other stipulations of the law were fulfilled. Even the quietest marriage ceremonies would be considered valid. Even those few confessions he heard on Saturday afternoons when no one else came to the Church would be valid. The reason is that factual, though not actual, error was present. This example should suffice to illustrate virtual common error. It may, however, profitably be added that such a virtual common error may exist in the minds of the faithful of a certain place after the announcement by the proper superior or a trusted individual concerning the advent of a confessor to some definite place at a definite time. The important point to bear in mind is that, when such announcements are publicly made to large groups, the generality of the people are inevitably led into error; for, the human mind is so constituted that it does not rest in a simple apprehension of truth, but necessarily assents, dissents or doubts.[189] And under normal circumstances, due to the mentality and disposition of the faithful and the trusted position of the person making the announcement, there is no doubt that the generality of those present make a judgment, however confused or implicit, about the competency of the newcomer to hear confessions or the like.

(e.) Practical or Speculative

The commonness of the error is not to be judged by the number of those who actually approach a certain agent for jurisdictional ministration. For, though it is true that the Church does not supply until the act is being posited and only for the duration of the act, it is likewise true that the Church does not supply in individual instances unless and until a certain condition is present: namely, a real danger to the common good of the faithful. But

[189] Kearney, *The principles of delegation*, p. 126.

this danger can, and does, exist from the very moment that a sufficiently large number of the faithful mistakenly believe that an incompetent agent has the powers necessary for the performance of certain jurisdictional acts. For, at the very moment these persons might go to this agent and correspondingly would receive an invalid ministration because of his lack of the necessary faculties.[190] Thus, even before a single individual approaches this agent, the state of common error, as required by canon 209, can exist. Thus, it is clear that common error need not be practical. Speculative error suffices, i. e., the error of those faithful who, because of their mistaken belief, *might* go to this putatively competent agent.

c. Measure of Common Error

The error must be *common*. As has been seen in the historical analysis, a very great discrepancy is to be found among the pre-Code authors with regard to the number or the proportion required to establish the commonness of error. Some identified common error with moral *unanimity*. Supporters of this train of thought may be found even among modern canonists and moralists.[191] Others demanded that the *majority* be in error. This school of canonists also has its upholders today.[192] Other authors, still stressing the fact that the purpose of this suppletory principle is to provide for the general and common good, have interpreted error in the light of the common good. And the common good is certainly involved in the good of *many*, insofar as it is opposed to the good of one private person or of a few such individuals.

This idea, as has also been shown in the historical analysis, was already entertained in the minds of some of the pre-Code authors. Since a number of good, reputable authors before the Code taught that common error was verified when *many* erred, one may con-

[190] Toso, "Jurisdictio quando ab ecclesia suppleatur,"—*Jus Pont.*, XVII (1937), 101.

[191] Cf., e. g., Chelodi, *Ius de personis*, n. 130; Marc-Gestermann-Raus, *Institutiones*, n. 1761; Pighi, *Cursus theologiae moralis*, lib. IV, n. 289; Woywod, *A practical commentary on the code of canon law*, I, 80.

[192] Cf., e. g., Knecht, *Handbuch des katholischen Eherechts*, p. 625.

clude to the existence of a *dubium* on this point. The Code, by simply demanding *error communis,* clearly did not solve the doubt. Therefore it is licit to follow this kindlier interpretation, not solely because the whole suppletory principle is a favor and therefore to be interpreted generously, but also in virtue of the second part of canon 209, which states that the Church will supply jurisdiction in positive and probable doubt of fact or of law.[193] Salvador feels that this opinion is grounded in strong probability and may consequently be followed as entirely safe in practice.[194]

But, granted that the error of *many* suffices for the application of canon 209 in view of the common good, the question immediately arises: How large a number of persons, or what proportionate section of a parish or community is required to constitute the *many* concerning whom some juridical determination remains to be made? A very precise or even mathematical answer to this question, it must be admitted, is not only difficult, but in fact impossible.

However, it must be granted that such a difficulty is naturally to be expected to persist despite any honest, serious effort that may be made to define the term as accurately as possible. For, groups differ in size and in character. The notion of common error is, therefore, necessarily elastic, and naturally connotes a proper proportion, a relative value, in respect not only of the numerical size, but also of the varied and characteristic milieu of the community in question. The numerical element sufficient to constitute a common error in a comparatively small community of religious, could certainly not be invoked for the detection and certification of common error in a comparatively large parish.

Several authors have done their utmost to set up some sort of a definite figure as a more or less absolute guide for various situations. For example, Vermeersch-Creusen in the first edition of

193 Merkelbach, *Summa,* III, n. 586; Génicot-Salsmann, *Theologia moralis,* II, n. 331; Schrattenholzer, "Beichtjurisdiktionszweifel,"—*LQS,* LXXX (1927), 331-333; Kearney, *The principles of delegation,* p. 124; Jombart, "L'erreur commune,"—*NRT,* L (1923), 172.

194 "Error communis et iurisdictionis suppletio ab ecclesia,"—*BE,* XVII (1939), 247.

their work, before their defection from the traditional teaching, stated that the error of one hundred persons living in a college would suffice.[195] In a similar way Vermeersch[196] suggested that the error of two hundred persons might be considered common anywhere. But, in reality, these attempts only show how impossible it is for any individual to set up a definite number, an exact mathematical formula for every possible case. Though such a formula might be useful, is it necessary?[197] In the majority of cases it will be possible for a priest to make a certain judgment without being forced to any laborious computation.

In the first place, it is generally admitted that the faithful in considerable numbers are unaware of the necessity of special faculties on the part of the priest for the valid performance of different jurisdictional acts.[198] Under such circumstances the priest can in most cases prudently judge that common error is present if apart from the lack of any cause to engender doubt in the minds of the faithful *there are present and known to the people* such conditions which, in consideration of their credulous mentality and limited powers of analytical reasoning, render the erroneous judgment *about his competence to act in a certain jurisdictional capacity* a practically assured reality.[199] Secondly, as has been explained

[195] *Epitome*, II, n. 154.

[196] *Theologia moralis*, III, n. 459.

[197] A. Salvador, "Error communis et iurisdictionis suppletio ab Ecclesia,"—*BE*, XVII (1939), 246: "Quod statuendum foret praevio *quot* numero errantes sufficiant singulis in casibus, nulla est ratio, nam etiam si melius esset, necessario tamen non requiritur. Revera Ecclesia iam ante Codicem iurisdictionem supplebat in errore communi et tamen numquam existimavit hoc ipsum esse necessarium."

[198] Kelly, *The jurisdiction of the confessor*, p. 135; Toso, "De errore communi,"—*Jus Pont.*, III (1923), n. 151; *IER*, XXI (1923), 299.

[199] Wilches, *De errore communi*, pp. 227-228: "Iamvero tamquam signum insufficiens erroris communis ad eius existentiam praesumendam vel probandam arbitramur simplex factum ex quo error multorum sequi potest; econtra si ex aliis adiunctis, v. c. ex diuturnitate temporis qua factum exsistit, vel ex aliis signis apparet factum iam in multorum vel maioris communitatis partis notitiam devenisse, non dubitamus adserere in talibus adiunctis errorem communem legitime praesumi vel probari posse. Remanet ergo, nostra sententia, definitio erroris communis traditionalis, idest iudicium falsum multorum vel maioris partis communitatis."

above, the mistaken judgment need not be explicit on the part of the faithful. A factual though only confusedly entertained error will suffice. Therefore, with all these things in mind a prudent man will be able in most cases to ascertain whether or not common error is present according as there were morally many or only a few people present for whom the occasion of an erroneous judgment obtruded itself. Furthermore, if in a certain case there be room for a prudent doubt about this matter, the second part of canon 209 will indirectly offer the requisite legal certitude.[200]

Such are the possibilities of cases where a priest, hitherto unknown to a certain group, arrives for the first time to minister to them and, for some reason or other, has failed to get the necessary faculties. It is readily seen that there can be numerous other kinds of cases where the error will truly be common even before the priest actually begins to exercise his jurisdictional power. Thus, for example, a priest whose arrival has sometime previously been announced by the pastor can validly perform jurisdictional acts on the strength of the error which virtually persists in the minds of the faithful of the locality.[201]

In conclusion, it may be stated that there is no need for anxiety or scrupulosity, since the Church supplies in cases of prudent doubt. The older canonists left such judgments to the prudence of the minister.[202] And quite rightly the upholders of the traditional concept of common error do the same in this day.[203]

d. Place of Error

In agreement with the teaching from almost the very beginning

[200] Cf. Claeys-Bouuaert, "De conceptu erroris communis in canone 209," —*Jus Pont.,* XVI (1936), 162.

[201] Vermeersch, *Theologia moralis,* III, n. 459, 1; Jombart, "L'erreur commune,"—*NRT,* L (1923), 172.

[202] D'Annibale, *Summula,* I, n. 242, note 49.

[203] Cf. Kearney, *The principles of delegation,* pp. 130-131; Jombart, "L'erreur commune,"—*NRT,* L (1923), 172-173; Vermeersch, *Theologia moralis,* III, n. 459, 1; Oesterle, *Praelectiones,* p. 112; Dalpiaz, "Vicariis cooperatoribus ipso iure potestas non competit assistendi matrimoniis,"—*Apoll.,* VIII (1934), 80-81; Claeys-Bouuaert, "De conceptu erroris communis in canone 209," *Jus Pont.,* XVI (1935), 160.

of the development of this suppletory principle *common error* may be verified in any locality, community or establishment when the people thereof can be classified as a distinct unit.[204] Thus common error can be verified in the whole world, in a diocese, quasi-diocese, parish, quasi-parish, town, church, order, province, college, convent, student-body, confraternity or among any similar unit of persons.[205] Vermeersch,[206] following Reiffenstuel[207] and Ballerni-Palmieri,[208] indicates that as long as a group is a distinct unit it does not matter if it is not very large; for, he notes that a community of *ten* persons constitute a *populus* sufficiently large and numerous to merit the benefit of the suppletory principle of canon 209.

e. Subjects of Error

Concerning this question much more will be specifically noted in the article treating of the licit use of supplied jurisdictional power. For the present, it may be sufficient to note that, just as the error of a few does not constitute common error, and, therefore, does not warrant the supplying of deficient jurisdiction by the Church, so too the consciousness of a few of the incompetency of a certain priest will not serve as any bar to their profiting by the presence of common error in their community. As shall be seen, the benefit of valid ministration because of the operation of the suppletory principle of canon 209 is forfeited only in cases, as in penance, wherein the approach to a confessor whom the penitent knows to be incompetent indicates the penitent's lack of the necessary dispositions for absolution.

B. Doubt

. . . aut in dubio positivo et probabili sive iuris sive facti, iurisdictionem supplet Ecclesia pro foro tum externo tum interno.

[204] Kelly, *The jurisdiction of the confessor*, p. 123.

[205] Kelly, *op. cit., p.* 122; Toso, "Jurisdictio quando ab ecclesia suppleatur,"—*Jus Pont.,* XVII (1937), 101.

[206] *Theologia moralis,* III, n. 459, 1.

[207] *Ius canonicum universum,* lib. V, tit. 1, n. 249.

[208] *Opus theologicum morale,* VII, n. 150.

This section of canon 209 explicitly declares that, in addition to common error, there is another condition under which the Church manifests her readiness to supply jurisdiction, namely, the condition of a positive and probable doubt of fact or of law.

In this manner the legislator sounded the death-knell to many pre-Code disputes. For as the reader readily recalls from the historical analysis before the Code all authors admitted that the Church supplied in cases of true probability. But many identified this *true probability* solely with doubt of law. In fact many of these authors demanded no less than the common authority of approved authors even for such probabilities of law.[209]

What is now termed doubt of fact was then, as Kearney observes, [210] generally regarded as properly doubtful jurisdiction. In such a case canonists and moralists quite generally denied that the Church would supply jurisdiction. Again, as the historical analysis has shown, and as Coronata observes,[211] before the Code only a few canonists, and these in the face of an overwhelming majority opposition, defended the autonomous character of probability as a condition for the application of the suppletory principle. Very many found it too difficult to divorce the efficacy of probability from that of common error and custom. In a few well chosen words canon 209 gives official and irrefutable approval to the contention of those who held that the Church supplies in positive and probable doubt of law and of fact. Thus, all controversies were banished in this regard. As in the case of common error, so here in the case of doubt, the Code raised the former doctrinal suppletory principle to the dignity of a codified law.

Comparing this latter phrase of canon 209 with the first, which treats of common error, one notes immediately a certain likeness and a certain difference. The disjunctive particle *aut* demonstrates beyond a prudent doubt that *common error* and *positive and probable doubt of fact and of law* are regarded on a par by

[209] Cf. St. Alphonsus, *Theologia moralis,* VI, 573; de Lugo, *Disputationes scholasticae et morales,* Disp. XIX, n. 29; D'Annibale, *Summula,* I, n. 80; Lehmkuhl, *Theologia moralis,* II, n. 388.

[210] *The principles of delegation,* p. 138.

[211] *Institutiones,* I, n. 292.

the legislator in reference to this supplying of jurisdiction.[212] But, while each of these factors is of itself sufficient to warrant this extraordinary bestowal of jurisdictional power, though of course a cumulative force can result from their junction in a given case, one notes that in the case of *common* error the Church supplies jurisdiction which is *certainly absent,* whereas in cases of doubt the supplying is *merely hypothetical.*[213] Moreover, it is universally admitted that the Church supplies in common error solely to protect the common good. From the very nature and circumstances of doubts, from the very fact that they can arise in the most private conditions, as, e.g., in the confessional, it becomes quite clear that, though this part of the canon is in no way intended to harm the common good, still it was formulated especially in favor of the priest, to make more remote the possibility of anxieties and scruples, and to afford him an authorized reflex principle by which practical certitude can be attained when he is confronted with doubts arising from the theoretical interpretation or the practical application of a law.[214] But while the Church manifests a willingness to aid the priest in such difficulties, there is no justification in canon 209 for condoning excessive latitude and for making too much allowance for the error of the priest, as shall be seen presently. With such an exposition in view, the present writer will offer several considerations about the following: *doubt; positive and probable doubt;* and, finally, *doubt of law* and *doubt of fact.*

I. DOUBT

Regarded subjectively, simply as a state of mind, the state of *ignorance*—implying, as it does, either the absence of all ideas (ignorance, simply), or the absence of assent to any judgment about a matter in question (doubt)—is intermediate between the

[212] Trombetta, *Ecclesia supplet,* p. 6.

[213] Noldin, *Theologia moralis,* III, n. 347, 2. a.

[214] Cf., e. g., Schrattenholzer, "Beichtjurisdiktionszweifel,"—*LQS,* LXXX (1927), 331; Couly, "La juridiction suppléée du canon 209,"—*Le canoniste,* XLVII (1925), 458; Vermeersch, *Theologia moralis,* III, n. 459, 2; Kearney, *The principles of delegation,* p. 143; Jone, "Suppletion der Beichtjurisdiktion bei einem dubium facti,"—*LQS,* LXXXI (1928), 576.

assent to a true judgment and the assent to an erroneous one about the same matter.[215] Doubt my be viewed in the strict sense of the philosopher or in its broader canonical acceptation.

Philosophically, doubt is a state of mind in which the mind hesitates between two contradictory propositions and feels incapable of giving forthright assent to either of them.[216] Any series of alternative propositions on the same subject may be enveloped in doubt at the same time; but, in strict parlance the doubt invests each proposition separately touching its affirmation and contradiction alike in non-committal fashion, that is to say, making allowance for each proposition to be or not to be true. It should be observed that doubt of itself signifies a purely internal psychological attitude, for to the mind alone does it belong to judge about facts. This action of the mind obviously has no influence on the facts themselves. Thus, a proposition or a theory, which is commonly regarded as doubtful, is simply one in regard to which sufficient evidence is as yet not available. In itself the proposition is true or false. However, if the doubt resides in a mind equipped with due knowledge, the doubt is called *objective;* if it resides in a mind lacking the knowledge which is its due, the doubt is termed *merely subjective,* i.e., in the sense that it has no foundation or basis whatever.[217]

Deliberate doubt always implies a judgment or judgments of the mind about the weight of the evidence for and against, together with the absence of any judgment about the main matter in question. Thus, the mind, when in a state of doubt in the strict philosophical sense, remains undecided. In this wise it is opposed: 1.) to *certitude,* or the adhesion of the mind to a truth without any prudent grounds for misgivings as to its truth; 2.) to *opinion,* which is a provisional assent of the mind to one of two contradictory judgments with more or less fear of error; and 3.) to mere *suspicion,* which signifies the assent of the mind to a judgment but with an exceedingly great fear of error.

[215] Coffey, *The science of logic,* p. 213.
[216] St. Thomas, *De veritate,* Q. XIV, art. 1.
[217] Blat, *Commentarium,* lib. I, n. 72.

These few considerations suggest mention of the more important divisions of doubt. Thus, doubt may be *positive* or *negative.* To be positive, a doubt must be occasioned by the presence of evidence that is so evenly balanced as to render any decision impossible. A positive doubt, as Michiels rightly observes,[218] by its very nature must be at least to some extent objective; for, if the reason for the doubt were purely subjective, there would be no question of the presence of anything but ignorance. Mere negative doubt exists when there are no grave reasons to claim the mind's assent for or against a certain proposition. It is possible, then, that a doubt may be positive on one side, and negative on the other (positivo-negative or negativo-positive), that is, in cases where the evidence on one side only is available and does not of itself amount to absolute demonstration.[219]

Doubt may likewise be either a *doubt of fact* or *a doubt of law.* A doubt of *law* exists when there is no certainty about the existence, permanence, force, or comprehension of the law.[220] A doubt of *fact* exists when, despite the full knowledge of the existence of the law and its theoretical comprehension and extension to a particular fact, one has not that same certainty as to the existence of that fact or of all the circumstances juridically required for the assumption of its existence.[221]

But while the abstract logician sees in doubt a perfect equilibrium effected by the equality of antagonistic forces, moralists and canonists, knowing that it is impossible to measure in concrete instances the exact strength and import of motives of different orders or of an extreme complexity, enlarged the notion of positive doubt a trifle and made it synonymous with a serious-minded probability.[222] Thus to St. Alphonsus,[223] and in fact to all moralists

[218] *Normae generales,* I, 332, note 3.

[219] St. Alphonsus, *Theologia moralis,* I, n. 67.

[220] Cf. Toso, *Ad codicem iuris canonici commentaria minora* (2. ed., Romae, 1921), I, p. 42. Hereafter this work shall be referred to simply as *Commentaria minora.*

[221] Michiels, *Normae generales,* I, 333.

[222] Jombart, "Le doute positif,"—*NRT,* XLVII (1921), 490.

[223] *Homo apostolicus* (Ed. nova, Mechliniae, 1858), Tractatus I, *De conscientia,* n. 12.

and canonists, *positive doubt* and *probable opinion* are identical terms.[224]

Since the expressions of the Code are to be interpreted more after the manner of canonists and moralists than according to the definitions of formal logic, it is to be concluded that *positive doubt* is verified when the mind rests in suspense under the reciprocal pressure of serious motives, *or* also when it chooses an opinion in virtue of serious motives without having to search out whether the contradictory opinion is more, or less, or equally, probable. *Negative* doubt is verified when there is an absence of motives capable of provoking prudent assent.[225] This state of mind, as Kelly well observes,[226] differs from the state of ignorance only in so far as doubt implies at least that the question has been entertained by the intellect, whereas ignorance implies no such implication. To illustrate such a negative doubt, one may take a confessor who knows only that he has temporary faculties. He asks himself whether these faculties have expired. No argument presents itself to his mind whereby he can gain any probability of opinion on this point. In a word he is simply in a state of ignorance. Canon 209 expressly, though implicitly, states that the Church does not supply in cases of purely negative doubt. In such a case the validity of any jurisdictional acts depends upon the objective truth.[227] But in regard to positive and probable doubt of law as well as of fact this canon can be used as a reflex principle to form a practically certain conscience. Thus the jurisdictional act is assuredly performed with the essentially necessary title. The validity is insured either in virtue of a title already possessed or because of the extra-

[224] Cf., e. g., Noldin-Schmitt, *Theologia moralis,* I, n. 197; Cappello, *De sacramentis,* II, Pars I, n. 497; Aertnys-Damen, *Theologia moralis,* I, 763; Wouters, *Manuale theologiae moralis,* I, n. 105, n. 3; Ferraris, *Prompta bibliotheca,* ad v. "*Conscientia,*" n. 22 ss.; Barbosa, *Tractatus varii,* ad v. "*Dubium,*" n. XIII, in *Tractatu de dictionibus frequentioribus;* Kelly, *The jurisdiction of the confessor,* p. 142; Kearney, *The principles of delegation,* p. 127; *NRT,* XLVII (1921), 491.

[225] Waffelaert, *De dubio solvendo in re morali* (Lovanii, 1880), n. 113.

[226] *The jurisdiction of the confessor,* p. 142.

[227] Wernz-Vidal, *Ius canonicum,* II, n. 382.

ordinary supplying of the needed jurisdiction by the Church.[228]

II. POSITIVE AND PROBABLE

Canon 209 is very specific in requiring that the doubt whether *of law* or *of fact,* in order to meet the stipulation required for the application of the suppletory principle, must be *positive* and *probable.* But, in precisely what sense is this requirement of positiveness and probability to be understood? It is clearly evident from the very nature of any opinion that it *might* be a false judgment, or the harboring of an erroneous view. It is also manifest that the lawmaker is entirely prepared for any such eventuality of error; otherwise it would seem quite pointless for him to express his readiness to supply whatever jurisdiction might be wanting in a given instance. Thus, then, undeniably, there is in canon 209 a definite indulgence shown by the lawmaker for the frailty of the human mind. Now, the question is: just how far is this spirit of indulgence intended to extend? When philosophers speak of a *positive* doubt, it is apparent that they speak of evidence, of ontological evidence which the mind grasps in its quest for a judgment about a certain question. When canonists speak of *true probability,* they are generally agreed that true probability requires *serious motives* plus a positive, conscientious judgment. The difficulty arises when certain canonists interject this possibility, namely, the the legislator would be content with the *subjective* conviction of a priest that his arguments are serious. In other words, these canonists would supplant the necessity of objectivity by upholding the sufficiency of subjective good faith.

Thus, for example, Girerd[229] is perfectly content with the subjective conviction on the part of a priest that his opinion in a given matter is probable. He willingly agrees, as has been noted above, that true probability must rest on serious motives and must entail a positive, conscientious judgment on the part of the priest. But Girerd is satisfied with the claim that it is juridically sufficient if a priest's reasons, though objectively weak and unconvincing, *seem* to him capable of being approved by

[228] Maroto, *Institutiones,* I, 731.

[229] "La juridiction probable,"—*NRT,* LVIII (1931), 916-920.

others. Girerd explicitly adds that it does not matter what the cause of the error might be. Even when the blunder in judgment is caused by gross negligence and ignorance, as long as the ignorance is not affected, Girerd contends that the Church will supply. He goes further. He claims that, if a priest should proceed to perform a jurisdictional act, because he feels certain that he has the proper power—in reality he does not possess it—even then the Church would supply on the ground that, if she supplies in mere subjective probability, there is more reason for her to supply in subjective, though false, certitude. In other words, the gist of Girerd's theory is that, as long as a priest acts in *good faith,* all his jurisdictional activity will be valid. Certainly, Girerd does not stand alone in this apotheosis of good faith as the ultimate condition necessary for the supplying of jurisdiction in cases of doubt.[230]

As Girerd himself admits, not many canonists have dared to venture very far in this field of probability. In fact, he regards his investigation and his conclusions as an important exploratory feat. Admitting that his is a comparatively new interpretation, Girerd insists that it is entirely in accord with the benignity of the Church, "which intended this singular enlargement of the domain of the priest's power so that he can now posit acts of jurisdiction without fearing that they might be invalid." [231]

When one reflects for a moment, and then remembers that Girerd extended the applicatory force of this suppletory principle to both *fora* and even to assistance at marriage, one cannot but be amazed at the juridical consequences that would follow from so liberal a view. Immediately doubt creeps into the mind regarding the feasibility and practicability of such a principle in jurisprudence. That phase will be treated subsequently when some attempt will be made to see what the practice of the Rota has been in similar cases.

[230] Cf., e. g., O'Donnell, "When does the Church supply jurisdiction?" See also *IER,* XVI (1920), 500-502, where the writer of the article testifies to the existence of similar views on the part of other canonists.

[231] "La juridiction probable,"—*NRT,* LVIII (1931), 917.

First of all, as as been seen, every doubt, in its philosophical sense, postulates a certain amount of *objective evidence* and presupposes a certain amount of *ignorance,* which together form the basis or reason for the mind's inability to form a *certain* judgment. According as the objective evidence is stronger in behalf of one or the other of the alternative propositions, the greater also becomes the degree of probability which attaches to that proposition. For, there is more objective reason to believe that in such a case a factually true judgment will be formed. On such a philosophical basis it is quite clear that any opinion based upon ignorance which is crass or supine can scarcely be termed truly probable. Hence, as Creusen indicates, it may be shown that there was always the general feeling among canonists that such ignorance would bar anyone from gaining the benefits of the suppletory principle.[232] The very formulation of the wording of the canon in the Code confirms the general teaching on this point by pre-Code authorities. No arguments are deducible from the context of the Code against such interpretation for the future. The common good is hardly jeopardized by following this view. Finally, the Rota would seem to indicate strongly that objective reasons are required if the validity of any jurisdictional act is to be upheld in the external forum.

1. *Pre-Code Interpretation*

As regards the pre-Code interpretation and understanding of true probability, there is little question that, whatever idea of probability the authors defended as the proper basis for the supplying of jurisdiction, the notion of probability had to rest upon serious and objective motives. Thus, as Castillon notes,[233] those who were loath to extend the suppletory principle to probability of fact, and found it hard to separate and distinguish probability and common error as independent conditions for the

[232] "Réponse du P. Creusen,"—*NRT,* LVIII (1931), 920.

[233] "La probabilité de fait en matière de juridiction pénitentielle,"—*NRT,* XLIV (1912), 534-555; 673-690; 718-727, and especially p. 552.

invocation of the suppletory principle,[234] demanded *public probability,* probability which had for its support the common teaching of approved authors. Likewise. in the minds of those canonists and moralists who extended the suppletory principle even to doubts *of fact,* true probability retained the motion of being supported by grave reasons of an objective character. Thus, for example, Mazzotta,[235] Elbel [236] and Reginald,[237] reflecting as they do the common teaching of their contemporaries, indicated most clearly the preservation of the concept of true probability in such a manner that it was never a probability divorced from objectivity. Certainly, in perusing the works of pre-Code authors one will never find such an apotheosis of subjectivism as advocated by Girerd. On the contrary, it was assumed by all that the basis of any probability had in some way to be identified with objectivity. That assumption was never questioned or argued. Argument arose only when authors differed as to *how many and how strong extrinsic reasons had to be adduced in defense and proof of an existent probability.*

2. *Text of the Code*

This traditionally accepted concept of true probability was significantly recognized and officially approved in the preparation of the text of the Code as it exists today. One has but to look into the history of the wording of canon 209 to find ample evidence for such a contention.

It is a matter of quite general knowledge that, before the Code made its official début before the world, first of all, schematic copies of what was hoped to become the future Code were sent out to all bishops for their perusal and approval or criticism.

[234] Cf., e. g., Suarez, *De poenitentia,* Disp. XXVI, sec. VI, n. 5; Cardenas, *Crisis theologica,* Pars IV, Diss. II, Cap. VI, art. II, nn. 137-146; Cap. VIII, art. II, n. 525.

[235] *Theologia moralis,* Tr. VI, D. II, q. I, c. II, par. III.

[236] *Theologia moralis sacramentalis tripartita,* Conferentia XII, nn. 310-311.

[237] *Praxis fori poenitentialis* (Coloniae, 1633), l. I, c. VIII, dub. X, nn. 102-103.

It is interesting to note the wording of this canon as it appeared in that schema:

> Canon 112: In errore communi **aut in dubio iuris iurisdictionem supplet Ecclesia in foro sive interno sive externo.**[238]

Even a most superficial glance at canon 209 reveals the striking change in the official Code:

> Canon 209: In errore communi **aut in dubio positivo et probabili sive iuris sive facti, iurisdictionem supplet Ecclesia pro foro tum interno tum externo.**

Whereas the schematic copy mentioned only *doubt of law,* the Code included also *doubt of fact.* But in so doing, the legislator very carefully inserted the two important qualifying adjectives: *positive* and *probable.* The least that can be said is that certainly no one may use the wording of this canon as a proof of a new, extreme liberalmindedness on the part of the legislator, and, therefore, as a reason for veering away from the traditional teaching concerning the character of positive and probable doubt. On the contrary, it is quite understandable how one could use the legislator's care in wording this canon as an argument that the law is intended to retain and to confirm officially the pre-Code ideas in this regard.

Indeed, canonists have manifested their consciousness of the lawmaker's painstaking care in formulating canon 209. Thus, for example, Jombart[239] thought that, by conjoining the adjectives *positive* and *probable,* the legislator wished to indicate emphatically that not any and every sort of doubt would suffice, and thus wished to restrain, as if by a double barrier, those who would push too far the application of the suppletory principle by being satisfied with merely subjective conviction. According to Jombart, the cases in which the Church wishes to supply the

[238] *Schema codicis iuris canonici* (sub secreto pontificio) Sanctissimi Domini Nostri, Pii, P.P.X., *Codex iuris canonici* cum notis Petri Gasparri, Romae, Polyglottis Vaticanis, MDCCCCXII.

[239] "Le doute positif,"—*NRT,* XLVIII (1921), 492.

needed jurisdiction always connote remedial intervention and therefore remain exceptional in their character as compared with and related to the cases of an ordinary character in which the Church is not called on to supply for any deficiency of jurisdiction. The legislator's condescension should not be interpreted as providing the source or the occasion or any pretext for arbitrary usage or license in this regard. Trombetta [240] in a similar vein regarded the joining of these two adjectives as an indication on the part of the lawgiver that he enacted this law with moral consciousness and concern. Oesterle [241] observed that the *positive* doubt does not coincide with the *probable* doubt of which the Code here speaks. Thus it is that in this instance the Code explicitly speaks of a doubt that is positive *and* probable. *Probable* denotes something objective. It implies that certain grave reasons militate for the objective truth of an allegation and that these reasons are of such a solid character that they are worthy of the assent of prudent men. As has already been seen in the exposition of the philosophical concept of positive doubt, Michiels certainly shares the same belief that true probability, inasmuch as it is based upon a positive and probable doubt, must possess the element of objectivity as an integral part of its essence.[242] Certainly, these are but a few examples of the post-Code canonists who persistently retain the old understanding of true probability; namely, by demanding that there always be verified a grave reason as the objective basis for true probability. One might mention that Blat,[243] Raus,[244] De Meester,[245] and a whole host of others who share this same view, by reiterating time and again that a *positive and probable doubt is one which is capable of gaining the assent of a prudent man.*[246]

[240] *Supplet ecclesia,* p. 7, n. 6.

[241] *Praelectiones,* I, 114.

[242] *Normae generales,* I, 332.

[243] *Commentarium,* II, 144.

[244] *Institutiones canonicae,* n. 78, II.

[245] *Juris canonici et iuris canonico-civilis compendium* (Nova Editio, Brugis, 1921-1928), I, n. 481. Hereafter this work shall be referred to simply as *Compendium.*

[246] Cf. *Coll. Brug.,* XXXIII (1933), 265-266; *Le canoniste,* XLVII (1925), 458.

This concept of the *objectivity* of the serious motives required by canon 209 is brought to the fore even more clearly when one examines the writings of post-Code canonists in which they definitely oppose any and every attempt at extreme liberalism of interpretation. That a doubt, due to and caused by personal ignorance, poor memory, light-mindedness, bad faith, or rashness be adjudged juridically sufficient to fulfill the requirements of canon 209, is not a thesis that finds much backing. Merkelbach [247] would deny such claims on the ground that in cases of this kind there really would be no doubt about jurisdiction, but rather about the personal knowledge of the confessor, in which case the Church can not be presumed to supply. Jombart, in a similar way, points out that such a conclusion assumes with entire gratuity that the Church allows favors to ignorance and its like.[248] The expression of this same view is shared almost *verbatim* by Michiels,[249] Kelly,[250] Pruemmer,[251] Noldin-Schmitt,[252] Chelodi,[253] and many others.[254]

3. *Consideration of the Context of the Code*

The ultimate reason, as Girerd frankly admits,[255] for their overemphasis of *good faith* and its juridical value in regard to the suppletory principle is the fact that Girerd and his followers feel that theirs is but the natural inference to be drawn from the benignity and liberality expressed by the law-maker in the Code. Thus, Girerd introduces as incontestable proof canons 2245, § 4,

[247] *Summa*, III, n. 586.

[248] "Juridiction et bonne foi,"—*NRT*, XLVII (1920), 548.

[249] *Normae generales*, I, 332, note 3.

[250] *The jurisdiction of the confessor*, p. 142.

[251] *Manuale iuris canonici*, p. 124, Q. LXX.

[252] *Theologia moralis*, III, n. 347.

[253] *Ius de personis*, n. 130.

[254] Cf., e. g., *Coll. Brug.*, XXXIII (1933), 265-266; *L'Ami du Clergé*, XLI (1924), 756; Knecht, *Handbuch des katholischen Eherechts*, p. 265; Nevin, "Subdelegated and interdiocesan faculties,"—*ACR*, VIII (1931), 231; M. J. Fallon, "Does canon 209 apply to delegation to assist at marriages?"—*IER*, LII (1938), 439.

[255] "La juridiction probable,"—*NRT*, LVIII (1931), 917.

and 2247, § 3, both of which he considers as illustrating the application of canon 207, § 2. These canons, he alleges, show the spirit of the legislator, a spirit of extreme condescension. In that spirit, Girerd concludes, all jurisdictional difficulties are to be settled. However, as Creusen correctly stated,[256] while it is true that they manifest a marvelous goodness on the part of the legislator, an examination of the canons cited above reveals that these canons hardly even indicate what Girerd claims that they *prove* beyond all prudent doubt.

Thus, canon 2245, § 4, views a very special case concerning the *reservation of a censure.* It deals with the restriction of jurisdiction which the priest would otherwise possess. It entails an aggravation of a penalty, and, therefore, must be strictly interpreted. In addition, it should be noted, that the text of 2245, § 3, clearly shows that the legislator does not qualify the necessary doubt with any adjectives such as *positive* or *probable.* He is content in this instance with any sort of doubt. A point further to note, with Creusen, is that this method of interpreting the reservation of censures was already admitted before the Code. On the other hand, this problem of supplying in the event of probability was the topic of widespread and heated controversy. If one further considers that in cases of such reservations the doubt, properly considered, often springs from the status of the penitent himself, as created, for example, by the indeterminate conditions and circumstances of the act posited by him, then one can readily perceive a wide disparity between this doubt and the doubt contemplated in the ruling of canon 209. From the penitent the confessor can hardly expect anything like a scrutinizing revelation of the nature of the doubt which troubled him. The confessor in all likelihood must in the end make liberal allowance for the presence of sincerity and good faith. With the presence of these taken for granted it matters not whether the penitent's sincere doubt was one that could be termed a *probable* doubt. Probable or improbable, his doubt was sincere,

[256] "Réponse du P. Creusen,"—*NRT,* LVIII (1931), 921.

and in this lies the assumption that the reservation does not obtain in his case.

Similarly in canon 2247, § 3, there is question of the *reservation* of jurisdiction. Incidentally, it might be noted that this canon postulates a case entirely different from that covered in canon 207, § 2. In the former case the Church does not maintain the reservation. In the latter case she declares how it is necessary to interpret the duration of a jurisdiction limited as to time. The Church declares that she will maintain such a jurisdiction up to the moment when the priest realizes that the time-limit of his possession of jurisdiction has lapsed, or, that the number of cases for which he was jurisdictionally authorized has been acquitted.

Fully admitting the liberality of the Church as manifested by these and by other canons in the Code,[257] O'Donnell,[258] warns against the tendency in interpretation which considers in substance, these canons as conclusive proof of the Church's intention to regard *good faith* under any circumstances of jurisdictional activity a sufficient juridical basis to enjoy the salutary benefits of canon 209. He observes, in full accord with the many authors to whom reference has already been made in this section, that this prospect of theology-made-easy puts a premium on ignorance and carelessness, and is totally out of harmony with the scientific principles insistently enunciated by theologians and reaffirmed by the Code. He further marks well that the above cited canons do make liberal allowances, but *for special cases,* when the spiritual welfare of the penitent is allowed to outweigh the advantages of strict consistency in the enforcement of jurisdictional laws and sanctions. But, he insists that these exceptions only prove the rule. The very care exhibited in marking off these special instances is the best indication that outside these limits the ordinary rules are to be applied. Indeed, if good faith were sufficient of itself, it seems rather pointless for canon 2247, § 3, to state that the provisions of this canon will hold for all reser-

[257] Cf., e. g., canons 2249, § 2; 882; 899, § 3; 900.

[258] "When does the Church supply jurisdiction?"—*IER* (1920), 500.

vations but those reserved *ab homine* or *specialissimo modo* to the Holy See, or for canon 207, § 2, to be so careful in stating that its concessions are limited to the internal forum and are applicable only when a priest acts with inadvertence to the fact that he is overrunning his jurisdictional time-limit or trespassing beyond the bounds demarcated by the indefinite number of cases for which he was authorized to act. The indication is plain: Whenever the legislator is not satisfied with mere good faith, then some other element in addition to good faith or in its place is required.

4. *Involvement of the Common Good*

Another argument advanced by Girerd is that the common good really demands this wider and more benign interpretation which he follows.[259] As in the case of the other arguments, so here Creusen quite effectively points out that the consideration is one of isolated instances existing apart from the possibility of common error. Thus, at the most, only the private good of the individual is at stake. Secondly, it may be seriously questioned whether it would be useful for the common good if the Church were to supply in cases where the priest's action would have nothing else to motivate it but crass or supine ignorance.[260] If the exercise of jurisdiction in a particular case were the sole means towards the salvation of a soul, then perhaps the liberal contention might boast of a strong argument in its favor. But in reality such is not the case. The Church has already made the most liberal provisions for such instances as is evident from canons like 882; 1043-1045; 1098, § 1; 2252. Outside such danger of death the difficulty besetting an individual because of the refusal of the Church to supply in a given case is never such as is not easily repaired. Especially in the sacrament of penance it should not be forgotten what an important rôle indirect absolution can play.

259 "La juridiction probable,"—*NRT*, LVIII (1931), 917.

260 "Réponse du P. Creusen,"—*NRT*, LVIII (1931), 922; cf. also Grosam, "Der Beichtvater ohne Jurisdiktion,"—*LQS*, LXXXII (1929), 124.

5. *The Practice of the Rota*

Toso[261] quite correctly observed that controversies concerning the supplying of jurisdiction in common error do not easily arise for solution by public authority. For, if there be question of a jurisdictional act posited in the internal forum, no one can really contest its validity except the one who posited it or his ecclesiastical superior, from whom the jurisdiction had been obtained. In the internal forum all things are done *coram Deo,* Who knows the hearts of men and can provide in the unusual way for the unusual case. But, if there should be question of a jurisdictional act posited in the external forum, and the act's validity is questioned on the ground of defect of jurisdiction and of common error, the presumption stands for the validity of the act and the burden of proof lies on the one attacking the act's validity. On parallel lines, one can say that difficulties and controversies will be rare in regard to supplying in doubt.

Indeed, there have been but a few cases—and most of them were settled within the last thirteen years—which were decided on the ground of the applicability or the non-applicability of the suppletory principle. In many ways it is not strange that all these cases revolved about marriage problems. But, inasmuch as Girerd[262] concedes the applicability of canon 209 to the case of assistance at marriage as well as to that of the hearing of confessions, and since there is quite a general feeling of agreement among canonists as to the applicability of this canon to assistance at marriage, the decisions of the Rota may be regarded as an authoritative confirmation of such an application. Because there will be more practical value in studying these cases individually when treating of *doubt of fact,* let it suffice for the present to note that certainly it is clear that the Rota has always sought for the *objective* motive before deciding to apply or not to apply canon 209 to a given case. The claim is here advanced that this is only to be expected in view of the historical origin and growth of the doctrine of supplying in cases of doubt.

[201] "De errore communi,"—*Jus Pont.,* III (1923), 149-150.
[267] "La juridiction probable,"—*NRT,* LVIII (1931), 917.

6. *Conclusion*

In view of all the foregoing considerations, it is quite clear that to be *positive* and *probable* a doubt must be objective in character. But, inasmuch as every doubt, of its very nature, involves something of a *subjective* character, Merkelbach[263] may be regarded a trifle strict when he says that "the doubt must be objective concerning the jurisdiction itself, and not concerning the doctrine or knowledge of the confessor about it." Canon 209 definitely does not mean that the doubt must be so serious that no one would be able to solve it. And if this be so, it would seem that the *dubium* must be at least to some extent subjective. The limit of subjectivity is determined by the time-honored phrase that, to merit the suppletory benefits of canon 209, it must always *be founded upon sufficient reason to gain the assent of a prudent man.*

As *L'Ami du Clergé*[264] and Creusen[265] agree that it is not always easy to draw with mathematical precision the line between the *positive and probable* opinion and one that is not such. So much is clear: a doubt proceeding from a crass or supine ignorance will hardly suffice to rally to its support the assent of prudent men or of men having at hand means necessary for ascertaining the objective statue of a certain qusetion. Therefore, this at least can be held without reserve, namely, that doubts arising from crass or supine ignorance can hardly be called positive and probable in the sense required by canon 209. As for defining the exact nature of the positive and probable doubt, namely, such as can gain the assent of a prudent man,no attempt will be made here to fulfill such a task. It is obviously a moral question depending upon circumstances that surround individual persons at individual occasions. Just as in the works of the moral theologians of the past and the present, so here is presented a merely moral guide to pass judgment in particular cases. However,

[263] *Summa,* III, n. 586, 3.

[264] XLI (1924), 756.

[265] "Réponse du P. Creusen,"—*NRT,* LVIII (1931), 920-921.

in the sections which will presently follow, an attempt will be made to give some further clarification by means of examples.

III. DOUBT OF LAW AND OF FACT

1. *Preliminary Notions*

a. Scope Limited to Ecclesiastical Laws Alone

When the Church, or more specifically the Roman Pontiff, is said to supply jurisdiction in any case whatsoever, be it in common error or in doubt, it is readily understood that the Pope acts in virtue of the plenitude of the jurisdictional power Christ entrusted to his person. Naturally it rests within the scope of such broad power to grant, to extend or to restrict the share of others in the exercise of this power in any way whatsoever, be it by the ordinary canonical commission or by the extraordinary supplying in certain emergencies. But it is important that just as in the case of common error, so in the case of doubt, the vast jurisdictional power of the Pope is limited to ecclesiastical laws alone. By this token divinely instituted laws, be they natural or positive, are outside the ambit or beyond the control of the Pope or any of his inferiors.[266] And thus, quite obviously canon 209 must be understood as applying exclusively to doubts that might arise from difficulties in the theoretical understanding or practical application of ecclesiastical laws.

b. Relation Between Canon 209 and Canon 15.

For a proper understanding of canon 209 in reference to the problem of doubt, whether of law or of fact, one must necessarily make some attempt to ascertain and to appraise the relation which certain canonists note as existing between canon 15 and canon 209.[267]

[266] Cf., e. g., canons 81; 107, § 3; 1069, § 2. Cf. also Michiels, *Normae generales,* I, 338.

[267] Cf. Wernz-Vidal, *Ius canonicum,* I, n. 189; Van Hove, *De legibus ecclesiasticis,* n. 231; Michiels, *Normae generales,* I, 339, footnote 2; Cicognani, *Canon law,* p. 591.

Like canon 209, canon 15 is limited in its consideration and application exclusively to ecclesiastical law. Canon 15 declares, first of all, that "in doubt of law, the law does not oblige." The legislator is clearly very careful to note that this rule does apply even to invalidating and incapacitating laws. The principle behind this law is identically the same as that adduced by the moralists in defense of probabilism, i.e., that it is not licit to restrict the natural liberty of man unless there be a *certain* obligation to that effect.[268] On the basis of the law of canon 15, any priest who is already in possession of some jurisdictional competence will retain the same in the event of any doubtful law demanding the forfeiture of his power. In regard to a case such as this, then, it is readily apparent that canon 209 follows the general prescript of canon 15 and applies its general norm, as applicable to any and all laws, to jurisdictional laws in particular. But there is a difference also, and a great one, between these two canons. While canon 15 may be regarded as a sort of defense of the *status quo,* a weapon against any undue infringement upon natural liberty or upon power already possessed, canon 209 applies not only when jurisdiction already possessed is threatened but also when there is some doubt concerning laws that would grant jurisdiction to one who never possessed it,[269] or increase such power in one who already enjoys a share in the Church's jurisdictional competence.[270] Thus, while canon 15 applies when there is question of an undue limiting of jurisdictional competence, canon 209 may be used for the purpose of obtaining or extending the same.

Yet even greater is the supplementary force of canon 209 in reference to doubts of fact. For, as the clear reading of canon 15 shows, the Code gives no general rule, nor any immediate application of the principle of probabilism to probable judgments about various facts. In canon 15 the legislator merely indicates

268 Michiels, *Normae generales,* I, p. 335; Bouquillon, *Theologia moralis fundamentalis,* n. 299.

269 E. g., canons 882; 1098, § 2.

270 E. g., canons 81, 523, 1043-1045, 2252-2254.

that, in the event of such doubts, the Ordinary can dispense provided there be question of laws from which the Holy Father is wont to dispense.[271] However, though the legislator was loath to state that in doubts of fact the law does not oblige, there are several particular instances wherein he has statements to that effect. Thus, for example, he decreed that in a doubt of law or of fact, the reservation of *latae sententiae* censures does not bind,[272] and that a penalty can be inflicted or imposed by the proper ecclesiastical superior only when there is certainty about the commission of a delict.[273] This certainty, however, can not be had in the face of any doubt, regardless of whether the doubt reflect uncertainty about a supposedly existing law or solely about the existence of a violation of an extant law. It is in this same manner that the legislator has decreed that the Church supplies jurisdiction, whenever needed, for the external and internal forum alike, in all cases of positive and probable doubt, in doubt of fact as well as in doubt of law.[274]

2. *Doubt of Law*

A doubt of law exists when there is no certainty about the existence, or the permanence, or the force, or the comprehension of some law in question.[275]

For the correct application of that part of canon 209 which treats of this specific case two very important considerations must be borne in mind. First of all, due attention and regard must always be given to the general principle of canon 6, n. 4. That canon states in effect that, if any doubt should arise as to whether some canon of the Code differs from the old law, there is to be no departure from the old law. This, of course, is to be understood of a doubt in regard to the comprehension or juridical extent of a law of the Code which is none too clearly

[271] Van Hove, *De legibus*, n. 231.

[272] Canon 2245, § 4.

[273] Canon 2233, § 1.

[274] Canon 209.

[275] Cf. Toso, *Ad codicem iuris canonici commentaria minora*, p. 42; Van Hove, *De legibus ecclesiasticis*, n. 228, 3.

identified with nor yet evidently differentiated from a previously existing law. On precisely such a basis as this must it be maintained that the traditional concept of common error must be retained and followed. If, however, there should be some doubt about the abrogation of an old law or a change in its obligatory character in as far as there is question, for example, of whether a penal or invalidating law has become merely preceptive or prohibitive in its character, then the principles of canon 15 are to be observed in harmony with the prescripts of canon 6, nn. 1 and 5 and of canon 11.[276] The second requirement, as has been shown in the preceding section, is that the doubt of law must be based upon true probability, upon such arguments that would, because of their objectivity, be able to gain the assent of a prudent man.

a. Kinds of Doubts of Law

From the point of view of its foundations a positive and probable doubt of law may be either *intrinsic or extrinsic.*

(a.) Intrinsic Probability

The probability is *intrinsic* if and when it is founded solely upon grave and solid reasons which are derived from a careful study of the problem at hand, an examination of its various properties, its causes and effects, the inconveniences of the opposite view, etc.[277] In a word, as *L'Ami du Clergé* very frankly expressed it,[278] because of the detailed knowledge and deep grasp of a subject that this thorough examination postulates and demands, it is readily seen how and why a judgment concerning the existence of a true probability of law on merely intrinsic grounds rests properly and solely within the office and province of those who are very learned.[279] Thereupon it is easily

[276] Michiels, *Normae generales,* I, n. 335.

[277] Vermeersch, *Theologia moralis,* I, n. 376; Merkelbach, *Summa,* II, n. 101, 2a; Michiels, *Normae generales,* I, p. 335.

[278] XLI (1924), 757.

[279] A noteworthy example of such an intrinsic probability of law was the doubt of law raised by Leitner (*Lehrbuch des katholischen Eherechts* [3. ed., Paderborn, 1920], p. 210) who was closely followed by Jone

understood how such a judgment is entirely beyond the competence and capability of the ordinary priest or confessor. It is the duty of any such priest, if his learning is only of an average status, to attempt to solve his doubt by seeking out the support of some extrinsic source. And, if a situation should arise wherein the priest cannot leave the faithful without ministering to them then and there as well and as far as he can do so, then, of course, it is clear that he should act as he would when possessed of some merely negative doubt in cases of grave need. This manner of acting, of course, must be accompanied by whatever safeguards and warnings the particular situation demands. The person ministered unto should be told, if it be necessary to do so, of the priest's uncertainty of validity in the case and advised to have the act ratified beyond all doubt at the earliest opportunity.

(b.) Extrinsic Probability

Concerning *extrinsic* probability, however, not only the very learned, but even those who possess only a mediocre learning can judge quite adequately. The probability is said to be extrinsic if and when it is based upon the authority of others. According as such probability is the result of the study, reflections, and research of some private individual or flows from the commonly admitted teaching of authorities, it is called *private* or *public* probability of law.[280] Since the Code does not distinguish the sort of probability of law that must be present, it follows that any probability will suffice which will qualify as *positive* and *probable.* In other words, just as intrinsic probability of law, for its juridical effectiveness, demands serious and objective rea-

(*LQS*, LXXX [1927], 556-559). Against the all but unanimous view of canonists, they had taken the position that it was not certain whether the phrases *ab acatholicis nati* in canon 1099, § 2, must be limited to those born of parents both of whom were non-Catholics. Cf. V. Schaaf, "An exemption from the canonical form of marriage,"—*AER*, LXXXIII (1930), 484-496; P. Maroto, "De vi verborum can. 1099, § 2: 'ab acatholicis nati'."—*Apoll.*, III (1930), 604. More will be said concerning this doubt of law subsequently.

[280] Michiels, *Normae generales*, I, p. 335.

sons as its basis, so too must extrinsic probability possess the very same qualifications of positiveness and objective evidence. Thus, the opinion of the authors does not gain strength from the mere fact that they espouse it. On the contrary, the sole reason why the authority of these authors is admitted and followed is because it is presumed that they have themselves constructed their opinion on good and sound, intrinsic arguments.[281] On this account authorities commonly teach the possibility of the Church's supplying in both instances: in probability of a private as well as of a public character.[282]

a°. Private Probability of Law

While authors admit the possibility of the Church's supplying of jurisdiction in cases of private probability of law, it is very important to note the general feeling among them that very seldom, in fact only in the case of a person who is gifted with intellectual and moral endowments in an unusual degree, will a personal survey and appreciation of a difficulty result in such a probability. This is not any new sort of position. If the reader will but recall the historical analysis of this point, he will remember that it was exactly on this basis that the majority of canonists opposed any and all application of the suppletory principle to any but public probability of law. And even those, like Verricelli [283] and Elbel,[284] who, as the reader also remembers, were among the first to contend in the face of almost overwhelming opposition that the juridically required element of probability could be verified even in the judgment of *one* man, were very careful to admit that it would need to be a *learned* man. This same qualification remains stressed by authors writing after the

[281] St. Alphonsus, *Theologia moralis,* lib. I, n. 80.

[282] Cf., e. g., Wernz-Vidal, *Ius canonicum,* II, n. 382; Couly, "La juridiction suppléée du canon 209,"—*Le canoniste,* XLVII (1925), 456.

[283] *Quaestiones morales et legales,* Tr. II, q. XXV, n. 15: "Quomodocumque opinio sit probabilis, sive extrinsece propter auctoritatem Doctorum, sive intrinsece propter solida fundamenta de novo *ab uno docto* considerata, sicuti licite ex tali probabilitate absolvit, ita et validissime."

[284] *Theologia moralis tripartita,* Conf. XII, nn. 310-311.

appearance of the Code. Thus, authors like Michiels,[285] Vermeersch [286] and Merkelbach,[287] repeat that the author of such a probability must be a very learned scholar of both the natural and positive law, prudent and diligent in his investigation, not a seeker after novelty, but adducing valid reasons, which others either have not considered or have not satisfactorily solved, and fittingly answering the objections to his opinion. Only then, continues Vermeersch, will the probability gain juridical value for reasons that are both intrinsic and extrinsic. He adds further, the more an opinion is considered doubtful and difficult, the more easily will the authority of a prudent and learned man opposing it suffice to make his opinion to be adjudged as sufficiently probable. Such a position is very clearly opposed to any and every contention that the works of recent and modern authors should be considered as presenting probable doctrine until such doctrine has called forth the criticism and reprobation of the Holy See. In fact, that opinion has long been condemned by Pope Alexander VII (1655-1667) in the list of condemnations that he levied against various Jansenistic teachings.[288]

b°. Public Probability of Law

An opinion is generally conceded to be extrinsically probable because of a public probability of law when at least five or six authors, approved and of great name, support it after really studying the question in point and not merely copying it one from the other without further personal examination.[289]

[285] *Normae generales,* I, p. 335.

[286] *Theologia moralis,* I, n. 376.

[287] *Summa,* II, n. 101, 2a.

[288] "Si liber sit alicuius iunioris et moderni, debet opinio censeri probabilis, dum non constet, reiectam esse a Sede Apostolica tamquam improbabilem"—Denzinger-Bannwart-Umberg, *Enchiridion symbolorum,* n. 1127.

[289] Merkelbach, *Summa,* II, p. 107, note 1: "Probabilitas extrinseca magis aestimanda est ex doctorum merito et eruditione, necnon ex studio et diligentia in rei veritate indaganda, *quam ex eorum numero;* possunt enim decem vel plures auctores tenere aliquam opinionem quorum auctoritas vix quidquam magis confert ad eius probabilitatem, quam auctoritas unius, quem forte illi sine rei examine ac discussione secuti sunt."

Concerning this it may be well added that authors are considered *approved* either because of the common reputation they enjoy to this effect or because they are so regarded by the Church, as manifested by specific judgment or by some other sign. Or, looking at this same point negatively after the manner of La Croix,[290] one would say those are not to be considered approved authors who: 1) uphold opinions, even though they be few, which are false because they are opposed to otherwise certain principles; 2) indulge in light and readily contestable, if not sophistic, arguments; 3) teach many things which are improbable or which have already been shown by other writers to rest upon futile and false reasons; 4) are mere compilers of opinions without undertaking the task of really appraising them by themselves. Thus, as Merkelbach points out,[291] "approved authors" cannot be identified with all those authors who have secured an *Imprimatur;* for, it is a matter of common knowledge that much that is futile and inconsistent is handed down in printed books, even in books that have such an *Imprimatur.*

In general, then, one might note that a probability of law is a juridical factor which is based upon a scientific basis. It is indeed, as Girerd observes,[292] a probability with an objective and universal value. Therefore, one can understand how Creusen, admitting as he did that there was considerable room for personal appreciation in probability of fact, insisted that such is not the case in probability of law.[293] And, on the basis of such a conviction on this score, Creusen warns the priest, in doubts of law, to go and to seek out the necessary information to solve the doubt and not to trust his own judgment. But, perhaps no one has been so outright in his statement as Michiels,[294] who states directly that no probability can be invoked against the obligation of a law unless it be *truly* probable, and that in questions of the external forum the probability must be seriously demonstrable. An

[290] *Theologia moralis,* I, n. 160.

[291] *Summa,* II, n. 108, footnote 4.

[292] "La juridiction probable,"—*NRT*, LVIII (1931), 916.

[293] "Réponse du P. Creusen,"—*NRT,* LVIII (1931), 922.

[294] *Normae generales,* I, p. 335.

opinion, however, will not be seriously demonstrable if for any reason it labors under an improbability of such a character that it must be regarded as only *doubtfully probable.* And, as Ballerini-Palmieri [295] observed, the doctors consider as negatively doubtful any opinion: 1) if there is doubt about the strength of the reasons adduced; 2) if those who are learned commonly doubt its probability; 3) if the authority of the doctors who affirm or regard this opinion as probable is of a doubtful character; 4) if the reasoning of the author defending it is not sufficiently strong; 5) if the opinion is singular in character and the author does not adduce sufficient reasons; 6) if one, or only a few, propose it while the greater part of the authors contradict it.

Before giving a few examples regarding this probability of law, this is the proper place to note a significant observation which was made by Merkelbach in regard to the question of how strictly all of these rules governing probability are to be applied. Certainly, it does seem that the rules of probability are to be strictly applied. For, it escapes no one that in this our day there are many and varied writings being published on theological and canonical topics. "Today, much more easily than in the past, five or six recent writers can be found to aver the sufficiency of the probability of any opinion. This is particularly true when these authors belong to the same school, especially since in most cases they do nothing more than copy some recent author." [296]

b. Examples

In consideration of all the vicissitudes of human legislation doubts of law are bound to arise. No human legislator, even when all adjuncts are favorable, can enunciate all his laws so clearly and so comprehensively as to preclude all possibility of doubt with regard to the existence, intent, extension or application of his laws.[297] Thus it is not at all surprising that such doubts can and do emerge from the laws in the Code. But prudent and

[295] *Opus theologicum morale,* Tom. I, *de conscientia,* n. 113.
[296] Merkelbach, *Summa,* II, n. 102, 4.
[297] Suarez, *De legibus,* l. I, c. 1, n. 5.

far-seeing as the Church is in her legistlation, fully conscious of the limitation of human law, she strives to remedy such inevitable lapses of the law by specific general provisions, of which canon 209 is perhaps the most important in respect of any deficient clarity in her jurisdictional laws.

Without an exhaustive enumeration of such doubts of law, it is entirely in order to present a few of them.

Thus, for example, canon 523 brings up the point as to whether the confessor, who is allowed in virtue of this canon to hear the confession of a gravely ill woman religious, needs jurisdiction from the Ordinary of the place wherein the confession is to be heard, or whether it suffices that he be approved for the confession of women by any Ordinary. The law is not clear as given in the Code. Canonists are divided. Worthy arguments are adduced on both sides. In virtue of this situation, in view of canon 209, the more lenient opinion can be followed in practice.[298]

Or again, can *ab homine latae sententiae* censures be absolved by reason of canon 2254, or must the possibility of absolving them be denied within the purview of this canon? The affirmative opinion has received wide support. From this external authority and from the fact that *ab homine latae sententiae* censures are not unquestionably excluded by the wording of canon 2254, it seems that there is at least a doubt of law and canon 209 can come into play.[299]

Again, has a priest who is delegated in virtue of cannons 1095, § 2, and 1096 to assist at all marriages within a parish, the power to dispense in cases wherein danger of death is present when time does not allow recourse to the Ordinary or to the pastor? O'Keefe,[300] presuming all the time of course that the in-

[298] For a fuller study of this point cf. Kelly, *The jurisdiction of the confessor*, pp. 205-209; McCormick, *Confessors of religious*, pp. 226-229.

[299] Cf. Moriarty, *The extraordinary absolution from censures* (The Catholic University of America, Canon Law Studies, n. 113: Washing-

[300] *Matrimonial dispensation, powers of Bishops, priests, and confessors* (The Catholic University of America, Canon Law Studies, n. 45: Washington, D. C., 1927), p. 116.

ton, D. C., 1938), p. 168.

dividual authors advocating the affirmative opinion have good reasons, thinks that their external authority is of sufficient gravity to justify the application of their opinion in practice. And certainly, the context of the law, particularly when canon 1044 and canon 1098, § 2, are studied more closely, bears out this conclusion. At any rate the doubt may be practically solved by canon 209.

Numerous other samples of doubts could be adduced. Thus, one could mention the doubt as to whether the law does or does not require the *acceptance* of a delegation to assist at marriage.[301] One could mention others, too. One could certainly not hope to give an exhaustive list of them all. Even if it were possible to do so, the number of samples would not add appreciably to the understanding of the prescript of the Code, namely, that each such doubt of law must be truly positive and probable. Still, it will not be amiss to cite another case to show how at times, while canon 209 will apply, great care must be taken that the supplying of jurisdiction will not be presumed to extend farther than the context of the Code will allow. Thus, Moriarty points out very carefully that it is the office of the confessor to verify whether or not a particular case is a *casus urgentior*.[302] If he has at least a positive and probable reason for considering one of the more urgent cases to be present, even though he have some doubt in this regard, he can validly absolve by virtue of canon 209 in particular conjunction with canon 2254. Yet, while canon 209 grants him the power to absolve a penitent from certain reserved censures, it does not empower him to absolve the penitent from the obligation of recourse. On the contrary, the priest must observe all the prescripts of canon 2254.

In regard to all doubts of law, of course, it is always to be understood that they cease immediately upon any authentic declaration of the Holy See. Canon 17, § 2, implicitly distinguishes authentic declarations of law as 1) declaratory; 2) explanatory;

[301] Cf. Payen, *De matrimonio*, II, n. 1779, 3; Kearney, *The principles of delegation*, p. 92; Carberry, *The juridical form of marriage*, p. 93.

[302] *The extraordinary absolution from censures*, p. 144.

3) restrictive; and 4) extensive. A merely *declaratory* interpretation simply reaffirms a point of law that is *in itself clear.* It requires no promulgation since it neither adds nor detracts from a law already in effect. For this same reason a merely declaratory interpretation has retroactive force. An *explanatory* interpretation is one that removes some obscurity inherent in the words of the law; for words may have a strict or a broad meaning. Such an interpretation requires a new promulgation insofar as it adds something that was not certainly in the law or detracts something that was not certainly beyond it, and in so far as it is equivalent to a new law. An *extensive* interpretation gives a law a wider scope than it originally had. A *restrictive* interpretation narrows the original scope of a law. Obviously the last two interpretations, since they change the law, need promulgation and are not retroactive.[303]

These few observations are not indicative of any attempt to probe very deeply into the rules of interpretation—that task is not properly within the scope of this work. However, they are quite necessary as a prelude to the consideration of a certain problem which was raised not long ago in regard to the correct interpretation of canon 1099, § 2, by the Pontifical Commission for the Authentic Interpretation of the Canons of the Code. This Commission issued two interpretations which, on the surface, seem to destroy the value of any probability of law. For, there was a dispute as to whether or not the term *ab acatholicis nati* embraced children born of a valid mixed marriage and baptized in the Catholic Church, if they had been raised from infancy outside the Catholic Church. The Commission, particularly in the later interpretation, seemed by calling it *declaratory* to assert that it was merely declaring a law that was *in itself certain.* Whereupon one wonders if the Commission did not entirely underestimate the value of the arguments adduced by the vast majority of canonists who would excuse from the canon-

303 Cf., e. g., Michiels, *Normae generales,* I, p. 384; Schaaf, "An exemption from the canonical form of marriage,"—*AER,* LXXXIII (1930), 491-492.

ical form of marriage only such children as are born of two non-catholics and baptized in the Catholic Church, but subsequently brought up outside the Catholic Church. An examination into the details of these two interpretations is almost indispensable from the point of view of this study.

First of all, it must be clearly born in mind that explanatory, extensive or restrictive interpretations are not retroactive. They must be promulgated and exert their juridical effect only upon due observation of the prescript of canon 9. Until the interpretation becomes juridically effective one may follow the *dubium iuris* on the side of leniency and still perform valid jurisdictional acts.

Secondly, interpretations that are merely declaratory are retroactive. As a sample of such an interpretation Schaaf [304] cited the declaration of the Commission to the effect that a "complete and continuous year" is necessary for the validity of a novitiate and that the reckoning of the novitiate year is to be made according to canon 34, § 3, n. 3.[305]

Thirdly it must be remembered that the Pontifical Commission possesses no power to legislate. At the same time it possesses the exclusive right to interpret the canons of the Code.[306] Certain authors, like Maroto, [307] would restrict the Commission's power to that of simple declaration of law. However, very many canonists feel that practical utility and efficacy demand that, over and beyond the power of mere declaration, this Commission possess at least the power to issue explanatory interpretations of obscure laws.[308] This last is a very important point to keep in

[304] "An exemption from the canonical form of marriage,"—*AER*, LXXXIII (1930), 490.

[305] *PCI*, 12 November, 1922, II—*AAS*, XIV (1922), 661.

[306] *Motu Proprio*, "Cum iuris canonici codicem," 15 September, 1917, II—at head of the Gasparri edition of the Code immediately after the constitution promulgating it. Cf. especially n. III of that *Motu Proprio*.

[307] *Institutiones*, I, 239.

[308] Cf., e. g., Van Hove, *De legibus*, n. 243; Michiels, *Normae generales*, I, p. 393; Schaaf, "An exemption from the canonical form of marriage,"—*AER*, LXXXIII (1930), 492-493; Nevin, "Marriage case arising from recent official interpretation of the phrase *ab acatholicis nati*,"—*ACR*, IX (1932), 263.

mind, particularly since upon it involves the retroactivity or non-retroactivity of any interpretation given by the Pontifical Commission, and consequently the validity or non-validity of any jurisdictional act that might have been posited on the strength of the *dubium iuris,* which the Commission chooses to define.

With these few principles in mind, one may consider the problem presented by the Pontifical Commission concerning the phrase *ab acatholicis nati* of canon 1099, § 2.

Contrary to the all but unanimous view of canonists who had carefully studied and discussed this point the Commission vindicated the opinion of Leitner[309] and of Jone,[310] who held that there was a real *dubium iuris* as to the meaning of the phrase *ab acatholicis nati* of canon 1099, § 2, and who maintained as a consequence, that those born of mixed marriages, baptized as Catholics but not brought up as such, did not fall under the invalidating and incapacitating prescripts of canons 1094-1099.[311]

When this official interpretation appeared, although a few like Maroto considered it of a purely declaratory character,[312] most canonists considered the decision as not purely declaratory, but explanatory, i.e., in the sense explained above.[313] They felt that a *dubium iuris* really existed concerning the phrase *ab acatholicis nati* of canon 1099, § 2. And in perfect harmony with cannonical doctrine, Schaaf observed that it was true that in this particular interpretation the reply of the Pontifical Commission led to the same conclusion as the reflex principle based on canon 15, namely, that the marriages entered into by the children of mixed marriages under the circumstances mentioned in canon 1099, § 2,

[309] *Lehrbuch des katholischen Eherechts* (3. ed., Paderborn, 1920), p. 120.

[310] *LQS,* LXXX (1927), 556-559.

[311] *PCI,* 20 July, 1929, ad II—*AAS,* XXI (1929), 573.

[312] "De vi verborum can. 1099, § 2: 'ab acatholicis nati'."—*Apoll.,* III (1930), 601-616.

[313] Cf., e.g., F. Hecht, "Quandonam lex peculiaris de forma matrimoniali in Germania ante cod. iuris can. vigens incipiebat?"—*Jus Pont.,* X (1930), 36; V. Schaaf, "An exemption from the canonical form of marriage,"—*AER,* LXXXIII (1930), 491.

without the canonical form of marriage between Pentecost of 1918 and 2 December, 1929, were valid. That was, however, only *per accidens.* The difference between the two, Schaaf observed, would be apparent if the reader supposed that the Pontifical Commission had given the opposite reply. Its decision would still be explanatory of a *dubium iuris* and would not have retroactive force and could not be used to settle cases of marriage before it took juridical effect on 3 December, 1929.[314] Thus, marriages before this date would be valid in view of the *dubium iuris* and canon 15. To digress for a moment, one may note that in the same fashion cannon 209 exerts its suppletory benefits in cases of doubts of law unless and until an authentic decision has been given and has taken juridical effect.

But to return to the main theme, one notes that the Pontifical Commission issued another interpretation which continued to occasion perplexity and amazement among canonists. This time the Commission stated that the interpretation given in 1929 was not extensive but *declaratory* in character.[315] As a result many canonists, like Schaaf,[316] received this decision as indicative of the fact that the earlier decision was retroactive in character.

But did the Commission intend to call this definition *declaratory* in the sense of canon 17, i.e., as one which "merely declares (*declaret tantum*) the meaning of a law which is neither obscure nor uncertain (*verba legis in se certa*)? With Nevin[317] one would rather agree that it is expecting much of a person asking him to admit that the words of a law are not obscure nor uncertain when practically everyone of the commentators—Ver-

[314] The Commission's answer to the doubt, given on July 20, 1929, was published in a fascicle of the *AAS* which bore the date of September 2, 1929. Allowing for the three months' *vacatio* stipulated by canon 9, one will correspondingly figure December 3, 1929, as the day on which the answer began to exercise its juridical effect.

[315] *PCI,* 25 July, 1931, ad II—*AAS,* XXIII (1931), 388.

[316] "Disparity of cult and the canonical form,"—*AER,* LXXXIX (1933), 69.

[317] "Marriage case arising from recent official interpretation of the phrase *ab acatholicis nati,*"—*ACR,* IX (1932), 263.

meersch, Creusen, Cappello, DeSmet, Vlaming, Vidal, Damen, Noldin—mistook their meaning. Therefore one cannot believe that the term *declaratory* as used by the Pontifical Commission to indicate the nature of the previous interpretation is the equivalent of the words *declaret tantum verba legis in se certa* of canon 17. There is all likelihod that *declaratory* is only to be taken in contradistinction to *extensive*. Evidently, the interpretation was not *restrictive*. Thus, there remains the one possibility that it was meant to be *explanatory*. Such would Nevin call it,[318] following a distinction made by St. Alphonsus[319] and incorporated by Ojetti in his commentary on canon 17.[320]

Ojetti distinguished between *declaratory* interpretations which were *pure tales* and *declaratory* interpretations which were *non pure tales*. The first "merely declare the words of a law in themselves certain,"; the latter explain an obscure text (*dubium explicant*. Applying this rule to the two interpretations of the Pontifical Commission, one believes with Nevin that they were indeed declaratory, but *non pure tales*. This, as Nevin puts it, "gets over the terminological difficulty and has the added merit of being in accordance with common sense." The result is that Nevin considered that these interpretations were not retroactive but would take juridical effects only upon due observance of the regulations of canon 9.

This view does not conflict with the fact that the Sacred Congregation of the Holy Office declared valid a marriage which without the observance of the canonical form took place in 1922 between a Lutheran and a girl who had been born of a mixed marriage, had been baptized, but had not been reared as a Catholic.[321] All the marriages contracted by persons like the one just mentioned were valid in virtue of canon 15. For there was a true *dubium iuris*, even though it was not exploited by

[318] "Marriage case arising from recent official interpretation of the phrase *ab acatholicis nati*,"—*ACR*, IX (1932), 264.

[319] *Theologia moralis*, lib. I, n. 200.

[320] *Commentarium*, p. 138.

[321] Cf. *Periodica*, XXI (1932), 14-16.

canonists. And, as Girerd aptly put it, a doubt of law is of universal value and character.[322]

3. *Doubt of Fact*

It is not quite correct to say that " . . . *dubium facti in dubium iuris converti potest,*"[323] for it is one thing to say that, in view of *doubt of fact,* one can by reflex principles conclude freedom from the obligation of a certain law, and quite another by that same process render doubtful a law that is clear and certain; that is mere quibbling which must destroy a clear understanding of the law.[324] A doubt of fact arises when with full and certified knowledge of the existence of a law and its theoretical comprehension and juridical extension to a particular fact, one has not that same certainty as to the existence of the fact in question or of all the juridically required circumstances.[325] This lack of certainty may be occasioned by any of the innumerable combinations of circumstances surrounding the priest. It may occur in regard to competency to perform acts in the external forum as well as in the internal forum. Clearly, as Creusen observes,[326] in doubts of fact there is much more room for personal appreciation of a set of circumstances on the part of the priest than there is in doubts of law which, according to the judgment of the prudent man, must be scientifically grounded if they are to have any juridical value. However, it must be insisted that, before the priest can validly posit any jurisdictional act on the plea of doubt of fact, he still must have some good objective reason, some real basis in support of the contention that he can act in this instance. This reason, this basis, as has already been, must be of a sufficiently objective character to be capable of gaining the *assent of a prudent man.*

It may be said in general that the authors have applied to such

[322] "La juridiction probable,"—*NRT,* LVIII (1931), 916.

[323] Michiels, *Normae generales,* I, p. 358.

[324] V. Schaaf, "Recent canon law study,"—*AER,* LXXXV (1931), 201-202.

[325] Michiels, *Normae generales,* I, p. 333.

[326] "Réponse du P. Creusen,"—*NRT,* LVIII (1931), 922.

doubts of fact the rule that they must represent more than a status of mere misapprehension or of simply subjective credence if they are to be juridically capable of making the benefits of the suppletory principle available for application and use. Thus, to illustrate the case of a positive doubt of fact, Vermeersch-Creusen [327] point to the juridical predicament of a priest who is not certain as to just when his faculties in a certain diocese will expire. But if this priest simultaneously knows for certain that in general the faculties like his are granted for a period of three years, which time has as yet not elapsed, Vermeersch-Creusen then conclude that such knowledge on the part of the priest establishes a sufficient objective basis for his belief that his faculties also will run that length of time. And, even though it were later shown that by way of exception his faculties were not intended to last that long, any act of jurisdiction which he had posited under the influence of this probability was valid because of the application of canon 209. In the same manner Coronata [328] considers the fact that in a certain diocese faculties are renewed on a particular day as a sufficient reason for a priest who had secured jurisdiction in that diocese to feel that he also has faculties until the day specified for the renewal of jurisdiction according to the custom and practice of that diocese.

Thus, whatever might be said of the value of the particular examples that these and other authors cite, so much is certain: they agree that there must be present a probability sufficiently objective to gain the assent of a prudent man. This attitude of the authors will be even better understood when the reader will study the article in reference to the licit use of jurisdiction under the conditions of canon 209. For the present it may be useful to note very summarily that, while the greater number of the authors requires a very good reason before conceding the liceitness of the use of jurisdiction in common error, these same authors require almost no special reason on the part of the priest to posit these same jurisdictional acts in cases of positive and

[327] *Epitome,* I, n. 284.
[328] *Institutiones,* I, 292.

probable doubt when the latter exists as a doubt both *of law* and *of fact.* In this conviction they certainly reflect their belief that the priest may have jurisdiction even independently of the Church's readiness to supply it were it really needed.[329] But the conviction that jurisdiction is possessed would be far-fetched and would amount to nothing more than inconsequential surmise if it rested exclusively on a sense of personal assurance and subjective certainty on the part of the priest. A true conviction, however, is a judgment based on a careful analysis of *evidence.* Such a judgment excludes all prudent fear of its deduction being untrue and therefore accepts as true the conclusion at which it has arrived. It is an interpretation of facts and circumstances that is truthlike, in harmony with reality, since the predicate of every opinion is the word "probable." [330]

a. Decisions of the Roman Rota

It will undoubtedly be a point of some interest to search into the decisions of the Rota and seek out several authoritative judgments regarding the value of personal certitude for the enjoyment of the benefits of the suppletory principle of canon 209. Of course, when one realizes that it was only since the issuance of the Code that it became a universally held doctrine that the Church will supply in cases of positive and probable doubt of fact, and that in reality only a few cases in regard to the possibility of using canon 209 as the deciding factor have appeared since that time among the decisions of the Rota, one understands that the Rota cases can hardly be said to present a complete picture, a complete authoritative handling of the problems that are bound to occur in regard to the applicability of canon 209 to doubts of fact. However, this much can not be gainsaid. The decisions of the Rota indicate two very remarkable points: first of all, in none

[329] Cf., e. g., Vermeersch, *Theologia moralis,* III, n. 459: " . . . dum *in dubio positivo et probabili* meae jurisdictionis, Ecclesia me vult securum reddere, ita ut etiam in meum favorem *ad cautelam* iurisdictionem suppleat."

[330] John Henry Cardinal Newman, *Grammar of assent* (London: Longmans, Green & Co., 1903), p. 60.

of the cases were the judges convinced that the presence of good faith or of subjective certitude on the part of the priest was in itself sufficient reason to urge the application of canon 209; and secondly, the instances in which the Rota affirmed the presence of true probability of fact certainly had enough objective arguments to convince any prudent man. But it will be best to present a few cases to demonstrate this attitude of the Rota.

On at least two rather recent occasions the Rota indicated, by its probing manner of examining whether or not delegation was really given, that it was not so much interested in the *certitude* or personal assurance which invited a priest to feel that he was juridically competent to perform a jurisdictional or quasi-jurisdictional act, as in the objective basis upon which the certitude was founded.

The first case here to be noted concerns a marriage, at which the Rector of an English, non-parochial church in Rome assisted. The marriage took place in his own church. However, it must be observed that this priest did not possess a complete authorization for his act of assisting at this marriage. And, while he did secure the permission of the pastor of the bride to assist at the nuptials, he did not secure the necessary delegation of the pastor of the place wherein his church was situated. After some time the marriage was impugned on the ground of lack and deficiency of due juridical form. Let it be noted carefully that the Rota revealed that it was fully ready to admit that this rector was in good faith at the time of the marriage, that he was truly convinced that he was juridically competent to assist at the nuptials. In fact, the Rota even carefully analyzed how, because of his old age, this priest could easily confuse the *proper* pastor of the Tridentine legislation, who could assist at the marriage of his parishioners anywhere, with the *proper* pastor of the Code, who could assist at marriages only within the limits of his territory, or how easily he could confuse *valid* assistance, for which the delegation of the territorial pastor is necessary, and *licit* assistance, for which the permission of the pastor of the bride is to be secured if the marriage is to take place outside the limits of his parish. Yet, as a matter of fact, in this case the Rota did not deem that there was a sufficient objective basis for a true probability even to consider the application of canon 209. Thus ignorance, confusion and false certitude were *not* considered enough. The marriage was declared invalid because of the lack of proper delegation.[331]

In another case, in which a priest assisted at the marriage of one of his brothers, it is similarly to be noted that he acted only because he was *certain* that he was legally capable so to do. In fact, as further testimony bore out, this priest testified that the basis of this action was the assurance of another of his brothers, a priest, who told him that it was not necessary to seek the delegation of the proper pastor, because everything was already taken care of. But, again, the mere existence of certitude on the part of the priest who assisted was not considered enough. The Rota very carefully examined the details of the case; and, when it verified that the proper pastor did not give, and under the circumstances could not have given, the proper delegation, it declared the marriage invalid.[332]

Indeed, not only these two cases, but others, such as those presently to be adduced, show quite definitely that Girerd[333] and his followers are quite unjustifiably liberal and excessively radical when they teach that the mere presence of subjective certainty on the part of a priest is sufficient guarantee of the validity of whatever jurisdictional acts he performs. These cases, reveal that in the instances where the Rota agreed that a true probability of fact was verified there are found real arguments, objective reasons leading a prudent man to believe that the priests possessed then and there the requisite jurisdictional competence.

Thus, in one case, which was ultimately decided on the grounds of common error, the Rota very much in detail asserted that this

[331] S. R. R., *Nullitas matrimonii,* 20 Jan. 1931, *coram R. P. D. Arcturo Wynen,* dec. XXIX—*Decisiones,* XXIII (1931), 257, esp. n. 19.

[332] S. R. R., *Nullitas matrimonii,* 7 Aug. 1931, *coram R. P. D. Iulio Grazioli,* dec. XLII—*Decisiones,* XXIII (1931), 360-371, esp. 18.

[333] "La juridiction probable,"—*NRT,* LVIII (1931), 919.

particular case could have reached the very same decision, i.e., of validity, if proof had been adduced merely from the point of view that there was a true probability of fact present at the time of the performance of the marriage ceremony. Because it is quite interesting to note how careful and exacting the Rota was in verifying the presence of an objective probability without requiring moral certitude, it will be altogether appropriate to note what details the Rota adjudged as sufficient to engender the juridically required positive and probable doubt of fact.

The case[334] involved a Catholic soldier who married a Protestant woman in Vladivostok in 1920 before a priest who up to a very short time before the marriage had been a military chaplain in the Austro-Hungarian army. But, due to the vicissitudes of army life and to the political changes which came about, the chaplain deserted the Austro-Hungarian army to join the Czecho-slovakian legions that he might thus remain near the soldiers with whose spiritual care he had previously been charged. The objective fact was that, as a result of the political upheaval, this priest had lost his chaplaincy and, consequently, whatever jurisdictional power he had possessed in virtue of his chaplaincy, the very moment he deserted. However, he continued to minister to the soldiers, and, among others things, joined this particular couple in wedlock. Ultimately this marriage was upheld as valid on the ground that common error was present and, that therefore, canon 209 applied. However, the Rota stated very clearly that it thought the priest in question had, under the circumstances, sufficient positive and probable doubt as to his competence to insure the validity of any and all of his jurisdictional and quasi-jurisdictional acts. For, under the circumstances, he could easily think that he was still chaplain of *those* soldiers, i.e., of those men who were directly entrusted to his spiritual care. Then, again, he was never dismissed from his position as chaplain by any act of personal authority. Finally, as reliable testimony proved, he

[334] S. R. R., *Nullitas matrimonii,* 22 Nov. 1927, *coram R. P. D. Andrea Jullien,* dec. XI—*Decisiones,* XIX (1927), 464, esp. n. 14.

kept on exercising his duties as field-chaplain of the Çzecho-Slovakian troops.[335]

In another marriage case, also recently solved by the Rota, there is apparent the same tendency to require and to look for the objective ground of an opinion before admitting the possibility of using the second part of canon 209. This case involved a pastor in Havana who wanted to officiate at the marriage of two of his parishioners. But, inasmuch as the ceremony was to take place outside of the territorial limits of his parish, he needed, and, therefore, sought the proper delegation. This the Vicar General granted him. Later, that marriage was attacked as invalid on the ground of lack of proper form. The plaintiff alleged that the pastor, though he had obtained the authorization of the Vicar-General, failed to comply with the condition clearly set in this authorization, namely, " . . . *con anuencia del Sr. Cura Parroco correspondiente y previo el pago de sus derechos parochiales.*" In regard to this case, it is to be noted, the pastor felt at the time of assisting at the marriage that he was acting with all proper authorization and permission. But this certitude again was not adjudged sufficient in itself to insure the validity of the assistance. For, the Rota thoroughly probed the clause in its various possible meanings. And only after the Rota had established to its own satisfaction that in all probability the clause above cited was not inserted for validity, only then did it affirm that the priest in question acted validly. Even if he had no other arguments in his favor, so the Rota clearly stated, he had enough probability on his side to insure the application of canon 209.[336]

In summary, then, it may be said that these last two cases particularly show that the Church is ready and willing to recog-

[335] Cf. I. Haring, "Error communis und Eheassistenz,"—*LQS*, XC (1937), 311-312.

[336] S. R. R., *Nullitas matrimonii,* 20 Iun. 1931, *coram R. P. D. Francisco Parrillo,* dec. XXVIII—*Decisiones,* XXIII (1931), 249, n. 23: " . . . Quae cum ita sint, etsi alia deficerent argumenta ad valorem praesentis matrimonii sustinendum, hoc unum sufficeret, nempe dubium positivum et probabile de vi clausulae in concessione appositae, quo in casu iurisdictionem ab Ecclesia suppleri, concors DD. sententia et Codex arcte tenet (can. 209)."

nize the presence of positive and probable doubts of fact. But, it is also very clear that she means this doubt to be founded upon a certain amount of objectivity. She does not require moral certitude, as the Vladivostok case proves. And above all, it is quite evident that mere subjective conviction is of itself no argument for the juridical validity of whatever jurisdictional acts performed.

b. Examples

There is little room to question the frequency and the variety of the doubts of fact that can arise. Because of this variety the present list of practical examples for purposes of clarification and illustration, will be limited to such doubts of fact as are most apt to occur in the life of the average priest.

First, there is the case of a priest who has confessional jurisdiction, but who wonders whether or not he can exercise it here and now. He is faced, for example, with the problem of trying to decide whether or not a penitent's sin—which as such he has the right to absolve—has attached to it a reserved censure that precludes the absolution of the sin without the previous absolution of the censure itself. To begin with, this priest knows a few general principles that will guide him in his decision. Thus he knows that penalties must be strictly interpreted.[337] He likewise knows that a penalty can not be inflicted unless there be clear evidence that a delicit has been committed and was not legitimately prescribed.[338] He knows full well the requirement for the commission of a delict,[339] the necessity of all elements, moral and material, to be verified.[340] He remembers above all the saving

[337] Canons 15 and 19.

[338] Canon 2233, § 1.

[339] Canon 2195.

[340] S. R. R., *In Recentiores,* Decis. 274, n. 16; D'Annibale, *Summula,* I, n. 317: "Itaque in poenis (et maxime in censuris) dubiis, semper pro reo respondendum est, seu factum (delictum), seu jus dubium sit, seu positivum sit dubium, seu negativum. Et (I) si factum; nempe si dubites: 1) utrum deliqueris, vel utrum graviter; sive 2) utrum delictum consummatum fuerit, vel utrum habuerit effectum; sive demum 3) si poena est f.s., utrum sententia lata fuerit, an minus. (II) Jus, idest: 1) cum

prescripts of cannon 2229. And, in regard to the reservation of the censure, he realizes that if there be any doubt of law or of fact as to its existence in a particular instance the reservation does not bind.[341]

Thus, in relation to the problem before him, the priest can have a real doubt as to whether the penitent, first of all committed a mortal sin, whether he committed a delicit in the sense of canon 2195, whether the prescripts of canon 2229 will come to his rescue, whether, finally, the reservation has been clearly determined in regard to this particular case. If on any of these points the priest has real doubt, so that there is real and objective probability on the side of the opinion which holds that the penitent did not contract the reserve censure, then the priest can lawfully and effectively absolve in virtue of canon 209.

Another rather common problem for the average priest is the determination of just when the juridically required conditions are verified in reference to canons 882, 1043-1045, 2252-2254. Again, the priest has the general principle to fall back upon, i.e., that his judgment need not of its essence be objectively correct, but that it must be based on reasons which are objective in character. For example, in general and ordinary conditions the disorder of a catarrhal cold or an attack of biliousness, or a natural indisposition brought on either by old age or general exhaustion, can not be considered a grave illness in the sense of these canons. On the other hand, certain sicknesses are very weakening and of such serious gravity that, although the danger of death is not imminent, they are liable soon to induce it. The confessor can certainly act in cases such as pneumonia, rheumatism (not merely pains concomitant with a chronic case of this), pleurisy, or stubborn siege of grippe when it is accompanied with numerous, though minor complications. Again there are other illnesses which are relatively grave because special circumstances weaken

non satis appareat, utrum poena sit adnexa delicto a te perpetrato; vel si constet esse adnexam. 2) utrum tu legi, vel poenae hujusmodi sis obnoxius; vel, si ei es obnoxius, 3) utrum sit latae an f.s."

[341] Canon 2245, § 4.

the powers of resistance on the part of the sick, e.g., the less malignant diseases in persons of self-piteous and non-resilient temperament, in persons whose physical constitution has been debilitated by age, or destitution, and in persons whose vitality is at low ebb in view of multiplied encroachments upon their health throughout the past, although of themselves these disorders would not constitute sufficient reason for the beneficial application of these canons. In such a situation a minister need not have physical certitude of the danger of death. If he has a prudent doubt, i.e., a doubt which rests on a commonly acknowledged foundation, he may act because, even should it prove that he was objectively wrong in his diagnosis, the Church supplies the necessary jurisdiction according to the prescripts of canon 209.[342]

All this bears out Creusen's observation[343] that, even though in probability of fact there is much more room for the priest's personal act of appraisal than in doubts of law, nevertheless the priest should not hastily feel himself committed secure in the probability of his doubt without having an objectively sufficient motive, i.e., a circumstance of fact which leads reasonably to believe in his likely possession of the necessary jurisdictional power. The true test of this probability, one must insist, is whether or not such a doubt of fact can be defended in the external forum as warranting the assent of a prudent man.

4. *Conclusion*

In conclusion it may be noted that it is the intention of the Church that her ministers be able and properly fitted for the task of fulfilling their mission. That is why she trains them and makes them undergo examinations. But she realizes that she can not immunize them against every likelihood of erroneous and mistaken judgments. And thus, to safeguard as well as she can the spiritual good of her faithful, to remedy the jurisdictional incompetency on the part of the minister, and to spare him all un-

[342] McCormick, *Confessors of religious,* pp. 222-223.
[343] "Réponse du P. Creusen,"—*NRT,* LVIII (1931), 922.

due anxiety the Church supplies her needed jurisdiction. But it is definitely not the Church's wish that any one should dare to presume any jurisdictional powers when he is certain that he is deprived of them, or even as long as he is plausibly uncertain that he is in possession of them. And thus all light, unsubstantial, negative, and therefore improbable doubts do not become beneficial factors for the supplying of jurisdiction, for they are all, taken singly or even collectively, juridically inadequate to make any rightful demands upon the jurisdictional favors which canon 209 is ready to bestow.

ARTICLE II. APPPLICATION OF CANON 209

It is quite evident that when authors expound the suppletory principle of canon 209 they almost invariably treat it with reference to the sacrament of penance. While it is perfectly true that the penitential forum offers an excellent field for the exemplification of this doctrine, and while it may be admitted that in this forum perhaps the most frequent use of this canon is apt to be made by the average priest in the course of his ministry, still there is a definite danger that some may, on that very account, more or less identify the doctrine of the supplying of jurisdiction with the penitential tribunal and thereby fail to realize that canon 209 has a much broader field of operation and application. As a matter of fact, it applies to *all kinds of jurisdictional activity*. It applies equally to the power to absolve from censures, to grant indulgences, to dispense from matrimonial impediments, to direct a judicial process, etc. Unless a person does realize the broad scope of this canon's applicatory force he will run the risk of adopting and following an interpretation that may not stand the test of textual and contextual criticism.

I. In Reference to the Twofold Forum

While it is true that the term *jurisdiction* comprises legislative, judicial and executive power, it has been noted with sufficient insistence that not always are these three phases of jurisdictional power to be found in one and the same person. On the contrary, any of these three powers may be given to individuals separately and in varying degrees. Likewise the Legislator may put even further limitations upon the exercise of this jurisdictional power, as, for example, in regard to the forum in which this power is to be exercised. Thus, a confessor enjoys jurisdiction in only the *internal* forum. Thus, the jurisdiction of the vicar-general is in the *external* forum.

Now, from the text of the law it is evident that the benefits of canon 209 are not restricted to sacramental jurisdiction. They are common to every use of jurisdictional power, regardless of the forum in which it is exercised. Of course, there is the ever present proviso that the requisite conditions of common error or of positive and probable doubt be fulfilled.

However, there must here be noted a certain precaution which, in all likelihood, is already apparent. As canon 202, § 1, very clearly states, an act of jurisdiction in the external forum, whether ordinary or delegated, holds also for the internal forum. But the act of one having jurisdiction for the internal forum only does not hold in the external forum. For example, the Pontifical Commission for the Interpretation of the Canons of the Code has authoritatively declared that an absolution granted in virtue of the power conferred upon any priest by canon 882 is limited to the internal forum and cannot be extended to the external forum.[1] The absolution from a censure, therefore, granted in virtue of the power of the said canon 882, has its effect only *coram Deo* and is not necessarily recognized *coram Ecclesia.*[2] Consequently, if a priest would employ the power which is accorded him by canon 882, namely, to absolve from some reserved and notorious censure when the penitent is in danger of death, but would use it in a case wherein, though full moral certainty is not had, yet a positive and probable doubt militates for the presence of such danger and thereby brings the suppletory principle of canon 209 into effective operation, it must be remembered that the absolution from the censure given in this case need not be recognized by the ecclesiastical Superior in and for the external forum unless the granting of it is established by proof, or at least by legitimate presumption.

In attempting to determine whether any power has been

[1] *PCI,* 28 Dec. 1927, *AAS,* XX (1928), 61.

[2] For it is true that the absolution need not be acknowledged in the external forum except upon the conditions mentioned by canon 2251: "Si absolutio censurae detur in foro externo, utrumque forum afficit; si in interno, absolutus, remoto scandalo, potest uti talem se habere etiam in actibus fori externi; sed, nisi concessio absolutionis probetur aut saltem legitime praesumatur in foro externo, censura potest a Superioribus fori externi, quibus reus parere debet, urgeri, donec absolutio in eodem foro habita fuerit."

granted for both *fora* or only for the internal forum, one will use the principle expressed in canon 202, §§ 2-3, that is to say, the restriction of a power exclusively to the internal forum will not obtain unless it is expressly so indicated or unless the nature of power conferred is such that the power can solely and simply be exercised in the internal forum. In the event that the power granted is not expressly restricted for use in the internal forum, such power is understod as given for both *fora,* unless its very operation can not be actualized except in the internal forum. Moreover, in the event that a power is granted for the internal forum, that power may be exercised in the non-sacramental as well as the sacramental forum, save in a matter that essentially requires the sacramental forum for its discharge, as would obtain whenever there is question of the power to absolve from sin or of a power which is granted to a confessor in his sole and exclusive capacity of confessor.[3]

B. In Reference to Ordinary and Delegated Power

Granting that the Church supplies jurisdiction in foth *fora,* canonists are not uniformly agreed in further defining the limits of the applicatory force of canon 209. Their points of difference may well be summed up under three headings. First of all, some canonists are not at all sure that the Church will not supply in any but strictly ordinary jurisdictional power. Others oppose any and all applicability of canon 209 to particular delegation. There is further disagreement as to whether or not the Church supplies any power other than that of jurisdiction. Specifically, in the light of the last mentioned disagreement, there has been considerable dispute concerning the applicability of the suppletory principle to the act of assistance at marriage.

This study, at the risk of some little repetition, will perhaps gain its purpose best by considering, first of all, the extent of canon 209's applicability to strictly jurisdictional acts. Ultimately, some treatment will be given to the question of its applicability to strictly non-jurisdictional acts. Because of the dis-

[3] Cf., e. g., canons 1043-1045.

putes about the peculiar character of the act of assistance at marriage, and because of the importance of this whole question in the external forum, detailed attention will be given to this problem midway between the treatment of the problem regarding strictly jurisdictional and strictly non-jurisdictional acts.

I. JURISDICTIONAL POWER

Introductory notions

When a person makes reference to the operation of the suppletory principle, he means that the power of jurisdiction which must be present for the validity of a certain act is wanting, and the Church must make up for this deficiency at the moment of the performance of the jurisdictional act. It does not matter for what reasons jurisdiction is lacking. It may be that this jurisdiction was never conferred upon the priest. It may have been conferred, but invalidly. It may have been conferred but does not extend to the territory in which he uses it or to the persons over whom he exercises it. Or it may have been conferred validly but was subsequently lost by the one who possessed it. A word may be said specially in regard to loss of jurisdiction by way of penalty.

With the exception of those who lay violent hands upon the person of the Holy Father [4] all others who possess jurisdiction may continue to exercise it validly, even though they have contracted the censure of excommunication, of suspension or of personal interdict. They may continue to do so in virtue of the direct prescripts of canons 2265, § 2, 2275, § 1, and 2284 until the penalty, or penalities, have been inflicted by a declaratory or condemnatory sentence. If, after such a sentence, anyone should venture to posit a jurisdictional act, he would act invalidly *unless* the conditions of canon 209 were fulfilled so as to insure the efficacious functioning of the suppletory principle.

As has already been seen in the preliminary notions, jurisdictional power may be ordinary or delegated. Delegated power, in

[4] Canon 2243, §1, 1°.

turn, may be *ad universitatem causarum* or for one or another case.

The problem of the applicability of canon 209 to the various kinds of jurisdictional power is not the same in cases where the Church supplies her jurisdiction because of common error as it is in cases of positive and probable doubts whether of law or of fact. The problem has many more angles in connection with common error. The reason for the difference can be ultimately ascribed to the fact that an entirely different purpose inspires the legislator to supply in the separate cases of common error and of positive and probable doubt. For, in the case of common error the intention of the legislator is to forestall a common loss or a peril to the common good when it is certain that the priest performing some act has not the jurisdictional competency required by the law for validity. In the case of probable and positive doubt it is not clear that the priest lacks jurisdictional competency in the matter in question. When positive and probable arguments are present to indicate the possession of the required jurisdiction, the Church supplies because she wishes to render the minister of the jurisdictional power secure and free from undue worry and anxiety.[5]

1. In Positive and Probable Doubt Either of Fact or of Law

Since the purpose of the law which supplies jurisdiction in cases of probable doubt, be it a doubt of fact or be it a doubt of law, may be pressing even in the case of a priest delegated for one case, it is quite clear that there are no restrictions in canon 209 in this regard. The only thing to remember is that the doubt must be of such a nature as to warrant its being called *positive* and *probable*. Some further elucidation will be offered in regard to this point in the consideration of the applicability of canon 209 to delegated assistance at marriage.

2. In Common Error

a. Ordinary Power

Ordinary power is that which is attached to an office by the

[5] Fink, "Eheassistenz und allgemeiner Irrtum,"—*Theologie und Glaube,* XXVI (1934), 594.

law itself. This power may be *proper* or *vicarious* according as the agent exercises it in his own name or in the name of the one whose vicar he is. But in either event it is a permanent power, at least in the sense that the incumbent thereof enjoys an abiding title to the same unless and until he be deprived of it either by law or by the decision of his legitimate superior.[6] Certain actions are presumed under the law to signify an incumbent's tacit renunciation of an office.[7] In like manner certain criminal actions—and they are few—bring upon their perpetrator an *ipso facto* deprivation of their offices,[8] and certain other actions—and these are many—carry with them a similar loss of office which loss, however, is not sustained until declared by the proper superior.[9] When an ordinary deprives a cleric of an office, the ordinary must very carefully distinguish the character of the office. And, according as that office is a removable one or an irremovable one, the ordinary must follow out the prescripts ot the law.[10]

There has never been, nor is there, any question in the minds of authors as to the applicability of canon 209 to the jurisdictional acts of one falsely believed by way of common error to possess ordinary power. Prescinding for the present from the dispute as to whether or not an *officium* in the strict sense is a term correlative with ordinary power, there is no question that in the case of ordinary power there is present an *officium* which is both *public* and *permanent* and concerning the possession of which even prudent men can be deceived. And regardless of whether the incumbent of such an office retain his position and continue to exercise his official duties in good faith or in bad, objectively his jurisdictional actions would be a source of real peril to the common good were they not validated from the very

[6] Canon 192, § 1.

[7] Canon 188.

[8] Canon 2343.

[9] Cf., e. g., canons 2177, n. 3; 2180; 2181; 2314, § 1, n. 2; 2331, § 2; 2324; 2336, § 1; 2336, § 2; 2340, §2; 2343, §2; 2345; 2346; 2354, § 2; 2359, §§ 2-3; 2368, § 1; 2384; 2394, n. 2; 2401; 2403; 2405.

[10] Canon 192, §§ 2-3. Cf. also canons 2157-2161, § 1; 2147-2153; 2401.

moment of their performance, by the suppletory principle of canon 209. The *raison d'être* of this canon may be said to be especially fulfilled in instances of the exercise of such power.

But, as Gasparri would seem to indicate,[11] and as the practice of the Sacred Congregation of the Council[12] and of the Tribunal of the Rota definitely betoken,[13] the mere possession of such a public office is not sufficient reason to argue that the principle of canon 209 immediately begins to function. On the contrary, the element of *common error* must first be a realized fact. Thus, for example, parish priests and bishops who solemnly take possession of their benefices are immediately from that moment considered by their subjects as the lawful possessors of said parishes and dioceses. In like manner, any other person solemnly and publicly installed in an office enjoys factually the common reputation on the part of the faithful of being the one to whom they are to have recourse in their needs.

On the other hand, all the others, who may be entrusted with a public office, but who are not so solemnly inducted or presented in some other way to the attention of the community as lawful incumbents of the office, simply cannot be said to appear to the community at large as legitimate office-holders. In fact, in such a case, even though it be true that their ecclesiastical office is public *de iure,* the people are not yet aware of their status. In cases such as these common opinion about an individual's position or power will develop only after he has performed repeated acts in his position with the tacit approval of his proper superior. Only then, when the error concerning the individual becomes sufficiently common, does the suppletory principle become effective in regard to his jurisdictional activity.[14] In other words, in order to create the deception of the

[11] *De matrimonio,* II, n. 936.

[12] S. C. Conc., Mar. 10, 1770, *Caesaraugustana matrimonii—Thesaurus resolutionum,* XXXIX (1770), 51-56.

[13] S. R. R., *Nullitas matrimonii,* 22 Nov. 1927, *coram R. P. D. Andrea Jullien,* dec. LI—*Decisiones,* XIX (1927), 453-465.

[14] Toso, "De errore communi ad normam can. 209,"—*Jus Pont.,* XVIII (1938), 168.

community there must be a cause of error which is not only public *de iure*, as verified in relation to every ecclesiastical office, but which is also public *de facto*. And it is readily understandable how such factually public common error would be easier to establish in regard to an episcopal or parochial office than in regard to a judicial or penitential office.

Once the common error is verified to the effect that a certain person is commonly regarded to be the legitimate incumbent of a certain office, it follows that all his jurisdictional acts are thereafter valid as long as this common error persists. Thus, for example, a commonly, but falsely, reputed pastor validly absolves from sin,[15] dispenses from the impediments of marriage,[16] and dispenses from the law of assisting at Mass on Sundays and holy days as well as from the law of fast and abstinence.[17] And, a very important point to keep in mind is that in virtue of the common error, which factually though only virtually exists among the parishioners, the confessions of lone individuals are valid, even though they should happen to be heard in extreme privacy. In the same manner, each and every possessor of ordinary jurisdictional power posits valid acts only if and when there is common error in regard to his competency.

However, it must be kept in mind that the law of canon 209 supplies only that jurisdictional power which the holder of the office would legitimately exercise, e. g., as canonical pastor or local ordinary.[18] In other words, supposing that X is falsely, but commonly, regarded to be pastor of parish Y, one concludes that all parochial jurisdictional activity of X is valid because of the operation of the suppletory principle. For, when the people

[15] Canon 873, § 1.

[16] Canons 1043-1045.

[17] Canon 1245.

[18] Cf. Toso, "Jurisdictio quando ab ecclesia suppleatur,"—*Jus Pont.*, XVII (1937), 104; C. Berutti, "De jurisdictione quae ipso jure delegatur ad audiendas fidelium confessiones,"—*Jus Pont.*, XIV (1934), 61: "Praeterea, non maior seu amplior iurisdictio ab ecclesia suppletur in errore communi, quam quae reapse in casu particulari correspondet muneri vel officio, cuius ratione error communis causatur."

erroneously consider X as legitimate pastor, there is an implicit, if not an explicit, judgment on their part that X, in view of his title as pastor, can perform all properly parochial functions. In such a frame of mind any of these people might approach the pastor for his ministration to them in their individual needs. Because the people are in a probable common error about a fact the Church supplies all the jurisdiction necessary to validate X's parochial activity. However, if X were to arrogate to himself powers greater than those which the Code confers upon pastors or if he were to exercise invalidly what powers he has, obviously he would be arrogating to himself powers beyond the scope of the title of the office which he is erroneously supposed to possesses legitimately. Quite clearly, X cannot plead the existence of a common error as a title insuring the validity of even such jurisdictional activity.

Thus, for example, the Code is very specific in stating that the pastor cannot validly grant the faculty of preaching in the parish to any one who does not possess the right to do so either by law, or *ex officio,* or by the delegation of the Ordinary of the place.[19] Again, even though a pastor has ordinary jurisdiction for hearing confession, he cannot in virtue of that power delegate another priest to hear confessions. Nor can he extend his jurisdiction beyond the limits within which it is restricted by law.[20] In a similar way a pastor would overstep the bounds of his power if he attempted to delegate someone other than a *vicarius cooperator* to assist at all the marriages in the parish,[21] or to delegate someone to take his place in witnessing the *sponsalia* of some couple in his parish.[22] For, although the pastor enjoys *ordinary* jurisdiction *pro cura animarum* in the internal forum, these are limitations which in accord with the prescript of canon 199, § 1, the legislator has very carefully specified. In a very similar way, a bishop would be acting invalid-

[19] Canons 1327, 1328, 1337.

[20] Cf. canons 199, § 1; 873, 878. Cf. also *PCI*, 16 Oct., 1919—*AAS*, X (1919), 477.

[21] Canon 1096, § 1.

ly if he would presume to appoint parish priests to parishes reserved to the Holy See for appointment,[23] or to disregard the laws in the Code concerning the appointment and reappointment of synodal and pro-synodal judges.[24] Obviously, as in the case of the pastor, so in the case of the bishop each and every attempt to arrogate to himself a power over and above his office will result in invalidity. And, in the event of such invalid appointments to parishes or to judgeships, it is to be remembered that subsequent common error about the competency of the person so appointed does not validate the invalid appointment. The common error merely brings into operation the suppletory principle. As a result the jurisdictional activity proper to the office which the person is thought legitimately to hold is validated.[25]

b. Delegated Power

It can not be doubted that the older canonists were agreed in holding that the jurisdictional acts of a person illegitimately holding a public office (*munus publicum*),[26] *officium . . . potestatis publicae*,[27] would be valid if and when the requisite conditions for the supplying of jurisdiction were fulfilled. That is a teaching that no canonists can, or would dare, gainsay.

However, there is evident among some canonists today too strong a tendency to insist upon the presence of such an *officium* as being identified with ordinary power, in accordance with the more frequent and almost general, though not altogether exclusive, acceptation of the term *officium* as defined and delineated in canons 145, § 1, and 197, § 1. Such a ten-

[22] Canon 1017; S. C. Conc., 28 (31) Mar. 1908—*ASS*, XLI (1908), 289, ad VI.

[23] Canon 1435, § 1.

[24] Canons 385-388 and 1574.

[25] Cf., for the sake of review, the considerations concerning the applicability of canon 209 in cases of common error of fact and in cases ol common error of law, as on pp. 163-167.

[26] Suarez, *De censuris*, Disp. XIX, sect. I, nn. 9-10; *De poenitentia*, Disp. XXVI, sect. VI, n. 7.

[27] Pirhing, *Jus canonicum*, l. II, tit. I, n. 83 ss.

dency, for example, is visible in Toso[28] and, to a much more notable degree, in the unsigned article written in *L'Ami du Clergé*.[29]

However, the historical analysis has shown us that, while the older authors argued for the application of the suppletory principle to persons enjoying a stable, public office, many of them argued also for the application of this self-same principle to persons enjoying simply delegated power. Thus, as can easily be recalled, Panormitanus,[30] Pontius[31] and Sanchez[32] are notable among the authorities who argued for the application of this suppletory principle to persons even when these were delegated for only one act of the exercise of jurisdictional power. Thus, others, as Guillermus de Cuno,[33] who would not go so far, taught nevertheless that the principle would be applicable to cases of delegation *ad universitatem causarum*.

As one studies the disputes of the older canonists on this score, it becomes apparent that the *crux* of the whole dispute centered about the question: Is the common good or public utility jeopardized or imperiled in a given case of jurisdictional activity? If the presence of such a danger had been proved to the satisfaction of the old canonists, indubitably their objection to this principle's application would have been swept away and they would have agreed to its application to every such instance of the exercise of jurisdictional power. Identically the same question faces the canonist today. Presently the evidence will be adduced which supports the different opinions concerning the applicability or non-applicability of canon 209 to cases of general and particular delegation.

[28] "Jurisdictio quando ab ecclesia suppleatur,"—*Jus Pont.*, XVII (1937), 100-102.

[29] XLVII (1930), 651.

[30] Ad c. 22, X, *de rescriptis*, I, 3, n. 3.

[31] *De sacramento matrimonii*, lib. V, cap. 19, n. 11.

[32] *De matrimonio*, Tom. I, lib. III, disp. 22, n. 61.

[33] Cf. Panormitanus, ad c. 22, X, *de rescriptis*, I, 3, n. 10.

(a.) Universal Delegation

Universal delegation (*delegatio ad universitatem causarum*) is delegation which extends to every species of power within the competence of the delegator or at least to one determined class of offices.[34] Thus, a delegated priest, commissioned by the pastor to take full charge of parochial affairs during the pastor's absence, or a delegated judge, authorized to proceed in all matrimonial cases of a certain place, or of a certain kind, or for a certain length of time, would be considered delegated *ad universitatem causarum.*[35]

Precisely because this section is intended to consider a priest who has no ordinary power, no *officium,* but only jurisdiction delegated *ad universitatem causarum,* it may be well to note with Toso[36] that power which is delegated *ad universitatem causarum* is sometimes conjoined with an ecclesiastical office and sometimes not. Thus, the jurisdiction to hear the confessions of the faithful—unless there be question of the office of the local ordinary and the canon penitentiary in relation to the faithful of their proper diocese, or of the office of a pastor in relation to the subjects of his proper parish—is certainly a power which is delegated *ad universitatem causarum,* i. e., for all cases brought to the sacramental forum except, of course, the isolated cases reserved either *a iure* or *ab homine.* And yet a cleric possessing such jurisdiction can not be said to have obtained an ecclesiastical office in the full, canonical and strict acceptance of the term. For there is no reception of such an office whenever the recipient does not simultaneously contract a *habitual obligation* of exercising its power. A priest's mere faculty of hearing confessions in a diocese does not give rise to any obligation that necessitates the use of his faculty, except under certain circumstances of need when the precept of christian charity, but not that of the

[34] D'Annibale, *Summula,* I, n. 71; Vermeersch-Creusen, *Epitome,* I, n. 280.

[35] Cf. Kearney, *The principles of delegation,* p. 59.

[36] "Jurisdictio quando ab ecclesia suppleatur,"—*Jus Pont.,* XVII (1937), 102.

virtue of commutative justice, may constrain him to employ his faculty with a view to filling an obligation in charity.[37]

On the other hand, many authors insist,[38] a true *officium* is conferred upon a cleric who is appointed as a *vicarius cooperator.* As a consequence, they declare that the " . . . parochial assistant . . . enjoys the radical potentiality of an ordinary vicarious power in the exercise of his subordinate parochial ministry. They are careful not to make their statement absolute and unconditional because of the evident possible limitations lurking in the clause *'nisi aliud expresse caveatur'* contained in the canon 476, § 6."[40]

This interpretation is not without its arguments to give it some recommendation. However, it seems that the intrinsic arguments against it are too strong to allow a person to hold it with any great amount of security. Moreover, the extrinsic testimony of authors who maintain that assistants have no other but delegated powers, and consequently no strict ecclesiastical office, could be multiplied on all sides.[41]

However interesting this question might be, and regardless of how it should ultimately be solved, only this needs to be said at this time: if the power of a *vicarius cooperator,* and if any other such universally authorized power attains to the dignity of an *officium,* then, in the presence of the requisite circumstances, as has just been seen in the preceding section, the suppletory principle will undoubtedly function. If, on the other hand, the power of the *vicarius cooperator* is merely a universally *delegated* power, and not at all an ordinary power, then it

[37] Canon 892, § 2.

[38] Fanfani, *De iure parochorum* (Taurini-Romae, 1924), n. 251, B, 6; Coronata, *Institutiones,* I, n. 492 3°, b; I. Stocchiero, "De jurisdictione vicariorum paroecialium,"—*Jus Pont.,* XI (1931), 228-231; Toso, "Jurisdictio quando ab ecclesia suppleatur,"—*Jus Pont.,* XVII (1937), 102.

[40] Bastnagel, *The appointment of parochial adjutants and assistants,* p. 142; cf. also footnote 48 on the same page for an enumeration of these authors.

[41] Cf. Bastnagel, *The appointment of parochial adjutants and assistants,* pp. 142-145, for a discussion regarding these points.

remains to be seen whether or not canon 209 will function in his regard or in regard to any other universal delegation of power.

First of all, it is to be noted that the text of canon 209 does not at all exclude delegated power from the ambit of its suppletory benefits. Indeed, canon 1606 explicitly declares that canon 209 is applicable to *delegated* judges. Thus, at least this is clear: the scope of canon 209 in its application is *not* limited to ordinary power. Therefore, provided the requisite conditions of common error or of doubt are fulfilled, there can be no doubt that canon 209 will apply to delegation *ad universitatem causarum.*

In opposition to those who would insist upon the presence of an *officium* before agreeing that the Church would supply, one might well note that many canonists who hold that an *officium* in the strict sense of canons 197, § 1, and 145, § 1, postulates the presence of some ordinary power do not consider it at all prejudicial to their theory to hold that canon 209 can apply even in cases where there is present no *officium* in the strict sense. Thus Chelodi,[42] De Meester,[43] Coronata[44] and Badii[45] readily hold that canon 209 can apply in cases of common error concerning delegated as well as ordinary power. While there might be some question as to whether these authors meant to say that they believe this principle to apply in cases of common error concerning even a particular delegation, there can be no doubt raised about these authors' conviction that canon 209 is applicable at least to cases of common error concerning universal delegation.

It might further be noted how others, like Toso,[46] in trying to maintain the necessity of an *officium* before the Church will begin to supply, finally yield ground and admit that the Church supplies in cases of delegation *ad universitatem causarum.* But, it is interesting to note how Toso defends his stand about the necessity of the *officium.* He does not say that the Church

[42] *Ius de personis,* n. 130.

[43] *Compendium,* I, n. 481.

[44] *Institutiones,* I, n. 291, I, 1.

[45] *Institutiones,* n. 149.

[46] "Jurisdictio quando ab ecclesia suppleatur,"—*Jus Pont.,* XVII (1937), 102.

supplies in such a case to safeguard the common good, which can be brought into jeopardy even by one who has not a strict *officium* . . . rather, says Toso, it is because power, so universally delegated, continually offers a foundation for the constitution of a public office.

Indeed, it seems more reasonable to hold, with Badii,[47] that it is quite easily demonstrable that in the case of a priest who is by common error thought to possess jurisdiction *ad universitatem causarum* the common good and public utility may be seriously jeopardized. And that is the ultimate reason why the Church will supply.

But here again, as in the case of ordinary power, it must be kept in mind that the mere fact that a priest invalidly possesses such a universal delegation is not sufficient evidence to argue to the immediate applicability of canon 209. On the contrary, the requisite condition of common error must be verified. And, again, it is easily understood how a solemn presentation to a parish or to a diocese might create common error from the very beginning. In the event that such a public fact, grasped by the faithful, is lacking, it can readily be seen that common error will not become a reality until and after repeated acts have been posited by the incumbent.

In brief summary, then, canon 209 may well be said to be applicable in the case of common error concerning universal delegation; for universal delegation, if invalidly given or received, may frequently indeed become an occasion of far-reaching evils and of disciplinary confusion, which the Church always wishes to avoid for the common good of the faithful.

(b) Delegation for One Case

The next problem to claim attention is concerned with the applicability of canon 209 in the case of particular delegation. Many authors, as will be seen more specifically in the study of this canon's applicability in the case of a particular delegation

[47] *Institutiones*, n. 149.

to assist at marriage, hold strongly that this suppletory principle can function even in the cases of error in which a priest is mistakenly thought to be delegated for one or the other case. But it is evident that extrinsic arguments are worth only as much as the intrinsic arguments upon which they are built. And the two important questions that must be satisfactorily answered are: 1) Is common error present in such cases? and 2) Is there a concomitant involvement of the common good?

Delegation for one or the other case constitutes a particular delegation. In view of the special, highly individual character of this kind of delegation it is difficult to see how such a delegation would occasion the common error and involve the common good to the extent of postulating the application of canon 209. For its must be maintained that before the Church will begin to supply jurisdiction in any case common error must be present. This common error must be real and not merely interpretative. To be real it must, of necessity, have a sense-perceptible cause. And, that such a cause be capable of producing so common an effect, as the Sacred Congregation of the Council[48] and the Tribunal of the Rota[49] clearly bear out, it is necessary, even in the case of a pastor or in an equivalent case of any other official person, that the cause of the error be public not only *de iure* but also *de facto*.

However, in consideration of the very nature of particular delegations, one sees quite clearly that in most cases there will be nothing more than a publicity *de iure*. In most cases the entire transaction will involve no more than one or a few individuals. And, when in exceptional instances there is present factual publicity, as shall be seen more in detail in regard to particular delegation to assist at marriage, the cause of the error, posited by the presence of a strange priest, will be so fleeting and momentary in character that there cannot be said to exist

[48] S. C. C., March 10, 1770, *Caesaraugustana matrimonii—Thesaurus resolutionum*, XXXIX (1770), 51-56.

[49] S. R. R., *Nullitas matrimonii*, 22 Nov. 1927, *coram R. P. D. Andrea Jullien*, dec. LI—*Decisiones*, XIX (1927), 453-465.

any danger to the common good at all. One may well with Cappello[50] maintain that in the case of a priest specially delegated for one case common error can scarcely ever be verified. Indeed, in the unusual exercise, in good faith or in bad, of a specially delegated power which was either conferred or received invalidly or not conferred at all, it is perfectly understandable that the Church will not supply the deficient jurisdiction, because the case remains distinctively private in character.[51]

If any one should counter, after the fashion of Ioannes of Imola[52] or of Panormitanus,[53] that public utility is involved by the mere fact of a commission of a power by a public person or of its execution in virtue of a public office,[54] one might well reply that it is not so certain that it would redound ultimately to the common good and public order of the Church if she were to supply in every case for the reason alleged. Would not such a practice nullify whatever jurisdictional laws and sanctions the Church has so carefully worked out? While it is true that, in accordance with Imola's and Panormitanus' views, a particular person would be spared his individual loss, ultimately confusion and disorder would intrude. To prevent the occurrence of such a general disturbance and disarray the Church has found it necessary and useful to enforce her jurisdictional laws when the immediate loss or the immediate danger of loss is only private. In reality such a loss is not beyond repair and, therefore, remains curable. The temporary inconvenience of the individual is permitted as an indirectly voluntary effect by the Church precisely in order that greater hardships and inconveniences might be spared the community as a whole.

Precisely on these grounds does Toso follow Innocent IV[55]

[50] *De sacramentis,* III, n. 671.

[51] D. (1. 3) 4: "Ex his, quae forte uno aliquo casu accidere possunt, iura non constituuntur."

[52] Cf. Felinus Sandeus, ad c. 22, X, *de rescriptis,* I, 3, n. 3.

[53] Ad c. 22, X, *de rescriptis,* I, 3, n. 10.

[54] Cf., e. g., Wilches, *De errore communi,* pp. 205-213, and especially p. 213.

[55] Ad c. 22, X, *de rescriptis,* I, 3, n. 1.

and Ioannes Andreae[56] in averring categorically that the Church never supplies in cases of particular delegation.[57] Salvador, completely won over by Toso's marshalling of his arguments, holds the same position.[58]

However, a word of consideration must be said in regard to the view expressed by Vermeersch.[59] Vermeersch held substantially the same position as Toso, namely, that the suppletory principle will ordinarily function only in regard to a person who possesses *habitual* power. However, he made an exception in regard to a person who had been delegated for one case but whose action by its very nature affects the entire community.

Thus, according to Vermeersch, if an assistant priest who is not validly delegated to dispense a whole community *per modum actus* from the obligation of fast or abstinence should nevertheless proceed, in good faith or in bad, to execute the delegation amidst the prevalent judgment on the part of the faithful that he has been properly empowered to act in this case, the provisions of canon 209 should be considered as functioning. In a similar manner, if a priest who is erroneously thought to be specially delegated to grant a certain community some extraordinary indulgence after the performance of the prescribed proper religious exercises should, notwithstanding the objective lack of such a delegation or the invalidity of its grant, proceed to confer the indulgence in question, his act would stand as valid.

Two reasons seem to militate against Vermeersch's view in this matter. First of all is the rare occurrence of such a case of common error. Admittedly this is not too strong an argument since the very essence of canon 209 postulates the presence of situations and problems which occur in the regular order of the day. Secondly, it seems that the maintenance of the common good by the

[56] Ad c. 22, X, *de rescriptis,* I, 3, n. 14.

[57] "Jurisdictio quando ab ecclesia suppleatur,"—*Jus Pont.*, XVII (1937), 102-105.

[58] "Error communis et iurisdictionis suppletio ab ecclesia,"—*BE,* XVII (1939), 375.

[59] *Theologia moralis,* III, n. 459.

aid of the suppletory principle is to be measured not by any negative factor which merely encompasses the failure of receiving some supererogatory benefit, though an entire community should miss gaining it, but by the positive factor which actually entails a veritable harm or detriment in respect of some service or ministration to which the faithful at large have a claim in equity, if not in justice itself. For these two reasons it seems to the author that the opinion of Innocent IV, as espoused by Toso and Salvador, is to be followed.

In conclusion, it may be said that canon 209 will probably not apply to cases of particular delegation, since there will not be the common error and the simultaneous perilous involvement of the common good.[60] If, in any case, it should be claimed that the suppletory principle does apply, in each instance it will be necessary to prove the verification of both these elements. An application and exemplification of this doctrine will be given soon in the forthcoming study concerning the applicability of canon 209 to delegation to assist at one marriage.

II. ASSISTANCE AT MARRIAGE

On account of the numerous controversies about the very practical question of assistance at marriage, it is imperative to trace the history of assistance at marriage; to demonstrate, if possible, what is the exact nature of such an act of assistance; to indicate how, and on what basis pre-Code authors applied the suppletory principle; and to show what is the post-Code understanding, teaching and practice on these points.

1. Historical Survey

The Christian teaching has ever stressed the sacredness of marriage. Christ had raised marriage to the dignity of a sacra-

[60] Cf., e.g., Jombart, "L'erreur commune,"—*NRT,* L (1923), 364; Creusen, "Preuve de l'erreur commune,"—*NRT,* L (1923), 366; Vermeersch, *Theologia moralis,* III, n. 459; Nevin, "Does doctrine concerning the supply of jurisdiction in *common error* apply in cases of matrimony?"—*ACR,* XIV (1937), 150.

ment,[61] and had declared it indissoluble.[62] This doctrine the Apostles preached to the world.[63] From the outset the Christians, conscious of the dignity of the married state, sought the blessing of their priest when embarking upon it.[64] It is only natural to inquire: Was this priestly blessing regarded as essential to marriage? Were marriage contracts which were entered into without this blessing considered invalid? As Carberry observes,[65] an examination of the Fathers, of the Pontiffs and of the early councils seems to indicate very strongly that the public celebration of marriage and the blessing of the priest were never considered as conditions affecting the validity of the marriage contract, but only as requisites for its lawful celebration. Secret marriages were admitted as valid, provided that the exchange of consent could be proved.

At the same time it must be noted that the Church did all in her power to persuade her children against the practice of clandestine nuptials. She even showed her serious attitude by means of various disciplinary measures.[66] There was also much particular legislation enacted to attain the same result.[67] But, because all these attempts, despite their good intentions, proved unavailing in stemming the tide of evils of clandestine marriages,

[61] Conc. Trid., sess. VII, *de sacramentis in genere,* can. 1; sess. XXIV, *de matrimonio, prooemium,* can. 1.

[62] Conc. Trid., sess. XXIV, *de matrimonio,* can. 2; sess. XXIV, *de reformatione matrimonii,* cap. 2.

[63] I Peter, III, 7; Ephes., V, 32.

[64] E. Westermarck, *Geschichte der menschlichen Ehe* (Jena, 1893), p. 429: "Der Begründer der christlichen Kirche hat für sie keinerlei Ceremonien vorgeschrieben, aber die Christen verlangten schon in den frühesten Zeiten aus freiem Willen den Segen ihrer Seelenhirten."

[65] *The juridical form of marriage* (The Catholic University of America, Canon Law Studies, n. 84, Washington, D. C., 1930), pp. 14-15.

[66] Cf., e. g., Compilatio II, c. 2, *de clandestina desponsatione,* IV, 3, wherein Alexander III strictly forbade marriage to be celebrated secretly. Cf. also can. 51 of the Fourth Lateran Council (1215)—*Collectio Regia,* VII, 58, or in c. 3, X, *de clandestina desponsatione,* IV, 3, which instituted the banns as a means of eradicating secret marriages.

[67] Cf. J. Carberry, *The juridical form of marriage,* p. 19.

the decree *Tametsi* was finally issued and the long sought for reform was in great measure accomplished.[68]

In substance the decree *Tametsi* declared null and void all marriages which were not celebrated before the pastor, or before the priest delegated by the said pastor or the local ordinary, and in the presence of two witnesses. The priest's presence was required *ad validitatem*. Canonists interpreted the words *praesente parocho* as referring to the proper pastor of either of the parties,[69] i. e., the pastor of the place where either of the parties had a domicile.[70] This teaching was confirmed by the Holy See.[71] After much disputation among the jurists in regard to quasi-domicile, it was decided by the Holy Office 1867 that a *parochus proprius* was also obtained by means of a quasi-domicile.[72]

There was never any serious difficulty encountered by canonists in determining the juridicial character of the priest's act of assistance at marriage. Thus Sanchez († 1610) plainly stated that the priest did not exercise any act of jurisdiction while assisting at a marriage. One of his strongest reasons was based on the fact that a marriage would have to be considered valid even though the witnessing priest were present emphatically against his will. This fact was of itself sufficient reason for regarding the act of assisting at a marriage as a non-jurisdictional act; for, as Sanchez reflected, jurisdictional acts could not be forced.[73]

Suarez († 1617) felt the same when he wrote that the pastor

[68] Conc. Trid., sess. XXIV, *de reformatione matrimonii,* c. 1.

[69] Carberry, *The juridical form of marriage,* p. 27.

[70] T. Sanchez, *De matrimonio,* Tom. I, lib. III, disp. 23, n. 1; J. M. Costello, *Domicile and quasi-domicile* (The Catholic University of America, Canon Law Studies, n. 60, Washington, D. C., 1930), p. 44.

[71] Urban VIII, Const. "Exponi vobis," 14 Aug., 1627—*Bullarium Romanum,* XIII, 537; Benedict XIV, const. "Paucis abhinc," 19 Mar., 1758—*Fontes,* n. 447.

[72] S. Cong. S. Off., *litt. encycl.,* 7 Jun., 1867—*Collectanea S. Congregationis de Propaganda Fide* (Romae: Ex Typographia Polyglotta, 1907), n. 1407.

[73] *De matrimonio,* Tom. I, lib. III, disp. 21, n. 4.

was only a *"testis qualificatus"*.[74] John De Lugo († 1660) further amplified this notion when he compared the task of the pastor as a witness to the function of a public notary, ". . . *ad quem non spectat examinare merita suscipientis, sed fidem facere et testari quae vidit.*"[75] Laymann († 1635) clarified the notion even more when he stated that this assistance was neither an act of jurisdiction nor an act of administration. To assist, according to him, was merely *"auctoritatem praebere."* [76] This concept of the character of the assistance of the priest at marriage was substantially held also by Benedict XIV († 1758).[77] Such, in fact, was the general teaching, as is further evidenced by the Salmanticenses,[78] Feije († 1894)[79] and Wernz († 1914),[80] and as illustrated in the *votum* given in a certain matrimonial case tried in Cologne.[81]

In fact there were but few who did not subscribe to this evaluation of the nature of the priest's act of assistance at marriage. There were certain so called "court theologians" of the Gallican and Josephinist school, who held that the presence of the priest constituted more than the act of a mere witness. They contended that the sacrament of matrimony was constituted by the blessing of the priest and that the contract was merely a necessary prerequisite. As Pohle-Preuss, however, remarked, this theory was contrived avowedly for the purpose of withdrawing matrimony from the jurisdiction of the Church and of handing it over to the state. Others, following the teaching of

[74] *Opera omnia* (Parisiis: Apud Ludovicum Vitte, 1861), Tom. XXIII, *De censuris,* Disp. XI, Sec. I, n. 24. Hereafter reference shall be made to this work with the title *De censuris.*

[75] *Disputationes selectae et morales,* Tom. III, *De sacramentis,* Disp. VIII, Sec. XIII, n. 216.

[76] *Theologia moralis* (Venetiis, 1719), lib. V, Tract. X, Pars II, cap. IV, n. 5.

[77] *De synodo dioecesana,* lib. XIII, c. 23, n. 6.

[78] *Cursus theologiae moralis* (Venetiis: Apud Nicolaum Pezzana, 1714), Tom. I, Tract. IX, cap. VIII, Punct. III, n. 33.

[79] *De impedimentis et dispensationibus matrimonialibus* (Lovanii: Typis Caroli Peters, 1885), n. 294.

[80] *Ius decretalium* (Romae, 1904), IV, nn. 176 and 180.

[81] S. C. C., 9 Sept., 1684—*ASS,* XXV (1892-1893), 656.

Melchior Cano († 1560), Estius († 1613), Sylvius († 1649), and Tournely († 1729), regarded the contract as the matter and the sacerdotal blessing as the form of the sacrament.[82]

A few other canonists regarded the priest's act of assisting at a marriage as an act of voluntary jurisdiction. In this vein Braun wrote.[83] He likened the assistance of a priest at a marriage to the presence of a judge at the process of emancipating a slave. He argued that as in the case of the emancipation so in the case of the marriage the official witness had to be present for validity. Therefore he concluded that such assistance was an act of voluntary jurisdiction. Convinced by such argument, F. Schmier († 1728)[84] also held the view that assistance at marriage was more than a mere act of witnessing, that it was an act of voluntary jurisdiction. However, despite these few dissenting voices the morally unanimous opinion before the Code, as St. Alphonsus testifies,[85] was that the priest assisting at a marriage was only an authorized witness and nothing more.

While this point, then, was generally admitted by jurists, there was a further difference of opinion in regard to the nature of the pastor's granting permission to another priest to assist at a marriage. Coninck († 1635), following Navarrus († 1586), considered such grants of permission acts of jurisdiction. Thus, also, Layman († 1635) clearly stated that he favored the view followed by Petrus de Ledesma († 1616) and by Coninck[86] But, again, the weight of authority regarded this granting of permission to assist at a marriage as not being an act of jurisdiction.[87]

[82] Cf. Pohle-Preuss, *The sacraments* (6. ed., St. Louis, Mo.: Herder, 1937), IV, 158.

[83] *Jurisdictio in genere et specie publica disputatione disposita* (Salisburgi, 1681), cap. IV, § 2, n. 32.

[84] *Jurisprudentia canonico-civilis* (Salisburgi, 1729), lib. I, Tr. V, cap. VIII, Sec. 2, nn. 44 ss.

[85] *Theologia moralis,* VI, nn. 1082, 1084, 1087.

[86] Laymann, *Theologia moralis,* lib. V, Tract. X, Pars II, cap. IV, n. 5.

[87] Cf., e. g., T. Sanchez, *De matrimonio,* Tom. I, lib. III, disp. 22, n. 7; Diana, *Coordinati, seu omnium resolutionum moralium tomi decem,* Tom. II, Tract. VI, res. 86, n. 2; Barbosa, *De officio et potestate parochi* (Ed. ultima, Lugduni, 1665), Pars II, Cap. XXI, n. 63; Wernz, *Ius decre-*

St. Alphonsus considered particularly apt and telling the reply of Sanchez to those who would consider the granting of permission to assist at a marriage as an act of jurisdiction. Sanchez noted that the faculty of granting such permission did not belong to the pastor in his capacity as pastor, but that it belonged to him in his capacity as the legitimate official witness designated as such by the Council of Trent and authorized with the power of substituting some other priest in his place.[88]

But, notwithstanding the non-jurisdictional character of the pastor's assistance at marriage, canonists nevertheless applied to this act of assistance the principle of the supplying of jurisdiction. That they did so quite universally is a matter of historical record that no one can reasonably gainsay.[89] This morally universal teaching of the canonists showed its traces in several decisions of the Roman Congregations concerning marriage cases which shall bear more minute examination as this study progresses.[90]

talium, Tom. I, n. 180, n. 11; Feije, *De impedimentis et dispensationibus matrimonialibus,* n. 294.

[88] St. Alphonsus, *Theologia moralis,* VI, n. 1084.

[89] Fagnanus, ad c. 1, X, *de schismaticis et ordinatis ab eis,* V, 8, n. 139; T. Sanchez, *De matrimonio,* Tom. I, lib. III, disp. 22, n. 61; Lessius, *De iustitia et iure,* lib. II, cap. 29, n. 67; Pontius, *De matrimonio,* lib. V, cap. 20, n. 9; Barbosa, *De officio et potestate parochi,* Pars II, cap. XXI, n. 53; *Collectanea doctorum in varia Concilii Tridentini decreta et canones,* ad sess. XXIV, *de ref.,* cap. 1, n. 79; Gonzalez-Tellez, *Commentaria perpetua in singulos textus quinque librorum decretalium* (Venetiis: Apud Nicolaum Pezzana, 1699), Tom. IV, tit. III, c. 3, n. 8; Pignatelli, *Consultationes canonicae,* Tom. IV, cons. III, n. 14; Reiffenstuel, *Ius canonicum universum,* lib. IV, tit. III, § II, n. 75; Schmalzgrueber, *Ius ecclesiasticum universum,* lib. II, Pars I, tit. 1, n. 22; Carrière, *De matrimonio* (Parisiis: Apud Mequignon Juniorem, 1837), Tom. II, n. 1320; Feije, *De impedimentis et dispensationibus matrimonialibus,* n. 291; P. Gasparri, *Tractatus canonicus de matrimonio* (Ed. altera, Parisiis, 1892), Tom. II, n. 913.

[90] Cf. Barbosa, *De officio et potestate parochi,* Pars II, Cap. XXI, n. 51 and n. 52, where he cited two matrimonial cases: one decided by the Sacred Cong. of the Council of Mar. 12, 1593; the other by the same Cong. on July 31, 1627. Both these cases upheld as valid the assistance of a putative pastor. Cf. also the report of a similar case on Mar. 10, 1770,

It stands to reason that, as a result of applying the suppletory principle to the case of assistance at marriage, there arose the same differences of opinion which have been individually studied earlier in this work. Thus, in reference to the necessity of a colored title, while authors rather commonly taught that common error would not suffice by itself to draw upon the benefits of the suppletory principle,[91] other authors, wielding a great influence despite their smaller numbers, insisted that a colored title was not an indispensable requisite.[92] The first school in its more rigid interpretation seemed to have the approval and confirmation of the Holy See; for, Pius VI in his Instruction to the Gallican Bishops declared that marriages contracted before a *parochus intrusus,* i.e., in the presence of one appointed to a pastorate by an incompetent authority, as was done by civil authorities in France towards the end of the 18th century, were invalid.[93] For that reason authors like Carrière, while recognizing the strength and authority of men like Pontius, Heislinger and Sambovius, felt that the more strict interpretation should be observed in practice.[94] However, he added that, in the event of a marriage contracted before a priest supported by common error

by this same Cong., in the *Thesaurus resolutionum,* XXXIX (1770), 51-56.

[91] Cf., e. g., Sanchez, *De matrimonio,* Tom. I, lib. III, disp. 22, n. 49; Feije' *De impedimentis et dispensationibus matrimonialibus,* n. 291; Kutschker, *Das Eherecht der katholischen Kirche nach seiner Theorie und Praxis* (Wien, 1857), IV, 383-385; De Becker, *De sponsalibus et matrimonio praelectiones canonicae* (Bruxellis, 1896), p. 94.

[92] Cf., e. g., Pontius, *De matrimonio,* C. XX, nn. 2 and 9; Heislinger, *De poenitentia,* casus XXI, n. 1 ss., and Sambovius, *Collationes Parisienses,* Tom. III, l. IV, cons. II, § 1—as cited by Carrière, *De matrimonio,* II, n. 1320.

[93] Cf. Pii VI Instr. *Laudabilem,* 26 Sept. 1791, ad epp. Gallos in Roskovány, *Matrimonium in ecclesia catholica* (Pestini: Typis Athenaei, 1870), I, 433. However, cf., Cerato, *De matrimonio,* n. 92; Cappello, *De sacramentis,* III, n. 661; Carberry, *The juridical form of marriage,* p. 55: "However, since no special title is required by the Code as a basis of common error, under the present law it may be possible to have a case of common error even though a pastor is a *parochus intrusus.*"

[94] *De matrimonio,* II, n. 1320.

alone, all hope should not be abandoned but, instead, recourse should be had to the Holy See for solution.

In a similar manner there came into the limelight the dispute about the applicability of the suppletory principle to the cases in which delegated power was mistakenly thought to be present. Thus, certain canonists, convinced that public utility was involved in the very act of assistance at marriage, taught that the Church would supply all requisite authorization in the cases wherein the lack of delegation for such assistance was commonly misapprehended.[95] But such a general conclusion did not seem so evident to all canonists. Many, as Carrière noted,[96] felt that there was real ground for doubt on this point, inasmuch as it did not seem to them that common utility was at stake in such individual instances. Certain canonists, like Kügler († 1721),[97] were quite ready to admit, however, that common utility would definitely be at stake in cases wherein a priest received a general delegation to assist at marriage. Hence, they felt that for such instances the suppletory principle would function.

Such, in brief resumé, was the state of affairs in regard to the priest's assistance at marriage under the decree *Tametsi*. Yet, although this decree did much to remedy the evils of clandestine marriage, it did not solve the problem in an altogether satisfactory manner. One of its serious drawbacks was the lack of its universal application as law, for the Council of Trent had left its promulgation to the prudence and discretion of the bishops the world over.[98] As a matter of later historical fact entire nations were left unaffected by this Tridentine decree, not to speak of the divergency of practice which sometimes occurred

[95] E. g., Sanchez, *De matrimonio,* Tom. I, lib. III, disp. 22, nn. 16 and 20; Pontius, *De matrimonio,* cap. XIX, n. 12.

[96] *De matrimonio,* II, n. 1324.

[97] As cited by Carrière, *De matrimonio,* II, n. 1324.

[98] Sessio XXIV, *de reformatione matrimonii,* cap. 1: "Ne vero haec tam salubria praecepta quemquam lateant, Ordinariis omnibus praecipit [ipsa Synodus Tridentina], ut *cum primum potuerint,* curent hoc decretum populo publicari, . . . " The italics (here inserted purposely) indicate the measure of prudence and discretion committed to the ordinaries.

in the same diocese. Moreover, in places where the decree had been formally published, jurisprudence invested it with an interpretation which caused innumerable doubts and anxieties.[99]

All too easily doubts could and did arise concerning the possession of a domicile or a quasi-domicile by either of the marrying parties. Yet, this was the one criterion set up by the decree *Tametsi* to decide the *parochus proprius,* who alone could validly assist or delegate some other priest to assist. If one but remembers that the conditions required for the acquisition of a domicile or a quasi-domicile were somewhat strict and very strictly enforced, one begins to see the perplexities that arose about the right and competency of priests to assist at definite marriages. It is, then, not surprising to learn that many bishops asked the Holy See for a modification of the decree *Tametsi.*[100] Indeed, at the Vatican Council it was even requested that the decree be abolished and that a return be made to the pre-Tridentine practices.[101]

Eventually, upon the accession of Pius X to the papal throne, the Holy See took cognizance of the need of a change; but only after more than two years of careful, painstaking examination, interpretation and formulation, the decree *Ne Temere* was evolved.[102] The new decree extended the law of the required canonical form throughout the entire Catholic Church.[103] Henceforth territory served as the primary basis for valid assistance at all marriages. Within the limits of his diocese a bishop could assist validly at all marriages. Within the limits of his parish a pastor could validly marry any one who came to him. All preceding dispensations along with the extension of the Bene-

[99] S. C. C., decr. *Ne Temere,* 2 Aug., 1907—*Fontes,* n. 4340.

[100] Cf. *Conc. Plen. Baltimoriensis II Acta et Decreta,* n. 340.

[101] Martin, *Coll. Documentorum Conc. Vaticani,* p. 163; *Collectio Lacensis,* VII, 842.

[102] Cf. Creagh, *A commentary on the decree "Ne Temere,"* p. 21.

[103] Special provision had already been made in 1906 for Germany. Cf. Pius X, litt. ap. *Provida,* 18 Jan. 1906—*Fontes,* n. 670. This particular law for Germany became binding on Easter Sunday, April 15, 1906, and continued in effect—with certain modifications—until the advent of the present Code.

dictine Declaration were abolished by the decree *Ne Temere,* with the exception of the Constitution *Provida,* which had been issued by Pope Pius X for Germany and was later extended to Hungary.[104] But even these exceptions were later abrogated by the Code of Canon Law, which in its legislation followed the decree *Ne Temere* very closely.[105]

2. *Post-Code Interpretation*

a. Non-jurisdictional Character of the Act of Assistance at a Marriage Ceremony

As Fink observes,[106] it is inaccurate and misleading to state after the fashion of Fabregas,[107] that all canonists and moralists unanimously teach that assistance at marriage is not an act of jurisdiction. As a matter of fact, the theory of Braun and Schmier, as explained above, boasts several followers even in our own day. Thus, Krüger,[108] following Konrad, Hilling and K. Hofmann,[109] claims that the act of assistance at marriage as an act of voluntary jurisdiction may be taken as fully proved. He further contends that the *licentia assistendi*—i.e., in the sense of canon 1095, § 2, and of canon 1096—is true delegation. J. Löhr,[110] while he balked at granting that the authorization given for valid assistance at marriage is true delegation, heartily approved, and indeed regarded as the only opinion to be followed under the present circumstances, the statement that assistance at marriage was an act of voluntary jurisdiction. Triebs,[111]

[104] S. C. C., *Romana et aliarum,* 1 Feb., 1908, ad IV—*Fontes,* n. 4344.

[105] Canons 1094-1099.

[106] "Eheassistenz und allgemeiner Irrtum,"—*Theologie und Glaube,* XXVI (1934), 585-597.

[107] "De componendo canone 1094 et 209,"—*Periodica,* XXII (1933), 117.

[108] *Die Delegation zur Eheassistenz* (Breslau: O. Borgmeyer, 1932), pp. 17 ss.

[109] *Die freiwillige Gerichtsbarkeit im kanonischen Recht,* Görresgesellschaft. Sektion für Rechts- und Staatwissenschaften, Heft 53, (Paderborn: F. Schöningh, 1929), p. 79.

[110] *Theologische Quartalschrift* (Tübingen), CXIV (1933), 573.

[111] *Praktisches Handbuch des geltenden kanonischen Eherechts* (Breslau, 1932), pp. 595-599.

observed that under the decree *Tametsi* it was necessary, and likewise sufficient, for the pastor to receive the consent. As long as the pastor was conscious, it did not make any difference if he were present willingly or under compulsion. Under the decree *Ne Temere,* however, according to Triebs, the work of the pastor became more active. He had to ask for and receive the consent of the bridal parties. Thus, under the latter decree there was effected more than an accidental difference between the pastor and the witnesses in their attendance on the marriage. The pastor was thenceforth made a *qualified* witness, while the other witnesses in their required attendance on the marriage still remained the ordinary witnesses they were in accord with the earlier law.

However, the result of a close study does reveal that modern authors quite generally consider the assistance at marriage as a non-jurisdictional act.[112] Such assistance is merely an act of a notary which is required by law for the validity of the marriage contract. For good reasons it is joined to the office of the pastor or of the local ordinary. But, in spite of this, it does not lose its legal character. Just as one does not call the acts of a notary or the acts of any witnesses acts of jurisdiction, so too one cannot consider the acts of assisting at a marriage an act of jurisdiction. By ecclesiastical jurisdiction one understands the power of ruling the Church in the internal or external forum in contrast to the legal idea of Orders or, as in this instance,

[112] Cf., e. g., Noldin-Schmitt, *Theologia moralis,* III, nn. 643-649; Cappello, *De sacramentis,* III, nn. 663-664; Vermeersch, *Theologia moralis,* III, n. 795; Blat, *Commentarium,* III, Pars I, n. 496; Carberry, *The juridical form of marriage,* p. 47; Wernz-Vidal, *Ius canonicum,* V, n. 332; Coronata, "L'errore commune nell'assistenza ad un matrimonio,"—*Palestra del clero,* IX (1930), 201 ss.; Linneborn-Wenner, *Grundriss des Eherechts* (Paderborn, 1933), pp. 355, 350, 2; Fabregas, "De componendo canone 1094 et 209,"—*Periodica,* XXII (1933), 117*; Hecht,—*Pastor Bonus,* XXXIV (1921-1922), 361; Koeniger, *Katholisches Kirchenrecht* (Freiburg i. Br., 1926), p. 320; Leitner, *Lehrbuch des katholischen Eherechts* (3. ed., Paderborn, 1920), p. 191; Schäfer, *Das Eherecht* (8. and 9. ed., Münster, 1924), p. 264; De Smet, *De Sponsalibus et matrimonio* (Brugis, 1927), p. 91.

in contrast to the legal idea of a notary. With all things, then, taken into consideration, it cannot but be concluded that the act of assistance at marriage is not an act of jurisdiction.[113]

b. Applicability of Canon 209 to Marriage

As the reader has seen, both the Code [114] and the Pontifical Commission for the authentic interpretation of the Code [115] have clearly indicated that the rules of delegation are to be applied to the act of assistance at marriage even though it be quite generally admitted that such an act of assistance does not comprise a strictly jurisdictional act. It stands to reason that there can be no talk of the need or of the possibility of the functioning of the suppletory principle except when and where the authority which the law requires for validity of assistance at marriage is lacking.

First of all, assistance at marriage is the proper function of the pastor and of the local ordinary. They attain this power the moment they take canonical possession of respective offices. They keep this power as long as they retain their benefice. Authorization to witness marriages may be lost by express and explicit resignation under conditions described in canons 184-187, and, likewise, by tacit resignation which occurs in circumstances mentioned in canon 188. In the event of a transfer, a former benefice is vacated when the new one is legitimately occupied unless otherwise determined by law or by the will of the superior.[116]

One, however, who lays violent hands upon the person of the Holy Father is *ipso facto vitandus* [117] and, according to the law, the customary conditions for declaring one *vitandus* [118] need not be observed. If a pastor or ordinary were guilty of this crime,

[113] Cf., Fink, "Eheassistenz und allgemeiner Irrtum,"—*Theologie und Glaube,* XXVI (1934), 588-590; Sipos, "Matrimonio contrahendo adsistentia an actus sit iurisdictionis,"—*Jus Pont.,* XV (1935), 41-45.

[114] Cf. canons 1096, n. 1, and 1094.

[115] *PCI,* 28 December, 1927—*AAS,* XIX (1928), 61.

[116] Canon 194, § 1.

[117] Canon 2343, § 1, n. 1.

[118] Canon 2258.

his competency to witness marriage would cease immediately. Over and above this case, it is the general opinion that excommunication, suspension from office, and personal interdict, are the only penalties which deprive the official witness of the competence to assist at marriages. Canon 1095, § 1, n. 1, names these penalties and no others. The disjunctive wording of the canon, " . . . *nisi per sententiam fuerint excommunicati,* **vel** *interdicti,* **vel** *suspensi ab officio* . . ." seems to strengthen the belief that the punishments which disqualify the pastor and others to witness marriage are listed taxatively.[119] Suspension from jurisdiction, therefore, or from orders, or *a divinis,* or from a benefice will not necessarily deprive one of his competence to assist validly at marriage. The view, therefore, of canonists[120] who would disqualify a priest from assisting if he had been deprived of jurisdiction by sentence seems to go beyond the limits of canon 1095, § 1, n. 1.[121] It may be noted that a general suspension, that is one, without any further qualification, includes suspension from office.[122] Hence a pastor who has been simply suspended by a declaratory or condemnatory sentence or decree is disqualified from acting as official witness of the Church at marriage.

As regards those who do not assist in virtue of the fact that they are the pastors or ordinaries of the place where the marriage occurs, no one of them can validly assist unless and until he has received the proper delegation demanded by the Code according to the prescript of canon 1096, § 1.

When one is sure that a priest acted without due competence or when one is not certain whether he had the necessary authorization then one turns to canon 209 to see whether or not the

[119] Gasparri, *De matrimonio,* I, n. 973; Wouters, *De forma . . . celebrationis matrimonii,* p. 18; Carberry, *The juridical form of marriage,* p. 67.

[120] Cf., e.g., Vermeersch-Creusen, *Epitome,* II, n. 393; De Meester, *Compendium,* III, pars 2a, n. 1782.

[121] Carberry, *The juridical form of marriage,* p. 67; Rainer, *Suspension of clerics,* p. 81.

[122] Canon 2278, § 2.

suppletory principle will supply whatever deficiency might be present in a given case.

Since the assistance of a priest at marriage is quite generally admitted not to be an act of jurisdiction, it is not difficult to find reasons to doubt the applicability of canon 209 to marriage.[123] In fact some canonists, few though they be, refuse to admit the *direct* applicability of canon 209 to assistance at marriage. Stressing the literal significance of the term *jurisdiction* in canon 209 and mindful of the non-jurisdictional character of assistance at marriage, these authors would, at the very most, allow only an indirect application of the salutary benefits of canon 209 to assistance at marriage. Thus Leitner[124] clearly and emphatically averred that there could not be in virtue of canon 209 any transmission of the capacity to assist at a marriage. Rather, according to their view, there could only be, under the requisite condition of common error, a supplying of jurisdiction to the pastor, who would become thereby the true pastor for assistance at a particular marriage. Schäfer,[125] Jone,[126] Linneborn-Wenner[127] and Cicognani[128] in like manner contend that in virtue of canon 209 the jurisdiction of the pastor is directly supplied. And then, only when and because this jurisdiction is present, does the priest in question become legally competent to assist validly at a marriage.

It cannot but be admitted that, beyond the literal significance of the text of canon 209, there seems to be little ground to accept this view in opposition to the more generally maintained opinion that canon 209 does *directly* apply to marriage. Certainly, it is true that the authors who propose this stricter theory do not give any details in support and explanation of their belief.

As has already been intimated, the vast majority of canonists

[123] Nevin, "Does doctrine concerning the supply of jurisdiction in *common error* apply in case of matrimony?"—*ACR,* XIV (1937), 146.

[124] *Lehrbuch des katholischen Eherechts,* p. 191.

[125] *Das Eherecht,* p. 175, note 2.

[126] "Error communis bei Eheassistenz,"—*LQS,* LXXXI (1928), 806.

[127] *Grundriss des Eherechts,* p. 350, note 2.

[128] *Canon law,* p. 764.

maintains that the principles of canon 209 regarding supplied jurisdiction in common error and in probable doubt either ot law or of fact may be applied to marriage.[129] In fact, some authors go so far as to claim that with the few exceptions enumerated above, *all* authors affirm the direct applicability of canon 209 to marriage.[130] The opinion as accepted by almost all the authors seems to be the sole tenable view to any one who examines the minds of the pre-Code authors on this matter, the similarity between assistance at marriage and jurisdiction, and finally the decisions that have been issued by the Sacred Congregation of the Council and by the Rota in reference to the application of canon 209 to marriage.

Fabregas [131] and Nevin,[132] have selected the three great masters of legal knowledge and culture, namely, Suarez,[133] Sanchez [134] and De Lugo,[135] and used them as models of contemporary legal thought. After a searching study both Fabregas and Nevin concluded that Suarez, Sanchez and De Lugo beyond any shadow of doubt believed the suppletory principle was to be extended to assistance at marriage as well as to strictly jurisdictional acts. And this in no roundabout way, as Leitner and his followers would insist. Because of their parallel placing of jurisdiction,

[129] Cf. e.g., Wernz-Vidal, *Ius canonicum,* V, n. 536; Payen, *De matrimonio,* II, n. 1763; Cappello, *De sacramentis,* III, n. 663; Noldin-Schmitt, *Theologia moralis,* III, n. 637, 2; Vermeersch-Creusen, *Epitome,* II, n. 392; Vlaming, *Praelectiones iuris matrimonialis,* II, n. 568; Wouters, *De forma . . . celebrationis matrimonii,* p. 8; Chelodi, *Ius matrimoniale,* n. 131; Trombetta, *Supplet ecclesia,* pp. 23-25; Fabregas, "De componendo canone 1094 cum 209,"—*Periodica,* XXII (1933), 192*-196*; Kearney, *The principles of delegation,* pp. 126-127; Carberry, *The juridical form of marriage,* p. 47; Salvador, "Error communis et iurisdictionis suppletio ab ecclesia,"—*BE,* XVII (1939), 375; Wilches, *De errore communi,* p. 203.

[130] E. g., Fabregas, "De componendo canone 1094 cum 209,"—*Periodica,* XXII (1933), 192*; Nevin, *op. cit.,—ACR,* XIV (1937), 146.

[131] *Periodica,* XXII (1933), 193*-195*.

[132] *ACR,* XIV (1937), 146.

[133] *De censuris,* Disp. XIX, Sec. I, nn. 9-10.

[134] *De matrimonio,* Tom. I, lib. III, disp. 22, nn. 60-65.

[135] *De justitia et jure,* Disp. XXXVII, Sec. III, n. 20.

of assistance at marriage and of documentary authentication, these old authors are to be understood as clearly speaking of a *direct* or equivalent *suppletio.*[136]

Since such was the understanding of this suppletory principle before the Code, the consequence is that the present law in canon 209 is to be interpreted in the self-same manner in virtue of the provision of canon 6, n. 2. And indeed, as both Nevin,[137] and Fabregas[138] cogently put it, if there was anyone who intimately penetrated the mind of the Code and understood it perfectly, that person was Cardinal Gasparri, its main compiler. And this eminent canonist wrote as follows on the point under discussion:

> "The mere fact that a priest is reputed to be a pastor does not of itself in absolute fashion confer upon him any right to assist at marriage. But, if he rules over and administers the parish under the circumstances of common error, he officiates validly, because in this case the Church supplies jurisdiction for the external and the internal forum alike according to the rule of canon 209. For, though assistance at marriage is not an act of jurisdistion, still in the favored elements of law (*in favorabilibus*) it is put on a par with jurisdiction, and thus arises the use of such terms as *delegation* and *delegated,* which in their proper and native application are employed in reference to the power of jurisdiction."[139]

This citation from Gasparri is important and interesting because it brings out the fact of the resemblance between an act of assistance at marriage and an act of jurisdiction. Indeed, the fact of this resemblance, as Carberry properly observes, is the motivating reason why the majority of canonists applies the suppletory principle to marriage directly.[140] And, indubitably, the resemblance is very close. For, upon this assistance depends

136 Fink, "Eheassistenz und allgemeiner Irrtum,"—*Theologie und Glaube,* XXVI (1934), 592.

137 *ACR,* XIV (1937), 147.

138 *Periodica,* XXII (1933), 192*-193*.

139 *De matrimonio,* II, n. 936.

140 Cf. Carberry, *The juridical form of marriage,* pp. 47-48.

the validity of the juridical act and the power to assist is possessed in virtue of a public office, i.e., a pastorate, which is an office of jurisdiction.[141] Furthermore, the Pontifical Commission for the Interpretation of the Code stated that a parish assistant with general delegation may subdelegate. But, in so doing, the Commission applied the general principle which governs the delegation of jurisdiction.[142] Again, the Code itself when speaking of assistance at marriage uses the words which apply to delegation, such as *"delegatio"* [143] and *"delegatus."* [144]

Finally, it will suffice to point out that the Sacred Congregation of the Council and the Tribunal of the Rota have issued decisions which seem to apply the suppletory principle directly to the act of assistance at marriage, not only in the case of common error [145] but also in the case of doubt.[146] Inasmuch as an extensive examination of these cases has already been made and still further reflections remain to be made, this alone might be noted here: There is no indication in any of the *vota* or decisions that the suppletory benefits of canon 209 were being applied indirectly, after the fashion suggested by Leitner and his followers. On the contrary, there is evidence in a case handled by the Rota that this august tribunal was ready, if there were need of so doing, to apply the suppletory power of canon 209 to the acts of an assistant, or—which is but another way of stating it—of a priest

141 Creusen, "Pouvoir dominatif et erreur commune,"—*Acta Congressus iuridicii internationalis,* IV, 188.

142 *PCI,* 28 December, 1927—*AAS,* XIX (1928), 61. Cf. also canon 199, § 3. One is best able to appraise this peculiar character of the act of assisting at marriage if and when he notes the decree of the Sacred Congregation of the Council to the effect that the pastor or the bishop could *not* delegate anyone to assist as a witness at *sponsalia*—S. C. Conc., 28 (31) Mar. 1908—*ASS,* XLI (1908), 289 ad VI.

143 Canon 1096, n. 1.

144 Canon 1094.

145 Cf. S. C. C., March 10, 1770—*Thesaurus resolutionum,* XXXIX (1770), 51-56; S. R. R., *Nullitas matrimonii,* 22 Nov. 1927, *coram R. P. D. Andrea Jullien,* dec. LI—*Decisiones,* XIX (1927), 453-465.

146 Cf. S. R. R., *Nullitas matrimonii,* 20 Jun., 1931, *coram R. P. D. Francisco Parrillo,* dec. XXVII—*Decisiones* XXIII (1931), 236-249.

who was not a pastor.[147] Surely, in such a case there is no question of a pastorate whose powers can be supplied directly, in order that canon 209 might indirectly wield its saving power. This brings up, therefore, still another objection to the opinion of Leitner and his school: namely, it would, without establishing proof for so doing, limit the saving grace of canon 209 to priests possessing an *officium.*

In conclusion, then, it may safely be held that the suppletory principle of canon 209 does apply directly to marriage.[148] How far this direct application will go will be the concern of the subsequent section.

c. Extent of Application to Marriage

If the suppletory principle is at all to be applied to marriage—and authors are commonly united in teaching that such an application is entirely in order, not only in virtue of canon 6, n. 2, but also by reason of canon 20—[149] it stands to reason that, as in the case of the performance of strictly jurisdictional acts, the requisite conditions must be verified: namely, common error, or a positive and probable doubt, either of fact or of law.

(a.) Ordinary Assistance

On the strength of the prescripts of canon 6, nn. 2 and 5, and of past cases settled by the Holy See,[150] it is entirely safe to hold the traditional teaching that a reputed local ordinary or pastor, commonly but erroneously considered as such by the faithful of the diocese or of the parish, assists validly at marriages con-

[147] S. R. R., *Nullitas matrimonii,* 30 Jan. 1931, *coram R. P. D. Ubaldi Mannucci,* dec. VI—*Decisiones,* XXIII (1931), 44.

[148] Jombart, "L'erreur commune,"—*NRT,* L (1923), 363: "Le principe est indiscutable. Il n'en vas pas même des applications."

[149] Fink, "Eheassistenz und allgemeiner Irrtum,"—*Theologie und Glaube,* XXVI (1934), 592; Claeys-Bouuaert, "De conceptu erroris communis in canone 209,"—*Jus Pont.,* XVI (1936), 160; Wilches, *De errore communi,* pp. 202-203, 213.

[150] S. C. C., 10 Mar. 1770, *Caesaraugustana matrimonii—Thesaurus resolutionum,* XXXIX (1770), 51-56; S. R. R., *Nullitas matrimonii,* 22 Nov. 1927, *coram R.P.D. Andrea Jullien,* dec. LI—*Decisiones,* XIX (1927), 453-465.

tracted within the diocese or parish, provided that there are verified those conditions in view of which the principle of canon 209 actualizes its suppletory force.[151]

The Code of Canon Law clearly defines the extension of the term "local ordinary." Accordingly all who come within its meaning are empowered by canon 1094 to assist at marriage. Besides the Roman Pontiff, the following are also classed as local ordinaries: residential bishops, abbots and prelates with territorial independence, the vicars general of these three classes of ordinaries, diocesan administrators, vicars and prefects apostolic, and, finally, those who by the enactment of law or in view of approved constitutions succeed to the office of the above mentioned when their office becomes vacant, or is otherwise impeded or frustrated in its fulfillment, so as to call upon these designated successors to assume its incumbency.[152]

With reference to the word "pastor" canon 451, § 1, offers the following descriptive definition: "A pastor is a priest or a moral person to whom a parish is in title entrusted with the care of souls which is to be exercised under the authority of the local ordinary." Nevin [153] quite appropriately observes that the potential benefits of canon 209 should be made available with equal results in reference to all who in law are declared equivalent in status with parish priests. In canon 451, § 2, two groups of priests are declared to enjoy an equivalent status: a.) quasi-pastors;[154] and b.) parochial vicars entrusted with full parochial authority. Classified as such are: the *actual vicar;*[155] the *administrator* of a vacant parish;[156] the *vicar substitute;*[157] the *vicar adjutant*[158] and any *parochial vicar* whose charge and station in

151 Cf. Wilches, *De errore communi,* p. 136.

152 Canons 198, § 1, and 309, § 2.

153 "Does doctrine concerning the supply of jurisdiction in *common error* apply in the casse of matrimony?"—*ACR,* XIV (1937), 147.

154 Canon 216, § 3.

155 Canon 471, §§ 1 and 4.

156 Canon 472, n. 1 and canon 473, § 1.

157 Canons 474 and 1923, § 3; 465, § 4; 465, § 5.

158 Canon 475, §§ 1-2.

a parish has been constituted on a canonical basis of permanence.[159]

The problem of the validity of marriages could very easily occur. This would be verified, for example, in the case of a newly appointed pastor who does not take *canonical possession* of his parish, or in the case of a pastor who has secured his appointment by simoniacal means. In cases such as these the mere possession of the office does not regularize the status of that pastor's pastorate; nevertheless, if his functions are performed amid the accompaniment of the conditions stipulated in canon 209 for the operation of the suppletory principle, then, it seems only logical to conclude that each and every marriarge at which he assists within the limits of the parish he holds will be recognized as valid in reference to the canonical form required for its contraction. Indeed, Fabregas declares,[160] the applicability of canon 209 in such instances is "so evident that it seems superfluous to insist upon it." For, it is obvious to all that the peculiar right of assisting at marriages, which is proper to pastors and which constituted them as qualified witnesses, invests them, as it were, with a certain public office or duty. And it is only fitting that the Church, in her wisdom and benignity, should obviate all the serious inconveniences, especially those of the spiritual order, which would otherwise befall many of the faithful, if the marriages contracted before such a priest reputed as pastor had to be pronounced invalid.

(b.) Delegated Assistance

a° Pre-Code Attitude

It is quite true, as *L'Ami du Clergé* [161] indicates, that in applying the suppletory principle to the priest's act of assisting at marriage pre-Code authors studied this problem in very great measure with reference to the pastor, i.e., whether he needed to have a colored title, whether it sufficed that he was merely a putative

[159] Canon 1412, 1°.

[160] "De componendo canone 1094 cum 209,"—*Periodica,* XXII (1923), 195 *.

[161] XLII (1930), 648.

pastor, and whether it was enough that he existed as an *intrusus,* in order that the benefit of a supplied power and authorization might accrue in the case. However, it is not equally true, as *L'Ami de Clergé* would have it, that it was only after the Code that authors applied this principle to an erroneously reputed delegation for assistance at marriage. As has been seen in the historical analysis of the problem dealing with the applicability of the suppletory principle to cases involving a false judgment of the presence of delegated power, there was always an articulate doctrine among some canonists which asserted that the common good of the faithful could be imperilled even by a person who did not hold an *officium,* as most understand it today in the strict terms of canon 197, § 1, and canon 145, § 1, and that in all such cases the Church would supply the needed power. This they taught also in regard to the act of assistance at marriage. Thus Pontius († 1629)[162] applied it, appealing to the old formula, *"Si servus. dum putaretur liber, ex* **delegatione** *sententiam dixit."* [163] Sanchez († 1619)[164] applied this principle even to the case in which a layman was delegated to assist at a marriage in view of being commonly regarded as a priest. De Lugo († 1660)[165] applied this principle to the case of a delegate without distinguishing between the universal and particular delegate. D'Annibale[166] apparently held the same opinion when he asserted that a deacon would assist invalidly at marriages whenever he was delegated to do so, unless he was commonly believed to be a priest. Arguing on the basis that the Church supplies the necessary competency whenever a colored title and common error are verified, Wernz († 1914) likewise taught that the act of assistance and the matrimonial contract would both be valid if and when a person assisted who was commonly regarded as a priest, even though in reality he were only a layman.[167] Admittedly following the teachings

[162] *De sacramento matrimonii,* V, cap. 19, n. 11.

[163] C. 1, C. III, q. 7.

[164] *De matrimonio,* Tom. I, lib. III, disp. 22, n. 61.

[165] *De justitia et iure,* Disp. XXXVII, n. 26.

[166] *Summula,* III, n. 328, note 50.

[167] *Ius decretalium,* IV, n. 180, II, note 213.

of Sanchez († 1619),[168] of Bonacina († 1631),[169] of Schmalzgrueber († 1731),[170] of Pichler († 1736),[171] of Rosset († 1902)[172] and of Wernz († 1914),[173] Gasparri also taught the applicability of the suppletory principle to delegated assistance at marriage. Indeed he maintained that the Church would supply even when the person commonly considered to be a priest were in reality a woman.[174]

In view of all this evidence the question of the applicability of this suppletory canon to cases of delegation for assistance at marriage can in no wise be regarded as a post-Code creation.

b° Attitude of the Code

As Dalpiaz[175] correctly observes, the Code makes no distinction whatever between ordinary and delegated power with regard to the extent of the applicatory force of canon 209. For that reason, as Fabregas[176] argues, there is no textual reason why any marriage—be it performed by a priest who is commonly, though falsely, reputed to possess either a general or a particular delegation to assist—should not be considered valid in virtue of canon 209 *if the prerequisite conditions of this canon are verified.*

a′ In Doubt

As has already been noted, though the Church supplies with equal efficacy in common error and in positive and probable doubt of fact or of law, still the two conditions are very much different. Each offers problems of its own as regards their proper verification.

[168] *De matrimonio,* Tom. I, lib. III, disp. 22, n. 61.

[169] *De matrimonio,* Q. II, punct. VIII, n. 30.

[170] *Ius ecclesiasticum universum,* lib. IV, tit. III, n. 188.

[171] *Ius canonicum,* lib. IV, tit. III, n. 22.

[172] *De sacramento matrimonii,* n. 2223.

[173] *Ius decretalium,* IV, n. 180, II, note 213.

[174] *Tractatus canonicus de matrimonio* (3. ed., Parisiis, 1904), II, n. 1129, note.

[175] "De conceptu erroris communis iuxta canonem 209,"—*Apoll.,* VII (1934), 490.

[176] "De componendo canone 1094 cum 209,"—*Periodica,* XXII (1933), 196*.

The purpose of the supplying by the Church in probability, i.e., the peace of mind of the ministering priest,[177] and the necessary condition, i.e., a positive and probable doubt, can easily be fulfilled in cases of delegation to assist at even one marriage. Therefore, with Cappello,[178] one must hold it not only as probable, or more probable, but as *certain* that canon 209 will apply in such instances of particular delegation.

Among the few Rota decisions there is one very recent one which shows a tendency on the part of the judges of that *turnus* to apply canon 209 to just such a doubt.[179] This case involved a certain pastor who, under the law of the decree *Ne Temere,* sought permission to assist at a marriage of his own parishioners in another man's parish. The Vicar-General granted the permission. Later the marriage was impugned on the ground that the formula of the grant of the permission required its recipient to secure also the permission of the pastor of the place wherein the ceremony was to occur. This, the plaintiff was careful to point out, the petitioning pastor failed to do. In the process of the trial it was shown that the formula granted by the Vicar-General was not clear in stating whether or not that added permission was required for validity. The arguments adduced against the necessity of obtaining that permission as a condition for validity of assistance were sufficiently strong to render doubtful the nature of the obligation whereby the permission was to be sought and obtained. The Rota very plainly asserted that canon 209 could be applied in this doubt.

b′ In Common Error

Far more complex and intriguing is the problem of the applicability of canon 209 when by way of common error some one is thought to possess delegation to assist at a marriage. On the one extreme there are those who press their interpretative

[177] Fink ,"Eheassistenz und allgemeiner Irrtum,"—*Theologie und Glaube,* XXVI (1934), 594.

[178] "De vicario substituto,"—*Periodica,* XIX (1930), 9*-10*.

[179] S. R. R., *Nullitas matrimonii,* 20 Jun. 1931, *coram R. P. D. Francisco Parrillo,* dec. XXVIII—*Decisiones,* XXIII (1931), 236-249, esp. 249.

theory to almost unlimited frontiers. They argue that as long as a cleric assists at a marriage it never enters the minds of those present to doubt his qualifications to assist. In other words, there is no one who even thinks that the cleric could or might act illegally in such a matter. Therefore, these would argue, there exists a public fact by which those present are misled and by which those absent would also be mislead if they were present.[180] On the other extreme there are those who restrain the application of their theory within an almost inhibitive province. They insist, and hold as certain, that the theory of common error is not applicable in the case of the delegation of a priest if he is not the pastor of one or the other of the bridal couple, or if he is not acknowledged by the Code as having an equivalent status. These writers stress the fact that whenever there is question of any delegated priest, though he be an assistant (*vicarius co-operator*) in a parish, then a merely private utility is at stake for the protection of which no factor of common error can invoke the suppletory principle of canon 209.[181]

In the midst of this disagreement one must always remember that the text of canon 209 does not exclude the applicability of its suppletory principle to delegated assistance at marriage. The lone condition required is common error. For that reason most authors agree that there is definite applicability of canon 209 to such assistance. However, as *L'Ami du Clergé* [182] judiciously observes, the authors express this belief in varying degrees of subjective certainty in relation to the varying manner in which the delegation was reputedly granted. Thus, for example, De Smet,[183] Arregui [184] and Cerato [185] seem to hold outright that canon 209 applies to delegated assistance of any kind. So also

[180] Concerning such theories cf. Toso, "De errore communi ad normam can. 209,"—*Jus Pont.*, XVIII (1938), 161-162; *L'Ami du Clergé*, XLVII (1930), 649.

[181] Cf., e.g., *L'Ami du Clergé*, XLVII (1930), 651.

[182] XLVII (1930), 648.

[183] *De sponsalibus et matrimonio*, n. 118.

[184] *Summarium*, p. 511.

[185] *De matrimonio*, p. 160.

Wilches maintains that canon 209 is to be applied to marriage without any peculiar limitation and expressly holds that it is applicable even to cases of delegation to assist at one marriage.[186] Claiming the support of Wernz, D'Annibale, Gasparri and others —to whom reference has only recently been made in this study— Coronata likewise teaches the applicability of the suppletory principle to cases of delegation to assist at one marriage.[187] Others more prudently state that almost the same principles apply to this authorization as to a veritable delegation of jurisdiction.[188] Still others, even more circumspectly and concisely, teach that the general principles which regulate the delegation of jurisdictional power must also be applied in the case of authorization for valid assistance at marriage, unless a contrary rule is established or unless such an act of authorization is of itself essentially precluded.[189]

Indeed, it may be logically argued that the text of the Code does not exclude the application of canon 209 to the cases of delegated assistance. If the required condition of common error is verified, it appears that the Church supplies the needed authorization, because that is all that she demands to be present. Upon the proper realization of common error, then, the solution of this whole problem rests.[190]

a Application to Universal Delegation to Assist at Marriage

There is no universal agreement, even among canonists who hold for a direct application of canon 209 to the case of assistance at marriage, as to the applicability of this same canon to the case of delegated assistance. Certain ones, as the writer in *L'Ami du Clergé*[191] are convinced and maintain as certain that

186 *De errore communi*, pp. 205, 208-214.

187 "L'errore commune nell' assistenza ad un matrimonio,"—*Palestra del clero*, IX (1930), 201 ss.

188 Cappello, *De sacramentis*, III, n. 672; Gougnard, *Tractatus de matrimonio*, p. 201.

189 Wernz-Vidal, *De matrimonio*, n. 538, footnote 38.

190 Dalpiaz, "De conceptu erroris communis iuxta canonem 209,"—*Apoll.*, VII (1934), 490.

191 XLVII (1930), 651.

the theory of common error does not apply in the case of any kind of delegated assistance. They exclude all but pastors and those holding an office equivalent to that of pastors from the salutary benefits of this principle on the ground that in all but cases involving pastors and their equivalents in law there would never be question of any more than merely private utility. Quite consistent in their position, they rule out even assistants (*vicarii cooperatores*) who might be commonly considered by the parishioners to possess faculties validly to assist at all marriages in the parish where they are stationed. For, so these canonists argue, even such assistants are never any more than helpers with a very restricted range of power. They have not *all* the parochial authority; they have no personal authority; they are not *alone* in the exercise of the parochial functions; the common weal will never be subordinated or abandoned to their activities.

Quite obviously this exclusion is based upon the argument the very core of which is rooted in the contention that public utility can never be endangered by the invalid ministrations of any priest unless he holds a parochial office or some other office equivalent in canonical status and effect. Such a contention seems to offer ample basis for challenging its argument and opposing its conclusion. One undoubtedly still remembers the very recent discussion in these pages concerning the pre-Code attitude on the question of the applicability of the suppletory principle to cases of delegated assistance at marriage. Was it not shown that there was a general teaching to the effect that this principle does apply to such delegated assistance? One can be fully ready to grant that there is no conclusive evidence that authors like Wernz and Gasparri wrote of particular delegation. This point will be searched into in due time. For the present, however, one must carefully note that the teaching of these pre-Code authorities certainly included at least universal delegation to assist at marriages within the scope of the applicability of the suppletory principle. And, as a matter of fact, of the vast majority of post-Code canonists who hold for the direct application of canon 209 to the case of assistance at marriage, by far the predominant number is convinced that at least in regard to assistants who are commonly but erroneously believed to possess the power to assist at all marriages, in the parish where they are appointed, the common good and public utility is sufficiently at stake to merit the benefit of the suppletory principle of canon 209.[192]

Consider, for example, a diocese where it is the rule for curates to receive a general delegation to officiate at marriages in the parish where they are appointed on the understanding that for the licitness of such acts they need the consent of their parish priest. Suppose that, for some reason, the curate's appointment is invalid, or that the general delegation given to curates according to the general rule is in a particular case omitted through an oversight. Further suppose that this curate is sent to a parish where the faithful, as a result of what they observed in the past, naturally conclude that this curate, too, can officiate at all marriages. In such a state of affairs, clearly, there would be present not only a common error but also the general danger of spiritual harm. Surely, one would have to admit that the delegation would be supplied in such a case.[193]

It is evident that multiple combinations of events could conspire and produce such a general error on the part of the people. In all such cases there will be verified the *object* of common error, as Jombart put it,[194] i.e., the quality, the authority, the habitual power of the priest . . . habitual, at least in the sense that it applies to all cases or to a series of analogous cases. It is under this very form that common error is analyzed with regard to the confessor, or putative pastor, or any other official. In every such

[192] Cf., e.g., Jombart, "L'erreur commune,"—*NRT,* L (1923), 172; De Smet, *De sponsalibus et matrimonio,* n. 118; Kearney, *The principles of delegation,* p. 135; Arregui, *Summarium,* p. 511; Cerato, *De matrimonio,* p. 160; Carberry, *The juridical form of marriage,* p. 91; Fabregas, "De componendo canone 1094 cum 209,"—*Periodica,* XXII (1923), 198*-199*; Fink, "Eheassistenz und allgemeiner Irrtum,"—*Theologie und Glaube,* XXVI (1934), 592; Claeys-Bouuaert, "De conceptu erroris communis in canone 209,"—*Jus Pont.,* XVI (1936), 160; Nevin, "Does doctrine concerning the supplying of jurisdiction in *common error* apply in the case of matrimony?"—*ACR,* XIV (1937), 150.

[193] Nevin,—*ACR,* XIV (1937), 150.

[194] "L'erreur commune,"—*NRT,* L (1923), 365.

case is present the *stability* of common error. For, as Toso expressed it, a stable cause or a permanent cause is always present in regard to those who enjoy ordinary power or are delegated *ad universitatem causarum.* In such cases, if the publicity of such a fact be clearly present, then, in regard to the common error already extant, there is no need of its further confirmation through the repetition of similar unauthorized acts which are commonly regarded by the faithful as valid ministrations.[195]

In confirmation of the doctrine which admits the application of the suppletory principle for the cases in which the factor of universal delegation is in question, it will prove to be of some interest and satisfaction to note a matrimonial case which was settled by the Tribunal of the Rota in 1931. The case revolved about a priest who officiated, sometime after the issuance of the decree *Ne Temere,* at a marriage of two people who belonged to the parish where this priest was stationed as an assistant in virtue of an oral and not officially recorded or published appointment by the bishop, due to the political situation around Vilno at the time. Later on the marriage was attacked on the ground that this priest did not possess the necessary delegation to assist. As a matter of fact, after a close study of testimony, the Rota was satisfied that the priest involved did have a sufficiently clear delegation to assist. But, for the purposes of this study, it is interesting to note that, of two arguments adduced *ad abundantiam,* one indicates that the "argument from common error would be, if there were need of that, a strong reason to uphold the validity of the marriage bond." [196]

Cappello [197] and Toso [198] both very judiciously point out that *common error,* as required by the prescript of canon 209, may likewise be easily verified in relation to a priest who often takes the place of the pastor (*qui saepe vices parochi suppleat*).

[195] "De errore communi ad normam can. 209,"—*Jus Pont.,* XVIII (1938), 168.

[196] S. R. R., *Nullitas matrim.* 30 Januarii, 1931, *coram R. P. D. Ubaldo Mannucci,* dec. VI—*Decisiones* XXIII (1931), 37-44, esp. 44, n. 9.

[197] *De sacramentis,* III, n. 671.

[198] "De errore communi ad normam can. 209,"—*Jus Pont.,* XVIII (1938), 168.

That canon 209 can apply in the case of an assistant (*vicarius cooperator*) who is falsely considered to have a general delegation to assist at marriages, is commonly accepted by canonists today.[199] However, some question does arise as to whether or not a priest who receives from a pastor of a parish the full spiritual care of his parishioners (*universa cura animarum*) for any period of time less than a week (*vicarius supplens infra hebdomadam*),[200] possesses in virtue of such a commission a general delegation to assist at marriages, and whether, in the event of some cause of invalidity in such a commission, canon 209 might be said to apply because of the existence of common error.

At the outset it is to be noted that a priest who takes care of a parish in this interval is not a vicar substitute, nor is he (it is presumed at present) an assistant with general delegation for assistance at marriage.[201] Also due cognizance is to be taken of the explicit and general determination by canon 1096, § 1, that a pastor cannot grant general delegation to assist at marriage to any priest other than an assistant in his parish.[202]

Without intending to impugn the generally accepted interpretation of canon 1096, § 1, i.e., by limiting the ability of a pastor to grant general delegation to assist at marriages to the assistants only, Cappello draws a distinction and asserts that the prohibition of canon 1096, § 1, refers only to the act of delegation *ad universitatem causarum* but is not to be extended to the act whereby a pastor delegates another priest to the full care of the spiritual welfare of his flock during his short absence.[203] A few other canonists, like Fermí de La Cot[204] and Coronata,[205] followed

[199] Cf. A. Salvador, "Error communis et iurisdictionis suppletio ab ecclesia,"—*BE*, XVII (1930), 375.

[200] In accordance with the prescription of canon 465, § 6.

[201] Cf. Carberry, *The juridical form of marriage*, pp. 52-53.

[202] *PCI*, 16 October, 1919—*AAS*, XI (1919), 477. Cf. Gasparri for his interpretation of canon 1096, § 1, in *Tractatus de matrimonio*, II, n. 950.

[203] *De matrimonio*, III, n. 650, 8, 2.

[204] "Casos I Consultes,"—*Estudis Franciscans*, XLII (1930), 97-98.

[205] *Institutiones*, I, n. 483; "L'errore commune nell' assistenza ad un matrimonio,"—*Palestra del Clero*, IX (1930), 201 ss.

Cappello in his understanding of what powers are to be considered included in the general spiritual care entrusted by a pastor to a priest who is to take his place for any period of time less than a week. Coronata in particular has been an ardent upholder of this teaching.

However, as Salvador appositely observes,[206] when Coronata alleges that neither the Code nor the authorities exclude such a general delegation to assist at marriage from the commission given by a pastor to a priest who is to watch over the spiritual good of his flock for any time less than a week, he is assuming the very point to be proven. And he can hardly use in support of his contention the fact that writers do not commonly consider this question. On the contrary, as Salvador indicates, if any argument at all is to be drawn from this general silence of the authors, it is that these authors understand the clear prescriptions of canon 1096, § 1, in such a manner that they do not feel that any exception is to be made in regard to general delegation to assist at marriage over and above the one already stipulated in the Code.

A further inspection of the intrinsic reasons upon which this contention of Cappello, de La Cot and Coronata is based emphasizes its lack of probability. For, while it is true that before the Code the general faculty to assist at marriages was contained in the commission of the *cura animarum* to the *vicarius supplens infra hebdomadam,* still in view of the clear wording of canon 1096, § 1, Coronata and his school must prove that the exclusion of all general delegation except for assistants, and even for these in relation to marriages to be contracted outside the parish wherein they are stationed, does not extend to a priest who is to take the pastor's place for a few days when the pastor commits to him the entire *cura animarum.* It seems altogether immaterial by what ingenious device the effect of a general delegation to assist at marriages is regarded as available for priests other than assistants. The general delegation—or what is really the same,

[206] "Error communis et iurisdictionis suppletio ab ecclesia,"—*BE,* XVII (1930), 377.

namely, the right to assist validly at all marriages similarly as if one had received a general delegation to do so—is by canon 1096, § 1, made available for assistants exclusively. If a delegation is granted to anyone else, it must be granted individually for a specific case, otherwise its granting is null and void of all juridical effect—*"secus irrita est."*

In regard to Cappello's unique distinction and interpretation in regard to the clause of canon 1096, § 1, "*. . . exclusis quibuslibet delegationibus generalibus,*" two important considerations must be kept in mind.[207] As regards the parochial vicars who in law come under the name of pastors, there of course can be no talk of delegation by the pastor. Such vicars obtain an office and with it the faculty and the power of assisting at marriages. As for the other parochial vicars, whatever powers they possess come through the delegation by the pastor or the local ordinary. However, in all these latter instances the norm of the sacred canons must be observed. And, it must be repeated, the canons clearly state that the pastor or the local ordinary can grant universal delegation to assist at marriages to assistants alone. Thus, the priest who is commissioned by the pastor to watch over the spiritual welfare of his parish for a few days, unquestionably has whatsoever faculties are delegable to him by the pastor. But he certainly has not any faculties which the pastor is incapable of delegating to him.

Over and above these arguments, it may be noted with Salvador [208] that there is no necessity of such a general delegation for the *vicarius supplens infra hebdomadam.* For the pastor could easily delegate this vicar for whatever specific marriages he foresees will occur within the short period of his absence. For the marriages which take place when one or the other or both of the contractants are in danger of death a very special provision is enacted in canon 1098. As regards the marriages of strangers who wish to be married in the parish, this vicar must

[207] A. Salvador, "Error communis et iurisdictionis suppletio ab ecclesia,"—*BE,* XVII (1930), 378, 380.

[208] "Error communis et iurisdictionis suppletio ab ecclesia,"—*BE,* XVII (1930), 380.

advise them either to go elsewhere or to wait for the proper pastor.

Thus, with Salvador [209] and Carberry,[210] it must be maintained that there is no *dubium iuris* regarding this question. The fact is that a pastor simply can not delegate the general faculty to assist at marriages to any priest other than an assistant. Hence the priest supplying for only a few days according to canon 465, § 6, cannot assist validly at marriages in general but only if and when he is delegated expressly for a definite marriage. Of course, if the pastor be delayed in his return, so that his absence from the parish will be protracted beyond a week, he will notify the local ordinary by letter of this emergency and indicate to him the reason for his continued, unavoidable absence. He will also make known the name of the priest who temporarily fills his place in the parish, and whom also he has retained in this position to act as substitute vicar for him in view of his absence for longer than a week. He will await the ordinary's mandate and then stand by whatever arrangement he might be called on to provide other than that already undertaken. As long as the ordinary makes no further demand in the case, the disposition previously made will in effect continue. In other words, the priest who was originally engaged to care for the needs of the faithful during the few days will thus, upon the absent pastor's notification to him of his retention at the parish for the added days, acquire the rightful status of a vicar substitute. The attainment of this status, however, brings with it the possession of an ordinary power in parochial ministrations. The *vicarius supplens infra hebdomadam* will thus become a *vicarius substitutus ultra hebdomadam,* whose office in the parish, temporary though it be, will essentially equip him with ordinary power to assist at any marriage to take place.[211]

[209] "Error communis et iurisdictionis suppletio ab ecclesia,"—*BE,* XVII (1930), 377, 380.

[210] *The juridical form of marriage,* pp. 52-53.

[211] Canon 465, § 5, and the authentic declaration of the Pontifical Commission for the Interpretation of the Canons of the Code under date of May 20, 1923 in reference to this canon. An affirmative reply is given to the question: "Utrum vicarius, seu sacerdos supplens, de quo in cit.

And therefore it must be concluded with Salvador [212] that, even were common error verified, i.e., if the faithful were to believe that this *vicarius supplens infra hebdomadam* could receive from the pastor the general delegation to assist at marriages, they would not be in a *positive* and *probable* error of law, as Cappello and Coronata believe. They would simply be in error of law, in which case the supplying of jurisdiction is not verified. The possibility of supplying, however, remains; for, the faithful could be in error concerning the possession by the priest of some title that is capable of furnishing the jurisdiction necessary and sufficient for the valid assistance at marriage.

β Application to Delegation to Assist at One Marriage

As has been seen regarding the application of canon 209 to the case of a reputed delegation to assist at marriages, there must, first of all, always be present on the part of the faithful a false judgment prevalent enough to deserve to be termed *common* error. This judgment must be concerned with the capacity or qualification of the priest to assist validly. But, there must also be simultaneously present a definite danger to the common good or to public utility. For, the *raison d'être* of the *Lex Barbarius,* and of the canonical suppletory principle the development of which it occasioned, admittedly was the safeguarding of the welfare, not of one or the other individual, but of an entire group or of a community. Today this self-same purpose persists: to prevent the danger of invalid acts that would cause an incredible, almost incurable confusion in and detriment to ecclesiastical discipline. Or, with the same thought put in

can. 465, § 5, id [licentiam assistendi matrimonio dare sacerdoti determinato ad matrimonium determinatum] possit ante Ordinarii approbationem." —*AAS,* XVI (1924), 114-115, V, ad 4. This answer implicitly acknowledges that the vicar substitute has the power to assist at any marriage to take place in the parish. His capacity to authorize another to assist at a specified marriage necessarily presupposes the possession of the same power for himself.

212 "Error communis et iurisdictionis suppletio ab ecclesia,"—*BE,* XVII (1930), 380.

another way, when the interest of only a few, or of a relatively small number of persons, is concerned, the Church will allow the prescribed consequences of her general laws to prevail.

In regard to delegation to assist at one marriage, there are authors of repute, who hold, with greater or lesser definiteness, that canon 209 does apply, even to delegations to assist at one marriage. Thus, while Kearney would not directly deny the conclusion of those authorities who would exclude the application of the suppletory principle to *any* particular delegation, precisely on the ground that the law considers only those matters which can cause damage to the common good, he [213] felt that in the rare instance when common error actually will be verified concerning a particular delegate it is probable that the Church will supply. Fink [214] likewise notes that it cannot simply be said that the validity of the acts of a priest delegated for one case will not be supplied, for there remains the possibility of the verification, even in such an instance, of the common error as required by canon 209. Moreover he claims that even in such a case a relation to the common welfare can be demonstrated. He admits that assistance at one marriage is, in a certain sense, a private affair. However, he adds that the authority to perform even one such individual marriage is connected with the *ius publicum*, and, under certain conditions, everyone who is prepared for marriage could come to the one falsely supposed to have the power to assist. In such a case, the *suppletio* would become a fact, precisely because of the common good.

The stand adopted by these two authors would seem to have even more decided champions in Arregui,[215] De Smet [216] and Cerato,[217] who express, without any reservation, their belief in the general applicability of canon 209 to the case in which there

[213] Kearney, *The principles of delegation*, pp. 135-136.

[214] "Eheassistenz und allgemeiner Irrtum,"—*Theologie und Glaube*, 595-596.

[215] *Summarium*, p. 511.

[216] *De sponsalibus et matrimonio*, n. 118.

[217] *De matrimonio*, p. 160.

is granted a delegation to assist at one marriage. Claiming the support of great pre-Code authorities, like Wernz, D'Annibale, Gasparri and others, Coronata holds this same thesis, namely, that the suppletory principle is applicable even in cases of delegation to assist at one marriage.[218] Jombart[219] once held this same belief, i.e., that canon 209 would supply in instances of particular delegation as well as in instances of delegation *ad universitatem causarum,* and rejoiced in such an applicability, because of the consequent lessening of declarations of nullity on the grounds of clandestinity. However, overcome by the criticism and arguments of some evidently respected authority whom he does not name, Jombart changed his view, convinced that, first of all, in such cases it would be very unlikely that there would be error truly common, that, in addition, the false judgment of the bridal parties and the few bystanders could hardly be considered as constituting common error, and finally that, even though there were error sufficiently common, the inconveniences and scandals resulting from an individual invalid marriage would not be of such a character as to endanger the common good.[220]

It must be said that the opinion finally espoused by Jombart seems to enjoy the more powerful extrinsic and intrinsic support. Thus, some authors, as Carberry[221] and Aertnys-Damen,[222] consider it at least very doubtful that in such a particular instance there could be common error of the sort exacted by canon 209. Others definitely exclude all possibility of the applicability of this canon to the case of a particular delegation to assist at marriage. To this group certainly belong Toso,[223] Claeys-

[218] "L'errore commune nell' assistenza ad un matrimonio,"—*Palestra del Clero,* IX (1930), 201 ss.

[219] "L'erreur commune,"—*NRT,* L (1923), 172.

[220] "L'erreur commune,"—*NRT,* L (1923), 363-364.

[221] *The juridical form of marriage,* p. 61.

[222] *Theologia moralis,* I, n. 836.

[223] "De errore communi ad normam can. 209,"—*Jus Pont.,* XVIII (1938) 165.

Bouuaert,[224] Fabregas,[225] Nevin [226] and Woywod.[227] Salvador likewise shares this view. To him Coronata's arguments appear inconclusive inasmuch as the texts of Wernz, D'Annibale and Gasparri—which Coronata adduced in support of the thesis that canon 209 is applicable even to cases of particular delegation to assist at marriage—could be rightly understood as applying only to the general faculty to assist at marriage.[228] Vermeersch, although he did not fulfill his promise to apply his rule to matrimony,[229] in all probability held this same thesis, i.e., the view denying the applicability of canon 209 to the case of a delegation to assist at one marriage, since he followed the general principle that before an invalid jurisdictional action could be said to be harmful to a community there would have to be error about an *habitual* power or jurisdiction of some one. This notion of Vermeersch certainly agrees with the point of view that Jombart [230] and Toso [231] hold on this same question. And it must be remembered that it was precisely because of this concept of common peril that Toso and Jombart staunchly opposed the application of canon 209 to the case of a delegation to assist at one marriage. Finally, one may adduce Cappello's statement that in such a case common error can *scarcely* be had.[232]

Since this particular point has been in the past, and, in all likelihood, will be in the future a source of concern and vexation

[224] "De conceptu erroris communis in canone 209,"—*Jus Pont.*, XVI (1936), 160-161.

[225] "De componendo canone 1094 cum 209,"—*Periodica*, XXII (1933), 199*-201*.

[226] "Does doctrine concerning the supply of jurisdiction in *common error* apply in the case of matrimony?"—*ACR*, XIV (1937), 148-151.

[227] "Does the Church supply jurisdiction for witnessing of marriages?" —*HPR*, XXX (1932-1933), 180.

[228] "Error communis et iurisdictionis suppletio ab ecclesia,"—*BE*, XVII (1939), 376.

[229] *Theologia moralis*, III, n. 459, 1.

[230] "L'erreur commune,"—*NRT*, L (1923), 365, n. 3.

[231] "De errore communi ad normam can. 209,"—*Jus Pont.*, XVIII (1938), 168.

[232] *De sacramentis*, III, n. 671.

to many priests in one capacity or another, having considered these different viewpoints of the authorities, one should spend at least a little time in making a summary review of the intrinsic arguments adduced against such an application of canon 209 and arrive at some appreciation of the manner of acting by the tribunals of the Holy See in regard to the question at hand.

Considering the essential purpose of canon 209, one can easily understand its application in cases where the common good is involved. Admitting that the invalidity of *one* marriage may cause inconveniences and hardships *the avoidance of which* urges extreme care on the part of pastors and bishops in watching over matrimonial alliances, one must nevertheless agree that, in the last analysis, the interest of only two individuals is at stake, and, furthermore, grave though the situation may be, still it can usually be remedied and repaired with comparative ease by means of convalidation of the marriage or even, in the more stubborn cases, by a radical sanation. One cannot avoid the conclusion that, if only such private, individual danger is involved, then there is no adequate reason to invoke the application of canon 209. It is true, as Fabregas points out,[233] that the law of canon 209 does not directly exclude its application to the case of such a particular delegation. The point that remains to be proved is that in such particular delegations common error can be verified in the sense exacted by the canon.

Error in regard to the competency of a priest delegated to assist at a particular marriage will not always be of the same degree and character. In some instances the error may be particular or shared by a few persons only; in others, common. In some cases the people may simply be in error concerning the delegated priest's competency to assist at some specified marriage; in others, the people may believe erroneously that the delegated priest may assist indiscriminately at any marriage in the parish or in the diocese. In the very last possibility which has been mentioned, the error may be occasioned by the fact that the

[233] "De componendo canone 1094 cum 209,"—*Periodica,* XXII (1933), 196*.

assisting priest seems to possess some office or some other title which gives him the necessary power. On the other hand, the erroneous judgment may arise simply because the people, in their ignorance of the law concerning the form of the celebration of marriage, consider that a priest does not need any special authorization to assist validly at any nuptials.

Primarily because the law in canon 1094 concerning the form of the celebration of marriage is so clear and certain, common error about this law must be considered unreasonable and not at all probable. Therefore, the Church will not supply the necessary authorization in such instances. As a matter of fact, such a common error will only rarely, if ever, arise since people of a marriageable age are aware, in however confused fashion this might be verified in individual cases, that the form of the celebration of marriage entails formalities that are more exact and defined than those which must be observed, for example, when one goes to confession. The people are generally aware of the fact that the celebration of marriage is a function reserved to their pastor or to the properly empowered assistants of the parish.

As regards error of fact in reference to the competence of a delegated priest assisting at a particular marriage, one must be very careful to observe the extent and the nature of the error. The error must be real and common. But, even before one begins to measure the number of persons who have fallen into an erroneous judgment, one must ascertain whether the error is concerned merely with the priest's capacity to assist validly at some specified marriage or whether the error is concerned with his power to assist indiscriminately at any and all other marriages in the parish or diocese.

There is little, if any, doubt that canon 209 does not apply in cases where the bridal couple, their families and other members of the wedding entourage participate in an erroneous judgment that such and such a delegated priest is validly assisting at their nuptials. Only recently the Rota has handed down decisions in

[224] S. R. R., *Nullitas matrimonii*, 20 Junii, 1931, *coram R. P. D. Arcturo Wynen*, dec. XXIX—*Decisiones*, XXIII (1931), 255-257; S. R. R., *Nullitas matrimonii*, 20 Junii, 1931, *coram R. P. D. Francisco Parrillo*, dec. XXVIII—*Decisiones*, XXIII (1931), 236-249.

two marriage cases which bear out this statement.[234] In both instances the bridal parties and even the priest were convinced that the ceremony was being performed validly and legitimately. Yet the Rota did not even consider the possibility of such an error being the deciding element in the solution of the problem of the validity or the invalidity of the marriage in question. Indeed, if such error were to be called common error, i.e., in the sense of canon 209, then the law regarding the authorization requisite for *valid* assistance would be rendered quite pointless; for, the intent of safeguarding and certifying the act of *valid* assistance would hardly ever be accompanied with the need of obtaining the express delegation which canon 1094 requires for the *valid* assistance at marriage.[235]

One might well agree with the decisions handed down by the Rota in these cases and still ask: What of the cases in which a marriage is contracted amidst great pomp, when all those present not only have no grounds to suspect the validity of the marriage being contracted but have, on the contrary, every reason to believe that the proper delegation has been secured, etc? Again, it is quite fortunate that there is available a case of the Rota to demonstrate that, even when there is truly common error in regard to a delegated priest's competence to assist at a specified marriage, it does not follow immediately that the Church supplies the authorization required for the validity of the marriage contract. In the aforementioned case settled by the Rota [236] a certain pastor of Havana was to assist at the marriage of two of his own parishioners, but outside the limits of his parish. Conscious of the need of the proper delegation, he sought and secured in 1914 from the Vicar-General the necessary authorization. According to the *ponens* of the case, the marriage ceremony took place "amidst great pomp and ceremony". The priest indubitably thought he was acting validly. So also thought the bridal couple and their party. So presumably thought the multitude of people

[235] Claeys-Bouuaert, "De conceptu erroris communi,"—*Jus Pont.*, XVI (1936), 160-161.

[236] S. R. R., *Nullitas matrimonii*, 20 Junii, 1931, *coram R. P. D. Francisco Parrillo*, dec. XXVIII—*Decisiones*, XXIII (1931), 236-249.

in attendance. Certainly in this instance there was a numerically common error with reference to the competence of the priest to assist at the nuptials in question. And yet, when, after almost nine years of married life, the marriage was attacked on the ground that the pastor who assisted had not obtained the permission of the pastor of the parish where the ceremony occurred, the securing of which was stipulated in the authorization granted by the Vicar-General, it is to be noted carefully that the argument for the validity of the marriage was in no way built up on the presence of common error concerning the priest's competence to assist at those nuptials. In fact the report of the case makes no reference to common error. This total absence of any mention of common error becomes more significant when one notes that the Rota did adduce the principle of the supplying of jurisdiction in probable doubt as a confirmatory argument.[287]

This omission on the part of the Rota of any mention of common error as an argument for the validity of the marriage ceremony in question cannot be regarded in any sense as a failure on the part of this august Tribunal to utilize a strong argument. The Rota did not adduce common error as an argument because, according to all the evidence of the case, common error, i.e., in the sense of canon 209, was simply not proved to have been present at the time of the performance of the marriage ceremony. The suppletory principle functions when the common good of the faithful of any community is jeopardized. That common peril does not exist except when the people of a community fall into error about some qualification or power which a priest is believed habitually to possess and which he might use to their common detriment. Thus, until they make a common judgment that X has the power to assist indiscriminately at the nuptials of any who might seek his ministration, there cannot be said to

[287] "Quae cum ita sint, etsi alia deficerent argumenta ad valorem praesentis matrimonii sustinendum, hoc unum sufficeret, nempe dubium positivum et probabile de vi clausulae in concessione appositae, quo in casu iurisdictionem ab Ecclesia suppleri, concors DD. sententia et Codex arcte tenet (can. 209)." — S. R. R., *Decisiones,* XXIII (1931), 249.

be any common danger present of their approaching him for his ministration and of suffering invalid matrimonial alliances. It was with such an understanding that the Sacred Congregation of the Council[238] and the Tribunal of the Rota,[239] before declaring the suppletory principle to have functioned in reference to the cases propounded to them, were particularly intent upon establishing the existence of error in the community in reference to the pastor's habitual right or title to assist at marriages in the parish indiscriminately and to perform all other properly parochial functions.

From the transitory character of particular delegations it is quite clear that the mere assistance of a delegated priest at a specified marriage can scarcely be termed a sufficiently probable basis or reason to consider him capable of assisting at any and all marriages in the community. At most, unless there should be sufficient evidence available indicating the possession of some title of jurisdiction or some office which enables him to assist at marriages in the parish or diocese indiscriminately—and, in this supposition, one would no longer deal with a merely delegated witness at a marriage ceremony—any judgment about such a general power could spring only from ignorance of the law. And as has been already seen, due to the clarity of the prescript of canon 1094, it is quite probable that the Church in such cases will not supply the necessary authorization.

III. NON-JURISDICTIONAL POWER

There is some dispute among canonists as to the precise sense in which the term *iurisdictio* of canon 209 is to be construed. On the one hand, certain canonists, like Coronata,[240] contend that this term is to be understood as contraposed to the power of Orders, and hence to include all acts which do not pertain to that

[238] S. C. Conc., 10 Martii, 1770, *Caesaraugustana matrimonii—Thesaurus resolutionum,* XXXIX (1770), 51.

[239] S. R. R., *Nullitas matrimonii,* 22 Nov. 1927, *coram R. P. D. Andrea Jullien,* dec. LI—Decisiones, XIX (1927), 453-465.

[240] "L'errore commune nell'assistenza ad un matrimonio,"—*Palestra del Clero,* IX (1930), 201ss.

power of Orders. On the other extreme, certain canonists, like Darmanin († 1939),[241] insist that *iurisdictio* is to be understood in its strict sense.[242]

Before any further consideration of this problem, it might justly be remarked that Darmanin's position appears too restrictive. The findings of this thesis have shown with some degree of certainty that the suppletory principle does apply over and beyond purely jurisdictional acts. For example, even though the act of assisting at marriage does not comprise a strictly jurisdictional act, all available evidence points to the fact that, under proper conditions, it does enjoy the benefits of canon 209.

1. *Non-jurisdictional Power Wielded by One who has an Office*

It may be summarily stated that, while the Church supplies any and all kinds of strictly jurisdictional power whenever the juridically required conditions are verified, she supplies likewise the necessary power and authorization whenever there is question of an authoritative act which flows, as it were, from jurisdiction or, rather, from an office to which jurisdiction is attached, and which requires for its validity a participation in that same office. On the basis that *accesorium sequitur principale,* the Church supplies all those things whose proper integration is joined with the valid exercise of all the powers inherent in an ecclesiastical office.[243].

This is not a teaching which one may term new. On the contrary, if the reader will but recall, when the actions of Barbarius

[241] "De promissione matrimoniali ad can. 1019 CIC,"—*Angelicum* VIII (1931), 347-348.

[242] I.e., according to the norm of canon 118.

[243] Cf., e.g., J. Nevin, "Does doctrine concerning the supply of jurisdiction in *common error* apply in the case of matrimony?"—*ACR,* XIV (1937), 146; A. Toso, "Jurisdictio quando ab ecclesia suppleatur,"—*Jus Pont.,* XVII (1937), 100; F. Claeys-Bouuaert et G. Simenon, *Manuale juris canonici* (4. ed., Gandae et Leodii, 1934-1935), I, n. 363; A. Salvador, "Error communis et iurisdictionis suppletio ab ecclesia,"—*BE,* XVII (1939), 381.

were declared as valid despite his servile condition, the validity of all of his acts . . . *"quae edixit"* and *"quae decrevit"* was upheld. There was no restriction to merely and purely jurisdictional acts.[244] Thus the old writers understood both the Church and the State to supply not only jurisdiction properly so called but whatever was necessary for the full administration of one's office. It was thus that Suarez, [245] Sanchez,[246] Lessius,[247] De Lugo [248] and Thesaurus-Giraldi [249] understood the *Lex Barbarius* and the ecclesiastical legislation built on the principle it involved.

In view of this doctrine, one might note to advantage a few examples for the sake of illustration. A pastor, for example, performs many official acts which are not of a jurisdictional nature and which do not imply an exercise of his power of Orders. Thus his assisting at marriage, his witnessing of *sponsalia,*[250] his contracts and all other administrative actions would be valid in view of canon 209.[251] In the same manner, the dominative actions of a religious superior, e.g., the investing of his subjects in the religious habit, the reception of their religious profession, the expulsion of them from the community, the various

[244] D. (1. 14) 3.

[245] *De censuris,* Disp. XIX, sec. I, nn. 9-10; *De poenitentia,* Disp. XXVI, sec. VI, n. 7.

[246] *De matrimonio,* Tom. I, lib. III, disp. 22, n. 61.

[247] *De iustitia et iure,* lib. II, cap. 29, n. 67.

[248] *De justitia et jure,* Disp. XXXVII, sec. III, n. 20.

[249] "Item procedit sc. iurisdictionis suppletio in errore communi in potestate conferendi beneficia, vel confirmandi, quia dicitur publicum officium potestate, et utilitate, et generaliter quod titulus coloratus cum errore communi reddat validos omnes actus iurisdictionis formaliter, ut assistentia parochi in matrimonio contrahendo, electiones, praesentationes, instrumenti publici confectiones . . . et idem dicendum est de actu admittendi ad professionem, qui non est actus iurisdictionis sed publici officii."—*De poenis ecclesiasticis,* Part. I, cap. VI.

[250] Canon 1017.

[251] In regard to a putative pastor witnessing the *sponsalia,* it is proper to note that, while Darmanin holds that the suppletory principle will not function, he admits that all other writers maintain the applicability of canon 209 in such a case.—"De promissione matrimoniali ad can. 1017 CIC,"—*Angelicum, VIII* (1931), 347.

contracts entered into in view of his official duties, would all be endowed with validity in virtue of the saving norm of canon 209, *if* the said superior holds an office in the strict ecclesiastical sense of canons 145, § 1, and 197, §1, as happens in the case of superiors in clerical exempt religious institutes.[252]

2. *Purely Dominative Power*

Dominative power, as has been seen in the preliminary notions, is readily distinguishable from jurisdictional power precisely on account of its eminently *private* character. Though distinct and separable, these two powers may reside simultaneously in the same person.[253]

Dominative power, as has been seen, may derive from one of three sources: 1.) from *nature,* as in the case of the power which a father has over his child; 2.) from *nature and contract,* as in the case of the power which a husband has over his wife; 3.) from a *contract,* as in the case of the power which a religious superior has over his or her subjects.

As Kearney points out, the Code is not interested with merely domestic or social power.[254] Thus, also, in the question of the applicability or non-applicability of canon 209 to cases of purely dominative power, there is no question of the dominative power which arises from the natural law. The question, instead, is concerning the validity or invalidity of juridical acts, that is to say, of acts whose consequences are established or specially sanctioned by the social power of the Church.[255] Thus, by way of illustration, there is question of the validity or invalidity of ad-

[252] Cf., Pruemmer, "An invalid election and its consequences,"—*HPR,* XXX (1929-1930), 74-74; V. Schaaf, "Profession under a superioress holding office invalidly,"—*AER,* CI (1939), 267; Parsons, *Canonical elections* (The Catholic University of America, Canon Law Studies, n. 118: Washington, D. C., 1939), p. 162.

[253] Schäfer, *Compendium de religiosis ad normam iuris canonici* (2. ed., Münster i. W., 1931), p. 179.

[254] *The principles of delegation,* p. 49.

[255] I. Creusen, "Pouvoir dominatif et erreur commune,"—*Acta congressus iuridici internationalis,* IV. 186.

missions by a reputed superior to the novitiate or to religious profession, of dismissals of religious, of contracts entered into by such superiors in the name of the community.

a. Pre-Code Background

An examination of pre-Code authors reveals that there was no law, anterior to the Code, which explicitly or implicitly provided for this difficulty in regard to canon 209's applicability or non-applicability to that form of dominative power which, either by direct establishment or indirect sanctioning by the Church, is required as the basis of the juridical validity of certain acts. As far as the teaching of these same authors is concerned, though it be true that the question of dominative power did not altogether escape their attention, still there is grave reason for doubting whether *any* of these pre-Code authors conceived and wrote about the same difficulty that has just been proposed on these pages.

There is found in Sanchez († 1610), a significant text concerning dominative power.[256] While he touched upon the problem of dominative power, it is to be carefully noted that he did so in reference to the power to annul *private* vows. In substance, Sanchez held that the annulment of a private vow as granted by an interloper who simulated the authority of a religious superior, of a father, or of a husband, would have to be declared invalid in its effects as soon as it was detected and proved as an act of counterfeit authority, despite its appraisal as a valid act of approved authority up to the time of the eventual denouement. Sanchez' reason, which, he alleged to substantiate his view, was drawn from the fact that the *Lex Barbarius* could not logically be argued to exert its suppletory force beyond the acts of strict jurisdiction to the acts of a non-jurisdictional character which derive their existence from an officially established or approved status endowed with a power of juridic dominance and authorized control. Besides revealing Sanchez' belief that the suppletory principle does not extend to the power to annul *private*

[256] *In decalogo,* IV, c. XXXII, nn. 15-16.

vows, this text gives the reader a fair sort of indication that this particular question of dominative power had not gained much attention from Sanchez' predecessors and contemporaries. For, though he is usually very profuse with citations of authors treating of the different points raised by him, in this particular question of dominative power Sanchez cites no one.

Bonacina († 1631),[257] in like fashion held that the *Lex Barbarius* did not apply to dominative power. But it is worthy of note, that while Sanchez wrote of the power of a superior, or of a husband, or of a father to annul private vows, Bonacina used the example of a private person selling something which he wrongly considered as his possession.

Castropalao († 1633),[258] speaking explicitly of dominative power, and claiming to follow Sanchez and Bonacina, stated in precise terms what his predecessors intimated more by way of example, namely, that he did not believe in the applicability of the *Lex Barbarius* to dominative power, simply because the laws made no provision for such an application. Thus, also, LaCroix († 1714),[259] following Sanchez, denied in very explicit fashion any such applicability on the ground that the analogy is not expressed in the law.

The Salmanticenses realized that one could not underestimate the authority of men like Sanchez, Bonacina, Castropalao, Truellench († 1664) and Leander († 1603), all of whom contended that the *Lex Barbarius* did not exert its suppletory influence over dominative acts. Although they readily granted the probability of this opinion, the Salmanticenses, for their own part,[260] claiming to follow Prado († 1668), argued the presence of the analogy which LaCroix strove to minimize as sufficient reason for applying the suppletory principle to dominative power, and insisted that the same *ratio* governs both cases, and that, therefore, in

[257] *De voto,* Disp. IV, Q. 2, p. 7, §2, n. 33.

[258] *De voto,* Tract. XV, Disp. II, punct. IV, n. 10.

[259] *Theologia moralis,* lib. VI, P. I. n. 113.

[260] *Cursus theologiae moralis,* Tom. IV, Tract. XVII, C. III, punct. VIII, n. 71.

all probability the *Lex Barbarius* applied both to jurisdictional and to dominative power.

St. Alphonsus [261] merely recorded the existence of these two opinions without choosing between them. Ballerini-Palmieri,[262] however, sided with Sanchez without giving any further reasons for so doing.

As Creusen well put it,[263] it may be summarily said that there existed no law, that there was no commonly taught or commonly received doctrine in the period before the Code concerning the point of this short study. Sanchez and Bonacina, it is true, wrote of dominative power. But, they wrote of definite, determined cases which would be decided today no differently from the way in which they were solved then. For, a *private* vow does not entail the juridical effects, the rights and the duties, recognized and sanctioned by public authority. Any annulment of such a vow affects only the conscience of the individual. The right to such annulling is based upon natural law or convention. The legislator cannot create this power. Nor, on the other hand, is it to his interest to free such individuals by making use of his jurisdictional power of dispensation.

Despite the greater precision of their words, it is not clear from the context that even Castropalao and LaCroix did not consider this problem of dominative power from identically the same perspective as did Sanchez and Bonacina. But, supposing for the moment that they did regard the problem from substantially the same point of view as does this short study, one must admit that the texts of these two, as well as of St. Alphonsus, Ballerini-Palmieri and the Salmanticenses, merely indicate that, as a general rule, canonists did not consider this problem. And, among the few who did consider the same there was a clear division of opinion.

[261] *Theologia moralis,* lib. III, n. 232.
[262] *Opus theologicum morale,* lib. VI, sect. III, cap. 3.
[263] "Pouvoir dominatif et erreur commune,"—*Acta congressus iuridici internationalis,* IV, 191-192.

b. Post-Code Doctrine

The Code does not make any explicit or implicit provision concerning the present problem. Even today this problem has not received treatment by many authors. As Schaaf correctly observes,[264] the general attitude among canonists is that canon 209 may be regarded as applicable even in the case of acts which are not properly jurisdictional, but only in the event that the power to perform such acts flows from jurisdiction or, rather, from an office to which jurisdiction is attached. And from a similar manner of expression of other canonists, like F. Claeys-Bouuaert—G. Simenon[265] and Toso,[266] it would seem that they wish to exclude the possibility of extending the application of canon 209 to the acts of any one who is erroneously reputed to possess purely dominative power. Thus, by way of illustration, these authors would deny the applicability of canon 209 in the case of superiors of non-exempt clerical religious institutes and of superiors, be they men or women, of lay religious institutes.

However, there are several authors of repute who hold that canon 209 should be applied in the case of dominative power as well as in that of strictly jurisdictional activity. Thus, Maroto,[267] studying the rubric of the Code in book II, title V, *De potestate ordinaria et delegata,* argues that the use of the generic term *potestas* signifies the legislator's intent that the canons under this title are not to be restricted to jurisdiction alone, but proportionately, should be applied to the administrative activity of pastors, to the dominative power of non-exempt religious superiors and to other such non-jurisdictional activities of the external forum. Some authors, like Kearney[268] and Coronata,[269] were evidently convinced that there was at least some cogency in this argument as

[264] "Profession under a superioress holding office invalidly,"—*AER,* CI (1939), 266.

[265] *Manuale juris canonici,* I, n. 363.

[266] "Jurisdictio quando ab Ecclesia suppleatur,"—*Jus Pont.,* XVII (1937), 100.

[267] *Institutiones,* I, 694.

[268] *The principles of delegation,* p. 49.

[269] *Institutiones,* I, n. 275, note 6. Cf. also "L'errore commune nell'assistenza ad un matrimonio,"—*Palestra del Clero,* IX (1930), 201ss.

deduced by Maroto. Others, as Creusen,[270] remained unconvinced of the cogency of such argumentation. However, despite their differences of opinion in evaluating the juridical import of the title, these authors, joined by a few others, agree that canon 209 should be applied to dominative power in virtue of the provisions of canon 20. Thus, among others, Creusen,[271] Coronata[272] and Vermeersch[273] are convinced that there exists a real analogy between the power of jurisdiction and this form of dominative power. Coronata, in particular, stresses the fact that he does not consider it an absurd but a truly juridical analogy. Goyeneche,[274] also noting this analogy between jurisdiction and this particular type of dominative power, holds that in either case there is present identically the same motive for the Church to supply: public utility. And he notes: *"Ubi eadem ratio est, eadem debet esse iuris dispositio,"* Creusen,[275] marshalling together, as it were, all these arguments, notes that:

1. such an application of canon 209 to this form of dominative power is *necessary* to safeguard the good of the community;
2. such an application is *possible* because the power which needs to be supplied is required exclusively by positive, human law;
3. there is a real analogy betwen jurisdictional power and this form of dominative power;
4. such an application of canon 209 is entirely in accord with the evolution of the doctrine and practice of the *Lex Barbarius* in ecclesiastical law;
5. there is nothing in pre-Code law in opposition to such an application.

[270] "Pouvoir dominatif et erreur commune,"—*Acta congressus iuridici internationalis,* IV, 184-185.

[271] "Pouvoir dominatif et erreur commune," *Acta congressus iuridici internationalis,* IV, 191.

[272] *Institutiones,* I, n. 275, note 6.

[273] *Epitome* (3. ed., Mechliniae, 1927), I, n. 274.

[274] "Consultationes,"—*CpR,* XIII (1932), 196-198.

[275] "Pouvoir dominatif et erreur commune,"—*Acta congressus iuridici internationalis,* IV, 191.

CONCLUSION

Surely a teaching held as *"valid"* by Maroto,[276] as *"certain"* by Kearney,[277] as *"fitting and necessary"* by Creusen [278] and as *"juridically acceptable"* by Coronata [279] and Vermeersch-Creusen,[280] cannot be cast aside without further ado. The whole problem in regard to dominative power involves, it is true, merely *private* power and concerns individual members of an *imperfect* society. The Church does not confer this power even when she approves the constitutions of religious institutes. The power arises from the subjection which the members owe to the superior in virtue of the vows they have taken. The Church is said merely to moderate that power.[281] On precisely this basis, certain authors aver that, pending an extensive interpretation of canon 209 by the Holy See, the suppletory principle does not apply to merely dominative power as exercised, for example, by a religious superioress.[282] Admittedly this theory rests upon a good argument. But it seems that the theory of Maroto, Kearney, Creusen and Coronata has at least a fair degree of probability. For it remains true that the validity of certain actions, performed in virtue of that private power, has been sanctioned and recognized by the *public* power of the Church. Therefore, it may be a bit hasty and premature to conclude to the non-applicability of canon 209 to merely dominative power. On the other hand, it might also be a mistake to conclude to such an applicability of the suppletory principle without any further proofs. But, it can at least be said, in the words of Goyeneche,[283] that it is by no means an *arbitrary* affirmation to

[276] *Institutiones,* I, 694.

[277] *The principles of delegation,* p. 50.

[278] "Pouvoir dominatif et erreur commune,"—*Acta congressus iuridici internationalis,* IV, 192.

[279] *Institutiones,* I, n. 275, note 6.

[280] *Epitome,* I, n. 274.

[281] J. Fernández, "Super instructione S. C. de Propaganda Fide diei 8 decembris, 1929,"—*CpR,* XII (1931), 284.

[282] E.g., Pruemmer, "An invalid election and its consequences,"—*HPR,* XXX (1929-1930), 72-75; Schaaf, "Profession under a superioress holding office invalidly,"—*AER,* CI (1939), 267.

[283] "Consultationes,"—*CpR,* XIII (1932), 196-198.

aver that canon 209 ought to, or does, apply to the case of dominative power.

What the correct solution of the problem is cannot be stated too definitely and positively. Of course, there is no difficulty in practice when there is doubt about the validity of certain acts, such as the act of admission to the novitiate and the act of receiving a religious profession, as long as the persons concerned are willing to apply for and obtain a radical sanation to ensure the effect of validity for these acts. A difficulty, however, arises when the interested parties attack the validity of their novitiate or of their profession with the hope of securing their freedom from further continuance in the religious life. In such an event it will seem best indicated to seek a solution of the problem directly from the Holy See. A case thus submitted may eventually offer an occasion for acquiring a more definite understanding of the extent to which the suppletory principle of canon 209 becomes operative in relation to cases wherein there is at stake the validity of acts entirely dependent on the use of dominative power.

ARTICLE III. LICIT USE OF CANON 209

Up to this point the entire discussion of this thesis has been concerned with determining the barest minimum required to insure the validity of jurisdictional acts performed under the circumstances covered by canon 209. However, over and above this question, another problem remains to be studied. It is a problem that is of much interest and importance to every priest and, although to a lesser degree for reasons soon to be seen, to all the faithful receiving any ministrations from a priest whose actions are valid only in virtue of the suppletory principle. The question concerns the conditions requisite for a licit use, i.e., the conditions requisite if the individual is to make use of the benefit of canon 209 wholly in accordance with the will of the legislator.

In brief resumé, it needs but be recalled that there is a marked difference in the supplying by the Church in the two cases included in canon 209. In the case of common error jurisdiction is supplied which is *certainly* absent. In the case of positive and probable doubt of fact or of law, however, the jurisdiction is supplied only *ad cautelam,* there being a strong presumption that the minister possesses it independently of any supplying by the Church.[1] This difference is fully reflected in the conditions required for licit participation in and reception of jurisdictional power in the two instances considered in canon 209. For this reason the attention of the reader shall first be focused upon the conditions requisite for the licit, premeditated application of canon 209, in cases of common error. Subsequently, consideration shall be given to the conditions similarly necessary in cases of positive and probable doubt whether of fact or of law. Finally, a brief inspection will be made of whatever penal sanctions the Code contains regarding unlawful use of this canon.

A. Common Error

The Church has made it very clear by her legislation that the demands of her jurisdictional system be seriously observed. For,

[1] Vermeersch, *Theologia moralis,* III, n. 459, 2; De Meester, *Compendium,* I, p. 325, footnote 2; Raus, *Institutiones canonicae,* n. 78, II.

note her very strict and definitive jurisdictional norms in general,[2] and her stringent, particular laws in reference both to the internal[3] and to the external forum.[4] The Church has found by her long experience that these laws are perhaps the best human safeguards for the good of the Church and of the faithful. She has enacted these laws to insure the faithful the proper sacramental and extra-sacramental ministrations by a properly equipped and carefully selected clergy. The sole objectionable feature of the exercise of jurisdiction under the circumstance of common error lies precisely in this that such usage forces the Church to deviate from the usual methods prescribed by law for the acquisition of jurisdictional power and to supply this power to any, even to the most unworthy priest. And even though the Church supplies willingly enough in such instances for the good of the faithful, still it is readily seen how such an extraordinary usage is definitely a deordination. For that reason the use of the jurisdictional power, secured in virtue of common error, is *per se* illicit, and will become licit only when there will be present a reason for acting which will counterbalance this disturbance of right order.[5] And just as it is illicit for the priest to act jurisdictionally under the prescripts of canon 209 without sufficient cause, in proportionate fashion, for substantially the same reasons, the reception of such ministration will be illicit for the faithful who know of the defect in the jurisdictional power of a particular priest and nevertheless seek him out and demand his services.

I. *Minister*

First of all, it is to be noted, authors quite generally agree that it is in no way licit for a priest actively to induce common error either directly or indirectly.[6] Noldin-Schmitt,[7] however, would

[2] Canons 196-210.

[3] Canons 872-900.

[4] Cf. canons 1043-1045; 1049-1052; 1094-1096; 1098, n. 2; 2236ss.

[5] Aertnys-Damen, *Theologia moralis*, II, n. 360.

[6] Vermeersch, *Theologia moralis*, III, n. 494, 6: ". . . intrinsice illicitum est, ut quis se fingat approbatum seu *errorem communem provocet.*" Cf. also, Jombart, "L'erreur commune,"—*NRT*, L (1923), 179; Oesterle, *Praelectiones*, p. 113, n. 3.

[7] *Theologia moralis*, III, n. 347.

allow a priest who is conscious of his lack of jurisdiction to provoke common error if he were morally unable to secure the necessary jurisdiction and, at the same time, could not decline the administration of the sacraments. The example they give is of a parochial vicar who, on the morning of a feast, with a large gathering of people waiting at the confessional, remembers that his jurisdiction has expired and yet cannot obtain the necessary faculty in suitable time.

But, once the condition of common error is verified, what reasons are necessary to warrant for the priest the licit use of the jurisdiction supplied by canon 209? That is a question that has not been settled entirely to the satisfaction of all. Thus Raus [8] properly criticized a statement of Jombart wherein the latter claimed that all canonists were agreed in demanding the presence of some *necessity* for the licit use of canon 209 in common error.[9] Génicot-Salsmans bear out Raus' contention; for they, too, were apparently aware of this lack of unanimity.[10]

Oesterle,[11] for example, did not at all consider the use of the jurisdiction supplied in virtue of the presence of common error as any kind of deordination. On the contrary, he rated jurisdiction thus secured on a par with jurisdiction secured by institution in an office, or by delegation, or by the confirmation of an election. In a similar manner Noldin [12] implicitly seemed to require no reason for the licit use other than the presence of common error. For he clearly wrote that he thought it would not be sinful for a priest, if he recalls with moral certainty that his jurisdiction had already expired, to continue hearing confessions. Noldin adjudged the presence of common error alone as sufficient reason for the priest to continue. Another group of canonists, of whom Cappello makes mention without naming them,[13] thought that it would not be more

[8] "Mangelnde Jurisdiktion und error communis,"—*LQS,* LXXV (1922), 298.

[9] "Juridiction et bonne foi,"—*NRT,* XLVII (1920), 549.

[10] *Theologia moralis,* II, n. 330.

[11] *Praelectiones,* p. 113, n. 3.

[12] *Theologia moralis,* (15. and 16. eds., Oeniponte, 1923), III, n. 346, 1, b.

[13] *De sacramentis,* II, Pars I, n. 492.

than venially sinful for a priest to use without sufficiently grave reason the jurisdiction supplied in virtue of common error. Cappello considered this opinion solidly probable and followed it himself. Thus, since he considered the use of this jurisdiction without any due cause no more than a venial matter, it is not difficult to see how Cappello considered the desire of the penitent to receive Communion on Sunday or on a feast-day of precept or on any extraordinary occasion sufficient cause to absolve in virtue of the common error of the faithful if an approved priest could not be secured, or even if one could be reached but only at a grave inconvenience. In like manner, faced with the objective fact that it is not easy in all cases to be sure of the presence of a grave necessity, especially on the part of a penitent, Cappello held that scruples and anxieties on this score are hardly ever to be entertained so long as the people willingly come and ask to have their confession heard or so long as some extraordinary set of circumstances comes into being.

Cappello's theory and the theories of Oesterle and of Noldin, have never enjoyed a numerous following among authors. Cavigioli,[14] for example, protested on the score that Cappello's view was too liberal and therefore not acceptable to the mind of the bishops who, after all, are the ordinary fount of jurisdiction. Cavigioli warned that, when reasoning seems safe but the consequences become clashing, it is highly advisable to retreat, to recheck all the steps in the argument and to find the flaw in the reasoning.

As Kearney [15] and Coronata [16] observe, the common opinion of the authors favors the necessity of the presence of a *grave cause* for the licit use of jurisdiction secured in virtue of common error. And it may be interesting to note that, while Cappello himself followed a more liberal view, still he regarded this opinion as the more common and the more acceptable.[17]

In studying the concepts of the individual authors as to what

[14] "Teologia morale,"—*La Scuola Cattolica,* XVI (1930), 220-221.

[15] *The principles of delegation,* p. 138.

[16] *Institutiones,* I, n. 293, 2.

[17] *De sacramentis,* II, pars I, n. 492.

constitutes a grave cause, it may be helpful to note that all of them follow, in whole or in part, the circumstances under which St. Alphonsus declared the use of probable jurisdiction licit.[18] As one inspects, after the fashion of Jombart,[19] the order in which St. Alphonsus drew up these circumstances, namely, grace necessity, great utility and a reasonable cause, one feels that he made a special effort to let the bars down as far as he could without depriving the Church of all her sanctions against real usurpation of jurisdiction. One can appreciate the existence of this same attitude of mind on the part of canonists and moralists, although they are not quite agreed among themselves as to what should be considered a sufficient cause. Some are content that *grave necessity* alone will warrant the licit use of jurisdiction secured in virtue of the existence of common error.[20]

Others admit *public utility* as a sufficient cause.[21] Vermeersch[22] sides with this opinion. He cites the example of a missionary priest who, while giving a public mission, suddenly realizes that the necessary jurisdiction was not secured for him by anyone, either because of forgetfulness or because of sheer negligence. Vermeersch would consider public utility sufficiently at stake to insure the licit use of canon 209. But he simultaneously inculcates the obligation, of course, of securing the necessary faculties as soon as at all possible. Others still, in an attempt at greater mildness stress the sufficiency of a *reasonable cause.*[23] Still others follow almost verbatim the three conditions set down by St. Alphonsus.[24]

In general, then, all the authors here mentioned hold that a *grave reason* will justify the licit use of the jurisdiction supplied in virtue

[18] Cf. *Theologia moralis,* VI, n. 573.

[19] "L'erreur commune,"—*NRT,* L (1923), 180.

[20] E.g., Vermeersch-Creusen, *Epitome,* I, n. 232; Wernz-Vidal, *Ius canonicum,* II, n. 382; Chelodi, *Ius de personis,* n. 130; Cocchi, *Commentarium,* lib. II, pars. I n. 134; Merkelbach, *Summa,* III, n. 586.

[21] Wouters, *Manuale,* I, n. 104; Jombart, "L'erreur commune,"—*NRT,* L (1923), 172.

[22] *Theologia moralis,* III, n. 494, 4.

[23] E.g., Maroto, *Institutiones,* I, 731, 5 d.

[24] E.g., Kelly, *The jurisdiction of the confessor,* p. 140; Badii, *Institutiones,* n. 149.

of common error. Nevertheless one must be prepared to find some authors a little more strict than others in admitting the presence of a sufficient cause. For example, while Guns would not consider the fact that a considerable number of people wishes to go to communion on a First Friday as a sufficient necessity or cause to warrant the use of supplied jurisdiction as a licit mode of procedure,[25] Aertnys-Damen [26] and Kearney [27] would seem to lean towards considering such an occasion as a sufficient cause for the lawful hearing of the penitents' confessions.

To set up an all inclusive enumeration of the cases that warrant the licit exercise of jurisdiction would be, as is readily seen, a task well-nigh impossible. However, it is entirely in order to note at least a few sample instances suggested by the authors to indicate the normal concept of what constitutes a grave cause. Badii [28] was content that a sufficient cause would be present if the penitent were in need of the help or counsel of a particular confessor who possesses no jurisdiction other than that made available in virtue of common error, or if the accomplice in a sin of the penitent were known to the confessor who possesses habitual faculties, but unknown to the confessor who can act only in virtue of common error, or if the precept of annual confession were binding, or again, if a singular indulgence were to be gained.

Aertnys-Damen [29] would consider the danger of scandal sufficient reason, as would Kearney.[30] In a similar way Jombart [31] would allow the hearing of confessions and the assisting at marriages under conditions of common error, if such an action were necessary to forestall or to avoid scandal, gossip, or malevolent insinuations against the clergy, the fiancés, or their families. Reiffenstuel († 1703) [32] and after him, Berardi († 1768) [33] considered any

[25] "L'erreur commune,"—*NRT,* L (1923), 536.

[26] *Theologia moralis,* II, n. 360.

[27] *The principles of delegation,* p. 138.

[28] *Institutiones,* n. 149.

[29] *Theologia moralis,* II, n. 360.

[30] *The principles of delegation,* p. 138.

[31] "L'erreur commune,"—*NRT,* L (1923), 181.

[32] *Ius canonicum universum,* lib. I, tit. XXXI, n. 210.

[33] *Praxis confessoriorum,* II, n. 4559.

danger of gravely exposing one's reputation as a sufficient reason for the priest to proceed. Thus, also, would Vermeersch-Creusen [84] consider licit the use of supplied jurisdiction in common error if otherwise grave loss would result for the priest or to the faithful. The Church, they contend, is to be considered as not urging her prohibition when such a grave loss on the part of the priest or of the faithful is at stake. For in such a case there is already absent every semblance of arrogant usurpation of jurisdictional power which the Church opposes so strongly. Negatively, Jone [85] stated that he did not consider as a sufficiently grave reason the fact that the refusal to act with a jurisdiction secured in conditions of common error would incur the displeasure of the pastor. Of course, it is to be understood, over and above what Jone says, that, if in a specific instance aggravating causes should exist, the exercise of supplied jurisdiction could then hardly be called illicit.

These few samples indicate at least what is fundamentally meant by a cause sufficiently serious to warrant the licit exercise of supplied jurisdiction. As long as the cause is reasonable, there need be no concern on the part of the priest. Any greater or stricter demands would be bound to cause the priest almost undue anxiety. for, as Wernz-Vidal [86] and Cappello [87] observed, in practice it is not always an easy thing to discern the presence of grave necessity, particularly on the part of the penitent. Unless one were satisfied with some reasonable probability about its presence, which reasonableness would incidentally not detract from the regard which should be had for the Church's plan of the ordinary dispensation of jurisdictional competence, a priest could hardly venture to act in border-line cases without committing sin.

II. *The Faithful*

In line with his view, whereby he considers that jurisdiction supplied in virtue of common error should not be restricted in its

[84] *Epitome,* I, n. 284, 5b.

[85] "Suppletion der Beichtjurisdiktion bei einem dubium facti,"—*LQS,* LXXXI (1928), 576.

[86] *Ius canonicum,* II, n. 382.

[87] *De sacramentis,* II, Pars I, n. 493, 1.

use and exercise any more than jurisdiction secured in the normal manner, Oesterle [38] would allow the faithful to avail themselves of the exercise of supplied jurisdiction if and when, under the existing condition of common error, they themselves were not unaware of the defect in the title of jurisdiction of the minister. According to Oesterle, the faithful could avail themselves of such supplied jurisdiction at their convenience. And they could even accept penitential ministration without receiving invalid absolution because of the lack of proper dispositions. Oesterle would ask for a grave reason on the part of the faithful only if and when they would have doubt about the presence of common error.

But this attitude seems hardly tenable in view of the general teaching of canonists on the matter. Quite appropriately authors commonly concede that the reason need not be as grave on the part of the faithful as on the part of the priest.[39] Nevertheless, they likewise commonly demand that there be some just reason, e.g., an urgent necessity, or some real difficulty in approaching another priest. De Meester [40] remarks in regard to this point that the just reason here required has to be proportionately greater or lesser according to the measure of the gravity of the jurisdictional acts. He stresses this factor especially in regard to the sacrament of penance; for, an absolution given in virtue of a supplied jurisdiction can nevertheless become invalid, not of course because the priest lacks the necessary jurisdiction but because of the readily imaginable lack of proper disposition on the part of the penitent, if the while he knows the real situation he still approaches the priest without reasonable cause, and thereby posits an *obex* to the efficacy of the sacramental absolution.

It may well be said that, as a general rule, authors are agreed that beyond the case of at least the positively probable verification of a reasonable cause, it would be illicit even for the faithful to

[38] *Praelectiones,* p. 113, n. 3.

[39] Coronata, *Institutiones,* I, n. 293, 2; Maroto, *Institutiones,* I, 731; Wernz-Vidal, *Ius canonicum,* II, n. 382, 4.

[40] *Compendium,* I, 482.

avail themselves of the exercise of jurisdiction supplied by the Church in common error.[41]

B. Doubt

Because the Church expressly, though implicity, excludes negative doubt as a condition or as a possible occasion for the supplying of any jurisdiction which might be wanting, the validity of jurisdictional acts performed in such a doubt depends in each individual case upon the objective presence or absence of the necessary competence. And since the lack of any positive and probable reasons renders the validity of the action highly dubious, it is *per se* illicit for the priest to act on the basis of such a doubt. Unless there be grave necessity for the priest to use even such negative probability because of his inability to defer the ministration to the faithful and of their dire need of such ministration at the moment, the priest is definitely not to posit any jurisdictional acts in such situations. Canonists are generally agreed that the priest could, for example, conditionally absolve a penitent in merely negative doubt on the score that Christ has instituted the sacraments in token of his benevolent helpfulness to man. But they all demand a grave necessity for so doing. Such a necessity, according to St. Alphonsus,[42] would be verified in the event that the obligation of yearly confession were binding, or the penitent were obliged to say Mass or receive Communion and could not postpone such actions without bringing disgrace upon himself, or a priest were obliged to say Mass in fulfillment of his duty. These causes other canonists have accepted up to this day. Cappello adds [43] that a grave necessity, allowing the use of jurisdiction that is only negatively doubtful, would be verified if otherwise a penitent would lack absolution for a long time. Of course, whenever a priest acts on the basis of such a doubt, he is bound, *ceteris paribus,* to warn the penitent to go to confession as soon as possible to a confessor who certainly possesses jurisdiction.[44]

[41] Bargilliat, *Praelectiones iuris canonici* (37. ed., Parisiis, 1923-1924), I, n. 309, b.

[42] *Theologia moralis,* VI, n. 571.

[43] *De sacramentis,* II, Pars I, n. 499.

[44] Vermeersch-Creusen, *Epitome,* III, n. 493.

But in regard to positive and probable doubt of fact or of law, wherein the Church will supply if necessary, there is a remarkable reduction in the demands of canonists regarding the sufficient reason that entitles the priest to exercise and the people to utilize a jurisdiction which at most needs to be supplied only conditionally.

Before the Code authors were wont to demand a *grave* cause.[45] Thus St. Alphonsus required the presence of *grave necessity,* or *special utility,* or a *reasonable cause,* lest the Church be wrongly construed as conniving with the unrestrained liberty of the priest. In like manner Lehmkuhl exacted grave cause.[46]

But since the Code authors are universally agreed that no grave reason is ever required for the licit use of probable jurisdiction. This is readily understandable when one considers that to be efficacious in its suppletory character a doubt has to be truly positive and probable, and not a mere figment of a priest's imagination, or the result of ignorance pure and simple. Nevertheless, while all are agreed that in a positive and probable doubt of law no cause whatsoever is required for the licit use of supplied jurisdiction,[47] certain authors, like Cappello,[48] require at least some cause in order to absolve licitly in a positive and probable doubt of fact. This view is open to some objection. First of all when a priest acts upon a positive and probable doubt of fact, he is not exposing the sacrament to the danger of nullity. Nor is he compelling the Church to supply jurisdiction against her will inasmuch as the concession of the second part of canon 209 is granted for the benefit of the priest as well as for the good of the faithful.[49]

This difference of opinion among authors is not to be unduly

[45] Cf. J. Brys, "De censurarum absolutione," — *Coll. Brug.,* XXXIII (1933), 266, note 4.

[46] *Theologia moralis,* II, nn. 390-391.

[47] Cf., e.g., Wernz-Vidal, *Ius canonicum,* II, n. 382; Vermeersch-Creusen, *Epitome,* I, n. 284; Cappello, *De sacramentis,* II, Pars I, n. 500; Kelly, *The jurisdiction of the confessor,* p. 144.

[48] *De sacramentis,* II, Pars I, n. 500.

[49] Cf., e.g., Kelly, *The jurisdiction of the confessor,* p. 144; Noldin-Schmitt, *Theologia moralis,* III, n. 347; Wernz-Vidal, *Ius canonicum,* II, n. 382.

magnified however. For all of the authors feel that in practice a priest's actual engaging in the legitimate exercise of his office or sphere of duties constitutes a sufficient reason for him to continue his jurisdictional ministration when he adverts to the not altogether certain, but still solidly probable, possession of the requisite jurisdictional power in view of some doubt attaching to the fact on whose actual existence the very possession of the jurisdiction depends.[50] This Cappello, writing of a truly probable doubt of fact entertained by a priest in the internal forum, and conscious of the existence of a controversy among authors regarding the necessity of a just cause, averred that in practice there will scarcely be any occasion or situation when such a cause will not be verified. The very fact of the person coming to confession, for example, would be a sufficiently just cause for the priest to proceed in hearing that confession and in granting absolution whenever the penitent is properly disposed.

As regards the faithful in these cases of doubt, there is little difficulty about how they should act. For, either they know that the jurisdiction is probable only or they have no inkling at all even as to the existence of the problem in the mind of the priest. In the latter case no one can attribute any sin to them if they ask for the priest's ministrations. In the former case, if they knew definitely that the priest was entirely wrong in his calculation and thus did not possess jurisdiction, they of course could hardly under any circumstances approach him in good faith and demand his serice. But, if they saw that the required qualities were present in the priest's probable opinion that he has jurisdiction, certainly they could approach him with even the slightest reason.

C. Penal Sanctions

The bishop, as pastor of his diocese, has the distinct duty of seeing to it that the prescripts of Church law will be faithfully observed by his subjects in accordance with the mind of the

[50] Wernz-Vidal, *Ius canonicum,* II, n. 382; Maroto, *Institutiones,* I, 731; De Meester, *Compendium,* I, n. 482; Cappello, *De sacramentis,* II, Pars I, n. 500, 2°; J. Brys, "De censurarum absolutione,"—*Coll. Brug.,* XXXIII (1933), 265-266.

supreme legislator. In this capacity the bishop can draw up the necessary disciplinary regulations and penal sanctions, always with due regard for canon 2222, § 1, to forestall or to punish any usurpation of power on the part of the clergy. But there is one form of jurisdictional usurpation which the Code singled out in particular, namely the usurpation of penitential jurisdiction, because it implies encroachment upon a most sacred domain. This usurpation the Code has severely penalized in canon 2366. This canon reads:

> **Sacerdos qui sine necessaria iurisdictione praesumpserit sacramentales confessiones audire, est ipso facto suspensus a divinis; qui vero a peccatis reservatis absolvere, ipso facto suspensus est ab audiendis confessionibus.**

At the outset it must be noted that this canon does not apply to bishops.[51] It applies solely and exclusively to priests, be they religious or secular.

For a proper understanding of this canon one must differentiate the separate penalties this canon involves. The text of canon 2366 reveals that the legislator here intends to penalize two distinct cases of usurpation of penitential jurisdiction:

I. The first case concerns a priest who without possessing penitential jurisdiction presumes to hear sacramental confessions. It does not matter for what reason the confessor lacks the necessary jurisdiction. Perhaps it was never conferred upon him, or perhaps he lost it. Perchance it does not extend to the territory in which he uses it, or to persons over whom he exercises it, as for example, when he hears the confessions of women religious without the required special delegation.[52]

II. The second case concerns a priest who ostensibly possesses the jurisdiction for hearing the general run of

[51] Canon 2227, § 2.

[52] Canon 876. But cf. canons 522 and 523.

> confessions but who presumes to absolve from reserved sins without the jurisdiction necessary to do so.

Of course, it is readily understood that if a priest were to presume both to hear confessions without the necessary jurisdiction and also to absolve from reserved sins, there would be verified in such a case a multiplication of delicts and, consequently, a multiplication of censures.[53]

I. Imputability of the Censure

To incur the censure of suspension *a divinis* it is not necessary for the priest to give absolution. It suffices that he *hear* any confession sacramentally made. On the other hand, to incur the suspension from hearing confessions it does not suffice merely to hear the confession of the reserved sin, but absolution must actually be imparted.

An important consideration arises at this point. Certain canonists, like Ayrinhac-Lydon [54] and Murphy,[55] Vermeersch-Creusen,[56] Salucci [57] and Augustine [58] contend that canon 2366 must be understood as speaking only of *reserved sins* in contradistinction to *reserved censures.* To bolster up this contention Ayrinhac-Lydon add that canon 2338 already provides for absolutions of reserved censures without authority. With all due regard to these canonists, and entirely mindful of the prescript of canon 2219, § 1, which urges the more benign interpretation of penal law whenever possible, it seems rather that the above interpretation leaves an unexplained lacuna in the law. Evidently, the legislator wishes to levy severe sanctions against any and all usurpers of jurisdiction. And while he clearly penalizes the usurpation of the power to absolve sins reserved on their own account and censures reserved to the Holy See in a special manner, it seems strange that he

[53] Canon 2224, § 1.

[54] *Penal legislation,* n. 329.

[55] *Delinquencies and penalties in the administration and reception of the sacraments,* p. 32.

[56] *Epitome,* III, n. 269, 2.

[57] *Diritto penale* (Subiaco, 1926), II, n. 330.

[58] *Commentary,* VIII, p. 433.

should not penalize usurpers of the competency to absolve from the other reserved censures. Because of the inadequacy of the explanation offered by Murphy and by Ayrinhac-Lydon, the present writer prefers the interpretation offered by canonists, like Chelodi,[59] Cappelo,[60] Cerato[61] and Coronata.[62] These canonists hold that the term *peccatis reservatis* must be understood in the general sense, i.e., as including not only sins reserved on their own account, but likewise sins reserved in view of a censure attached to them. According to them it matters not if the reservation be made by common law or by diocesan statute.

II. *The Sanctions*

The penalty levied by the Code against any priest who *presumes* to hear confession without the necessary jurisdiction is suspension *a divinis.* This suspension, according to canon 2279, § 2, 2°, forbids any act of the power of Orders which one has received either by ordination[63] or by special privilege.[64] The penalty levied by the Code against any priest *presuming* to absolve from reserved sins is suspension from hearing confessions. And any priest who acts in violation of the suspension which has been placed upon him becomes irregular.[65]

III. *Applicability of Canon 209*

It is quite apparent from the foregoing pages that the absolutions imparted by any priest will be valid—even though he himself may not have received the proper faculties—provided that the conditions required for the operation of canon 209 are verified. Those conditions, as has also been seen, are twofold: 1.) common error; 2.) positive and probable doubt of law or of fact.

[59] *Ius poenale,* n. 89, 3.

[60] *De censuris,* n. 178.

[61] *Censurae vigentes,* n. 118.

[62] *Institutiones,* IV, n. 2077, III, 1.

[63] Cf., e.g., canons 738-741.

[64] Cf., e.g., canons 239, § 1, 5°; 239, § 1, 6°; 294, § 2; 239, § 1, 23°; 323, §2; 349, §1, 1°; 782, §§ 2-3; 951; 957, § 2; 1147, § 1.

[65] Canon 985, 7°.

There is not so much difficulty with regard to the supplying of jurisdiction in instances of positive and probable doubt as there is in regard to the supplying of the necessary jurisdiction in common error. For, once there is a probable doubt of law or of fact concerning his power to act in a certain case, the priest can act without any further cause and the Church will indubitably supply the jurisdiction that might be wanting. The difficulty exists to a marked degree in the proper understanding of the Church's supplying of jurisdiction in the case of common error. Treatment of this is now in order.

There is no jurisdiction that the Church cannot supply. There is no jurisdiction which the Church will not supply, provided that the proper conditions are verified. But as Berutti well points out,[66] no greater nor any more jurisdiction is supplied by the Church in the case of common error than that which in reality corresponds to the measure and coincides with the content either of the jurisdictional competence associated with some entrusted function (*munus*) or of the authorized powers inherent in some established office (*officium*), when it is solely to the extent of that function and office that the common error of the faithful has been occasioned.

For example, if a simple priest arrives in a parish and is commonly regarded as duly authorized to hear confessions, there can be no doubt that all of his absolutions are valid in virtue of canon 209, even though in reality he does not possess the necessary faculties. In the same manner if a certain priest has held the office of the canon penitentiary in a diocese for a long time, the objective fact of the invalidity of his appointment would hardly impede the validity of his absolutions from reserved cases. The simple reason for the validity of the absolution in either case is the very same. The people are in common error of fact. In each case the Church supplies the power which is commensurate with the jurisdictional competence associated with the function or the office which the priest is commonly supposed to possess. In a word the Church supplies in common error of fact.

[66] "De jurisdictione quae ipso jure delegatur ad audiendas fidelium confessiones,"—*Jus Pont.*, XIV (1934), 61.

To illustrate this point further the writer will suppose that the same priest in the conditions stipulated above attempts to absolve from reserved sins. These absolutions are certainly invalid. The reason for the invalidity is different according as the people commonly do or do not think that this simple priest has such power to absolve from reserved cases. If the people consider that a simple priest can absolve from reserved cases without any further authorization, they are in a common error of a clear and certain law. Because the objective law in regard to competency in such cases is clear, the common error of law cannot in any instance be called probable. Therefore the Church does not supply. One must not make any hasty, undue conclusions. One fully admits the possibility that this same simple priest could by some act whose consequences are not foreseen lead the people to believe that he has received the necessary jurisdiction for absolving from reserved sins. But in such a case there would no longer be an error of law. It would be an error of fact and the Church will supply. If, on the other hand, the people do not commonly think that this simple priest can absolve from reserved cases, there is no danger whatsoever of their approaching him for such absolution. Here, again the Church will not supply the needed jurisdiction simply because there is no common error of fact.

IV. *The Necessary Jurisdiction*

First of all, canonists are agreed that the penalties threatened in canon 2366 do not apply to priests acting in cases of positive and probable doubt.[67] For the use of jurisdiction which in all due probability is legally possessed does not imply a presumptuous act nor does it constitute a delict of any kind. But, as will soon be seen, there is no similar uniformity of doctrine among canonists concerning the extent to which the penalties threatened in canon 2366 apply in regard to a priest who absolves in circumstances of common error.

From the preceding considerations it is clear that if a simple priest presumes to absolve from *reserved* sins, his absolution from

[67] Cf., e.g., Chelodi, *Ius poenale,* n. 89, 3; Ayrinhac-Lydon, *Penal legislation,* n. 328.

such sins is invalid, regardless of such jurisdiction on his part as would enable him to absolve from non-reserved sins, whether in view of his proper delegation by the ordinary in accordance with the rule of canon 872, or in view of a supplied jurisdiction in virtue of the suppletory principle of canon 209 operating in a given case of common error.[68] In fact, as long as the faithful consider him a simple confessor without any special authorization in his penitential jurisdiction, there simply *cannot* be present that common error of fact which is required as a condition to ensure the validity of his absolutions from any reserved sins. It is manifest that such a priest would incur at least the censure of suspension from hearing confessions.

But the question arises in regard to this simple priest who under the stipulated conditions of common error absolves only unreserved sins, and in regard to the canon penitentiary who, contrary to popular belief, is invalidly in office but continues to exercise the functions proper to that office by absolving from reserved sins. No doubt, in either case the absolutions imparted are valid. But can it be said, that, because each has the jurisdiction necessary to ensure the validity of his absolutions, he likewise has the jurisdiction necessary to enable him to elude the penal sanction of canon 2366? Or does the simple priest still contract the suspension *a divinis,* and the canon penitentiary the suspension from hearing confessions?

For the remainder of this study consideration shall be given almost solely to the simple priest absolving under conditions of common error from unreserved sins. One should bear in mind, however, that the very same principles hold in regard to the canon penitentiary who is invalidly in office, not only with reference

[68] In this connection it will be recalled, of course, that a confessor who is ignorant of the reserved censure will nevertheless validly absolve the penitent from both the censure and the sin, as long as there is not a question of a censure *ab homine* or of a censure most specifically reserved to the Holy See. Cf. canon 2247, § 3. But, it must be remarked simultaneously that in the case of sins reserved *ratione sui* ignorance on the part of the confessor concerning their reservation does not occasion the same benefit of a valid absolution, unless—which is altogether unlikely—the superior who reserved the sin has specifically and expressly provided for it.

to the latter's presumptuous hearing of confessions, but also in respect to his presumption in absolving from reserved sins. If the simple priest does not escape the suspension *a divinis,* neither does the supposititious canon penitentiary. Again, if the simple priest, despite his valid absolution from non-reserved sins in virtue of the suppletory benefit of canon 209 in the case of common error, nevertheless can be said to *presume* this act *without the necessary jurisdiction,* then the same must also be said of the non-qualified canon penitentiary in the valid absolution which in the circumstances of common error he administers for the *reserved,* as well as the non-reserved sins. For him the presumptuous though valid absolution from a reserved sin will be an act performed without the necessary jurisdiction demanded by canon 2366 and there automatically follows his suspension from the hearing of confessions, if indeed he had any penitential jurisdiction.

As has been seen in the treatment of the licit use of a jurisdiction that is supplied in common error, certain canonists, like Oesterle,[69] would not even concede the possibility of applying these penalties to priests who hear confessions or absolve in virtue of common error. These authors are so convinced that a jurisdiction which is secured in virtue of common error is eminently proper jurisdiction that they require no further cause for its licit exercise. While Cappello[70] and the authors of whom he makes mention without naming them do not go so far as Oesterle, nevertheless they consider it no more than venially sinful for a priest to act without a sufficient cause. Certainly, such reasoning could hardly lead to the admission that the penalties of canon 2366 can be visited upon a priest who either hears confession or absolves from reserved sins when a common error is present to occasion the supplying of the needed jurisdiction or faculty. Cappello reasoned in just this manner, for he determined to change his earlier and stricter view on this point,[71] and excused such a priest from incurring the censures inflicted by canon 2366.

[69] *Praelectiones,* p. 113, n. 3.
[70] *De sacramentis,* II, Pars I, n. 492.
[71] Cf. *De censuris,* n. 177.

Another group of canonists—although entirely in harmony with the opinion that demands the presence of a grave cause for the licit exercise of jurisdiction secured in virtue of the presence of common error—carefully examining the words of canon 2366 holds that such a priest does not incur the penalties precisely because he does not absolve without the necessary jurisdiction, since the Church supplies the power when common error is verified.[72] This opinion Jombart considered seriously probable. It may be helpful to note his direct words rather closely, since he pithily sums up the case of all who, like Ayrinhac-Lydon,[73] are content to state that the whole matter is not certain, and hence the censure is doubtful.

"True," Jombart writes, "a priest acting in circumstances wherein common error exists sins gravely if he acts without any special reason. But does he incur the censure levied by canon 2366 against priests presuming to hear confessions without the necessary jurisdiction? Some have thought that he does; some still think so." Thus the opinion which holds that such a priest does not incur the censure seemed to Jombart to be seriously probable. For, he asks: "When jurisdiction is supplied, should one say that the necessary jurisdiction is lacking? Necessary for what? For validity? That certainly is not lacking. For its licitness? Assuredly, that is lacking." According to Jombart "the words of the Code are ambiguous, inasmuch as they allow this double interpretation." And therefore he is content to apply the axiom: *"In poenis benignior est interpretatio facienda."* [74]

Nevertheless, and quite rightly, the greater number of canonists holds that the penalties of canon 2366 apply to the priest who proceeds to hear confessions or to absolve from reserved

[72] Woywod, "Supplied jurisdiction for hearing confessions,"—*HPR,* XXVII (1926), 67; "Unauthorized administration of the sacraments,"—*HPR,* XXXVIII (1938), 848-849; Wouters, *Manuale,* I, n. 104. Nor does Vermeersch look askance at this opinion: "Pro benigniore tamen sententia dici potest eum, cum Ecclesia suppleat, necessaria jurisdictione non carere."—*Epitome,* II, n. 157.

[73] *Penal legislation,* n. 328.

[74] Canon 2219, § 1.

cases solely on the basis of common error, though there be no necessity for his doing so.[75] To canonists such as these, in view of the normal and grave condition imposed by canon 872, namely, that the power of jurisdiction is necessary for the validity of sacramental absolution, and in view of the reason which prompts the Church to supply in common error, the opinion of Oesterle seems altogether incorrect. For the same reasons they find Cappello's opinion untenable and devoid of probability.[76]

First of all, these canonists and moralists point out that a priest who without sufficient reason exercises jurisdiction which is supplied by the Church in the case of common error violates the normal and general ruling of canon 872, which demands the *direct* possession of jurisdiction for the valid granting of absolution from sin, and that he trespasses upon the right whereby authorized superiors have reserved to themselves the absolution of a specified sin in accordance with the discretional option granted them by canon 893. In the cases here outlined the priest actually compels the Church through the sheer constraint of her benevolent will to supply her otherwise withheld jurisdiction, for the Church has invoked the potential benefit of the suppletory principle not in favor of the priest but for the good of the faithful.

These same authors also insist that the Church supplies the needed jurisdiction neither before nor after but only at the moment when the absolution is imparted. Therefore, if a priest, holding no jurisdiction in the locality and acting without a sufficient cause, hears confession and grants sacramental absolution simply in view of the common error concerning his actually unauthorized status, he incurs the suspension *a divinis,* for canon

[75] Cf., e.g., Kelly, *The jurisdiction of the confessor,* pp. 137-139; Murphy, *Delinquencies and penalties in the administration and reception of the sacraments,* pp. 27-28; Wernz-Vidal, *Ius canonicum,* VII, n. 501; Ferreres, *Institutiones,* II, n. 1168; Chelodi, *Ius poenale,* n. 89, 3; Génicot-Salamans, *Theologia moralis,* II, n. 331; Raus, "Mangelnde Jurisdiktion und error communis"—*LQS,* LXXV (1922), 301; *Institutiones,* I, n. 731; Berutti, "De jurisdictione quae ipso jure delegatur ad audiendas fidelium confessiones,"—*Jus Pont.,* XIV (1934), 61.

[76] Cf. Kelly, *The jurisdiction of the confessor,* p. 138.

2366 inflicts the censure of this particular kind of suspension upon any priest who presumes to *hear* confession without the necessary jurisdiction.[77]

A natural corollary of this theory is exemplified in the following case. If a priest while hearing confessions should recall with moral certainty that the time of his jurisdiction has elapsed, he would be obliged to discontinue hearing confessions until he had obtained express, direct jurisdiction. For, to continue without first having secured a sufficiently grave cause for continuing, he would certainly fall under the censure of canon 2366.[78]

V. *Presumption*

As the text of canon 2366 plainly indicates, *presumption* is required on the part of the priest before he will incur the penalty or penalties prescribed by this canon. And, as Roberti points out,[79] such a presumption can never be verified without absolute *dolus*. Any sort of cause, therefore, that will diminish this *dolus* will excuse from the penalty threatened by the legislator. Thus, any sort of confusion, excitement, uncertainty, perplexity, fear, ignorance, even though crass or supine, provided that it be not affected, any sort of forgetfulness, distraction or negligence will excuse the priest from the censure. For then there will not be present the consummate malice and contempt required by the plain prescript of canon 2229, § 2.[80]

[77] Cf., e.g., Chelodi, *Ius poenale,* n. 89, 3; Kelly, *The jurisdiction of the confessor,* pp. 139-140.

[78] Farrugia, *Commentarium in censuras latae sententiae,* n. 291; Génicot-Salsmans, *Theologia moralis,* II, n. 330; Chelodi, *Ius poenale,* n. 89, 3; Raus, "Mangelnde Jurisdiktion und error communis,"—*LQS,* LXXV (1922), 301.

[79] *De delictis et poenis* (Romae, 1938), I, Pars II, n. 246.

[80] Cf., e.g., Blat, *Commentarium,* lib. V, n. 49; Augustine, *A Commentary on canon law,* VIII, p. 432-433; Raus, "Mangelnde Jurisdiktion und error communis,"—*LQS,* LXXVIII (1925), 299-301; Pistocchi, *I canoni penali,* p. 334.

CONCLUSIONS

The following items seek to set down in summary fashion some of the conclusions which have been reached in the course of the study and composition of this thesis concerning canon 209:

1.) The development of the suppletory principle is due principally to the teaching and work of the decretalists.

2.) Canon 209 is new as statute law. It is old insofar as it represents the results of centuries of jurisprudential thought and development.

3.) The rules set down by canon 6, nn. 2-5, are to be followed in the interpretation of canon 209.

4.) The Church in all probability does not supply in common error about a clear and certain law. The Church does not supply in common error of law unless that error is built upon a basis of genuine probability. In such an event the second phase of canon 209 becomes operative.

5.) The common error must be about the existence of a particular office or about the validity of the possession of jurisdiction by some particular person or persons. Common error must, then, be *particularized*.

6.) The Code has abolished the need of a colored title. But if common error about any fact is to exist, it must, of philosophical necessity, be occasioned by the presence of some kind of title.

7.) There is no *legal* argument available to support the embracing and the following of either the interpretative theory or of the theory which attempts to identify error and ignorance as far as the application of canon 209 is concerned.

8.) The common error must be *factual*. It can be that and still be only implicit, speculative and virtual.

9.) Though common error in the strict, traditional sense is possible, it is not verified as easily as many authors are wont to think. For the suppletory principle is for emergency situations. Canon 209 is not intended as an ubiquitous law nullifying the force of all invalidating laws.

10.) The interpretation of the *PCI*, given on July 25, 1931, and terming the definition of July 20, 1929, "declaratory", is to be understood as intending to designate the definition of the phrase *"ab acatholicis nati"* as *explicative* and not as *purely declaratory,* in the sense of simply stating the meaning of words in themselves certain and clear.

11.) Positive and probable doubt postulates more than subjective certitude. It demands, in addition, at least some objective evidence to support and to justify the subjective belief in the existence of the jurisdictional power about which there is question.

12.) A doubt of law, even though it be adduced by only *one* person, has universal efficiency as has been shown in the case of Leitner's interpretation of the phrase *"ab acatholicis nati"*.

13.) The position that the benefits of canon 209 are limited to the strictly jurisdictional sphere of activity is untenable.

14.) The application of canon 209 to the act of assistance at marriage is to be regarded as *direct.*

15.) It is probable that canon 209 does not apply in any case of delegation for one act of jurisdiction. It is highly probable that canon 209 does not apply to delegation to assist at one marriage.

16.) The evidence is inconclusive for one to be able to aver the immediate application of canon 209 to acts of purely dominative power.

BIBLIOGRAPHY

Sources

Acta Apostolicae Sedis, Commentarium Officiale, Romae, 1909—

Acta Conciliorum et Epistolae Decretales ac Constitutiones Summorum Pontificum, Ed. Regia, 10 vols., Parisiis: Ex Typographia Regia, 1714-1715.

Acta Sanctae Sedis, 41 vols., Romae, 1865-1908

Bullarii Romani Continuatio Summorum Pontificum, 19 vols., Prato, 1756-1883.

Bullarium SSmi. Domini nostri Benedicti XIV, 4. ed., 4 vols., Venice, 1778.

Canones et Decreta Sacrosancti Oecumenici Concilii Tridentini, Romae: Ex Typographia polyglotta S. C. de Propaganda Fide, 1882.

Codex Iuris Canonici Pii X Pontificis Maximi iussu digestus Benedicti XV auctoritate promulgatus, Romae: Typis Polyglottis Vaticanis, 1917.

Codicis Iuris Canonici Fontes cura Emi. Petri Card. Gasparri Editi, 9 vols., Romae (postea Civitate Vaticana): Typis Polyglottis Vaticanis, 1923-1938. (Vol. VII, VIII et IX ed. cura et studio Emi. Iustiniani Card. Serédi).

Collectanea S. Congregationis de Propaganda Fide, 2 vols., Romae, ex Typographia Polyglotta Vaticana, 1907.

Corpus Iuris Canonici, ed. Lipsiensis 2., Aemilius Ludouicus Richter—Aemilius Friedburg, ed. anastatice repetita, 2 vols., Lipsiae: Tauchnitz, 1928.

Corpus Iuris Civilis (Kreuger-Mommsen-Scholl-Kroell), 5. ed., 3 vols., Berolini, 1928-1929.

Decretales D. Gregorii Papae IX, una cum Glossa Restitutae, Romae, 1582.

Decretalium Gregorii Papae IX Libri V, Moguntiae: Petr. Schoeffer, 1473.

Decretum Francisci Gratiani cum glossa Bartholomaei Brixiensis, Venetiis, Andreas Calabrensis, 1491.

Denzinger, Henr., et Bannwart, Clem., et Umberg, Joan., *Enchiridion Symbolorum, Definitionum, et Declarationum de Rebus Fidei et Morum,* 21-23. ed., Friburgi Brisgoviae: Herder, 1937.

Friedberg, Aemilius, *Quinque Compilationes Antiquae,* Lipsiae, 1882.

Harduin, Jean, *Acta Conciliorum et Epistolae Decretales ac Constitutiones Summorum Pontificum,* 12 vols., Parisiis, 1715.

Mansi, J. D., *Sacrorum Conciliorum Nova et Amplissima Collectio,* 53 vols., Paris, Leipzig-Arheim.

Pallottini, S., *Collectio omnium Conclusionum et Resolutionum Quae in causis propositis apud Sacram Congregationem Cardinalium S. Concilii Tridentini interpretum Prodierunt ab ejus institutione anno MDLXIV ad MDCCCLX, distinctis titulis alphabetico ordine ber materias digestas,* 18 vols., Romae, 1868-1895.

Thesaurus Resolutionum Sacrae Congregationis Concilii, 167 vols., Romae, 1718-1908.

Reference Works

Ācta Congressus Iuridici Internationalis, 5 vols., Romae, 1935-1937.

Aertnys-Damen, *Theologia Moralis,* 11. ed., 2 vols., Taurinorum Augustae: Marietti, 1928.

Alphonsus Liguori, St., *Theologia Moralis,* ed. L. Gaudé, 4 vols., Romae, 1905-1912.

Alterius, Marius, *Disputationes de Censuris Ecclesiasticis,* 2 vols., Romae, 1616.

Arquer, M. de, *El Error Commun y la jurisdiccion eclesiastica,* 2. ed., Barcelona: Editorial Poliglota, 1927.

Aristotelis Opera, 5 vols., Berlin, 1831-1870.

Arregui, A., *Summarium Theologiae Moralis,* 12. ed., Bilbao, 1934.

Bączkowicz, F., *Prawo Kanoniczne,* 2. ed., 2 vols., Warszawa: Nakładem Ksiezy Misjonarzy, 1924.

Badii, Caesar, *Institutiones Iuris Canonici,* 3. ed., Florentiae, 1931.

Baldus de Ubaldis, *In Decretalium Volumen Commentaria,* Venetiis: Apud Juntas, 1580.

Barbosa, Augustinus, *De Officio et Potestate Parochi Tripartita Descriptio,* Lugduni, 1665.

Bartolus a Saxoferrato, *Opera, quae extant, Omnia,* Venetiis, 1690.

Bastnagel, Clement Vincent, *The Appointment of Parochial Adjutants and Assistants,* The Catholic University of America, Canon Law Studies, n. 58, Washington, D. C., The Catholic University of America, 1930.

Beste, Udalricus, *Introductio in Codicem,* Collegeville, Minn., St. John's Abbey Press, 1938.

Blat, Albertus, *Commentarium Textus Codicis Iuris Canonici,* 6 vols., 1921-1927.

Böckhn, Placidus, *Commentarius in Jus Canonicum Universum,* 5 vols., in 3, Salisburgi, 1776.

Bonacina, Martin, *Opera Omnia,* 3 vols., Venetiis, 1687.

Bouix, Dominicus, *Tractatus de Judiciis Ecclesiasticis,* 2. ed., 2 vols., Parisiis, 1855.

Tractatus de Jure Regularium, 2 vols., Bruxellis, 1867.

Braun, F., *Jurisdictio in genere et specie publica disputatione disposita,* Salisburgi, 1681.

Bucceroni, Ianuarius, *Casus Conscientiae,* 4 ed., Romae, 1901.

Buckland, W. W., *A Text-book of Roman Law from Augustus to Justinian,* 2. ed., Cambridge: The University Press, 1932.

Buonocore, Giuseppe, *Il 'Titulus Canonicus',* 2 vols., Napoli, 1933.

Cappelli, A., *Lexicon Abbreviaturarum,* Milano, 1899.

Cappello, Felix M., *De Censuris iuxta Codicem Iuris Canonici,* Augustae Taurinorum: Marietti, 1919.

Tractatus canonico-moralis de sacramentis, 3. ed., 3 vols. in 4, Taurinorum Augustae: Marietti, 1933-1935.

Carberry, John J., *The Juridical Form of Marriage,* The Catholic University of America, Canon Law Studies, n. 84, Washington, D. C.: The Catholic University of America, 1934.

Cardenas, Joannes de, *Crisis Theologica sive Disputationes Selectae—Ex Morali Theologia,* 3 vols., Venetiis, 1700.

Carrière, Josephus de, *De Matrimonio,* 2 vols., Parisiis, 1837.

Castropalao, Ferd., *Opus Morale,* 6 vols. in 3, Lugduni, 1682.

Cavigioli, Joannes, *De Censuris Latae Sententiae Quae in Codice Iuris Canonici Continentur Commentarium,* Taurino: Libreria Editrice Internazionale, 1918.

Cerato, Prosdocimus, *Matrimonium a Codice Iuris Canonici Desumptum,* 4. ed., Patavii: Typis Seminarii, 1929.

Censurae Vigentes, 2. ed., Patavii, 1921.

Chelodi, Joannes, *Ius de Personis iuxta Codicem Iuris Canonici,* 2. ed., Tridenti: Libr. Editr. Tridentum, 1927.

Ius Poenale et Ordo Procedendi in Iudiciis Criminalibus iuxta Codicem Iuris Canonici, 4. ed., Tridenti: Libr. Moderna Edit. A. Ardesi, 1935.

Ius Matrimoniale a Codice Iuris Canonici Desumptum, 3. ed., Tridenti: Libr. Edit. Tridentum, 1921.

Cicognani, Amleto, *Canon Law,* authorized English Version by J. O'Hara and F. Brennan, Philadelphia: Dolphin Press, 1934.

Cipollini, A., *De Censuris Latae Sententiae,* Turini, 1925.

Ciprotti, P., *De Consummatione Delictorum Attento Eorum Elemento Obiectivo in Iure Canonico,* Romae, 1936.

Claeys-Bouuaert, F. et Simenon, G., *Manuale Juris Canonici,* 4. ed., 3 vols., Ghent-Liège, 1934-1935.

Coady, John J., *The Appointment of Pastors,* The Catholic University of America, Canon Law Studies, n. 52, Washington, D. C.: The Catholic University of America, 1929.

Cocchi, Guidus, *Commentarium in Codicem Iuris Canonici ad Usum Scholarum,* 5 vols. in 8, Taurinorum Augustae, Vols. III-VII, 3. ed., Vol. II et VIII, 4. ed., Vol. I, 5. ed., Augustae Taurinorum: Marietti, 1931-1938.

Coninck, Aegidius de, *De Sacramentis ac Censuris,* Antuerpiae: Apud Haeredes Martini Nutl., 1619.

Connolly, Nicholas P., *The Canonical Erection of Parishes,* The Catholic University of America, Canon Law Studies, n. 114, Washington, D. C.: The Catholic University of America, 1938.

Coronata, Matthaeus Conte a, *Institutiones Iuris Canonici,* 5 vols., Taurini (Italia): Marietti, vol. III, *De rebus,* 1933; vol. IV, *De processibus,* 1935; vol. V, *De delictis et poenis,* 1936; vol. I, *Normae generales* et vol. II, *De personis,* 2. ed., 1939.

Costello, John M., *Domicile and Quasi-Domicile,* The Catholic University of America, Canon Law Studies, n. 60, Washington, D. C.: The Catholic University of America, 1930.

Covarrubias, Didacus, *Opera Omnia,* Antuerpiae, Apud Joannem Meursium, 1638.

D'Annibale, J., *Summula Theologiae Moralis,* 2. ed., 3 vols., Mediolani, 1881.

Summula Theologiae Moralis, 3. ed., 3 vols., Romae, 1892

Summula Theologiae Moralis, 5. ed., 3 vols., Romae, 1908.

Davis, Henry. *Moral and Pastoral Theology,* Heythrop Theological Series, II, 4 vols., New York: Sheed and Ward, 1935.

De Angelis, Phillipus, *Praelectiones Iuris Canonici ad Methodum Decretalium Gregori IX Exactae,* 4 vols. in 6, Romae, 1877-1887.

De Lugo, J., *Disputationes Scholasticae et Morales,* Ed. nova, 8 vols., Parisiis, 1868.

De Meester, Alphonsus, *Juris Canonici et Juris Canonico-Civilis Compendium,* nova ed., 3 vols. in 4, Brugis, 1921-1928.

De Smet, Aloysius, *Tractatus Theologico-Canonicus De Sponsalibus et Matrimonio,* 4. ed., Brugis: Beyaert, 1927.

Diana, Antonius, *Omnium Resolutionum Moralium Tomi Decem,* 10 vols. in 5, Venetiis: Ex Typographia Balleomania, 1728.

Eichmann, E., *Lehrbuch des Kirchenrechts auf Grund des Codex Iuris Canonici,* 4. ed., 2 vols., Paderborn: Schöningh, 1934.

Fagnanus, Prosper, *Commentaria in Quinque Libros Decretalium,* 4 vols., Romae, 1661.

Feije, Henricus J., *De Impedimentis et Dispensationibus Matrimonialibus,* 3. ed., 2 vols., Lovanii, 1885.

Felinus, Sandeus, *Commentaria Iuris Canonici in Quinque Libros Decretalium,* 3. vols., Venetiis, 1570.

Ferreres, Joannes B., *Compendium Theologiae Moralis ad Normam Codicis Canonici,* 14. ed., 7. ed. post Codicem, 2 vols., Barcinone: Eugenius Subirana, 1928.

Ferraris, F. Lucius, *Prompta Bibliotheca, Canonica, Juridica, Moralis, Theologica necnon Ascetica, Polemica Rubricistica, Historica,* ed. Migne, 8 vols., Parisiis, 1860-1863.

Frances, Didacus Antonius, *Tractatus de Intrusione,* Lugduni, 1660.

Gasparri, Petrus, *Tractatus Canonicus de Matrimonio,* 2. ed., 2 vols., Parisiis, 1892.

Tractatus Canonicus de Matrimonio, 3. ed., 2 vols., Parisiis, 1904.

Tractatus Canonicus de Matrimonio, ed. nova ad mentem Codicis I. C., 2 vols., Romae: Typis Polyglottis Vaticanis, 1932.

Génicot, E.,—Salsmans, I., *Institutiones Theologiae Moralis,* 2 vols., Bruxellis: Alb. DeWit, 1927.

Giraldi, Ubaldus, *Expositio Juris Pontificii iuxta Recentiorem Ecclesiae Disciplinam,* 3 vols. in 2, Romae, 1769.

Gobat, Georgius, *Operum Moralium Tractatus Octo Priores,* 3 vols. in 2, Duaci, 1770.

Gonzalez-Tellez, Emmanuel, *Commentaria Perpetua in Singulos Textus Quinque Librorum Decretalium Gregorii IX,* 5 vols. in 4, Lugduni, 1715.

Gougnard, Armand, *Tractatus de Matrimonio,* 7. ed., Mechliniae: Dessain, 1931.

Grabowski, Ignacy, *Prawo Kanoniczne Według Nowego Kodeksu,* 2. ed., Lwów, 1927.

Hohenlohe, Constantin, *Einfluss des Christentums auf das Corpus juris civilis,* Wien: Hölder-Pichler-Tempsky, 1937.

Hostiensis, Cardinalis (Henricus de Segusio), *Commentaria in Quinque Decretalium Libros,* 5 vols. in 3, Venetiis, 1581.

Innocent IV, *In Quinque Libros Decretalium Necnon in Decretales Per Eundem Innocentium Editas, Quae Modo in Sexto earundem volumine sunt Insertae, et in hujus operis Elencho ut cunctis pateant adnotatae Commentaria Doctissima,* Venetiis, 1578.

Joannes Andreae, *In Sex Decretalium Libros Novella Commentaria,* 6 vols. in 5, Venetiis, 1581.

Kearney, Raymond A., *The Principles of Delegation,* The Catholic University of America, Canon Law Studies, n. 55, Washington D. C.: The Catholic University of America, 1929.

Kelly, James P., *The Jurisdiction of the Confessor According to the Code of Canon Law,* The Catholic University of America, Canon Law Studies, n. 43, Washington, D. C.: The Catholic University of America, 1927.

Knecht, August, *Handbuch des katholischen Eherechts,* Freiburg im Breisgau: Herder, 1928.

Kober, F., *Der Kirchenbann nach den Grundsätzen des kanonischen Rechts,* Tübingen, 1863.

Koeniger, A., *Katholisches Kirchenrecht,* Freiburg im Breisgau, 1926.

Kutschker, Johann B., *Das Eherecht der katholischen Kirche nach seiner Theorie und Praxis,* 5 vols., Wien, 1856-1857.

LaCroix, Claudius, *Theologia Moralis,* 3 vols., Venetiis, 1761.

Laymann, Paul, *Theologia Moralis,* Venetiis, 1719.

Lea, Henry C., *A History of Auricular Confession and Indulgences in the Latin Church,* 3 vols., Philadelphia, 1896.

Leage, R. W.-Ziegler, C. H., *Roman Private Law,* 2. ed., London: MacMillan and Co., Ltd., 1937.

Lega, M., *Praelectiones in Textum Iuris Canonici de Iudiciis Ecclesiasticis,* 2 vols., 2. ed., Romae, 1905.

Lega, M.—Bartoccetti, V., *Commentarius in Iudicia Ecclesiastica iuxta Codicem Iuris Canonici,* 2 vols., Romae, 1938-1939.

Lehmkuhl, Augustinus, *Theologia Moralis,* 11. ed., 2 vols., Friburgi Brisgoviae, 1900.

Leitner, M., *Lehrbuch des katholischen Eherechts,* 3. ed., Paderborn, 1920.

Lessius, Leonardus, *De Iustitia et Iure,* Antuerpiae, 1612.

Leurenius, Petrus, *Forum Ecclesiasticum in quo Jus Canonicum Universum Explanatur,* 5 vols. in 3, Venetiis, 1729.

Linneborn, J.,—Wenner, J., *Grundriss des Eherechts nach dem Codex Iuris Canonici,* 4. and 5. eds., Paderborn, 1933.

MacKenzie, E., *The Delict of Heresy in Its Commission, Penalization, Absolution,* The Catholic University of America, Canon Law Studies, n. 77: Washington, D. C., 1932.

Marc-Gestermann-Raus, *Institutiones Morales Alphonsianae,* 18. ed., 2 vols., Lugduni: Typis Emmanuelis Vitte, 1927.

Maroto, Philip, *Institutiones Iuris Canonici ad Normam Novi Codicis,* 3. ed., 2 vols., Romae: Apud Commentarium Pro Religiosis, 1921.

Mascardus, J., *Conclusiones Probationum Omnium,* 3 vols., Venetiis, 1593.

Maupied, Franciscus L. M., *Juris Canonici Compendium,* 2 vols., Paris, 1863.

Merkelbach, Benedictus H., *Summa Theologiae Moralis ad Mentem D. Thomae et ad Normam Iuris Novi,* 2. ed., 3 vols., Parisiis: Typis Desclée, De Brouwer et Soc., 1935-1939.

Michiels, Gommarus, *Normae Generales Juris Canonici,* 2 vols., Lublin: Universitas Catholica, 1929.

Migne, P. J., *Patrologiae Cursus Completus,* Series Graeca, 161 vols., Parisiis, 1856-1866.

Patrologiae Cursus Completus, Series Latina, 221 vols., Parisiis, 1858-1864.

Theologiae Cursus Completus, 28 vols., Parisiis, 1863-1866.

Navarrus (Martin de Azpilcueta), *Opera Omnia,* Romae, 1590.

Consilia et Responsa, Lugduni, 1594.

Noldin, H., *Summa Theolgiae Moralis Iuxta Codicem Iuris Canonici,* 15. and 16 ed., 3 vols., Oeniponte, 1923.

Noldin, H.,-Schmitt, A., *Summa Theologiae Moralis Iuxta Codicem Iuris Canonici* 21. ed., 3 vols., Oeniponte, 1932.

Oesterle G., *Praelectiones Iuris Canonici,* Vol. I, Romae, 1931.

Ojetti, B., *Commentarium in Codicem Iuris Canonici,* 4 vols., Romae: Univ. Greg., 1927-1931.

Ottaviani, Alaphridus, *Institutiones Iuris Publici Ecclesiastici,* vol. I, *Ius Publicum Internum,* ed. altera emendata et aucta, Romae: Typis Polyglottis Vaticanis, 1935.

Pallavicinus, Sforza, *Vera Concilii Tridentini Historia,* Antuerpiae, 1670.

Panormitanus, Abbas (Nicholaus de Tudeschis), *Commentaria in Quinque Libros Decretalium,* 5 vols. in 7, Venetiis, 1588.

Perathoner, A., *Das kirchliche Gesetzbuch,* 3. ed., Brixen, 1923.

Petavius (Petau) Dionysius, *De ecclesiastica hierarchia libri tres,* Paris, 1643.

Pichler, Vitus, *Jus Canonicum secundum Quinque Decretalium Titulos Explicatum,* 2 vols., Ravenna, 1741.

Pighi, J. *Cursus Theologiae Moralis,* 4. ed., Veronae: Sorores Cinquetti Filiae Felicis, 1926.

Pascuccio, Carminus Thomas, *Compendium et Index ad Consultationes Canonicas D. Jacobi Pignatelli,* 2 vols., Romae, 1619.

Pignatelli, Jacobus, *Consultationes Canonicae,* 12 vols. in 6, Coloniae Allobrogum, 1700.

Pirhing, Henricus, *Jus Canonicum Novo Methodo Explicatum,* 5 vols. in 4, Dillingae, 1674-1678.

Piscetta, A.,—Gennaro, A., *Elementorum Theologiae Moralis Summarium,* Torino, 1933.

Pistocchi, Mario, *I Canoni Penali del Codice Ecclesiastico,* Torino: Marietti, 1925.

Praelectiones Juris Canonici Habitae in Seminario Sancti Sulpitii, 6. ed., 3 vols., Parisiis, 1886.

Prümmer, Dominicus M., *Manuale Iuris Canonici,* 4. et 5. eds., Friburgi Brisgoviae: Herder, 1927.

Manuale Theologiae Moralis secundum Principia S. Thomae Aquinatis, 4. et 5. ed., 3 vols., Friburgi Brisgoviae, Herder, 1928.

Rainer, Eligius G., *Suspension of Clerics,* The Catholic University of America, Canon Law Studies, n. 111, Washington, D. C.: The Catholic University of America, 1927.

Raus, Joannes B., *Institutiones Canonicae juxta Novum Codicem Juris,* 2. ed., Lugduni: Apud Vitte, 1931.

Reiffenstuel, Anacletus, *Ius Canonicum Universum,* 5 vols. in 7, Parisiis, 1864-1882.

Roberti, F., *De Delictis et Poenis,* 2. ed., Romae, 1938.

Roskovány, A. de, *Matrimonium in Ecclesia Catholica,* 5 vols., Pestini, 1870-1882.

Sabetti, A., Barrett, T., *Compendium Theologiae Moralis,* 34. ed., Neo-Eboraci, Pustet 1939.

Sägmuller, I., *Lehrbuch des katholischen Kirchenrechts,* 4. ed., Vol. I, 4 fascicles, Freiburgi Br., 1925-1935.

Salmanticenses, *Cursus Theologiae Moralis,* 6 vols. in 4, Venetiis, 1728.

Salmeron, Alphonse, *Doctrina de Jurisdictionis Episcopalis Origine et Ratione,* Moguntiae, 1871.

Sanchez (Sanctius) Joannes, *Selectae, Illaeque Practicae Disputationes De Rebus in Administratione Sacramentorum,* Venetiis, 1639.

Sanchez, Thomas, *De Sancto Matrimonii Sacramento Disputationum Libri Tres,* Lugduni, 1669.

Santi, Franciscus, *Praelectiones Juris Canonici,* 2 vols., Ratisbonae, Neo-Eboraci, Cincinnati, 1886.

Sasserath, Reinerus, *Cursus Theologiae Moralis,* 6. ed., 4 vols., Augustae Vindelicorum, 1787.

Schäfer, T., *Das Eherecht nach dem Codex Iuris Canonici,* 6. and 7. eds., Münster, i. W., 1921.

Schmalzgrueber, Franciscus, *Ius Ecclesiasticum Universum,* 5 vols. in 12, Romae, 1843-1845.

Schmier, F., *Jurisprudentia Canonico-Civilis,* Salisburgi, 1729.

Schulte, Joannes F. von, *Die Geschichte der Quellen und Literatur des kanonischen Rechts von Gratian bis auf die Gegenwart,* 3 vols., Stüttgart, 1875-1880.

Smith, Mariner T., *The Penal Law for Religious,* The Catholic University of America, Canon Law Studies, n. 98, Washington D. C.: The Catholic University of America, 1935.

Soto, Dominicus de, *De Iustitia et Iure Libri Decem,* Salmanticae, 1556.

Sperelli, A., *Decisiones Fori Ecclesiastici,* Coloniae, 1667.

Sporer, Patritius, *Theologia Moralis Super Decalogum,* 3. ed., 3 vols. in 1, Salisburgi, 1710.

Suarez, Franciscus, *Opera Omnia,* 26 vols., Parisiis, 1856-1866.

Taberna, Joannes, *Synopsis Theologiae Practicae,* Coloniae Agrippinae, 1705.

Tamburini, Thomas, *Opera Omnia,* Venetiis, 1702.

Thesaurus, Carolus, *De Poenis Ecclesiasticis Praxis Absoluta et Universalis,* ed. U. Giraldi, Romae, 1760.

Toso, Albertus, *Ad Codicem Iuris Canonici Commentaria Minora,* 5 vols., Romae: Marietti, 1920-1934.

Triebs, Franz, *Praktisches Handbuch des geltenden kanonischen Eherechts in Vergleichung mit dem deutschen staatlichen Eherecht für Theologen und Juristen,* Breslau, 1933.

Trombetta, Aloysius, *Supplet Ecclesia seu Commentarium in can. 209 Codicis Iuris Canonici,* Neapoli: Ex Typis M. D'Auria, 1931.

Van der Velden, Pio, *Principia Theologiae Moralis,* 2 vols., Parisiis, 1882.

Van Hove, A., *Commentarium Lovaniense in Codicem Iuris Canonici,* vol. I, *Prolegomena,* Mechliniae: H. Dessain, 1928; vol. II, *De Legibus Ecclesiasticis,* Mechliniae: H. Dessain, 1930.

Verricelli, A., *Quaestiones Morales et Legales in Octo Tractatus Distributae,* Venetilis, 1653.

Vermeersch, A., *Theologiae moralis principia, responsa, consilia,* 2. ed., 3 vols., Brugis: Firme Charles Beyaert, 1926-1927.

Vermeersch, A., - Creusen, J., *Epitome Iuris Canonici,* 3 vols., Mechliniae: H. Dessain, vol. I, 5. ed., 1934; vol. II, 5. ed., 1936; vol. III, 6. ed., 1937.

Wernz, Franciscus X., *Ius Decretalium,* 6 vols., Romae et Prati, 1898-1905.

Wernz, F. — Vidal, P., *Ius Canonicum* 7 tom. in 8 vols., Romae: Apud Aedes Universitatis Gregorianiae, 1923-1938.

Westermack, E., *Geschichte der menschlichen Ehe,* Jena, 1893.

Wilches, F., *De Errore Communi in Iure Romano et Canonico,* Romae: Apud Pontificium Athenaeum Antonianum, 1940.

Wohlhaupter, Eugen, *Aequitas Canonica,* Paderborn: Ferdinand Schöningh, 1931.

Wouters, Ludovicus, *Manuale Theologiae Moralis,* 2 vols., Brugis: Carolus Beyaert, 1932-1933.

Woywod, S., *A Practical Commentary on the Code of Canon Law,* 2 vols., New York: Jos. F. Wagner, 1925.

Articles

d'Angelo, S., "De aequitate in codice iuris canonici,"—*Periodica,* XVI (1927), 210*-224*.

A.D.S., "An et quare sacerdos absolvere potest cum jurisdictione dubia?"—*Coll. Brug.,* IV (1899), 639-644.

Adloff, "L'erreur commune et la jurisdiction suppléée,"—Bull. Ecclésiastique du Diocèse de Strasbourg, XLVI (1927), 254 ss.

Berlière, U., "L' exércise du ministère, paroissial par les moines dans le haut moyen-âge,"—*Revue Bénedictine,* XXXIX (1927), 227-250.

Berutti, C., "De jurisdictione quae ipso jure delegatur ad audiendas fidelium confessiones,"—*Jus Pont.,* XIV (1934), 51-66.

Brys, J., "De Censurarum absolutione,"—*Coll. Brug.,* XXXIII (1933), 264-267.

Cappello, F., "De vicario substituto,"—*Periodica,* XIX (1930), 1*-10*.

Castillon, P., "La probabilité de fait en matière de jurisdiction pénitentielle,"—*NRT,* XLIV (1912), 534-555; 673-690; 718-727.

Cavigioli, G., "Teologia morale,"—*La Scuola Cattolica,* XVI (1930), 216-221.

Citati, A., "Supplere, nei testi giuridici,"—*Studia et Documenta Historiae et Iuris,* I (1935), 153-187.

Claeys-Bouuaert, F., "De conceptu erroris communis in canone 209,"—*Jus Pont.,* XVI (1936), 157-164.

Coronata, M. a, "L'errore commune nell' assistenza ad un matrimonio,"—*Palestra del Clero,* IX (1930), 201 ss.

Couly, A., "La jurisdiction suppléée du canon 209,"—*Le canoniste,* XLVII (1925), 450-459.

Creusen, I., "La jurisdiction probable. Réponse du P. Creusen,"—*NRT,* LVIII (1931), 920-923.

"Preuve de l'erreur commune,"—*NRT,* L (1923), 365-366.

"De extensione c. 209 ad potestatem dominativam,"—*Apoll.,* VII (1934), 359.

"Pouvoir dominatif et erreur commune,"—*Acta congressus iuridici iternationalis,* IV, 181-192.

Dalpiaz, V., "De conceptu erroris communis iuxta canonem 209,"—Apoll., VII (1934), 490-492.

"Vicariis cooperatoribus ipso iure potestas non competit assistendi matrimoniis,"—*Apoll.,* VII (1934), 77-82.

Darmanin, A., "De promissione matrimoniali ad can. 1017 CIC,"—*Angelicum,* VIII (1931), 305-375.

Fabregas, M., "De componendo canone 1094 et 209,"—*Periodica,* XXII (1933), 113*-122*; 191*-201*.

Fallon, M., "Does canon 209 apply to delegation to assist at marriages?" —*IER,* LII (1938), 438-439.

Fernández, J., "Super instructione S.C. de Propaganda Fide diei 8 decembris, 1929,"—*CpR,* XII (1931), 284-285.

Fink, P., "Eheassistenz und allgemeiner Irrtum,"—*Theologie und Glaube,* XXVI (1934), 585-597.

Girerd, M., "La jurisdiction probable,"—*NRT,* LVIII (1931), 916-920.

Grazioli, F., "De errore communi et defeçtu iurisdictionis in confessario," —*Palestra del Clero,* X (1931), 177-178.

Grosam, W., "Der Beichtvater ohne Jurisdiktion,"—*LQS,* LXXXII (1929), 120-124.

Guns, A., "L'erreur commune,"—*NRT,* L (1925), 533-541.

Hilling, N., "Begriff und Umfang der potestas jurisdictionis ordinaria und delegata nach geltendem Kirchenrecht,"—*AKKR,* CIV (1924), 181-205.

Jombart, E., "L'erreur commune,"—*NRT,* L (1923), 169-182.

"L'erreur commune,"—*NRT,* L (1923) 363-365.

Jone, H., "Suppletion der Beichtjurisdiktion bei einem dubium facti," —*LQS,* LXXXI (1928), 576.

"Error communis und Suppletion der Beichtjurisdiktion,"—*LQS,* LXXXI (1928), 140-143.

"Error comunis bei Eheassistenz,"—*LQS,* LXXXI (1928), 806-809.

Kerchhove, M. Van de, "De notione jurisdictionis in jure romano,"—*Jus Pont.,* XVI (1936), 49-65.

"Notio jurisdictionis apud decretistas et priores decretalistas."—*Jus Pont.,* XVIII (1938), 10-14.

La Cot, Fermí de, "Casos I Consultes," —*Estudis Franciscans,* XLII (1930), 97-99.

Lehmkuhl, A., "Kirchliche Jurisdiktion und das Supplieren derselben," —*Zeitschrift für katholische Theologie,* VI (1882), 659-691.

Lo Grasso, I., "Solutio casus propositi pag. 20*,"—*Periodica,* XXIII (1934), 254-256.

Löhr, J., Review of "*Die Delegation zur Eheassistenz* von Gregor Krüger," —*Theologische Quartalschrift,* CXIV (1933), 573-574.

Maroto, P., De vi verborum can. 1099, § 2: '*ab acatholicis nati*'," —*Apoll.,* III, (1930), 601-616.

Necchi, P., "La giurisdizione nell' errore commune," —*Palestra del Clero,* VII (1928), 279-280.

Nevin, J., "Subdelegated and Interdiocesan Faculties," —*ACR,* VIII (1931), 231-232.

"Does Doctrine concerning the Supply of Jurisdiction in *Common Error* Apply in the Case of Matrimony?" —ACR, XIV (1937), 143-151.

"Marriage Case Arising from Recent Official Interpretation of the Phrase *ab acatholicis nati,*"—ACR, IX (1932), 261-267.

O'Donnell, M., "When Does the Church Supply Jurisdiction?" —*IER,* XVI (1920), 499-502.

Oesterle, G., "Eheassistenz und error communis,"—*LQS,* XC (1937), 311-312.

O'Neill, P., "The Meaning of 'Common Error'," —*IER,* XXI (1923), 299-300.

Prümmer, D., "An Invalid Election and Its Consequences," —*HPR,* XXX (1929-1930), 72-75.

Raus, J., "Mangelnde Jurisdiktion und error communis," —*LQS,* LXXV (1922), 297-301.

"Die Gültigkeit einer Delegation und Subdelegation zur Eheassistenz," —*LQS,* XCI (1938), 103-109.

Riccobono, S., "Cristianesimo e diritto privato," —*Rivista di diritto civile,* III (1911), 37 ss.

Salvador, A., "Error communis et iurisdictionis suppletio ab ecclesia," —*BE,* XVII (1939), 77-91; 175-183; 238-253; 371-383.

Saucedo, P., "Exercitium Jurisdictionis et Superiores Laici Ex Ordine Hospitalario S. Joannis de Deo," —*CpR,* XIII (1932), 51-61; 106-114; 224-231; 291-302.

Schaaf, V., "An Exemption from the Canonical Form of Marriage," —*AER,* LXXXIII (1930), 484-496.

"Disparity of Cult and the Canonical Form," —*AER,* LXXXIX (1933), 69-76.

"Profession under a Superioress Holding Office Invalidly," —*AER,* CI (1939), 261-268.

Schmitt, A., "Probabilismus und supplierte Jurisdiktion,"—*Zeitschrift für katholische Theologie,* XXXIX (1915), 34-64.

Schrattenholzer, A., "Beichtjurisdiktionszweifel,"—*LQS,* LXXX (1927), 331-333.

"Jurisdiktionsfragen,"—*LQS,* LXXIX (1926), 128-132.

Stocchiero, J., "De jurisdictione vicariorum paroecialium,"—*Jus Pont.,* XI (1931), 144-150.

Toso, A., "De errore communi,"—*Jus Pont.,* III (1923), 148-152.

"Jurisdictio Quando ab Ecclesia Suppleatur,"—*Jus Pont.,* XVII (1937), 98-105.

"De Errore Communi ad Normam Can. 209,"—*Jus Pont.,* XVIII (1938), 161-169.

Van Overbeke, P., "De relatione ordinem iuridicum inter et ordinem moralem,"—*ETL,* XI (1934), 289-346.

Vermeersch, A., "Quam late sit locus can. 209 de Ecclesia supplente iurisdictionem in errore communi,"—*Periodica,* XXIII (1934), 59*-61*.

Woywod, S., "Supplied jurisdiction for hearing confession,"—*HPR,* XXVII (1926), 67.

"Unauthorized administration of the sacraments,"—*HPR,* XXXVIII (1938), 848-849.

Periodicals

Angelicum, Romae, 1924—

Apollinaris, Romae, 1928—

Archiv für katholisches Kirchenrecht, Innsbruck, 1857-1861; Mainz, 1862—

Australasian Catholic Record, The, Manly, 1923—

Boletin Eclesiastico, Manila, 1923—

Collationes Brugenses, Brugis Flandrorum, 1895—

Commentarium pro Religiosis (later *Commentarium pro Religiosis et Missionariis*), Romae, 1920—

Ecclesiastical Review, The (originally *The American Ecclesiastical Review*), Philadelphia, 1889—

Ephemerides Theologicae Lovanienses, Lovanii, 1923—

Estudis Franciscans, Barcelona-Sarrià, 1907—

Homiletic and Pastoral Review, The, New York, 1900—

Irish Ecclesiastical Record, Dublin, 1864—

Jus Pontificium, Romae, 1921—

L'Ami du Clergé, Paris, 1878—

La Scuola Cattolica, Milano, 1873—

Le Canoniste, Paris, 1878—

Nouvelle Revue Théologique, Paris, 1869—

Palestra del Clero, Rovigo, 1922—

Periodica de Re Canonica et Morali utili Praesertim Religiosis et Missionariis, Bruges, 1905—

Revue Bénedictine, Lille et Bruges, 1884—
Rivista di Diritto Civile, Romae, 1909—
Studia et Documenta Historiae et Iuris, Romae, 1935 —
Theologie und Glaube, Paderborn, 1909 —
Theologische Quartalschrift, Tübingen, 1819 —
Theologisch-praktische Quartalschrift, Linz, 1832 —
Zeitschrift für katholische Theologie, Innsbruck, 1876 —

Abbreviations

AAS — *Acta Apostolicae Sedis.*
ACR — *Australasian Catholic Record,* The
AER — *American Ecclesiastical Review.*
AKKR — *Archiv für katholisches Kirchenrecht.*
ASS — *Acta Sanctae Sedis.*
BE — *Boletin Eclesiastico.*
C. — *Codex* (Iustinianus).
c. — Canon.
cc. — Canones.
Coll. Brug. — *Collationes Brugenses.*
Coll. S.O.P.F. — *Collectanea S.C. de Propaganda Fide.*
CpR — *Commentarium pro Religiosis et Missionariis.*
D. — *Digestum* (Iustinianum).
ETL — Ephemerides Theologicae Lovanienses.
Fontes — *Codicis Iuris Canonici Fontes cura . . . Gasparri editi.*
G. — *Gaius.*
Harduin — *Acta Conciliorum* etc.
HPR — *Homiletic and Pastoral Review.*
IER — *Irish Ecclesiastical Record.*
Jus Pont. — *Jus Pontificium.*
LQS — *Theologisch-praktische Quartalschrift* (Linz).
Mansi — *Sacrorum Conciliorum Nova et Amplissima Collectio.*
MPG — Migne, *Patrologia Graeca.*
MPL — Migne, *Patrologia Latina.*
N. — *Novellae* (Iustinianae).
NRT — *Nouvelle Revue Théologique.*
Periodica — *Periodica de Re Canonica et Morali Utili praesertim Religiosis et Missionariis.*
PCI — *Pontifical Commission for the Authetic Interpretation of the Canons of the Code.*
S.C.C.—*Sacred Congregation of the Council.*
S.R.R. Dec. — *Sacrae Romae Rotae Decisiones seu Sententiae.*
Thesaurus resolutionum — *Sacrae Congregationis Concilii Resolutiones* (1718-1908).

BIBLIOGRAPHICAL NOTE

Francis S. Miaskiewicz was born on September 20, 1911, at Salem, Massachusetts. He attended the St. John the Baptist parochial school of that city for his elementary education. His high school course was made under the tutelage of the Xaverian Brothers at St. John's Preparatory College at Danvers, Massachusetts. He matriculated at Boston College, Boston, Massachusetts, in the fall of 1928. After two years of college training he entered St. John's Boston Ecclesiastical Seminary, Brighton, Massachusetts, where he made his philosophical and theological studies from 1930 to 1937. He was ordained to the priesthood on May 21, 1937. In September of that year he entered the School of Canon Law at the Catholic University of America, where he received the degree of the Baccalaureate in Canon Law in June, 1938, and the degree of the Licentiate in Canon Law in June, 1939.

ALPHABETICAL INDEX

Ab acatholicis nati, interpretation of, 205-210.
Absolution from reservation in ignorance 144-145, 181, 191, 203-204, 306.
Ad evitanda of Martin V, significance of, 50, 57, 60-61.
  text of, 60.
Administrative acts, and jurisdiction, 12-13, 21.
  applicability of suppletory principle to, 279-282, 286-289.
Approbation, jurisdiction differs from, 12.
Approved authors, means of distinguishing, 201.
Assistance at marriage, applicability of suppletory principle to,
  before the Code, 244-247, 253-254, 258-260, 271.
  after the Code,
    direct applicability, 252-256.
    extent of applicability,
      in common error,
        delegated assistance, 260-263.
          particular delegation, 271-279.
          universal delegation, 263-269.
        ordinary assistance, 256-258.
      in doubt, 256, 260-261.
Assistant *(vicarius cooperator),* question of the applicability of suppletory principle to,
  in assistance at marriage,
    in common error, 256-266.
    in doubt, 260.
  in strictly jurisdictional acts, 235.
  status, 232-233.
Authorization to assist at marriage, limitation of general, 267.
  nature of, 240.
  necessity of, 251.
Benignity of Church, as exemplified by her laws, 28-29, 144, 150, 191,196.
Canon 209 and canon 15, 194-196.
Canon 209, a repetition of the pre-Code law, 113, 132, 146, 154, 156, 186-187, 256.
Canon 209, and other liberal grants of jurisdiction in the Code, 28-29; 218.
Censure, absolution from,
    in ignorance, 144-145, 181, 191, 203-204, 306.
    in inadvertence, 28, 133, 144-145, 155, 191.
    without necessary jurisdiction, 301-310.
  and the exercise of,
    jurisdictional power, 19, 224.
    power to assist at marriage, 250-251.
Church, possessor of plenitude of jurisdiction from Christ, 8, 21, 41.
Clerics, and jurisdiction, 18-19.
Colored title, definition of, 15.
  question of necessity of,
    before the Code, 53, 56-57, 67, 81-87.
    after the Code, 107.
Common error, occasion of supplying of jurisdiction, as understood by,
  Roman jurists, 67-68, 153.
  Gratian, 69, 153.
  glossators, 53, 69.
  other canonists up to the Code, as to,
    extent, 74-78.
    measure, 78-80.
    place, 70-72.

quality, 69-70.
subjects, 72-74.
canonists since the Code,
interpretative theory, 121-124.
ignorance theory, 151-152.
traditional theory,
argument, 157-159, 160-161, 162.
genesis of common error, 168, 174, 304.
judgment as to its presence, 137-138, 174-175.
proof of its existence, 168.
qualifications,
actual or virtual, 169-171.
explicit or implicit, 169.
extent, 163.
measure, 172-175.
place, 175-176.
practical or speculative, 171-172.
probable, 169.
real, 168-169.
subjects, 176.

Common error of fact, supplying of jurisdiction in, 27, 74-78, 167.

Common error of law, supplying of jurisdiction in, 27, 74-78, 163-167.

Common good, the motivating cause of the suppletory principle, 34, 36, 41, 43, 62-67, 105, 131, 132, 143, 144, 146-147, 150, 157-162, 172, 178, 231, 237, 265, 275.

Competence, jurisdiction differs from, 12.

Concept of jurisdiction, crystallization of,
civilly, 4-6.
ecclesiastically, 7-8.

Convalidation, and the supplying of jurisdiction, 27.

Danger of death, and jurisdictional competence, 28-29, 144-146, 150, 159, 191, 218, 222.

Delegated power, essence of, 16.
applicability of suppletory principle to,
in cases of strict jurisdiction,
before the Code, 62-67.
after the Code,
in common error, in
particular delegation, 236-239.
universal delegation, 235,
in doubt, 225.
in assistance at marriage,
before the Code, 258-260.
after the Code,
in common error, in
particular delegation, 271-277.
universal delegation, 263-267.
in doubt, 260-261.
kinds of, 17.

Delict, doubts concerning comission of, 217-218.

Dictum of Gratian, doctrinal significance of, 48.
importance of, 47-48.
text of, 46-47.

Dominative power, and jurisdiction, 10-11.
applicability of suppletory principle to,
before the Code, 283-285.
after the Code, when this power is
joined with an ecclesiastical office, 280-282.
apart from an ecclesiastical office, 286-289.
definition of, 282.
illustrations of, 10-11.
kinds of, 282.

Doubt, definition of, 179.
differs from,
certitude, 179.

opinion, 179.
suspicion, 179.
kinds of,
merely subjective, 179.
objective, 179.
of fact, 180.
of law, 180..
Ecclesiastical jurisdiction, source of, 8, 21, 41.
Epikeia, role of—, in interpretation of jurisdictional laws, 161-162.
Equity, role of—, in development of suppletory principle in
Roman law, 36, 39.
ecclesiastical law, 34, 39-41, 43, 48, 146, 151.
Error, definition of, 116, 152.
differs from,
doubt, 115-116.
ignorance, 115, 152.
nescience, 115.
kinds of, 116, 163-164.
Examples of positive and probable doubts,
of fact, 212-219.
of law, 202-210.
Excommunicates and jurisdiction. 19, 50, 51, 59, 62.
Excommunication, its effects upon possession and exercise of jurisdiction,
up to *Ad evitanda,* 50, 57.
after the *Ad evitanda,* 60-61.
Exempt, non-clerical religious superiors, nature of power of, 18.
Forum, applicability of suppletory principle to,
internal forum, 55-56.
internal and external *fora,* 56-57, 134, 155, 221-223.
Glossators' rôle in development of suppletory principle, 50-54.
Good faith and censures, 189-190, insufficient to validate jurisdictional acts, 23, 144, 187-188, 190, 213-216, 226-227.
Hospitalers of St. John, nature of power of superiors of, 11, 18.
Hypothetical character of supplying of jurisdiction in doubt, 178, 291.
Ignorance, and error, 115, 152.
Ignorance theory,
arguments for, 151-152.
evaluation and criticism of, 152-156.
Imperium, 3.
Inadvertence, supplying of jurisdiction in, 28, 133, 144-145, 155, 191.
Influence, of Church on Roman Law, 6-7, 34, 39-40.
Roman Law upon development of suppletory principle, 30-31, 39-40.
Interpretation of law, authentic, 204-205..
by *PCI*
character of, 206-207.
examples cited,
canon 34, § 3, n. 3,—206.
canon 882—222.
canon 1096—250, 255.
canon 1099, § 2—205-210.
Interpretative theory, appraisal of, 130,
contextual arguments,
context of the Code, 143-148.
difficulties against traditional theory, 135-143.
sequels of, 148-151.
gist of, 121-130.
Jurisdiction,
ambit of, 12-13, 21, 59, 221.
and title, 14-15, 23, 81-87, 107-110
crystallization of concept of,
in civil law, 4-6
in ecclesiastical law, 7-8
definition of,
canonically, 8, 221

civilly, 3, 6
etymologically, 3
differs from,
approbation, 12
competence, 11-12
dominative power, 10-11
power of Orders, 9-10
division of, as to
extent of application
particular, 14
universal, 14
forum,
external, 13
internal, 13
non-sacramental, 14
sacramental, 14
manner of exercise
contentious, 14
voluntary, 14
origin,
false, 17
true, 17
title,
delegated, 16-17
personal, 17
real, 17.
ordinary, 16
proper, 16
vicarious, 16
importance of, 22
normal requirements for possession and exercise of, 21-22.
required for validity of acts, 22.
subjects of
clerics, 18-20
laics, 18-19
Jurisdictional laws, purpose of, 23.
Laics, and jurisdiction, 18-19.
Lex Barbarius, importance of, 39-40, 30-31.
interpretation of, 38-40.
text of, 33-34.
Licit use of canon 209, in common error, by
faithful, 296-298.
minister, 291-296.
doubt, 298-300.
Maiestas, 3.
Negative doubt, notion of, 181.
supplying in, 181.
Non-baptized persons, and jurisdiction, 8-9, 19.
Non-jurisdictional power, question of applicability of suppletory principle to, 279-280.
Notio, 3.
Officium, question of
essence of, 226, 230-234.
necessity of—for supplying of jurisdiction, 226-228, 230-231, 234-235.
Orders, power of,
beyond Church's jurisdictional control, 24, 26, 27, 57-62.
differs from power of jurisdiction, 9-10.
Ordinary power, applicability of suppletory principle to,
in assistance at marriage,
in common error, 256-258.
in doubt, 260-261.
in strictly jurisdictional acts,
in common error, 225-230.
in doubt, 225.
nature of, 16, 225-226.
Particular delegation, question of applicability of suppletory principle to,
in assistance at marriage,
in common error, 271-279.
in doubt, 260-261.
in strictly jurisdictional acts,
in common error, 236-239.
in doubt, 225.
Pastors, applicability of suppletory principle to,
in assistance at marriage,
in common error, 258.

in doubt, 260-261.
in strictly jurisdictional acts,
in common error, 225-230.
in doubt, 225.
necessity of common error, 258.

Penal sanction against usurpation of jurisdiction, in any case, 300-301.
in tribunal of penance, 301-310.

Positive and probable doubt, identified as probable opinion, 180-181.
kinds of,
doubt of fact, 180, 210.
doubt of law,
intrinsically probable, 197-198.
extrinsically probable, 198-202.
privately, 199-200.
publicly, 200-202.
supplying in,
before the Code, 87-103.
after the Code, in doubt
of fact, 210-220.
of law, 196-210.

Probability, indispensable for supplying of jurisdiction,
in common error, 69-70, 169.
in doubt, 182-194.

Public, as to be distinguished from *common*, 138-140.

Public power, question of verification of,
in dominative power, 10-11, 288.
in jurisdiction, 8.

Purpose of the suppletory principle, 23, 25, 113-114.

Quasi-pastors, application of suppletory principle to assistance at marriage by, 256-258.

Radical sanation, and supplying of jurisdiction, 27.

Reasonable cause, required for licit use of canon 209,
in common error,
by faithful, 296-298.
by minister, 291-296.
in doubt, 298-300.

Rota cases, involving questions of common error, 119-121, 133, 135, 153, 168, 227, 236, 255, 256, 266, 276, 277.
doubt 192, 210-217, 261, 255-256.

Sacred Congregation of the Council, case solved by, 153, 227, 236, 244-245, 255, 256, 279.

Slavery in Rome, 32.

Supplying of jurisdiction,
canonical notion of, 27-28, 224, 304.
development of doctrine of—in doubt and common error,
Roman law, 32-40.
before Gratian, 41-45.
Gratian, 46-49.
glossators, 50-54.
canonists up to the Code, 55-114.
different instances in Code of, 28-29.
effect of, 25, 27.
limits of, 24, 26-27, 57-62, 194, 228-230, 304.
purpose of, 23. 35, 113-114.

Title, definition of, 14-15.
kinds of, 15-16.
necessity of colored title, question of,
before Code, 53, 56-57, 67, 81-87.
after Code, 107.
necessity of some title, 108-112, 167, 168.

Universal delegation, application of suppletory princple to,
in assistance at marriage,
in common error, 263-268.
in doubt, 260-261.

in strictly jurisdictional acts,
in common error, 235.
in doubt, 225.

Vicarius supplens infra hebdomadam, question of supplying of authorization to assist at marriage, 269-271.

Virtual error, in sense of
interpretative theory, 128-130.
traditional theory, 170-171.

Women, and jurisdiction, 18-19.

CANON LAW STUDIES

1. Freriks, Rev. Celestine A., C.PP.S., J.C.D., Religious Congregations in Their External Relations, 121 pp., 1916.
2. Galliher, Rev. Daniel M., O.P., J.C.D., Canonical Elections, 117 pp., 1917.
3. Borkowski, Rev. Aurelius L., O.F.M., J.C.D., De Confraternitatibus Ecclesiasticis, 136 pp., 1918.
4. Castillo, Rev. Cayo, J.C.D., Disertacion Historico-Canonica sobre la Potestad del Cabildo en Sede Vacante o Impedida del Vicario Capitular, 99 pp., 1919 (1918).
5. Kubelbeck, Rev. William J., S.T.B., J.C.D., The Sacred Pentitentiaria and Its Relations to Faculties of Ordinaries and Priests, 129 pp., 1918.
6. Petrovits, Rev. Joseph J.C., S.T.D., J.C.D., The New Church Law On Matrimony, X-461 pp., 1919.
7. Hickey, Rev. John J., S.T.B., J.C.D., Irregularities and Simple Impediments in the New Code of Canon Law, 100 pp., 120.
8. Klekotka, Rev. Peter J., S.T.B., J.C.D., Diocesan Consultors, 179 pp., 1920.
9. Wanenmacher, Rev. Francis, J.C.D., The Evidence in Ecclesiastical Procedure Affecting the Marriage Bond, 1920 (Printed 1935).
10. Golden, Rev. Henry Francis, J.C.D., Parochial Benefices in the New Code, IV-119 pp., 1921 (Printed 1925).
11. Koudelka, Rev. Charles J., J.C.D., Pastors, Their Rights and Duties According to the New Code of Canon Law, 211 pp., 1921.
12. Melo, Rev. Antonius, O.F.M., J.C.D., De Exemptione Regularium, X-188 pp., 1921.
13. Schaaf, Rev. Valentine Theodore, O.F.M., S.T.B., J.C.D., The Cloister, X-180 pp., 1921.
14. Burke, Rev. Thomas Joseph, S.T.D., J.C.D., Competence in Ecclesiastical Tribunals, IV-117 pp., 1922.
15. Leech, Rev. George Leo, J.C.D., A Comparative Study of the Constitution, "Apostolicae Sedis" and the "Codex Juris Canonici," 179 pp., 1922.
16. Motry, Rev. Hubert Louis, S.T.D., J.C.D., Diocesan Faculties According to the Code of Canon Law, II-167 pp., 1922.
17. Murphy, Rev. George Lawrence, J.C.D., Delinquencies and Penalties in the Administration and Reception of the Sacraments, IV-121 pp., 1923.
18. O'Reilly, Rev. John Anthony, S.T.B., J.C.D., Ecclesiastical Sepulture in the New Code of Canon Law, II-129 pp., 1923.

19. Michalicka, Rev. Wenceslas Cyrill, O.S.B., J.C.D., Judicial Procedure in Dismissal of Clerical Exempt Religious, 107 pp., 1923.
20. Dargin, Rev. Edward Vincent, S.T.B., J.C.D., Reserved Cases According to the Code of Canon Law, IV-103, pp., 1924.
21. Godfrey, Rev. John A., S.T.B., J.C.D., The Right of Patronage According to the Code of Canon Law, 153 pp., 1924.
22. Hagedorn, Rev. Francis Edward, J.C.D., General Legislation on Indulgences, II-154 pp., 1924.
23. King, Rev. James Ignatius, J.C.D., The Administration of the Sacraments to Dying Non-Catholics, V-141 pp., 1924.
24. Winslow, Rev. Francis Joseph, A.F.M., J.C.D., Vicars and Prefects Apostolic, IV-149 pp., 1924.
25. Correa, Rev. Jose Servelion, S.T.L., J.C.D., La Potestad Legislativa de la Iglesia Catolica, IV-127 pp., 1925.
26. Dugan, Rev. Henry Francis, A.M., J.C.D., The Judiciary Department of the Diocesan Curia, 87 pp., 1925.
27. Keller, Rev. Charles Frederick, S.T.B., J.C.D., Mass Stipends, 167 pp., 1925.
28. Paschang, Rev. John Linus, J.C.D., The Sacramentals According to the Code of Canon Law, 129 pp., 1925.
29. Pointek, Rev. Cyrillus, O.F.M., S.T.B., J.C.D., De Indulto Exclaustrationis necnon Saecularizationis, XIII-289 pp., 1925.
30. Kearney, Rev. Richard Joseph, S.T.B., J.C.D., Sponsors at Baptism According to the Code of Canon Law, IV-127 pp., 1925.
31. Bartlett, Rev. Chester Joseph, A.M., LL.B., J.C.D., The Tenure of Parochial Property in the United States of America, V-108 pp., 1926.
32. Kilker, Rev. Adrian Jerome, J.C.D., Extreme Unction, V-425 pp., 1926.
33. McCormick, Rev. Robert Emmett, J.C.D., Confessors of Religious, VIII-266 pp., 1926.
34. Miller, Rev. Newton Thomas, J.C.D., Founded Masses According to the Code of Canon Law, VII-93 pp., 1926.
35. Roelker, Rev. Edward G., S.T.D., J.C.D., Principles of Privilege According to the Code of Canon Law, XI-166 pp., 1926.
36. Bakalarczyk, Rev. Richardus, M.I.C., J.U.D., De Novitiatu, VIII-208 pp., 1927.
37. Pizzuti, Rev. Lawrence, O.F.M., J.U.L., De Parochis Religiosis, 1927. (Not printed).
38. Bliley, Rev. Nicholas Martin, O.S.B., J.C.D., Altars According to the Code of Canon Law, XIX-132 pp., 1927.
39. Brown, Mr. Brendan Francis, A.B. LL.M., J.U.D., The Canonical Juristic Personality with Special Reference to Its Status in the United States of America, V-212 pp., 1927.

40. Cavanaugh, Rev. William Thomas, C.P., J.U.D., The Reservation of the Blessed Sacrament, VIII-101 pp., 1927.
41. Doheny, Rev. William J., C.S.C., A.B., J.U.D., Church Property: Modes of Acquisition, X-118 pp., 1927.
42. Feldhaus, Rev. Aloysius H., C.PP.S., J.C.D., Oratories, IX-141 pp., 1927.
43. Kelly, Rev. James Patrick, A.B., J.C.D., The Jurisdiction of the Simple Confessor, X-208 pp., 1927.
44. Neuberger, Rev. Nicholas J., J.C.D., Canon 6 or the Relation of the Codex Juris Canonici to the Preceding Legislation, V-95 pp., 1927.
45. O'Keefe, Rev. Gerald Michael, J.C.D., Matrimonial Dispensations, Powers of Bishops, Priests and Confessors, VIII-232 pp., 1927.
46. Quigley, Rev. Joseph A.M., A.B., J.C.B., Condemned Societies, 139 pp., 1927.
47. Zaplotnik, Rev. Johannes Leo, J.C.D., De Vicariis Foraneis, X-142 pp., 1927.
48. Duskie, Rev. John Aloysius, A.B., J.C.D., The Canonical Status of the Orientals in the United States, VIII-196 pp., 1928.
49. Hyland, Rev. Francis Edward, J.C.D., Excommunication, Its Nature, Historical Development and Effects, VIII-181 pp., 1928.
50. Reinmann, Rev. Gerald Joseph, O.M.C., J.C.D., The Third Order Secular of Saint Francis, 201 pp., 1928.
51. Schenk, Rev. Francis J., J.C.D., The Matrimonial Impediments of Mixed Religion and Disparity of Cult, XVI-318 pp., 1929.
52. Coady, Rev. John Joseph, S.T.D., J.U.D., A.M., The Appointment of Pastors, VIII-150 pp., 1929.
53. Kay, Rev. Thomas Henry, J.C.D., Competence in Matrimonial Procedure, VIII-164 pp., 1929.
54. Turner, Rev. Sidney Joseph, C.P., J.U.D., The Vow of Poverty, XLIX-217 pp., 1929.
55. Kearney, Rev. Raymond, A., A.B., S.T.D., J.C.D., The Principles, of Delegation, VII-149 pp., 1929.
56. Conran, Rev. Edward James, A.B., J.C.D., The Interdict, V-163 pp., 1930..
57. O'Neil, Rev. William H., J.C.D., Papal Rescripts of Favor, VII-218 pp., 1930.
58. Bastnagel, Rev. Clement Vincent, J.U.D., The Appointment of Parochial Adjutants and Assistants, XV-257 pp., 1930.
59. Ferry, Rev. William A., A.B., J.C.D., Stole Fees, V-135 pp., 1930.
60. Costello, Rev. John Michael, A.B., J.C.D., Domicile and Quasi-domicile, VII-201 pp., 1930.
61. Kremer, Rev. Michael Nicholas, A.B., S.T.B., J.C.D., Church Support in the United States, VI-1930.

62. Angulo, Rev. Luis, C.M., J.C.D., Legislation de la Iglesia sobre la intencion en la application de la Santa Misa, VII-104 pp., 1931.
63. Frey, Rev. Wolfgang Norbert, O.S.B., A.B., J.C.D., The Act of Religious Profession, VIII-174 pp., 1931.
64. Roberts, Rev. James Brendan, A.B., J.C.D., The Banns of Marriage, XIV-140 pp., 1931.
65. Ryder, Rev. Raymond Aloysius, A.B., J.C.D., Simony, IX-151 pp., 1931.
66. Campagna, Rev. Angelo, Ph.D., J.U.D., Il Vicario Generale del Vescovo, VII-205 pp., 1931.
67. Cox, Rev. Joseph Godfrey, A.B., J.C.D., The Administration ot Seminaries, VI-124 pp., 1931.
68. Gregory, Rev. Donald J., J.U.D., The Pauline Privilege, XV-165 pp., 1931.
69. Donohue, Rev. John F., J.C.D., The Impediment of Crime, VII-110 pp., 1931.
70. Dooley, Rev. Eugene A., O.M.I., J.C.D., Church Law On Sacred Relics, IX-143 pp., 1931.
71. Orth, Rev. Raymond Clement, O.M.C., J.C.D., The Approbation of Religious Institutes, 171 pp., 1931.
72. Pernicone, Rev. Joseph M., A.B., J.C.D., The Ecclesiastical Prohibition of Books, XII-267 pp., 1932.
73. Clinton, Rev. Connell, A.B., J.C.D., The Paschal Precept, IX-108 pp., 1932.
74. Donnelly, Rev. Francis B., A.M., S.T.L., J.C.D., The Diocesan Synod, VIII-125 pp., 1932.
75. Torrente, Rev. Camilo, C.M.F., J.C.D., Las Processiones Sagradas, V-145 pp., 1932.
76. Murphy, Rev. Edwin J., C.PP.S., J.C.D., Suspension Ex Informata Conscientia, XI-122, pp., 1932.
77. Mackenzie, Rev. Eric F., A.M., S.T.L., J.C.D., The Delict of Heresy in its Commission Penalization, Absolution, VII-124 pp., 1932.
78. Lyons Rev. Avitus E., S.T.B., J.C.D., The Collegiate Tribunal of First Instance, XI-147 pp., 1932.
79. Connolly, Rev. Thomas A., J.C.D., Appeals, XI-195 pp., 1932.
80. Sangmeister, Rev. Joseph V., A.B., J.C.D., Force and Fear as Precluding Matrimonial Consent, V-211 pp., 1932.
81. Jaeger, Rev. Leo A., A.B., J.C.D., The Administration of Vacant and Quasi-vacant Episcopal Sees in the United States, IX-229 pp., 1932.
82. Rimlinger, Rev. Herbert T., J.C.D., Error Invalidating Matrimonial Consent, VII-79 pp., 1932.
83. Barrett, Rev. John D.M., S.S., J.C.D., A Comparative Study of the Third Plenary Council of Baltimore and the Code, IX-221 pp., 1932.

84. Carberry, Rev. John J., Ph.D., S.T.D., J.C.D., The Juridical Form of Marriage, X-177 pp., 1934.
85. Dolan, Rev. John L., A.B., J.C.D., The Defensor Vinculi, XII-157 pp., 1934.
86. Hannan, Rev. Jerome D., A.M., S.T.D., LL.B., J.C.D., The Canon Law of Wills, IX-517 pp., 1934.
87. Lemieux, Rev. Delisle A., A.M., J.C.D., The Sentence in Ecclesiastical Procedure, IX-131 pp., 1934.
88. O'Rourke, Rev. James J., A.B., J.C.D., Parish Registers, VII-109 pp., 1934.
89. Timlin, Rev. Bartholomew, O.F.M., A.M., J.C.D., Conditional Matrimonial Consent, X-381 pp., 1934.
90. Wahl, Rev. Francis X., A.B., J.C.D., The Matrimonial Impediments of Consanguinity and Affinity, VI-125 pp., 1934.
91. White, Rev. Robert J., A.B., LL.B., S.T.B., J.C.D., Canonical Ante-Nuptial Promises and the Civil Law, VI-152 pp., 1934.
92. Herrera, Rev. Antonio Parra, O.C.D., J.C.D., Legislation Ecclesiastica sobra el Ayuno y la Abstinencia, XI-191 pp., 1935.
93. Kennedy, Rev. Edwin J., J.C.D., The Special Matrimonial Process in Cases of Evident Nullity, X-165 pp., 1935.
94. Manning, Rev. John J., A.B., J.C.D., Presumption of Law in Matrimonial Procedure, XI-111 pp., 1935.
95. Moeder, Rev. John M., J.C.D., The Proper Bishop for Ordination and Dismissorial Letters, VII-135 pp., 1935.
96. O'Mara, Rev. William A., A.B., J.C.D., Canonical Causes For Matrimonial Dispensations, IX-155 pp., 1935.
97. Reilly, Rev. Peter, J.C.D., Residence of Pastors, IX-81 pp., 1935.
98. Smith, Rev. Mariner T., O.P., S.T.L., J.C.D., The Penal Law For Religious, VII-169 pp., 1935.
99. Whalen, Rev. Donald W., A.M., J.C.D., The Value of Testimonial Evidence in Matrimonial Procedure, XIII-297 pp., 1935.
100. Cleary, Rev. Joseph F., J.C.D., Canonical Limitations on the Alienation of Church Property, VIII-141 pp., 1936.
101. Glynn, Rev. John C., J.C.D., The Promoter of Justice, XX-337 pp., 1936.
102. Brennan, Rev. James H., S.S., A.M., S.T.B., J.C.D., The Simple Convalidation of Marriage, VI-135 pp, 1937.
103. Brunini, Rev. Joseph Bernard, J.C.D., The Clerical Obligations of Canons, 139 and 142, X-121 pp., 1937.
104. Connor, Rev. Maurice, A.B., J.C.D., The Administrative Removal of Pastors, VIII-159 pp., 1937.
105. Guilfoyle, Rev. Merlin Joseph, J.C.D., Custom, XI-144 pp., 1937.
106. Hughes, Rev. James Austin, A.B., A.M., J.C.D., Witnesses in Criminal Trials of Clerics, IX-140 pp., 1937.

107. Jansen, Rev. Raymond J., A.B., S.T.L., J.C.D., Canonical Provisions for Catechetical Instruction, VII-153 pp., 1937.
108. Kealy, Rev. John James, A.B., J.C.D,, The Introductory Libellus in Church Court Procedure, XI-121 pp., 1937.
109. McManus, Rev. James Edward, C.SS.R., J.C.D., The Administration of Temporal Goods in Religious Institutes, XVI-196 pp., 1937.
110. Moriarity, Rev. Eugene James, J.C.D., Oaths in Ecclesiastical Courts, X-115 pp., 1937.
111. Rainer, Rev. Eligius George, C.SS.R., J.C.D., Suspension of Clerics, XVII-249 pp., 1937.
112. Reilly, Rev. Thomas F., C.SS.R., J.C.D., Visitation of Religious, VI-195 pp., 1938.
113. Moriarty, Rev. Francis E., C.SS.R., J.C.D., The Extraordinary Absolution from Censures, XV-334 pp., 1938.
114. Connolly, Rev. Nicholas P., J.C.D., The Canonical Erection of Parishes, X-132 pp., 1938.
115. Donovan, Rev. James Joseph, J.C.D., The Pastor's Obligation in Prenuptial Investigation, XII-322 pp., 1938.
116. Harrigan, Rev. Robert J., M.A., S.T.B., J.C.D., The Radical Sanation of Invalid Marriages, VIII-208 pp., 1938.
117. Boffa, Rev. Conrad Humbert, J.C.D., Canonical Provisions for Catholic Schools, X-211 pp., 1939.
118. Parsons, Rev. Anscar John, O.M. Cap., J.C.D., Canonical Elections, XII-236 pp., 1939.
119. Reilly, Rev. Edward Michael, A.B., J.C.D., The General Norms of Dispensation, X-156 pp., 1939.
120. Ryan, Rev. Gerald Aloysius, A.B., J.C.D., Principles of Episcopal Jurisdiction, XII-172 pp., 1939.
121. Burton, Rev. Francis James, C.S.C., A.B., J.C.L., A Commentary on Canon 1125.
122. Miaskiewicz, Rev. Francis Sigismund, J.C.L., Supplied Jurisdiction According to Canon 209.
123. Rice, Rev. Patrick William, A. B., J.C.L., Proof of Death in Prenuptial Investigation.

www.ingramcontent.com/pod-product-compliance
Lightning Source LLC
LaVergne TN
LVHW050259080826
844660LV00012B/659

* 9 7 8 0 8 1 3 2 2 3 1 1 7 *